THE ARAB UPRISINGS EXPLAINED

Columbia Studies in Middle East Politics

Columbia Studies in Middle East Politics

Marc Lynch, Series Editor

Columbia Studies in Middle East Politics presents academically rigorous, well-written, relevant, and accessible books on the rapidly transforming politics of the Middle East for an interested academic and policy audience.

Sectarian Politics in the Gulf: From the Iraq War to the Arab Uprisings, Frederic M. Wehrey

Edited by MARC LYNCH

THE ARAB UPRISINGS EXPLAINED

NEW CONTENTIOUS POLITICS IN
THE MIDDLE EAST

 COLUMBIA UNIVERSITY PRESS   NEW YORK

Columbia University Press

Publishers Since 1893

New York   Chichester, West Sussex

cup.columbia.edu

Copyright © 2014 Columbia University Press

All rights reserved

Library of Congress Cataloging-in-Publication Data

The Arab uprisings explained : new contentious politics in the Middle East / edited by Marc Lynch.

      pages cm. — (Columbia studies in Middle East politics)

   Includes bibliographical references and index.

   ISBN 978-0-231-15884-8 (cloth : alk. paper) — ISBN 978-0-231-15885-5 (pbk. : alk. paper) — ISBN 978-0-231-53749-0 (ebook)

   1. Arab Spring, 2010–   2. Revolutions—Arab countries—History—21st century.

   3. Democratization—Arab countries—History—21st century   4. Arab countries—Politics and government—21st century.   I. Lynch, Marc, 1969–

   JQ1850.A91A826 2014

   909'.097492708312—dc23

                                  2014009250

COVER DESIGN: Martin Hinze

COVER IMAGE: © Getty

References to websites (URLs) were accurate at the time of writing. Neither the author nor Columbia University Press is responsible for URLs that may have expired or changed since the manuscript was prepared.

Contents

Acknowledgments

This book originated in the May 2011 annual conference of the Project on Middle East Political Science (POMEPS), which I direct at George Washington University. Convened only a few months after the outbreak of the Arab uprisings, the workshop brought together more than thirty leading political scientists specializing on the Middle East, along with half a dozen specialists on other regions. Following those intensive discussions, I invited the participants to submit proposals for what eventually became this book. A smaller group, including many of the authors in this volume, then convened at the American University of Cairo for a conference on the Egyptian revolution, which POMEPS organized with Lisa Anderson. We discussed in depth the draft chapters at the May 2012 POMEPS annual conference and also at an October 2012 GW workshop comparing the Arab uprisings with the post-Soviet revolutions.

In addition to the authors who contributed to this volume, I would like to thank the many outstanding scholars who commented on the draft chapters or participated in the conferences along the way. My thanks go to Holger Albrecht, Michael Barnett, Mark Beissinger, Eva Bellin, Lindsey Benstead, Dina Bishara, Jason Brownlee, Rex Brynen, Melani Cammett, Sheila Carapico, Janine Clark, Daniel Corstange, Jill Crystal, Emma Deputy, Kristin Diwan, John Entelis, Eleanor Gao, Gregory Gause, Henry Hale, Michael Herb, Manal Jamal, Toby Jones, Charles Kurzman, Adria Lawrence, Rabab el-Mahdi, Peter Moore, Gwenn Okruhulik, Anne Peters, Wendy Pearlman, Dina Rashed, Glenn Robinson, Etel Solingen, Josh Stacher, Shibley Telhami, Lisa Wedeen, Stacy Yadav, and Sean Yom. Many more contributed either directly or indirectly.

The conferences and research for this volume were made possible through the generous support of the Carnegie Corporation of New York and the Social Science Research Council. I would particularly like to thank Hilary Wiesner and Thomas Asher for their enthusiastic support for POMEPS over the years. Mary Casey and Maria Kornalian played a pivotal role in organizing and running the POMEPS network and conferences and offered editorial assistance on the Middle East Channel. Shana Marshall helped organize several of the key conferences. Susan Glasser and Blake Hounshell supported *Foreign Policy*'s Middle East Channel, a key part of the POMEPS initiative. Cara Beining and Gregory McGowan provided editorial assistance in the preparation of this manuscript. Finally, my thanks to Anne Routon of Columbia University Press for believing in this book and making it the foundation of our new series, Columbia Studies in Middle East Politics.

Above all, my thanks to the entire intellectual community of the political science of the Middle East. Despite a wide range of methodological, theoretical, and political differences, these scholars have managed to construct powerful explanations for extremely important political developments and to offer useful, effective guidance for those attempting to fathom their meaning. The last few years have proven more than ever before that this is an intellectual mission worth pursuing.

THE ARAB UPRISINGS EXPLAINED

1

Introduction

MARC LYNCH

The period of contentious politics unleashed by Mohammad Bouazizi's self-immolation in December 2010 in Tunisia has reshaped the terrain of regional politics and challenged the theories that have dominated the literature on the comparative politics of the Middle East. The broad outlines of the story are familiar.[1] In the face of massive popular protests, the Tunisian president, Zine al-Abidine Ben Ali, was deposed, followed a month later by the removal of the Egyptian president, Hosni Mubarak. A wave of protest then swept across the region as Arab citizens, inspired by the example of change broadcast on al-Jazeera and spread over increasingly ubiquitous social media, rose up to challenge their own entrenched authoritarian rulers. By the end of February 2011, virtually every country in the Arab world was beset by tumultuous demonstrations demanding fundamental political change.

Whereas Ben Ali's and Mubarak's regimes gave in, the next wave of challenged leaders fought back. Some, like Morocco's king, offered limited, pre-emptive political concessions, while some wealthy regimes like Saudi Arabia's combined repression with lavish public spending. Others, determined not to share the fate of their deposed counterparts, responded to peaceful challenges with brutal force. Libya's Muammar al-Qaddafi unleashed the full force of his army on peaceful protesters, triggering a virtually unprecedented international military intervention to prevent a slaughter of rebels in the city of Benghazi. In Bahrain, a carefully negotiated political power-sharing bargain collapsed as Gulf Cooperation Council (GCC) troops poured in to the tiny island and the al-Khalifa dynasty began a systematic purge of its political opponents. The Yemeni president, Ali Abdullah Saleh, clung to power as virtually every sector of society and even the military turned against him. Syrian troops unloaded the fury of a Baathist regime on protesters in Deraa, which led to the escalation of protests across the country. The viciousness of these responses to popular challenges suggested that the institutions of authoritarian rule had not lost their relevance. Some regimes seemed to right themselves quickly, while others appeared to slide toward civil war.

Like most of the regimes and almost all U.S. policymakers, American political science was ill prepared for this tumult. For the last several decades, the political science literature on the region concentrated on the resilience of entrenched authoritarianism, the relative weakness of civil society, and the apparently limited effect of the diffusion of novel norms and ideas through new information and communications technologies. The first responses to the uprisings probably overstated their novelty and scope in the heat of enthusiasm for long-denied popular challenges. Now, however, political scientists should take stock of the uprisings and what they did and did not signify.

Whether the upsurge in contentious political action will bring enduring political change remains highly uncertain. We also cannot yet define and measure the political changes that have occurred. Even the fall of the dictators in Tunisia and Egypt only opened the door to new political struggles, which left many of the revolutionaries at home and observers abroad deeply concerned. In Egypt, the old regime reasserted itself through a military coup on July 3, 2013, which overthrew the elected government of Mohamed el-Morsi. The dizzying pace of the Arab spring has now slowed to a gritty, desperate, and increasingly bloody set of interlocked battles for power. A counterrevolution led by Saudi Arabia and the monarchies of the GCC has at least temporarily blocked further change. As a result, "most of the Arab political openings are closing faster and more harshly than happened in other regions—save for the former Soviet Union, where most new democratic regimes quickly drifted back toward autocracy."[2] Does this mean that the protests of 2011 will resemble most closely the postcommunist experience of highly mixed political outcomes following a regionwide wave of protests?

This volume has three principal goals. First, it seeks to bring together the best political science analysis of factors relevant to regime change and contentious politics. To that end, we revisit various literatures to determine where the prevailing hypotheses seem to be supported and where revisions to widely accepted propositions may be warranted. Second, we compare the region's upheavals with those of other regions and historical periods.[3] We hope to avoid the mistakes made by earlier scholars attempting to explain previous waves of political change, such as the neglect of the old-regime autocrats in the study of post-Soviet revolutions, or the extrapolation from the highly unusual Spanish transition, in which a pact was reached without massive mobilization. We thus make no assumptions about the outcomes of these protests, nor do we subscribe to a teleology of democracy or an assumption of inevitable failure. Finally, in order to avoid monocausal or overdetermined explanations, we look closely at the wide range of actors, sectors, and structural forces affecting the region's politics.

We argue that the Arab upheavals of 2011 require a dynamic model of political contention that takes into account the interaction of diverse actors across multiple levels of analysis. We place considerable emphasis on the timing, sequence, and pace of events, which undermine an easy comparative method based on the characteristics of specific cases. The integrated political and media space in which these revolutions unfolded may be one of the most distinctive aspects of this period, rooted in the long-term growth of the pan-Arab media such as al-Jazeera and the consolidation of transnational activist networks in the years leading up to the protests.[4] But those common themes played out in distinct political arenas, each with a unique institutional history, ethnic and sectarian composition, and political balance of forces.[5] The force of these protests eventually ran aground in the face of the strength and determination of those regimes that did not succumb to the original ferocity, revealing important patterns in the nature of regime resilience and the value of different forms of survival resources.

We distinguish three phases in the uprisings, each with its own dynamics and logic. The first is *mobilization*, the process by which virtually unprecedented levels of popular contention exploded across a highly diverse set of Arab countries nearly simultaneously. We seek to account for both the commonalities in this regional mobilization, especially changes in the information environment and the international context, and the national and subnational variations in the protests' timing and composition. Here we explore a wide range of factors, including questions of ongoing mobilization during the transition, different approaches to former regime officials and institutions, accommodations to the military and entrenched elites, and the role of regional and international actors.

Second, we explore the *regimes' responses*, ranging from accommodation to repression, abdication to civil war. We consider the importance of the strength and durability of state institutions; of divisions within the regime, including unanticipated splits between militaries and political regimes; and tension between hard-liners and moderates, public sector and private sector, in the policy arena. The decisions made by the militaries have played a particularly important role.

Finally, we offer necessarily preliminary thoughts on *political outcomes*, keeping in mind that the enduring nature of those outcomes in even the most advanced cases of change, such as that in Egypt and Tunisia, will not be known for years. Nevertheless, we believe it likely that these political outcomes will be highly heterogeneous, with some regimes shifting toward more democracy and others sustaining some version of an autocratic status quo, and that this variety merits explanation. We also warn against the premature coding of cases. The short-term fall or survival of particular leaders may be ultimately less important than the deep underlying structural transformations of the regional and domestic political environments in these countries.[6] Thus, theories built on the "outcomes" of monarchical survival may come to look foolish in the medium range if these underlying forces continue to build, and some of the seemingly transitional regimes may come to uncomfortably mimic their predecessors. Egypt's "outcome," for example, looked very different before the military coup of July 3, 2013.

The Puzzle: What Needs Explanation?

The new wave of contentious politics should be seen as a partial but serious challenge to much of the conventional literature on the comparative politics of the Middle East. The uprisings destabilized not only the regimes themselves but also the findings of a sophisticated literature that developed over the previous decade to explain the resilience of authoritarian Arab states.[7] The political science of the Middle East in 2011 faced a situation similar to Sovietology in 1991, when extremely few scholars correctly predicted the timing and nature of change, even though in immediate retrospect such change came to seem inevitable and, at the time of the writing, the fate of the Soviet Union was not yet known.[8] As in those earlier cases of unexpected change, we seek to find out how the impossible became the inevitable.

The distinctive changes that demand explanation in this volume are not the fates of specific regimes but the *speed and magnitude of mobilization across multiple countries* and the *divergent political outcomes*. As in Africa and the postcommunist realm, a relatively synchronized wave of political ferment across multiple countries seems likely to produce highly heterogeneous outcomes. But the developments of the last few years clearly warn against any easy assimilation of these cases into a "transitions to democracy" literature.[9]

Although most contemporary political science on regime change begins with the literature that grew out of the transitions in Latin America and southern Europe in the 1970s and 1980s, these paradigmatic cases of pacted democratic transition seem to be less useful comparisons. Focused on the prospects of deal making between regime soft-liners and opposition moderates, these studies tended to conclude that democracy was most likely to emerge where a rough balance of power existed among political forces and that mobilization during the transition would make democratic outcomes less likely. As Daniel Brumberg points out in chapter 2, the assumptions and distinctive conditions that informed the "transitology" literature have less resonance in the turbulent conditions of today than the postcommunist world after 1989, the varieties of political change in Africa in the early 1990s, and the "color revolutions" in the 2000s in Eastern and Central Europe. Even though they differ significantly, these waves of regional change produced a heterogeneous mix of outcomes—some democratic, some authoritarian, and many complex hybrid regimes with old patterns of informal power layered beneath new formal institutions.

It overstates the case to claim that political scientists focused on the Middle East completely missed the potential for mobilization. Political scientists were keenly aware of disruptive forces such as al-Jazeera and Arab satellite television, a global trend toward democratization, a youth bulge and a crisis of employment, transnational Islamism, globalization, and the upsurge of civil society and the demands for democracy from within and abroad. But they noted that in almost every case, Arab autocrats had proved to be more capable than their global counterparts at resisting such pressures. A robust and closely observed set of explanations for how these authoritarian states had managed those challenges bred skepticism about the ability of mobilization to defeat entrenched regimes.[10]

This literature pointed to a variety of factors to explain authoritarian resilience: access to oil and strategic rents, overdeveloped security forces, sophisticated strategies of dividing and co-opting the opposition, and political culture. These Arab states seemed to have demonstrated their capacities to adapt to a wide range of challenges and to perpetuate their dominant position in both domestic affairs and foreign policy. Fueled by strategic rents and the vast influx of oil revenues in the 1970s, Arab states constructed large and oppressive apparatuses for state control, surveillance, and repression. Their close reliance on overdeveloped and self-protective militaries, along with massive intelligence services, seemed to allow regimes to withstand challenges that might have threatened autocrats outside the region. Political opposition was expertly co-opted, divided, repressed, and contained to the point that opposition parties served as much to maintain the political status quo as to articulate grievances or push reforms.[11] As Eva Bellin argued, "It is the stalwart will and capacity of the state's coercive apparatus to suppress any glimmers of democratic initiative."[12] This will and capacity seemed adequate to meet the successive challenges of the 2000s, and by 2009/2010, the authoritarians seemed to have a decisive upper hand.[13]

At the same time, some parts of the literature had been tracking the dynamics of contentious politics across the region. The literature on civil society and democratization that had dominated the 1990s had lost momentum.[14] But studies of Islamist movements captured the changing scope of political opportunity, as well as the intricate linkages between cultural and electoral politics.[15] Studies of popular and youth culture, urban politics, and popular protests such as Egypt's Kefaya movement captured the sense of agency and frustration spreading throughout Arab political society.[16] Studies of the new media and public sphere captured some of the degree to which the terms of political debate and the balance of power between state and society were shifting. Almost all analyses of the region pointed to the long-term risks of closing political systems at a time of institutional decay, a growing gap between rich and poor, and a rising generation of frustrated, disenfranchised, and impatient youth. But few predicted the precise nature of the eruption. This was not because of a failure to observe the trends, but rather a tendency to accord inadequate weight to these discordant trends or else an entirely appropriate scholarly caution in the face of popular and activist enthusiasm.[17]

It is, of course, too soon to tell whether the literature's focus on robust authoritarianism was misguided. Hybrid authoritarianism has proven more resilient than many hoped or expected in the early days of 2011. Indeed, the ferocity of the pushback against popular mobilization across the region following the fall of Hosni Mubarak, the descent of multiple cases into civil wars rather than smooth transitions, and the continuing power of the old guard in both Egypt and Tunisia all suggest the continuing relevance of authoritarian structures. The vexed and complex relationship between state formation and regime type seems to be particularly salient here, as very strong states in Egypt and Tunisia saw their regimes jettisoned; very weak states in Libya and Yemen fell into civil conflict; and regimes managing divided societies, including Syria and Bahrain, dug in their heels and reacted assertively and violently. Continued focus on the resilience and strength of state institutions may help Middle East specialists avoid mistakes in other regions by not surrendering to enthusiasm for the democrats and keeping a close eye on the autocrats. At the same time, this continued focus on the real power of states and authoritarian regimes may blind us to the manifest changes in the tenor and substance of politics across the region. Most Arab autocrats may have survived thus far, but almost all are offering previously unthinkable concessions, and their people are more mobilized than at any time in the recent past.

The Speed and Magnitude of Mobilization Across Multiple Countries

The dramatic and rapid upsurge of popular mobilization did not come out of nowhere, as some people may have imagined.[18] Indeed, for most of the decade of the 2000s, popular protest had increasingly characterized Arab politics: protests about Israeli-Palestinian conflicts and the invasion of Iraq between 2000 and 2003, protests focused on domestic political change from Egypt to Lebanon and the Gulf in the mid-2000s, labor and judicial protests in Egypt, and economic protests across North Africa in the late 2000s.[19] But the mobilization of 2011 had several distinctive qualities. It was *massive*, incorporating sectors of society that had not previously joined protests and linking together protest sectors that had previously remained isolated from one another. It was *surprising*, often shocking both the regimes and the protest organizers themselves. It was *fast*, with protests going from minimal to overwhelming national convulsions seemingly overnight. They were often (though not always) driven by *new protest actors*, a self-conscious "youth" category of social action that used distinctive means (social media, SMS [short message service, or texting], popular coordinating committees) to challenge the rules and red lines of traditional political engagement. In addition, they mobilized previously nonmobilized sectors into the streets, particularly the urban middle class, which had previously remained sullenly aloof from political protest.

The *regional* nature of the mobilization, with clear diffusion and imitation effects across multiple countries, is important as well (see chapter 3).[20] Each incident of protest mobilization cannot be explained in terms of unique national conditions. Instead, they erupted nearly simultaneously, despite national differences. They displayed common repertoires of contention such as identical slogans, the use of Friday prayers as protest focal points for "days of rage," and the occupation of central urban nodal points. Without prejudging the explanation for these shared features, al-Jazeera's coverage in particular seemed to unite the political space in unusually intense ways. The very definition of these upheavals as "Arab" may presuppose analytical conclusions that should be left open: were Iran's Green movement protests of 2009 part of the same wave? What about the rising contentious politics in Africa, Spain, or—for that matter—Wisconsin?

The *surprising* nature of the mobilization also points to hypotheses developed in response to the rise of protests "out of nowhere" in Eastern Europe in 1989.[21] Both Timur Kuran and Suzanne Lohmann contend that the act of protest can lead to the revelation of previously falsified preferences across society.[22] Protest by a small number of early movers signals to others in society, who are privately dissatisfied but less willing to take risks, that others share their grievances. If those early movers go unpunished, it raises their confidence about the riskiness of expressing their dissent. As more people join the ranks of the protesters—including, for Lohmann, people understood as "like us" rather than professional activists or a clearly marked sectarian or ethnic group—then people with higher thresholds of risk will join in. At a certain point, societal incentives shift, and a cascade dynamic sets in as huge numbers of people flip from the previously socially safe position (regime support) to the newly socially safe position (protest). In the Arab uprisings, framing the protests around demands for "dignity" permitted joining the jobless and the employed, the highly educated and the poorly trained, the rights advocates and the religious activists, men, women, young and old. (Of course, this remarkably inclusive mobilization proved particularly difficult to sustain as politics routinizes and different groups made different kinds of claims.)

But as several chapters in this book note, this cascade model only imperfectly captures the dynamics. The extent of popular discontent was well known in Egypt and many other Arab states (see chapters 5 and 15), with pervasive and open criticism of leaders rather than the fearful silence assumed by Kuran. The cascade may have been driven more by updating the calculations of the prospects for success than by new information about the distribution of preferences (see chapter 4). This mobilization also contained an element of emotion and anger; it was not simply the revelation of thresholds but the transformation of underlying preferences for and beliefs about the moral legitimacy of regimes. The demand for dignity and the shattering of the barrier of fear—two slogans often heard—speak more about changing identities and values than about updating calculations of risk and opportunity.[23]

The course of these mobilizations also varied widely, as we explore in this book. In some cases, protests built and grew (Egypt, Yemen, Tunisia, Bahrain), while in others they petered out (Jordan, Saudi Arabia). In yet others, they flagged only to reignite after being given up for dead (Morocco). In some cases, activists failed repeatedly to spark protest before finally breaking through, often in response to ill-advised regime violence (Syria). In some cases, protesters turned to violence, whereas in others they practiced an impressive degree of nonviolent self-restraint. In some cases, protests began in rural areas (Tunisia) before moving to the cities, whereas in others they were primarily an urban phenomenon. Distinctive urban geographies, such as the existence of a central public square to seize, profoundly shaped the possibility of protest (see chapter 9). In some cases, the protest remained confined to either traditional opposition parties or to youth movements, but in others it grew to encompass wide sectors of society. In Bahrain, for instance, some 60 percent of the citizen population, by some measures, had joined the protests by early March 2011.

Then there were the dogs that did not bark. Lebanon and Iraq, two traditionally unstable and turbulent political arenas, remained surprisingly insulated from the regional turmoil. Protests in Jordan did not catch on to form a large-scale popular challenge. Calm in Qatar and the United Arab Emirates (UAE) may not be surprising given their great wealth and small populations, but the same cannot be said for Saudi Arabia, which had many of the antecedent conditions that would predict turbulence (large underemployed youth population, media censorship combined with high satellite TV and Internet penetration, divisions within the royal family, unpopular foreign policy).

One argument that we assess is the distinctive role of youth in shaping and driving these protests (see chapter 14).[24] Some analysts argue that across many Arab countries, "youths," as self-aware and self-identified actors, have even become a novel category for political analysis. These analysts point to objective grievances of the youth sector, such as underemployment and the difficulties of marriage, noting that they may have been disproportionately disadvantaged by neoliberalism. They also point out that many of these young people, especially urban youth, are "digital natives," conversant with information technology of all sorts and socialized into communicative norms completely at odds with the long-standing traditions of the internalized deference and self-censorship characteristic of Arab authoritarian societies.[25] In some cases, these youth activists were clearly the agents of the uprisings, but it is less obvious that they were necessary for the uprisings, to say nothing about being sufficient. As protests spread throughout the region, countries with few previously prominent youth activists seemed just as prone to sudden outbreaks of protest as did those with many activists. Evidence from Egypt even shows that middle-aged people participated at a higher rate than did youth in the protests during the revolution.

Crucially, mobilization took different forms, and its success cannot be judged solely on the survival or failure of regimes.[26] Kuwait, for instance, did not see regime change but did witness the largest and most enduring political protests in its modern history, forcing the resignation of a long-serving prime minister and the dissolution of its parliament. Although Moroccan and Jordanian protesters failed to dislodge their kings, they nonetheless reshaped the terms of political action. The new levels of political engagement, circulation of information and opinion, and willingness to challenge the political status quo that have become political norms may prove to be a more enduring transformation than the fate of any one regime.

Another argument concerning mobilization pertains to the importance of labor movements in channeling economic grievances and bringing into the streets people who had little interest in formal political institutions. In Tunisia, for instance, such labor movements seemed to play a critical role, and in Egypt, wildcat strikes had spread rapidly for years and politicized a wide swath of urban society (see chapter 10). In the 1980s, economic protests against reforms mandated by the International Monetary Fund (IMF) were a common feature of political life and helped drive significant democratic moves in several countries, including Jordan and Tunisia. Many analysts point to the pervasive impact of neoliberal economic reforms, which hollowed out the middle class while enriching a new class of well-connected insiders and impoverishing the already struggling poor. Highly visible corruption and conspicuous consumption during hard times may have provided one of the many sparks for the uprisings.

Islamist movements were a distinct actor in most of these cases, typically with a higher level of organizational strength than other challengers and also with a particular ability to trigger regime and international fears (see chapter 11).[27] The discussion about transition to democracy is heavily shaped by those fears, as many analysts continue to believe that Islamists are distinguished by their lack of true commitment to liberal democracy. The near future will test many previously held assumptions about Islamist movements. The removal of the hard ceiling on their ability to gain power tested their oft-stated commitments to democracy, pluralism, and tolerance, and Egypt's military coup and bloody repression of the Muslim Brotherhood will test its commitment to nonviolence. It is too soon to know whether the common assumption that they will dominate free elections in perpetuity will prove correct. Having evolved to survive repressive environments, they may or may not adapt successfully to radically changed opportunities and constraints, and their organizational advantages in "getting out the vote" may be swamped by a high turnout in transitional elections. They may face internal divides; they may be forced to choose between appealing to a conservative religious base or a mainstream public; or they themselves may not know how far to push their ideological commitments.

Finally, in explaining the nature of this mobilization in 2011, we must explain the failure of earlier protests to develop the same momentum. As we noted earlier, there is a long history of mobilization in Arab societies but few examples of their successfully forcing regime change. Why did the protests against IMF reforms in Jordan and several North African countries in the late 1980s not lead to more enduring political transformation? Why didn't the labor strikes in Tunisia between 2004 and 2008 catalyze a movement back then? Why did Egyptian protesters consistently fail to mobilize large-scale protest from 2006 to 2010 despite the manifestly growing discontent and increased repression? Indeed, on the eve of Egypt's January 25 uprisings, most protest organizers were frustrated by their inability to spark large-scale participation and by the regime's self-confident repression and political manipulation.

The ability to create master frames linking disparate social forces into a single protest movement may be a critical intervening variable explaining the successful mobilization.[28] In the past, according to this argument, different forms of protest could be seen all over the region, but they did not "link up" into a single identifiable movement with clear demands and a master narrative. Again, the discourse of demands for human dignity, personal respect, and government accountability extended the appeal of these movements well beyond the "interest groups" that had animated labor protests, student strikes, Islamist rallies, and previous efforts to mobilize opposition.[29] It remains very much an open question whether two decades of international democracy assistance and civil society building programs contributed in a meaningful way to the emergence of the individuals and groups with the competencies to effectively challenge their regimes.[30]

Decisions about nonviolence and violence, and the general breaking of taboos and red lines, lay at the heart of the contentious nature of politics.[31] It always has been misleading to speak of "nonviolent" revolutions in Egypt or Tunisia, where thousands of citizens were killed in street clashes and countless police offices and Egypt's National Democratic Party (NDP) headquarters were torched. But there is a key difference between the non-militarized uprisings and the decision by Libyan and Syrian protesters to take up arms. Why some protest movements turned to armed insurrection while others remained relatively peaceful even in the face of extreme provocation is one of the most vital questions raised by these cases. Is peaceful mobilization more effective by commanding moral force with the international community and persuasive appeal to fence-sitters in the population and the regime? Is armed insurrection more likely to rapidly shatter the regime or to attract international support?

Responses by Regimes

Why did some regimes respond to the outburst of protest with political concessions and preemptive dialogue, and others take hard lines? Why did the military sometimes decide to shoot at the protesters and, in other cases, exercise restraint?[32] Why did some regimes decide to sacrifice their leaders (Egypt, Tunisia) in hopes of protecting their core interests, and others (Syria) remain loyal?

In two key cases of significant change, Egypt and Tunisia, the president and top regime officials abandoned power—or were sacrificed by their armed forces—in the face of a mobilized population, leaving the military to broker a transition to a new regime. The case that best fits the "pacted" model is probably Yemen, in which Ali Abdullah Saleh was eventually eased from the presidency after long, internationally facilitated negotiations, and his replacement was ratified in a popular referendum. Efforts at a pact failed in Bahrain, however, when a deal between soft-liners in the regime with moderates in the opposition failed in the face of provocations by opposition radicals, a pushback by regime hard-liners, and the Saudis' forceful intervention to tip the balance back toward the minority-dominant autocracy.

The credibility of regime reform offers also is important. Although Morocco's constitutional reforms did not affect the core of monarchical rule, they did reshape the political debate, divide and co-opt parts of the opposition, and help the king ride out the storm. In other countries, however, offers of reform were quickly dismissed. Under what conditions do oppositions accept such offers as credible and binding, and when do they reject even generous offers in favor of continued protests? Here the shadow of the past weighs heavily, as in the Yemeni opposition's dismissal of sweeping reform offers from President Saleh on the grounds that he had made and broken such promises many times in the past. Mechanisms of signaling credible commitment or the emergence of third parties to enforce bargains also may have worked in the past, although to date the former have been difficult to generate, and the latter (primarily the role of the military in Egypt and Tunisia) have proven contentious as well. On the flip side, the Saudi regime proved successful in heading off large-scale protests, in part by throwing huge amounts of money at both economically frustrated citizens and the Islamist networks and institutions that might otherwise have taken the lead in mobilizing dissent.[33]

The very uneven strength and penetration of the state apparatuses across the region shaped the regimes' responses. In Egypt and Tunisia, where we find relatively strong states, the rebellions were met with disciplined responses and prompt decisions to sacrifice the regime, or at least its incumbents, in favor of the stability of the state itself. In the countries with the weakest states—Libya, Yemen—the prospect of removing the regime signaled the collapse of the state, and the rulers' ineffectual resistance led to prolonged and ineffective rebellion. Where the regime's project is state building itself, in countries like Algeria and Syria, the regimes (and their military forces) see themselves as the builder and protector of the state, and they are prepared to be brutal in putting down rebellions that they see as challenges, not merely to their regimes, but also to the coherence and autonomy of the state itself. This is particularly true for relatively large unwieldy states in which sectarian and ethnic divisions have bedeviled politics in the recent past.

What about the monarchical exception? It is striking that all of the region's monarchies have survived, compared with the collapse of five nonmonarchical regimes. Some have used this pattern to argue for a particular logic of monarchical institution that provides for greater legitimacy, more flexibility, or more effective cross-national cooperation.[34] But others point to confounding factors. The monarchies of the GCC enjoyed several distinct advantages not shared by the regimes that fell. Oil and gas revenues bestowed financial advantages that allowed these regimes to co-opt or crush the opposition and to offer economic incentives to angry citizens. The geostrategic position of these regimes also gave them greater international support, as oil-dependent and Iran-fearing Western governments shied away from challenging Gulf regimes. Finally, these regimes cooperated more effectively than is the norm in Arab politics, with Saudi Arabia and the wealthier GCC states providing cash, media and political support, and, in extremis, military intervention to protect their own.

The regimes' use of violence seems to be an inflection point in the fate of mobilizations. Regimes have faced the classic repression/dissent nexus with fascinating results.[35] The failure to repress forcefully allows mobilization to escalate, which could trigger an informational cascade like that described by Kuran and Lohmann. But violent repression—particularly when images are captured and disseminated through social media and al-Jazeera—seems also to trigger protest escalation and to spread dissent into previously quiescent quarters by generating outrage and revealing the "true face" of the regime. For decades, most Arab regimes seemed to have found a "Goldilocks equilibrium" of just the right amount of violence and repression to deter challengers. But in 2011, some lost that equilibrium and repeatedly misjudged the timing and extent of repression.

International positions vis-à-vis regimes and violence also raise important questions and reveal great variation. Why did the United States and the European powers move to sanctions against some regimes but not others? Why a military intervention in the name of a "responsibility to protect" in Libya but not in Syria or Yemen or Bahrain? Why did the United States push for a transition away from Hosni Mubarak, a key regional ally, relatively quickly, despite the massive interests at stake for both itself and Israel? Why did it hold back from similar calls against King Hamad of Bahrain? Why did Saudi Arabia and the GCC intervene so forcefully in Bahrain? Often, the answers to these questions are not surprising: there are few options for military action in Syria; Saudi oil makes it unlikely that any U.S. president could oppose it on a matter defined as existential; and so forth. But the popular expectations of the United States do not necessarily factor in those practical limitations, and nervous regimes may lack confidence in what seems obvious.

Political Outcomes

It would be premature to define the dependent variable as "revolution," much less "democratic transition" (see chapter 2). As yet, only Tunisia has the makings of a true revolution, and even that remains uncertain. Other states, from Egypt to Yemen to Syria, may yet experience genuine political transformations that bring to power different ruling elites and incorporate social groups into the ruling bargain in different ways. But this has not yet happened, and it is not possible at this point to conclusively code the outcome of political change in any of the Arab cases. Core conceptual questions still need more attention: How heavily should we weigh the departure of leaders against the perpetuation of the old regime's institutions? Do elections signal an end to the transitional period, and if so, does it matter whether those elections are won by the opposition, by old regime figures, or by popular forces unpopular with other protesters, such as Egypt's Muslim Brotherhood (see chapter 12)? Are "outcomes" best seen at the level of society rather than the official political realm?

The "transitions" literature argued that democracy was most likely to result from a painful and costly stalemate among political forces that led them to accept political rules allowing for the peaceful resolution of an uncertain conflict. But Michael McFaul's work on postcommunist transitions found quite the opposite: "It was situations of unequal distributions of power which produced the quickest and most stable transitions from communist rule. In countries with asymmetrical balances of power, it was the ideological orientation of the more powerful party that largely determined the type of regime to emerge."[36] This points to an important question for comparative research: What is the balance of power among social forces in transitional cases, and what outcomes do they tend to produce?

McFaul also points to the ideological preferences of the more powerful parties as a crucial factor, with democracy most likely to result when "democrats" have the upper hand and impose that system. In the Middle Eastern cases, the most powerful party is likely to be either Islamist or the remnants of the old regime, neither known for their deep commitment to democracy. What is the balance of power in each case between democrats and autocrats (and, for that matter, Islamists)? The optimistic case for Egypt is that like the success stories of postcommunism, the democrats have the upper hand as long as mobilization is sustained, given the high value placed on democracy in the public sphere and the long struggle for democratic reforms by an array of social forces over a decade. In Tunisia, the Islamists of al-Nahda and an array of leftist and liberal trends seem, at least for now, united around a commitment to creating a democratic constitution. In other cases, this is far less clear, and in some places, there may be very little ideological competition at all, as political actors compete merely to protect and advance their own personal interests or clientelistic networks. In Jordan, Morocco, and many Gulf states, a case can be made that there is significant popular and elite support for the status quo, which gives autocrats the upper hand against even mobilized democrats. In such cases, the main battle is not between democrats and autocrats but among competing princes and between the regime and conservative Islamist networks.

Then there is the question of continued mobilization. The emergence of turbulent, contentious societies may ultimately be more important than who sits in the presidential office. McFaul argues that continued mobilization is positive, not negative (despite the transitions literature), for producing democratic outcomes, since it can prove that the balance of power is in the opposition's favor, imposing democracy on elites. Mobilization is one of the few ways for publics to assert their power and preferences over those of entrenched elites, but it also can have major economic costs (such as the collapse of tourism in Egypt and Tunisia) and can alienate mainstream publics.[37] This is a very active debate in Egypt, in particular, where activists have questioned whether maintaining street protests effectively pressured Egypt's Supreme Council of the Armed Forces (SCAF) or alienated those who supported the revolution but yearn for a return to normality. The Muslim Brotherhood faced a virtually identical strategic dilemma following the Egyptian coup, as it mounted sustained protests to prevent the consolidation of a new order.

Constitutions and the judiciary have emerged as surprisingly central to these transitions (see chapter 15).[38] The upheavals generated uncertainty about the rules of the political game and raised the stakes for defining new rules in a transitional moment that could not last. In the absence of the clear rules for ensuring government accountability that are typically inscribed in constitutions, one of the few effective ways of holding governments to account is continued, albeit uninstitutionalized, popular mobilization expressed in protests, demonstrations, and marches. But such mobilization may itself undermine hopes for reaching a consensus on new rules that might allow a return to political normality.

Outcomes may also be shaped by the focus on political issues—from democratic elections and constitutional design to foreign policy—rather than on questions of political economy. Economic grievances may have been crucial to driving discontent, but few of the transitional governments have been able or willing to respond effectively. This may be because the economic challenges are technically more complex or because they are politically more contentious, a possibility suggested by the likely hostile

popular response to the conditions attached to offers of desperately needed foreign economic assistance from the United States, the Group of Eight
(G8), and the IMF.

Thus, the impact of the economy's condition may be felt most keenly in
the second, rather than the first, posttransition election. No government
in Egypt, Tunisia, or other potential cases of transition seems likely to be
able to deal effectively in the short term with the massive problems of debt,
underemployment, and uncompetitive economies that caused the underlying frustration.[39] The international aid offered by the United States, the
G8, the World Bank, the IMF, and the Gulf states to support these transitions all comes with strings attached, and these strings will pull in different directions. International aid from industrialized countries and international financial institutions is likely to be pegged specifically to demands
for further neoliberal reforms, which some analysts believe contributed
to many of the current problems (such as rising inequality, a deteriorating
social safety net, corruption, and low levels of job creation). This could create openings for populists of all stripes, whatever the short-term outcome
of the political transition.

The question of how to deal with figures of the old regime hangs heavily over the Arab cases, as it did in earlier cases of political change.[40] The
memory of de-Baathification in Iraq, which turned out hundreds of thousands of state functionaries and well-armed fighters into the streets, offers a
cautionary tale to those who seek revenge against the old order. More immediate and urgent is the question of guarantees of immunity for top regime
officials. For those who seek revenge, the prosecution of the Mubarak family is very satisfying, whereas the GCC's offer of immunity to Yemen's President Ali Abdullah Saleh was repugnant. But for those who seek more rapid
transitions, such prosecutions may send a dangerous message: If surrendering power means prosecution and execution, why shouldn't autocrats fight
to the end? The lesson of South Africa, Chile, and other countries may be
that truth and reconciliation commissions later may be more conducive to
real transitions than immediate prosecution. But such arguments are difficult to sustain in the heat of a revolution. The role of the International
Criminal Court adds a new dimension to this, with indictments of figures
like Qaddafi and Asad becoming an instrument of leverage but also potentially blocking the path to peaceful transfers of power.

The importance to these political outcomes of widely held individual
beliefs and preferences is worth considering (see chapter 13). Polls have
consistently shown that more than 80 percent of the Arabs surveyed have

consistently expressed support for democratic forms of government.[41] They also show high levels of support in many countries for basing legislation on *sharia*. Do such findings matter for the political outcome? By what mechanism might a generalized but inchoate preference for "democracy" affect the strategic gamesmanship of elites or the power struggles among competing trends?

Finally, the role of international actors and factors may matter more in the Middle East than elsewhere, given the region's geopolitical centrality and the long tradition of deep foreign involvement in its internal politics. Unlike the postcommunist world, from which the Soviet Union quite literally disappeared, the United States remains closely involved in the internal dynamics of the Arab cases and has not declared its indifference to political outcomes in its client states—but it has gone further in accepting political change and advocating reform than many analysts might have expected.[42] What is more, regional actors tend to be far more entangled in the domestic affairs of others in the emerging environment, a "new cold war" in which political struggles involve competitive mobilization and patronage. The Saudi and UAE role in preempting Bahraini reform and supporting egypt's coup is the most obvious example, but more subtle interventions are widespread across the region. This will pose a powerful test of very old questions about the Middle East's strength, stability, and legitimacy: Are political outcomes shaped more by internal factors or by regional and international forces?

A Dynamic Framework for Understanding the Uprisings

This book's framework is designed to organize analyses of the 2011 Arab upheavals and to isolate particular hypotheses, actors, and issues. Because the variation in political outcomes may be explained at several different levels, we concentrate on the dynamic, strategic interaction across these levels. Protesters who initially were focused on getting Egyptians into the streets quickly turned to choosing how best to persuade the military to side with the people rather than Mubarak and how to best shape international responses to their challenge. Bahrain's turbulent political dynamics seemed to be moving toward an agreement until negotiations broke down and Saudi Arabia forcefully intervened.

Sequence and timing matter enormously, along with the pace of events. Egypt could not have happened without the Tunisian example. It matters that Libya's challenge came to a head just as the world was focused on the successful transition in Egypt and captured the attention of al-Jazeera and the Arab publics at a volatile moment. Had Syria's challenge broken before Libya's, or if Libyan violence had peaked two weeks earlier, the international response might have been very different. Indeed, the impact of the immediate on international actors' decisions to intervene is probably underappreciated: In the absence of hindsight and in the heat of the moment, what appears to be urgent may drive policy assessments that later have unintended ramifications. The dynamics of making major policy adjustments quickly (especially in the "fog of war") is a factor that merits attention, particularly, for example, in the United States' decision to support intervention in Libya, which was much more about the impact of a rebel defeat in Egypt and Tunisia than it was about what was likely to happen in Libya itself. As a result, the United States is left with the consequences of a decision to intervene that has taken on a life of its own.

Timing and sequence matter at the local level as well. In many cases, including Egypt and Yemen, weeks into the protests leaders offered wide-ranging reforms that might have been happily accepted at the outset but that did little to quell popular anger when finally advanced. Repression sometimes squashed dissent before it took root and, at other times, spurred much greater challenges. The uncertainty about rules of the game is paramount here. Without constitutions or legitimate institutions, the actors were forced to play a complex and unsettling game in which they simultaneously struggled for immediate advantage and argued over long-term political rules.

General patterns of inequality or poverty may be less significant in driving unrest than are very short-term changes such as rapidly growing inequality, explosive growth in Internet access, or a rising cost of living. Generically dissatisfied publics may have rapidly and dramatically changed their willingness to join protests based on new information about the distribution of preferences in society (through Facebook groups or observations of others protesting) or about the likelihood of success (the fall of Tunisia's Ben Ali persuading those on the fence that it was worth the risks of joining the protests).

Highly local factors may account for differential patterns within these general environmental conditions, even if they are sufficient for explaining the timing and nature of the protest wave itself. For instance, variations in the sectarian balance within a country may be adequate to explain why Jordanians shied away from joining a major protest wave but Tunisians or Moroccans did not, or why assessments of the strength of the state apparatus and relations between the military and civilian wings of government shaped the regimes' ability and willingness to use violence. Even as local a factor as the presence of central squares like Tahrir where protesters could congregate and consolidate a presence may help explain the endurance of some movements rather than others.

Different dynamics, as well, should be expected during different stages. The initial outbreak of protests, and whether they accelerate or fizzle, should be treated as one phase. The immediate political outcome may be a second distinct phase, as regimes fall, strike a deal with their challengers, or successfully (at least for the short term) repress. Whether violence is introduced is a key variable at this phase. A third phase may be the postmobilization political scene: Do protesters demobilize? Do incumbents honor deals made during the mobilization phase? Does the old guard find ways to recapture state power from challengers who succeeded in earlier phases? How is accountability defined, and how is it embodied in actions and institutions? Is there a transition to stable, institutionalized democracy?

In addition, the international dimension represents a vital overlay to the strategic, mobilizational, and ideational dynamics inside each Arab country. The turbulence in individual countries simply cannot be understood in isolation from the broader regional moment. While the main drivers of protest were domestic in each case, the simultaneity of their eruption points to the relevance of systemic variables. These systemic variables may be both global and regional and could include both structural variables (the distribution of power, the institutional environment, norms, and identities) and process variables (imitation and diffusion, transnational networking). Even highly domestic and local factors often had an international component: local labor strikes breaking out in response to economic conditions shaped by the global financial crisis, protests with an eye on influencing interventions by the United States or the United Nations for or against regimes.

The broadest context comes from the structure of the international system, which might best be described as a declining American unipolarity. For at least two decades, the Middle East had been powerfully shaped by this unipolarity and by 2010 had a robust alliance structure that included every Arab government except Syria's. But by 2009/2010, the financial crisis had undermined the United States' standing and capabilities, and a global power shift toward Asia (particularly China) and the BRICS (Brazil, Russia, India, China, and South Africa) seemed well under way. The legacy of the Bush administration was extremely high levels of anti-Americanism across the region, and massive, expensive military deployments in Iraq and Afghanistan, as well as a widespread belief across the region that President George W. Bush's grand words supporting democracy had been revealed as hypocritical by his reaction to the electoral victory of Hamas in the Gaza Strip. The Obama administration attempted to assuage the anti-Americanism and withdrew more than 100,000 troops from Iraq, but escalated the number of forces in Afghanistan and continued or expanded many of the "global war on terror" activities (such as drone strikes).

The Obama administration's response to the outburst of protest mattered a great deal, in that it signaled to both regimes and opposition groups about whether to expect serious intervention for or against the regime. This was relatively minor in Tunisia, where Europe's role was more significant. But in Egypt, the Obama administration moved remarkably quickly away from the Mubarak regime, calling on its most trusted regional ally to step down only a week into the protests.[43] This suggests a hypothesis: that the United States' moves on Mubarak sent a signal across the region comparable to the decision by the Soviet Union's president, Mikhail Gorbachev, to not intervene to save the Communist government of East Germany in April 1989. This could not satisfy Egyptian protesters, of course, who demanded more and faster action than the United States could possibly have offered, but it did arguably signal to opposition groups across the region that if they rose up effectively and sustained their protest long enough—preferably with nonviolent means—then they might gain American and international protection and support. Regimes similarly may have begun to doubt the value of U.S. commitments: reports abound of Gulf leaders complaining about Mubarak's being "discarded like a used handkerchief"—and acting accordingly.

The importance of the international role led to strategic interaction and framing battles around international intervention. In each case, both protesters and regimes struggled to frame each case: were these terrorists threatening an American ally or peaceful democracy protesters? Shia challengers backed by Iran or a nonsectarian human rights and democracy movement? Although this does not mean that the United States or any other international actor caused the uprisings, it makes little sense to suggest that those outside actors were irrelevant to the course of the political struggles.

At the regional level, the regional polarization of the Bush years remained well in force going into the Arab upheavals. Terrified of Iran, the Arab Gulf states increasingly openly turned to Israel and the United States in an alliance of "moderates" against Iran and its allies. This set them against the dominant trends in public opinion and, in some cases—such as the Mubarak regime's enforcement of the Gaza blockade—clearly contributed to popular condemnation. Cutting against that polarization was the emergence of new "swing states"—particularly Qatar and Turkey—able to appeal effectively to Arab public opinion while maintaining solid working relationships with the United States and the West. As states change domestically, their foreign policies will likely change as well, but within limits. Egypt under Morsi demonstrated more independence from the United States and Israel but maintained the peace treaty and sought to reassure foreign powers about continuity in core policy areas.

The intervention question came into sharpest focus around Libya and Syria. The Libyan regime's violent repression of its protest movement rapidly generated an unusually unified regional call for international intervention, a UN Security Council resolution authorizing action, and then a NATO air campaign in support of the opposition. Ultimately, this limited military intervention allowed the rebels to triumph and overthrow the Qaddafi regime. In Syria, by contrast, the regime's violence prompted significant international condemnation and eventually significant regional support for an armed insurgency against Assad, but not Western military intervention.

Finally, outcomes should be understood in a longer time frame and broader political context than has usually been the case. The unfolding transformations are reshaping the relationship between state and society, the nature of transnational connections, and the flows of political information through multiple networks. The initial wave of revolutionary enthusiasm ended with mixed results, but the deeper transformations continue to unfold in unpredictable ways. Kuwait, for instance, did not have a revolution in February 2011 but, over the next two years, experienced the greatest political crisis of its modern history.

Conclusion

The upheavals in the region do not yet constitute revolutions. Nor do they yet disconfirm findings about the resilience of Arab authoritarian regimes. But they do pose a potent challenge to political scientists specializing in the region, unsettling core findings in the literature and demanding new theoretical approaches. This volume represents an important first step in placing these developments into broader comparative perspective, isolating specific mechanisms and actors, and building toward a preliminary theoretical understanding of these exceptional events. The chapters in this book demonstrate the complexity of the Arab uprisings and the uncertainties about both their causes and their long-term effects. There is little reason to believe that the uprisings will lead neatly to more democratic regimes or that the wave of mobilization will continue to unfold in linear fashion. Indeed, the initial wave of mobilization that erupted in December 2010 has likely peaked, as most Arab arenas bogged down in murky political battle, the regional agenda fragmented, and the bloodshed and sectarian politics of Syria overshadowed the rest of the region. But the events from 2010 through 2014, across multiple countries and sectors, have already generated important variations that allow for useful comparative analysis.

NOTES

1. For a detailed narrative, see Marc Lynch, *The Arab Uprising: The Incomplete Revolutions of the New Middle East* (New York: PublicAffairs, 2012).
2. Larry Diamond, "A Fourth Wave or False Start?" *Foreign Affairs,* May 22, 2011, available online only at http://www.foreignaffairs.com/articles/67862/larry-diamond/a-fourth-wave-or-false-start; Edward Mansfield and Jack Snyder, "Democratization and the Arab Spring," *International Interaction* 38, no. 5 (2012): 722–33; Alfred Stepan and Juan Linz, "Democratization Theory and the Arab Spring," *Journal of Democracy* 24, no. 2 (2013); Alfred Stepan, "Tunisia's Transition and the Twin Tolerations," *Journal of Democracy* 23, no. 2 (2012): 89–103.
3. Sami Zubaida, "The Arab Spring in the Historical Context of Middle East Politics," *Economy and Society* 41, no. 4 (2012): 568–79; Agnieszka Paczynska, "Cross-Regional Comparisons: The Arab Uprisings as Political Transitions and Social Movements," *PS* 46, no. 2 (2013): 217–21.
4. On the Arab public sphere, see Marc Lynch, *Voices of the New Arab Public* (New York: Columbia University Press, 2006), and Lynch, *The Arab Uprising*; on transnational activist networks, see Kathryn Sikkink and Margaret Keck, *Activists Beyond Borders* (Ithaca, N.Y.: Cornell University Press, 1998).
5. Lisa Anderson, "Demystifying the Arab Spring," *Foreign Affairs*, 90, no. 3 (May/June 2011): 2–54 .
6. Olivier Roy, "The Transformation of the Arab World," *Journal of Democracy* 23, no. 3 (2012): 5–18.
7. Eva Bellin, "Arab Authoritarianism in Comparative Perspective," *Comparative Politics* 36, no. 2 (2004): 139–57; Fred Halliday, *The Middle East in International Relations* (New York: Cambridge University Press, 2003); Nazih Ayubi, *Over-Stating the Arab State* (London: I. B. Tauris, 1995); Michele Angrist Penner and Marsha

Pripstein Posusney, eds., *Authoritarianism in the Middle East* (Boulder, Colo.: Lynne Rienner, 2005); Jason Brownlee, *Authoritarianism in an Age of Democratization* (New York: Cambridge University Press, 2007).

8. Mark Beissinger, *Nationalist Mobilization and the Collapse of the Soviet State* (New York: Cambridge University Press, 2002).

9. On Eastern Europe, see Michael McFaul, "The Fourth Wave of Democracy and Dictatorship: Noncooperative Transitions in the Postcommunist World," *World Politics* 54, no. 2 (January 2002): 212–44. On Africa, see Michael Bratton and Nicolas van de Walle, *Democratic Experiments in Africa: Regime Transitions in Comparative Perspective* (New York: Cambridge University Press 1997).

10. Eva Bellin, "Reconsidering the Robustness of Authoritarianism in the Middle East: Lessons from the Arab Spring," *Comparative Politics* 44, no. 2 (2012): 127–49.

11. Ellen Lust-Okar, *Structuring Conflict in the Arab World* (New York: Cambridge University Press, 2005).

12. Penner and Posusney, *Authoritarianism in the Middle East,* 26.

13. Steven Heydemann, "Upgrading Authoritarianism in the Arab World," Saban Center for Middle East Policy Analysis Paper no. 13 (Washington, D.C.: Brookings Institution, October 2007); Daniel Brumberg, "The Trap of Liberalized Autocracy," *Journal of Democracy* 13, no. 4 (October 2002): 56–68; Jason Brownlee, "Portents of Pluralism: How Hybrid Regimes Affect Democratic Transitions," *American Journal of Political Science* 53, no. 3 (July 2009): 515–32; Marsha Pripstein Posusney, "Enduring Authoritarianism: Middle East Lessons for Comparative Politics," *Comparative Politics* 36, no. 2 (2004): 127–38.

14. Lisa Anderson, "Searching Where the Light Shines: Studying Democratization in the Middle East," *Annual Review of Political Science* 9 (2006): 189–214; Vickie Langohr, "Too Much Civil Society, Too Little Politics: Egypt and Liberalizing Arab Regimes," *Comparative Politics* 36, no. 2 (January 2004): 181–204; John Waterbury, "Democracy Without Democrats? The Potential for Political Liberalization in the Middle East," in *Democracy Without Democrats? The Renewal of Politics in the Muslim World,* ed. Ghassan Salamé (New York: I. B. Tauris, 1994), 23–47; Rex Brynen, Baghat Korany, and Paul Noble, eds., *Political Liberalization and Democratization in the Arab World: Theoretical Perspectives* (Boulder, Colo.: Lynne Rienner, 1995).

15. Jillian Schwedler, *Faith in Moderation: Islamist Parties in Jordan and Yemen* (New York: Cambridge University Press, 2006); Mona El-Ghobashy, "The Metamorphosis of the Egyptian Muslim Brothers," *International Journal of Middle East Studies* 37, no. 3 (August 2005): 373–95; Rabab El-Mahdi, "Enough!: Egypt's Quest for Democracy," *Comparative Political Studies* 42, no. 8 (August 2009): 1011–39.

16. Asef Bayat, *Life as Politics* (Stanford, Calif.: Stanford University Press, 2009).

17. For discussion of this literature, see F. Gregory Gause III, "The Middle East Academic Community and the 'Winter of Arab Discontent': Why Did We Miss It?" in *Seismic Shift: Understanding Change in the Middle East,* ed. Ellen B. Laipson (Washington, D.C.: Henry L. Stimson Center, 2011): 11–26.

18. Joel Beinin, "Egyptian Workers and January 25: A Social Movement in Historical Context," *Social Research* 79, no. 2 (2012), 323–50.

19. Asef Bayat, "The 'Street' and the Politics of Dissent in the Arab World," *Middle East Report* 226 (spring 2003): 10–17; Marc Lynch, "Beyond the Arab Street," *Politics and Society* 31, no. 1 (March 2003): 55–92.

20. Henry E. Hale, "Regime Change Cascades: What We Have Learned from the 1848 Revolutions to the 2011 Arab Uprisings," *Annual Review of Political Science* 16 (2013): 331–53; Roger Owen, "The Arab 'Demonstration' Effect and the Revival of Arab Unity in the Arab Spring," *Contemporary Arab Affairs* 5, no. 3 (2012): 372–81; Kurt Weyland, "The Arab Spring: Why the Surprising Similarities with the Revolutionary Wave of 1848?" *Perspectives on Politics* 10, no. 4 (2012): 917–34; Stephen Saideman, "When Conflict Spreads: The Arab Spring and the Limits of Diffusion," *International Interaction* 38, no. 5 (2012): 713–22.

21. Charles Kurzman, "The Arab Spring Uncoiled," *Mobilization* 17, no. 4 (2012): 377–90; Asef Bayat, "The Arab Spring and Its Surprises," *Development and Change* 44, no. 3 (2013): 587–601.

22. Timur Kuran, "Now Out of Never: The Element of Surprise in the East European Revolution of 1989," *World Politics* 44, no. 1 (October 1991): 7–48; Susanne Lohmann, "The Dynamics of Informational Cascades: The Monday Demonstrations in Leipzig, East Germany, 1989–91," *World Politics* 47, no. 1 (October 1994): 42–101.

23. Wendy Pearlman, "Emotions and the Microfoundations of the Arab Uprisings," *Perspectives on Politics* 11, no. 2 (2013): 387–409; Reinoud Leenders, "Collective Action and Mobilization in Dar'a: An Anatomy of the Onset of Syria's Popular Uprising," *Mobilization* 17, no. 4 (2012): 419–34; Tova Benski and Lauren Langman, "The Effects of Affects: The Place of Emotions in the Mobilizations of 2011," *Current Sociology* 61, no. 4 (2013): 525–40; Talal Asad, "Fear and the Ruptured State: Reflections on Egypt After Mubarak," *Social Research* 79, no. 2 (2012), 271–300.

24. For an outstanding discussion of the Egyptian mobilization, see Mona El-Ghobashy, "The Praxis of the Egyptian Revolution," *Middle East Report* 41, no. 258 (spring 2011): 3–11; and Dina Shehata, "The Fall of the Pharaoh," *Foreign Affairs* 90, no. 3 (May/June 2011): 26–32.

25. Lisa Wedeen, *Ambiguities of Domination: Politics, Rhetoric, and Symbols in Contemporary Syria* (Chicago: University of Chicago Press, 1999).

26. Ingo Forstenlechner, Emilie Rutledge, and Rashid al Nuaimi, "The UAE, the Arab Spring, and Different Kinds of Dissent," *Middle East Policy* 19, no. 3 (2012): 84–98; Thierry Desrues, "Mobilizations in a Hybrid Regime: The 20th February Movement and the Moroccan Regime," *Current Sociology* 61, no. 4 (2013): 409–23; Mona El-Ghobashy, "Politics by Other Means: In Egypt, Street Protests Set the Political Agenda," *Boston Review* 36, no. 6 (2011): 39–44; Sari Hanafi, "The Arab Revolutions: The Emergence of a New Political Subjectivity," *Contemporary Arab Affairs* 5, no. 2 (2012): 198–213; Anja Hoffmann and Christoph Konig, "Scratching the Democratic Facade: Framing Strategies of the 20 February Movement," *Mediterranean*

Politics 18, no. 1 (2013): 1–22; Reinoud Leenders and Steven Heydemann, "Popular Mobilization in Syria: Opportunity and Threat, and the Social Networks of Early Risers," *Mediterranean Politics* 17, no. 2 (2012): 139–59.

27. The role of Communist movements in Latin American cases may offer some useful comparative perspective; also see Quintan Wiktorowicz, ed., *Islamic Activism: A Social Movement Theory Approach* (Bloomington: Indiana University Press, 2004). On Islamist movements in the Arab uprisings, see Khalil Anani and Maszlee Malik, "Pious Way to Politics: The Rise of Political Salafism in Post-Mubarak Egypt," *Digest of Middle East Politics* 22, no. 1 (2013): 57–73; Nathan Brown, "Contention in Religion and State in Postrevolutionary Egypt," *Social Research* 79, no. 2 (2012), 531–52; Rikke Hostrup Haugbølle and Francesco Cavatorta, "Beyond Ghannouchi: Islamism and Social Change in Tunisia," *Middle East Report* 262 (2012): 20–25; Khalid Madhi, "Islamism(s) and the Arab Uprisings: Between Commanding the Faithful and Mobilising the Protestor," *Journal of North African Studies* 18, no. 2 (2013): 248–71; Jillian Schwedler, "Islamists in Power? Inclusion, Moderation and the Arab Uprisings," *Middle East Development Journal* 5, no. 1 (2013): 1–18.

28. On framing, see Doug McAdam, Sidney Tarrow, and Charles Tilly, *Dynamics of Contention* (New York: Cambridge University Press, 2001).

29. Jeffry Halverson, Scott Ruston and Angela Trethewy, "Mediated Martyrs of the Arab Spring: New Media, Civil Religion, and Narrative in Tunisia and Egypt," *Journal of Communication* 63, no. 2 (2013): 312–32; Naila Hamdy and Ehab Gomaa, "Framing the Egyptian Uprising in Arabic Language Newspapers and Social Media," *Journal of Communication* 62, no. 2 (2012): 195–211.

30. Sheila Carapico, "Foreign Aid for Promoting Democracy in the Arab World," *Middle East Journal* 56, no. 3 (summer 2002): 379–95; Thomas Carothers and Marina Ottaway, eds., *Uncharted Journey: Promoting Democracy in the Middle East* (Washington, D.C.: Carnegie Endowment for International Peace, 2005); Tamara Wittes, *Freedom's Unsteady March: America's Role in Building Arab Democracy* (Washington, D.C.: Brookings Institution Press, 2008).

31. Chibli Mallat, "The Philosophy of the Mideast Revolution, Take One: Non-Violence," *Middle East Law and Governance* 3 (2011): 136–47; Sharon Erickson Nepstad, "Mutiny and Nonviolence in the Arab Spring: Exploring Military Defections and Loyalty in Egypt, Bahrain and Syria," *Journal of Peace Research* 50, no. 3 (2013): 337–49.

32. Holger Albrecht and Dina Bishara, "Back on Horseback: The Military and Political Transformation in Egypt," *Middle East Law and Governance* 3 (2011): 13–23; Zoltan Barany, "The Role of the Military," *Journal of Democracy* 22, no. 4 (2011): 24–35; Risa Brooks, "Abandoned at the Palace: Why the Tunisian Military Defected from the Ben Ali Regime in January 2011," *Journal of Strategic Studies* 36, no. 2 (2013): 205–20; Phillipe Droz-Vincent, "Prospects for Democratic Control of the Armed Forces? Comparative Insights and Lessons for the Arab World in Transition," *Armed Forces and Society* 2013; Hillel Frisch, "The Egyptian Army and Egypt's 'Spring,'" *Journal of Strategic Studies* 36, no. 2 (2013): 180–204; Florence Gaub, "The

Libyan Armed Forces Between Coup-Proofing and Repression," *Journal of Strategic Studies* 36, no. 2 (2013): 221–44; Michael Knights, "The Military Role in Yemen's Protests," *Journal of Strategic Studies* 36, no. 2 (2013): 261–88; Laurence Louer, "Sectarianism and Coup-Proofing Strategies in Bahrain," *Journal of Strategic Studies* 36, no. 2 (2013): 245–60; Derek Lutterbeck, "Arab Uprisings, Armed Forces, and Civil-Military Relations," *Armed Forces and Society* 39, no. 1 (2013): 28–54; Curtis Ryan, "The Armed Forces and the Arab Uprisings: The Case of Jordan," *Middle East Law and Governance*, 4, no. 1 (2012): 153–67.

33. On the Saudi strategy, see the comments by Stephane Lacroix and Steffen Hertog in *The Arab Uprisings: The Saudi Counter-Revolution* (POMEPS Briefs #5, August 9, 2011, available at http://pomeps.org/2011/08/arab-uprisings-the-saudi-counter-revolution/); Stephane Lacroix, "Is Saudi Arabia Immune?" *Journal of Democracy* 22, no. 4 (2011): 48–59; Madawi Al-Rasheed, "No Saudi Spring: Anatomy of a Failed Revolution," *Boston Review* 37, no. 2 (2012): 32–39; Madawi Al-Rasheed, "Sectarianism as Counter-Revolution: Saudi Responses to the Arab Spring," *Studies in Ethnicity and Nationalism* 11, no. 3 (2011): 513–26.

34. Sean Yom and F. Gregory Gause III, "Resilient Royals: How Arab Monarchs Hang On," *Journal of Democracy* 23, no. 4 (2012): 74–88; Victor Menaldo, "The Middle East and North Africa's Resilient Monarchs," *Journal of Politics* 74, no. 3 (2012): 707–22.

35. Christian Davenport and Will Moore, "The Arab Spring, Winter, and Back Again? (Re)Introducing the Dissent-Repression Nexus with a Twist," *International Interaction* 38, no. 5 (2012): 704–13; Mauricio Rivera Celestino and Kristian Gleditsch, "Fresh Carnations or All Thorn, No Rose? Nonviolent Campaigns and Transitions in Autocracies," *Journal of Peace Research* 50, no. 3 (2013): 385–400.

36. Michael McFaul, "The Fourth Wave of Democracy and Dictatorship: Noncooperative Transitions in the Postcommunist World," *World Politics* 54, no. 2 (January 2002): 212–44.

37. For an earlier discussion of this issue, see Larbi Sadiki, "Popular Uprisings and Arab Democratization," *International Journal of Middle East Studies* 32, no. 1 (February 2000): 71–95.

38. Nathan Brown, *Constitutions in a Nonconstitutional World: Arab Basic Laws and the Prospects for Accountable Government* (Albany: State University of New York Press, 2002).

39. Clement M. Henry and Robert Springborg, *Globalization and the Politics of Development in the Middle East* (New York: Cambridge University Press, 2010).

40. Priscilla Hayner, *Unspeakable Truths: Transitional Justice and the Challenge of Truth Commissions*, 2nd ed. (New York: Routledge, 2011).

41. Mark Tessler, Amaney Jamal, and Michael Robbins, "New Findings on Arabs and Democracy," *Journal of Democracy* 23, no. 4 (2012): 89–103; Mark Tessler and Eleanor Gao, "Gauging Arab Support for Democracy," *Journal of Democracy* 16, no. 3 (2005): 83–97.

42. The fullest statement of U.S. thinking on the Arab upheavals came in the speech delivered by President Barack Obama at the U.S. Department of State, May 19, 2011. For the full text of the speech, see http://www.whitehouse.gov/the-press-office/2011/05/19/remarks-president-middle-east-and-north-africa.

43. Marc Lynch, "America and Egypt After the Uprisings," *Survival* 53, no. 2 (April 2011): 31–42; Jason Brownlee, *Deterring Democracy* (New York: Cambridge University Press, 2012).

2

Theories of Transition

DANIEL BRUMBERG

Momentous political events often undermine cherished assumptions. The collapse of the Soviet Union was one such occasion, as with its demise the field of Sovietology virtually disappeared. Caught unaware, social scientists were cast in a sea of paradigms, unsure of which to grab as a "third wave" of change transformed entire political landscapes.[1] More than twenty years later, scholars of the Arab world are suffering their own paradigm crisis. Surprised by mass political rebellions that few saw coming, beyond asking hard questions about the theories that had informed our work, we are once again trying to decide just how our geographic area fits into the wider field of comparative politics itself.

This question of "fit" is hardly unique to our field. Whether studying Asia, the Middle East, sub-Saharan Africa, or Latin America, all regional scholars must strike a balance between more generalized theories that emphasize the structures, dynamics, and logics that cross geographic boundaries and the geographically focused inquiries that highlight the particulars of local cultures, identities, and social structures. Because politics is always both exceptional and universal, finding this conceptual sweet spot is an occupational preoccupation (or hazard). Thus it should come as no surprise that Middle East scholars—who seem especially prone to conceptual envy—have periodically suffered bouts of fractious analytical introspection.[2]

What distinguishes this latest round of academic self-flagellation is the scope of political change provoked by 2011 Arab rebellions. After a decade of regionally focused work that probed the assumed resilience of autocracy, the exhilaration of mass revolt inspired scholars and policymakers alike to dust off grand theories of democratization and regime transition. Even the very term "Arab spring" spoke to this embrace of a universalistic conceptual optimism, one that suggested an Arab world catching up with history itself.

I wrote the first draft of this chapter in the crucible of this analytical enthusiasm. Although I hoped that the young people massing in Cairo's Tahrir Square and in other Arab capitals would prevail, I concentrated on the enduring obstacles to democratization and, in turn, the limitations of deductive models that are said to capture such dynamics. Yet if the ensuing trajectories of revolt seem to warrant this guarded view, I am not calling for a return to the dead end of "Arab exceptionalism." The term is as ahistorical—and thus as useless—as notions of global democratization. What we need instead is a more "bounded" approach, one that looks at how political change, contestation, and negotiation in the Arab world are conditioned by local, national, or regional forces. Among these forces, the role of identity conflicts is a crucial variable, one that merits more serious conceptualization within a broader (if midrange) theory of change.

To set out this argument, I begin by discussing the evolution of the comparative politics field after World War II. This brief examination of "modernization theory and its discontents" may seem like an unnecessary detour. In fact, however, the emergence of the transitions paradigm is closely connected to this story. Indeed, the transitions paradigm tried to transcend the highly polarized debate between the advocates of modernization theory, who focused on grand social and political structures, and the advocates of culturalist analysis, who emphasized local or national symbols, values, and traditions. Transitions theory sought to exit this debate by envisioning democratization as a rational process by which competing elites embrace democratic procedures not because they have intrinsic value but because they provide a means to peacefully resolve violent conflicts over economic policy. Seemingly devoid of any of cultural, economic, or institutional "prerequisites" for democracy, the transitions paradigm posited what seemed like a universal theory that could be applied to any geographic or national arenas.

This quest for universal relevance has been assailed for its failure to account for cases in which identity, cultural, or religious factors shape political behavior and actions. Although I share this concern, I shall try to show that paradigm has been widely misunderstood. Far from deploying an acultural or "rationalist" approach, it modifies rather than transcends mainstream modernization theory. Indeed, the transitions paradigm retains the former's focus on the structural conditions that can create openings for democratic change but adds a useful conceptual edge by highlighting the role that leaders play in forging agreements that help realize the potential created by structural change. This emphasis on agency was thus a corrective rather than a fundamental paradigm break. Its great advantage was both theoretical and practical: the authors of the transition paradigm focused on leadership because they wanted to help opposition elites create strategies for negotiating with military regimes that were being subject to severe legitimacy crises. Their fourth volume in the *Transitions from Authoritarianism* series was, in fact, a kind of self-help book.[3]

This focus on praxis had clear conceptual limitations: largely based on the evolution of a handful of Latin American cases over a short period of time, the transitions paradigm cannot account for much variance in regard to outcomes. Why does pact making succeed in some cases, fail in others, or take place only to be followed by authoritarian regression in yet other cases? To explain such diversity, we must move from a short-term strategic focus on the choices that elites use to overcome inherited structural barriers to collective action and look instead at how the legacies of specific types of autocracies structure political change. Multiple histories—rather than any one notion of one grand history—must be brought back in.

The "post-transitions literature" that emerged in 2000 and beyond attempted to do precisely this kind of more nuanced, historically informed work. But this effort to theorize the dynamics of semiauthoritarian regimes also unfolded in tandem with an equally strenuous bid to sustain the quest for more expansive, deductive theories that emphasized universal over local structures and logics. Thus many studies of semiauthoritarianism offered conceptual extensions rather than clear breaks with transitions theory. Their great asset is that they reveal many regime dynamics that this paradigm was not equipped to illuminate.

But in theorizing such variance, the post-transitions studies also recapitulated the conceptual bias of their predecessors, namely, a striking incapacity to theorize the role of local cultures, political logics, or ideologies in either regime change or stasis. For the Arab world, such conceptual continuity has shoehorned distinctive cases into larger deductive theories, thus yielding insights that are always conceptually eloquent but frequently empirically misleading.

What does all this mean for theorizing the 2011 Arab uprisings? First and foremost, it means accounting for factors that many scholars have explained away as epiphenomenal, residual, or even irrelevant. Chief among these, as I just suggested, is the conceptually slippery but vital reality of identity conflicts and their manipulation by what I call "protection racket autocracies." The legacies of such manipulative strategies have weighed heavily on the Arab revolts. In Tunisia they have undercut but not precluded political accommodation and democratization. In Egypt they facilitated pact making between the military and resurgent Islamists in ways that may be leading to a new form of autocracy, or a new form of military rule after this entente broke down. In Syria, Libya, and perhaps Yemen, they are inviting internal domestic conflict that, in the first case, has led to civil war. As for the cases of the dogs that did not bark, the manipulation of identity conflicts by the Arab world's semiauthoritarian regimes has undercut opposition efforts to construct viable alternatives to the fragile status quo. While prediction is a dangerous game, my guess is that in the coming years, the leaders of Morocco, Algeria, Jordan, Saudi Arabia, and the Gulf states will have at their disposal a range of tools and strategies for deflecting pressures for dramatic political change.

Modernization Theory and Its Discontents

Until the early 1970s, the field of comparative politics was dominated by the teleological assumptions of modernization theory. That theory assumed that one great path of history is driven by genetic code that is both socioeconomic and cultural. Indeed, modernization theory suggested a dynamic by which a rising middle class would become the vanguard for global democratization.[4] Critical to it was the assumption that modernization would produce a process of "cultural secularization" by which all particularistic identities—ethnic, religious, or linguistic—would find expression in a private sphere away from the rational exigencies of democratic politics and market economics.

History did not work out this way. If the universal forces of urbanization, markets, literacy, communications, and social mobilization were unstoppable, their political outcome was rarely what Daniel Lerner and his colleagues expected. On the contrary, by generating instability, violence, and intensified ethnic or religious conflicts, modernization made it possible for "dangerous demagogues" to manipulate both the masses and their particularist ideologies for totalitarian ends.[5] Under these dangerous conditions Samuel Huntington and Clifford Geertz, among others, prescribed a modernizing autocracy that could limit political participation, thus creating the space to grow the very symbolic, economic, and cultural prerequisites that modernization theory envisioned.[6]

The postmodernization thesis took many forms in Middle East studies, almost of all which pivoted around the assumption that the cultural, symbolic, or ideological terrain of the Arab-Muslim world did not easily support liberal democratic politics. For example, although he was a partisan of modernization theory, Michael Hudson argued that by politicizing competing forms of authority, rapid social change created an endless search for legitimacy that invited instability, weak states, and personalistic rule.[7] With the subsequent rise of Islamic activism, this failure to create a democratic foundation for legitimacy was attributed to factors supposedly intrinsic to Islam, in particular to its assumed drive to link religious precepts to political institutions, secular law, and the state itself.[8] While some analysts believe that the resulting barrier to secularization was a significant obstacle to democracy, others hold that Islam had its own intrinsic concept of democracy that could not be judged according to one "universal" yardstick.[9] But whatever the premises of these various postmodernization arguments are, they all suggest that modernization theory in its global version was unlikely to be realized in an Arab world in which particularistic religious, ethnic, or tribal identities seemingly reigned supreme.

This culturalist shift was hardly unique to Middle East studies. On the contrary, it was anticipated by a similar trend that occurred in other corners of comparative politics, including Latin American studies.[10] Not surprisingly, this shift provoked retaliation from Marxist scholars, whose theories of dependency located autocracy not in the cultural or even the social soil of the region or a particular country but in the global division of capitalist labor and exploitation. If this argument did not convince culturalists, it nevertheless revealed an emerging consensus regarding the difficulties of advancing democracy in developing states.

This widening conceptual gloom was brief. Indeed, political openings in the Southern Cone and especially the fall of the Berlin Wall and the democratization of much of Eastern Europe compelled comparativists to transcend the "culture-structure" debate. By the early 1990s, transcendence was seemingly achieved in a new paradigm that demonstrated the capacity of political leaders to negotiate their way out of social and political conflicts that previously had seemed structurally preordained. Thus was born the transitions paradigm.

The roots of this conceptual metamorphosis can be traced to the efforts of Guillermo O'Donnell to explain why Latin American bureaucratic authoritarian regimes like Brazil's had in fact adopted political openings.

In making this shift, O'Donnell pointed out, these regimes sought to regain some measure of democratic legitimacy while sustaining unpopular market reforms. This enterprise seemed to amount to a squaring of the circle, since political openings could invite popular mobilization against economic austerity measures. But O'Donnell and his colleagues contended that these social tensions could be mitigated through political "pacts" by which oppositions guaranteed the property rights of regimes and in return obtained formal political rights. This instrumentalist view—which in its pure form conceived of democratic institutions and rules as mechanisms for peacefully containing advancing socioeconomic struggles—provided one core assumption for a theory of transitions whose conceptual validity reached beyond the shores of Latin America.

The second, and closely related, master assumption concerned the logic that would eventually compel regime and opposition leaders to negotiate a pact. Embracing the universal premises of rational choice theory, O'Donnell and his colleague Adam Przeworski argued that repeated cycles of military rule and weak democracies would eventually produce a regime-societal stalemate that would compel regime and opposition moderates to embrace democracy as a "second-best" solution. Borrowing from the earlier work of Dankwart Rustow, the transitions paradigm holds that no level of economic, social, cultural, or religious development was necessary to at least begin a transition.[11] Setting out what other scholars later called a theory of "democracy without democrats," O'Donnell and his colleagues seemed to postulate a broad rationality that political leaders in all societies could eventually learn—whether experientially, from repeated iterations of bloody conflict, or intellectually, from reading the fourth volume of the *Transitions from Authoritarian* series itself.[12]

Ten assumptions underlay this vision of transitions:

1. Transitions *begin* as a consequence of repeated but inclusive bouts of conflict over economic issues between regimes and oppositions. These conflicts produce splits within regimes and successive efforts of regime soft-liners to reach out to opposition moderates and forge a vision of or program for political change.

2. At least at the outset, elite preferences do not reflect or derive from any philosophical, social, or even economic interests. In short, no prerequisites are needed to get the ball rolling. What counts most is recognition by elites that they all would be better off using democratic rules and institutions to resolve conflicts rather than suffering an endless stalemate.

3. This recognition of democracy as a second-best option is a necessary but insufficient condition for transitions. The latter requires elites with the organizational skills, political will, and vision to overcome multiple obstacles to collective action. Even though leadership and strategy are not determinative, the choices of leaders can be fundamental to moving beyond any short-term or regime-initiated limited political opening.

4. At some point in the transition, elite strategies and choices are affected by a filtering down of the economic, social, and institutional structures that survived the cracking of the regime and the subsequent contest to define new democratic rules. In the early stage of a transition, the institutional, economic, and coercive power accruing to the ruling elite gives it a bargaining advantage, thus facilitating the efforts of incumbents to compel opposition leaders to accept a pact that protects the social and political interests of the regime's incumbents.

5. The "resurrection" of civil society groups gives the opposition the leverage to collectively counter the regime's efforts to severely limit the scope of the transition.[13] Thus even though regime transitions begin with regime-controlled political liberalizations, moving toward substantive democratization requires popular mobilization that is organized independently of the state.

6. Transitions pivot around "four player games" that involve different degrees of implicit or explicit coordination within and between regime soft-liners and hard-liners on one side and opposition radicals and moderates on the other. Regime moderates need regime hard-liners, as the threat posed by the latter offers the regime soft-liners leverage to encourage the opposition moderates to negotiate. Similarly, opposition moderates can invoke the threat posed by opposition radicals to gain leverage with regime soft-liners. For a transition to move forward, however, opposition moderates and radicals must secure a minimal consensus on a common strategy and objective as the transition unfolds.

7. Transitions are "uncertain," in that their outcome is partly a function of nonstructural or random factors such as the elite's skills and choices. They also are uncertain to the extent that information about opponents' relative strength is often murky, and thus any mistakes and miscalculations can have the unintended consequences of either advancing or slowing a transition.

8. State-initiated political openings or decompressions can be only unstable equilibria that are destined to break down, thus setting the stage for reverting to full autocracy or advancing to competitive democracy. Thus, even though they are not unilinear, transitions do entail a linear dynamic

in which a new equilibrium is reestablished in favor of either autocracy or democracy.[14]

9. While pragmatic or instrumental concerns provide the initial basis for a political pact or a "democracy without democrats," in the long run consolidating and sustaining a democracy requires a commitment from elites and the wider populace to democracy as an end rather than a means. This commitment can evolve pragmatically or constitutively; in other words, it can be learned and absorbed through the repeated practice of democratic politics itself.[15]

10. Transitions are unlikely to succeed beyond their initial stage unless elites have a common vision of national identity. If pacts are only tactical recipes for communal power sharing or "consociational democracy," they are unlikely to provide a springboard from which competitive democracies can emerge.

The Transitions Paradigm: Agency and Structure Combined?

This list includes many more assumptions than are usually ascribed to the paradigm itself. Critics of the paradigm, such as Daniel Levine and Thomas Carothers, have described it as an "actor-oriented" model that supposedly highlights the elite's short-term bargaining at the expense of conceptualizing the economic, social, institutional, and cultural forces that proceeded it.[16] In effect, they argue for "bringing history back in."

This critique is valid to the extent that the transitions paradigm appears to emphasize agency. But a closer excavation of its deeper roots reveals something else, namely, the dynamic way in which the paradigm embeds a core set of assumptions about the logic that produces a "democracy with democrats" in a wider account of the social and economic forces that set the stage for pact making. Indeed, if Dankwart Rustow's notion of a "mutually hurting stalemate" provided the conceptual pivot of their theory, this was because O'Donnell and his colleagues rooted pact making in patterns of social and economic conflict whose roots (and the constraints they generated) were deeply structural and whose ultimate effect on elite action was central. Thus their apparent focus on the "uncertainties" of transition was something of analytical smoke screen. Far from describing an open game, they assumed that the ruling elite would inherit sufficient economic, institutional, and coercive power that opposition elites would have to accept a warped compromise that ultimately protected the regime's property rights. Moreover, by arguing that opportunities that the "resurrection of civil society (a term closely associated with the growth of an autonomous, educated urban sector) could give opposition leaders the leverage to push for greater democratic participation, the founders of the transitions paradigm implicitly placed classic modernization variables into the heart of their analysis. The result was a dynamic paradigm that sought to transcend the "agent/structure" problem by showing how opposition leaders might avoid the constraints and use the opportunities inherited from the proximate past and, in so doing, find themselves "on the uncertain path toward the construction of democratic forms of political organization."

This venture into what the authors admitted was a form of analytical prescription or praxis was geared to a very specific notion of elite logic born of a particular historical context.[17] Indeed, their paradigm implicitly echoed Rustow's basic assumption, that the creation of a political pact ensues from a "hot family feud" that pivots on pragmatic issues of class conflict rather than on existential questions of national, ethnic, or religious identity. In short, the paradigm assumes certain structural prerequisites but also suggests that their potential must be ultimately realized through the strategic action of leaders. As a product of a distinct set of social forces that rise to a particular type of autocracy, this notion of rationality could be stretched only so far through time and space.

The thorny issue of "conceptual stretching" is hardly limited to the Middle East. On the contrary, whenever political conflicts have been shaped by factors other than class or social-economic divisions, the conceptual limitations of the transitions paradigm become apparent. Whether we are studying the Balkans, the Middle East, sub-Saharan Africa, or other regions, the role of culture, identity, or even ideology present challenges for which the paradigm is not easily prepared.

John Waterbury's essay "Democracy Without Democrats" was the first to evaluate the relevance of transitions theory to the Arab world. He used the 1991–1999 conflict in Algeria to evaluate the relevance of the transitions paradigm in general and its rationalist assumptions in particular. Using Poland as a contrasting case, Waterbury set up the following puzzle:

> In Poland, the seizure of power by General Jaruzelski in 1981 may be seen as a first step in the transition to democracy. Nearly a decade of stalemate followed, in which the armed forces and the police were pitted against Solidarity. During those years . . . civil society began to create political space for itself.

Could the aborted elections in Algeria and the seizure of powerful by the military and technocrats signal the beginning of a similar transition?

This narrative is animated by the key assumptions that form the rationalist core of the transitions paradigm: the effort of an authoritarian regime to impose itself on an alienated society; the emergence of a stalemate between the regime and the opposition, the ensuing resurgence of civil society, and, finally, the negotiation of a pact. But Waterbury did not conclude that the stalemate in Algeria was likely to produce a dynamic that echoed the Polish experience. It would not do so, he observed,

> primarily because the FIS, aside from its popularity, in no way resembles Solidarity. . . . The FIS and many other Islamic organizations elsewhere in the Middle East do not oppose . . . incumbent power blocs because they are undemocratic but because they have no sense of mission. Moreover, religious political groups . . . are non-democrats *of a peculiar kind*. Non-religious, non-democratic groups . . . may alter their perceptions over time and in light of experience. . . . [But] where the scriptures are both holy and explicit, as is the case in Islam, pragmatic compromise will be very difficult.[18]

Although the language echoes many of the culturalist assumptions characteristic of the "Orientalist" enterprise, elsewhere in the same essay Waterbury shifts the analysis away from the study of Islam per se and instead examines the role of a state ideology. Deploying an argument that Ghassan Salamé set out elsewhere in the same volume, Waterbury locates the resistance to democracy in the "mission-oriented" vision of state authority disseminated by Arab nationalist regimes. By mission oriented, Waterbury means an ideology that upholds rulers and state institutions as the ultimate enforcers of a "sacred" ethos of unity and conformity against all domestic, regional, and global challengers. This authoritarian ideology, he contends, choked off the symbolic and institutional space for a more pluralistic politics, thus leaving the rulers of mission states with a narrow range of options (and allies) should they choose to open up the political and ideological space.

Regardless of one's judgment of the "mission state" thesis, the point here is that Waterbury's and Salamé's conceptualization of states and political actors departs significantly from the universalistic assumptions of transitions theory. Embedded in a macrostructural analysis that suggests a universal set of preferences independent of or "exogenous" to any given political system, this theory is not equipped to handle the local, bounded, or endogenous forces that shape political preferences and even distinctive authority structures and ideologies. While not using the language of "New Institutionalism," Waterbury and Salamé effectively anticipate the rise of this eclectic school of analysis by daring to suggest that not all political logics are universal and that they instead can be rooted in local, national, or regional political structures that generate distinctive notions of legitimacy.

I believe that for the Arab world, this shift to a more historical-institutional approach is fundamental to grasping the particular challenges of pact making and transitions in the region. Here, two factors loom large, the first being structural and the second ideational and institutional. The structural factors have been discussed extensively by Waterbury himself and many other scholars. They stem from the capacity of many Arab regimes to use direct and indirect rents, as well as indigenous resources, to purchase the political quiescence of diverse constituencies and even to fund a "patronage state" that avoids the escalating economic crises and social struggles that the transition literature views as root causes of both conflict and pact making.[19]

But such structural explanations must also consider the ways in which such local distributional strategies were propped up and legitimated by political leaders and their ruling institutions. This was done through regime-led cultural-symbolic strategies that shifted to the terrain of social conflict away from class and then to a range of local (and sometimes global) identity conflicts. In some cases, these conflicts were cultural and ideological. The most pervasive examples of the latter is the cleavage between Islamist and secular found in many Arab states, particularly in North Africa where this divide is magnified by the linguistic and cultural differences between those who speak French and identify with Europe and those who emphasize the Arabic language and their Arab-Muslim heritage. Farther east, the divide is sectarian, as is the case in Bahrain, Iraq, and Syria, where autocracies representing vulnerable minorities (Sunnis in the first two cases and Alawites in the third) imposed their will on the majority. Elsewhere, such strategies were enhanced by regime efforts to curry favor with exposed religious or ethnic minorities. The monarchs of Morocco enhanced their power by selectively defending the cultural or linguistic rights of Berbers, while in Syria, Iraq, and Egypt, regimes secured the tacit or explicit allegiance of Christian and other religious minorities by promising to protect them from the uncertainties of a truly open political process and the threat of majority rule by a dominant group.

As should be obvious, my conceptualization of identity politics does not locate their political significance in culture, religion, or ethnicity per se but in the instrumental (and often deliberate magnification) and institutionalization of available identity cleavages by autocracies seeking to enhance their capacity for maneuver. The advantages that accrue to regimes from such manipulative strategies include the following:

First, as noted, they fit nicely with patronage-distributional strategies designed to undermine or detract from class conflict or new distributional coalitions aimed at ruling regimes. Even regimes whose primary goal has been to defend the core interests of a vulnerable minority—such as the Alawite-Baathist regime in Syria—could expand their room for maneuver by channeling patronage to Sunni businessmen, thus compensating them for not challenging the pro-Alawite status quo.[20]

Second, identity politics can sometimes offer potential opposition groups a useful device for mobilizing social support, but without necessarily creating a lethal threat that might invite regimes to repress dissent. This has long been the great advantage of Islamist groups in the Arab world. Their moralistic focus on communal values and Islamic law facilitated efforts by Islamist movements to form a constituency of capitalists, urban poor, and rural actors, but without calling attention to these structural contradictions. By reducing the potential for class conflict—or for creating cross-cutting class alliances that could be mobilized in opposition to the promarket reforms that Arab regimes began pushing in the 1990s—the ideologies of mainstream Islamist groups have often made regimes less vulnerable to severe social or economic crises.[21]

Third, regime manipulation of identity conflicts magnifies vulnerable groups' perceived risks of losing the regime's patronage. Vulnerable identity groups can grasp the economic and institutional benefits (and costs) of relying on autocracies for patronage, but they can imagine the risks of losing that support only in a context of an open or even "pacted" democratization.

Fourth, on a more symbolic or psychological level, such concrete fears are magnified by vulnerable groups' difficulty imagining how a negotiated exit will shield their cultural, linguistic, or ideological interests. In contrast to the transitions paradigm—which sees pact making as pivoting on a pragmatic divvying up the spoils of economic or even political power—a focus on the mechanics of identity politics points to the difficulties of reaching a consensus amid existential concerns.

Even a cursory look at the multiple trajectories of the 2011 Arab uprisings reveals how such fears and the history of their systematic manipulation have complicated the quest of competing groups to nego-tiate a transition from autocracy. In Egypt, divisions in the Islamist and non-Islamist camps undermined the opposition's capacity to negotiate a pact with the military that would secure basic democratic rights. Instead, a de facto—and ultimately unsustainable—pact between the Muslim Brotherhood and the military emerged, only to be overturned by mass protest and a military coup. In Tunisia, the divide between Islamist and non-Islamist has perhaps been less corrosive, in part because there was no politicized military to manipulate both camps, thus forcing them to negotiate.

But these two cases stand in stark contrast to Bahrain and Syria, whose minority regimes have concluded that no agreement will ensure their political or even physical survival. This calculation has fed a brutal sec-tarian war in Syria, one that has been abetted by a fragmented opposition led by Islamist militants. Meanwhile, in Bahrain, a Sunni minority regime has repressed its Shiite opponents while engaging in a "national dialogue" whose chances of success seem remote. In both Syria and Bahrain, the zero-sum polarization of sectarian conflict has created little or no space for the soft-liners that the transitions paradigm envisions as crucial to pact mak-ing. Elsewhere, a multitude of identity conflicts based on region, tribe, and sectarianism have hindered political pact making. In Libya, the division between East and West—compounded by competing tribal loyalties, ten-sion between Islamists and non-Islamists, and the predominance of militias that reflect and channel these divisions—threatens to overthrow the peren-nially weak central government. Similarly, in Yemen—which has seen two civil wars, as well as a breakaway revolt among the Shiite Houthis in the north—a "national dialogue" has endured despite the centrifugal forces threatening to pull the country apart. Still, the future of Yemen as a unified state seems up for grabs.

This brief account of the impact of identity conflicts helps account for factors that the transition paradigm does not theorize, and it also shows the various trajectories that cannot be explained by identity conflicts alone. On the contrary, these dynamics are a consequence of a number of institutional factors, including the ways in which different authori-tarian regimes structure identity conflicts. Thus the remaining question we need to ask is how to theorize these different trajectories in a con-ceptually meaningful way that speaks to local logics and dynamics while underlining processes of political change relevant beyond the Arab world itself. To address this question, we must first consider "post-transitions" studies and where and how political dynamics in the Arab world fits into the study of "semiauthoritarianism."

Post-transitions Theory: The Dynamics of Semiauthoritarianism

At first glance, the dramatic changes in the global political map that unfolded during the late 1990s were good news for Middle East scholars. Indeed, by then the trajectories of authoritarian regimes had sufficiently diverged from the modal path envisioned by the transitions paradigm so that comparativists were beginning to look for new analytical frameworks. The principal development that provoked this paradigmatic shift was the survival of the autocracies, particularly those whose endurance could be partly attributed to their mix of autocratic, pluralistic, and democratic mechanisms. Seen through the transitions paradigm, these semiauthoritarian systems constituted "unstable equilibrium," or as Samuel Huntington put it, "halfway" houses that could "not stand." But rumors of their inevitable collapse were vastly exaggerated. As Larry Diamond noted, while the number of fully closed autocracies dropped dramatically in the 1990s, by 2002 hybrid regimes constituted at least 45 percent, and perhaps as much as 60 percent, of all regime types.[22] Because most Arab countries were ruled by semiautocracies, it appears that the rest of the world was in fact catching up to the Middle East rather than surpassing it along some linear trajectory to democracy.

Here I break down the study of semiautocracies into two large groups, "formalist" and "configurative." Formalistic approaches are deductive and expansive in their reach (if not their grasp) and thus focused on a far wider range of cases than was originally studied by scholars of regime transitions. By theorizing a multitude of outcomes, including negotiated transitions, regimes collapse, and authoritarian resilience, formalistic approaches highlight institutional factors that are central to mainstream political analysis, such as the differential impact of electoral systems, the relative degrees of institutional unity or disunity in regimes and oppositions, the "survival strategies" that regimes use to deflect opposition dissent or regime defections, and the strategies that opposition leaders use to engage potential regime interlocutors.[23] This focus on formal politics was matched by the growth of a political economy literature that investigated the socioeconomic dynamics that the transitions paradigm had considered only in passing. Among them, perhaps the most important was the degree of success or failure that autocracies had registered in their bid to advance market economic reforms and, by association, the impact of such divergent economic legacies on efforts to build political consensus and regime-opposition pacts.[24] This global focus was further paralleled by studies emphasizing how international political, social, and even ideological linkages between local political actors and global powers, either autocratic or authoritarian, enhanced or limited the leverage of would-be democratic actors seeking to advance transitions.[25]

This shift from the study of transitions to the study of the political change in semiautocracies captured variances in outcomes that the transitions paradigm could not. For example, studies of "electoral autocracy" theorized a dynamic of within-system change that resulted when oppositions finally took control of electoral machines that had been previously controlled by dominant single parties. This dynamic often involved a measure of implicit pact making or negotiations between regime reformers and opposition moderates. But what counted most was the existence before the transition of a set of formally democratic institutions, laws, and even constitutions whose potential could be realized only when oppositions had overcome the dominant parties' patronage machine. This dynamic pointed, in turn, to the crucial role of political leaders taking advantage of available political openings or opportunity structures. Indeed, as Marc Howard and Phillip Roessler note in their large-N study of semiauthoritarian regimes, regime splits were a necessary but insufficient condition for a "liberalizing outcome." The sufficient condition was the capacity of political leaders to unify the opposition and thus sustain pressure on ruling regimes.[26]

By linking structural conditions and political agency Howard, Roessler, and other scholars took on a conceptual challenge that the transitions paradigm had noted but did not elaborate. But in tackling the agency-structure question, much of the post-transitions literature stuck to the formalist approach, which did little to explain the deeper causes or motivations behind the particular choices and strategies adopted by regime and opposition elites. While some of these choices can be traced to an exogenous means/end logic that cuts across national boundaries and regions, they can also grow out of an endogenous logic that has at least some link to local cultures, ideologies, or identities.

It is hardly surprising that the post-transitions literature that does address such local, bounded logics largely focused on geographical regions. These "configurative approaches" point out the ways in which a diverse set of formal and informal institutional, economic, social, and cultural/ideological variables that are present in particular regions are reinforced over time, thus yielding distinct types of local or regional political systems that cannot be reduced to any specific constituent elements.[27] Accordingly, they are animated by a ground-up, inductive analysis of particular countries in specific geographic regions. Inspired by historical institutionalist and configurative approaches, scholars such as Michael Bratton, Nicolas van de Walle, Joy Langston, Steven Heydemann, and myself feature the interlocking effects of economic, social, cultural, ideological, and/or institutional forces as they evolved in specific national or regional arenas during specific historical phases. This focus on endogenous forces and the "bounded" logics they spawn eschews universal paradigms in favor of more conceptually modest midrange theories. For example, in their study of sub-Saharan Africa, Bratton and van de Walle identified a core set of economic and institutional formations that created a distinct pattern of "neopatrimonialism." This legacy, they assert, has promoted a two-player, zero-sum game between regime and opposition, whose dynamics can be understood only by tracing their roots backward, rather than forward, to some universal logic of negotiation between regime and opposition.[28]

Each of these approaches has advantages and disadvantages. By tracing the survival or transformation of regimes to a historically specific configuration of autocracy, configurative approaches replace the master path of grand theorizing with a multitude of path-dependent narratives. Depending on one's own theoretical proclivities, one can argue that this enterprise amounts to little more than a vast storytelling enterprise. However, I would argue that such liabilities are compensated for by the tendency of large-N deductive studies to assume that the universal institutional or structural variables that they use actually account for outcomes. Indeed, precisely because the evolution of semiautocracies is always shaped to an extent by local logics, institutions, and cultures, relying on universal models invites empirical and conceptual shoehorning of the more particular into the more universal.

Shoehorning is bound to loom most forcefully the more we stretch theories to cover regions that are vastly different. This much is clearly revealed by the effort to analyze the evolution of Arab regimes in large-N studies of semiauthoritarian regimes. For example, Jason Brownlee's work offers a comprehensive adaptation of the semiauthoritarian literature that falls clearly in line with the deductive, theory-building orientation of institutional or formalistic approaches. For this purpose, he mines large-N comparative studies of electoral authoritarianism examining the conditions under which the manipulation of electoral systems by competitive and hegemonic autocracies opens up or narrows the space for ruling and opposition elites to reimpose autocracy or, alternatively, to redefine its institutional rule and boundaries that advance democracy. Extending the geographical reach and time horizon of Barbara Geddes's earlier work, Brownlee concludes that while the institutional differences between electoral and hegemonic regimes "exhibit no substantial differences in their propensity for regime break-down," electoral autocracies "substantially improved the likelihood" that regime breakdown "would be followed by electoral democracy."[29] Such con-clusions, he notes, echo the findings of Marc Howard and Philip Roessler, which show that the single most important variable in predicting whether elections would advance an "liberalizing outcome" in competitive autocra-cies is the capacity of oppositions to "overcome inherent . . . divisions and build a broad-based coalition."[30] This result, Brownlee agrees, reveals the critical role of leadership and choice in facilitating democratization, as the transitions paradigm argues. But, he adds in a crucial qualification, coalition building matters only when there is a split in the ruling party that creates an opportunity for oppositions to push elections. Because parties sustain effec-tive coalitions, they—rather than elections or prior levels of liberalization under autocracy—"are the foundation of political stability today."[31]

It is from this elemental premise that Brownlee compares Egypt, Malay-sia, Iran, and the Philippines. These cases affirms his master assumption, inasmuch as ruling elites maintained unity in Egypt and Malaysia, whereas in the Philippines the ruling party split, thus making room for the opposi-tion. For Iran, Brownlee holds that factional politics created the opening for President Mohammad Khatami and his reformist allies. But, he con-cludes, Khatami's failure to support the 1999 summer student uprising deprived him of the leverage that he—as a regime soft-liner—might have gained from a radical opposition. This conclusion reaffirms his overall model, which he clearly offers as a more robust and comprehensive exten-sion of the transitions paradigm: a "complete explanation of the varying regime outcomes of developing countries."[32]

Though an impressive achievement, this study also exemplifies the shortcomings of the formal institutional approach. At first, it seems to con-firm the importance of political parties in creating (or narrowing) the space for negotiations. But in many countries, like Egypt, the ruling parties—as well as the electoral system through which they operate—are only one node in a complex, interlocking *system* of autocracy, many elements of which are far more important than the formal party or electoral system. Moreover, by tracing one necessary, albeit insufficient, condition of autocratic survival to the regime and the opposition's unity or fragmentation, Brownlee settles on a variable that is more often a symptom of the actual forces shaping the choices or rulers and their opponents. These forces are not fully revealed in a historical or "path-dependent" analysis of the evolution of weak, strong, or even failed political parties. As the products of a wider web of local forces and logics, their power in the Middle East is in the informal dynamics of patronage politics, a mix of explicit and implicit power rules, and the elite management (or manipulation) of identity politics.

As one example of the deleterious effects of conceptual shoehorning, consider Iran. The effort to fit the Islamic Republic into a global model of elite unity or fragmentation in electoral autocracies misses the key drivers of the overall political system that include—but cannot be reduced to—factional politics. The latter is one part of a wider, integrated web of "reserved power domains" through which essential institutional actors—first and foremost the Office of Supreme Leader, followed by the Revolutionary Guards, and the Council of Guardians—negotiate, define, or limit the boundaries of political contestation.

Moreover, this complex dynamic is generated not merely by a rational struggle over economic interests. Rather, it pivots on a state ideology rooted in the fundamental principle that the Islamic Republic exists to defend and disseminate the cultural, religious, and identity foundations of Shiite Iran as defined by a clerical vanguard and its lay allies. Thus to attribute the endurance of autocracy to the vulnerabilities of factional politics or the failure of "moderate" leaders like Khatami to make the kinds of choices that would otherwise exploit such vulnerabilities to advance a reform agenda misses the deeper local logic of Iran's political system. In this system, no matter how much reformists advocate negotiation process within the existing system's rules and institutions, for the ruling elites that occupy the system's reserved domains, any real compromise threatens to slide into ideological dissolution. It is for this reason that Iran's dynamics are not fully illuminated by universalistic models of regime change or stasis, whether rooted in the "four player" games of the transitions paradigm or the paradigm's theoretical progeny, that is, large-N comparative studies of competitive authoritarianism or electoral autocracy.

Protection Racket and Identity Conflicts in the Middle East

Although Iran's political system appears to differ radically from those of the Arab world, the preceding account suggests that in the Middle East a systemwide view of the integrated ecology of autocracy that includes—but does not reduce to—ideology and identity politics provides the most compelling vantage point from which to assess the dynamics (and limitations) of political change. Identity politics, as well the statist ideologies that sometimes attach to such politics, has a structural importance insofar as all the autocratic states of the Middle East, regardless of their institutional and even ideological differences, have one common political function: to protect the particular identity, religious, or ideological groups that might otherwise be politically disenfranchised, or even physically endangered, by a transition to majoritarian democracy. It is in this sense it can be said that the Supreme Leader of Iran, the Commander of the Faithful in Morocco, and the former presidents of Tunisia and Egypt operate according to a similar logic that, borrowing from Charles Tilly, can be called "protection racket politics."[33]

This does not mean that local institutional, cultural, or ideological differences do not matter. On the contrary, and as I have noted, the different ways that conceptually distinct types of autocracies structure identity conflicts is a crucial issue. In the Arab world, protection racket politics is manifest in two conceptually distinct autocracies: "liberalized autocracies" and "full autocracies."[34] Because the Arab spring has unfolded in both, I next outline the main features of liberalized and full autocracy and then show how the distinctive legacies arising from each protection racket system have promoted very different trajectories of political change since January 2011. As an example, I contrast Tunisia and Egypt.

Liberalized autocracies are political systems in which the ruling elite uses a mix of overlapping formal and informal institutions to structure a political game in which contending groups are allowed to express themselves—and sometimes even compete for votes—but not to gain sufficient political clout to undermine the foundations of autocratic rule. While such a system would seem to have much in common with the "electoral autocracies" analyzed by Andreas Schedler and others, formal electoral systems and ruling parties play an important, but not the decisive, role in sustaining liberalized autocracy in the Arab world. Indeed, apart from their reliance on coercion and the central role of the military, the leaders of a liberalized autocracy have sustained their power not by relying on a single-party political machine but, rather, by manipulating a dense network of formal and informal bodies that funnel various benefits to myriad constituencies organized in diverse array of institutions, including parliaments, parties, professional associations, charitable organizations, and nongovernmental organizations or civil society groups.[35]

One key to the survival of liberalized autocracies is to tolerate—if not promote—a level of state-managed quasi pluralism through a host of arenas, thus producing a level of conflict and fragmentation in society that abets autocratic rule. The resulting protection racket does not privilege any one identity group. Rather, it encourages a process by which all groups ultimately are compelled to engage in a game of negotiation, accommodation, or cooptation with their respective patrons in the ruling state apparatus.[36] This negotiating dynamic finally is mediated by the state through a powerful military and or powerful executive located in the bureaucratic office of the president or on in the political apparatus of a powerful monarchy. These centers of "reserved power" compel all competing identity groups to look to the state, rather to themselves, for their ultimate political salvation.

Even though this system functions as an organic system rather than a "regime"—in other words, through the integrated dynamics of its many constituent elements—the particular nature of the formal political regime does matter. A liberalized autocracy that functions partly through a presidential system backed by a military-security apparatus has clear disadvantages over many (but not all) monarchies. By virtue of their role as arbiters that sit at some remove from the formal political arena, monarchs have an institutional tool for promoting a divide-and-rule strategy that their presidential counterparts lack. Wed to a ruling-party apparatus, in the lead-up to the Arab spring, the presidents of Egypt and Yemen—two good examples of liberalized autocracy—became the shared and supreme targets for opposition movements that were otherwise divided along religions, cultural, tribal, or ideologies lines. By contrast, with the exception of Bahrain, not a single Arab monarchy has thus far faced a systemwide challenge. Instead, the leaders of Jordan and, especially, Morocco have reworked rather than disbanded the mechanisms of liberalized autocracy in order to sustain the protection racket game.[37]

The room for maneuver afforded by liberalized autocracy is conspicuously absent in "full autocracies." The autocracies in Syria, preinvasion Iraq, Libya, and Tunisia functioned through formal political machines that reproduced "electoral victories" while exhibiting little or, in some cases, no tolerance of organized opposition or civil society autonomy. This quest for total hegemony was buttressed by long-standing, sharp identity conflicts whose particular structure worked against the very strategies of state-controlled pluralism used by liberalized autocracies. Indeed, in Syria, Iraq, and Tunisia, the near total dependence of vulnerable identity groups— Alawites in the first, Sunnis in the second, and secularists in the third—on the state for total protection from their rivals was secured through regimes that, by their very nature, could envision reform only as a slippery slope to political suicide.

Paradoxically, this zero-sum worldview was magnified by the purely coercive role of the security apparatus in full autocracies. In these systems, the military did not play the mediating role that the military and bureaucratic ruling apparatus played—or pretended to play—in Egypt. Indeed, because the only role of the security apparatus in full autocracies is to protect the regime rather than manage a divide-and-rule dynamic with diverse patrons, the coercive apparatus is not well placed to initiate (much less sustain) the kind of "reform" game characteristic of liberalized autocracies. In the latter, regimes not only are used to periodically proclaim a new age of reform; they also see state-managed reform as their means of survival. Accordingly, the *marhalla intiqaliyya* (transitional phase) has been celebrated for years, if not decades, in Egypt, Jordan, Kuwait, and Morocco. By contrast, the efforts of the so-called reformers in Bahrain and (even more so) in Syria have been short lived. In those states, a sectarian security apparatus either survives with the existing regime or goes down with it.

It is far too early in the evolution of the Arab revolts to draw definitive conclusions about how the institutional, social, and ideological legacies bequeathed by such markedly different ecologies of protection racket autocracy will be manifested in the Arab world. But a quick contrast of the Egyptian and Tunisian cases offers some interesting and perhaps counterintuitive food for thought.

In Egypt, the survival of a multipolar institutional field dominated by the military created opportunities for manipulation that all the principal players found irresistible. If the military's initial efforts to use the divide between Islamists and secularists to reimpose its authority were not at all successful, the divisions between and within both the Islamist and the secular camps greatly complicated the negotiation of a clear set of institutional, legal, and constitutional rules for guiding a democratic transition forward. Indeed, with the emergence of the Salafists as major electoral force, the Muslim Brotherhood's Freedom and Justice Party felt no pressure to negotiate seriously with non-Islamists. Instead, it rammed through a new constitution, which among other things, sustained and even enhanced the institutional and social foundations of the military's power. Left in its current form, this particular form of pact making could have set the stage for a transition from liberalized autocracy to an Egyptian form of electoral authoritarianism or, if this failed, to increasing instability and social conflict, a dynamic that—as it now turns out—has helped facilitate the return of the military.

By contrast, Tunisia illustrates the somewhat paradoxical possibilities that can arise from a system of total autocracy that had very few of the institutional instruments available to a liberalized autocracy. Having suppressed nearly all vestiges of meaningful institutional and ideological pluralism, the regime of former President Zine al-Abdine Ben Ali became dependent on the blunt and inflexible instruments of a strong party machine and a security apparatus that was separated from—and even antagonistic to—the depoliticized, professional military. This centralized, coercive apparatus gained a measure of legitimacy from the secular, professional urban middle class by providing it with political protection and economic opportunities and rewarding its tacit support by cutting out the Islamists from any formal means of legal political organization or expression. Deprived of the chance to advance the kind of protection racket politics that in Egypt had both Islamists and secularists looking to the state for their salvation, before the 2011 "Jasmine revolution," the growing alienation of important elements of the professional urban secular elite left the regime increasingly isolated. When the army then refused to intervene on the side of the president and his allies, the ruling authorities not only faced a mass revolt that linked almost everyone in opposition to it; it also lacked the institutional tools to sustain a divide-and-rule strategy against the opposition. Thus in Tunisia, much of the old protection racket collapsed, in contrast to that in Egypt where it was effectively revived in a new institutional configuration. Indeed, because Tunisia's military did not have the experience, tools, or will to emulate the quasi-arbitrating role of Egypt's Supreme Council of the Armed Forces, Tunisia's civil society and political leaders eventually had to face each other and negotiate a common vision of political change, rather than look to the remnants of the ancient regime for protection.

This outcome was facilitated by the exiled Islamist party, al-Nahda, which had never had to engage in the accommodation-cooptation games that Egypt's Muslim Brotherhood had long pursued with the Egyptian state. At the same time, however, the sudden emergence of the Salafists put al-Nahda in a difficult position as it attempted to maintain its credibility among non-Islamist political forces while at the same time trying to demonstrate its "Islamic" credentials and selectively integrate Salafists into the political process. During 2012, this difficult balancing act alienated secular groups and almost led to a complete breakdown in negotiations over a constitution. Nevertheless, absent any other arbitrating center, all parties were forced to return to the negotiating table, thus producing in March 2013 a compromise constitution that, while far from perfect, provides real democratic guarantees and rights. While negotiations over this document and the associated question of a common road map for advancing the transitions have been difficult, it is likely that Tunisia's leaders will get closer to transition than any of their Arab counterparts have.

This brief comparison of Egypt and Tunisia reminds us that in any situation of regime change, we must simultaneously take into account two dynamics or logics. One such logic, captured by the transitions paradigm and some of its most ambitious successors, is a more global or exogenous logic and institutional dynamic that is assumed to shape, frame, or otherwise constrain the actions of political leaders under some set of structural conditions. The second logic is local and endogenous to a particular national or regional setting. It is a product of a web of institutional, cultural, ideological, social, and political forces that have emerged over time to create a distinctive system. No effective analysis of regime transitions can proceed without taking into account *both* logics and how they interact.[38] Particularly in the Middle East, where identity conflicts are part of a more elaborate structure of autocracy, the allure of rationalist analysis must be balanced by a deeper appreciation of the more distinctive or even particularistic rationalities that coexist with the more "universalistic" dynamics of political life and change. Understanding the link between the two, rather than falling prey to either one, is the first step in moving beyond the trap of "Arab exceptionalism," on the one hand, or the cul-de-sac of equally strident analytical universalism, on the other.

The purpose of coming to conceptual and empirical terms with both logics is to understand rather than forecast political dynamics. From a scholarly perspective, it is a fool's errand to blame the post-transitions literature on authoritarian resilience for failing to "predict" the Arab spring. The key contribution of this literature—as with the wider literature on hybrid regimes—was to compensate conceptually for the failure of the transitions paradigm to adequately theorize how authoritarian institutions and ideologies structure the dynamic of regime change (or stasis). The experience of Egypt—not to mention those liberalized autocracies that have thus far survived the Arab spring—shows that these structures can endure despite, or because of, the legitimate efforts of political oppositions to topple regimes. The past is not a single guide to the future, but it is certainly an important element in grasping how regimes do or do not change after autocracies are challenged. Moreover, as the multiple trajectories of the Arab spring attest, a regime crisis or even toppling is only the beginning of a transition. What remains is the arduous task of building consensus in political systems that had previously relied on protection racket politics to block any such unity. Where and when this legacy can be overcome—or, to put it more prosaically, where and when Arab political systems move from autocratic to democratic protections—requires attention to local logics and institutional dynamics that universalistic models of transitions only partly grasp.

NOTES

1. See Leon Rabinovich Aron, "The 'Mystery' of the Soviet Collapse," *Journal of Democracy* 17, no. 2 (April 2006): 21–35.

2. See Pinar Bilgin, "What Future for Middle Eastern Studies?" *Futures* 38, no. 5 (June 2006): 575–88.

3. On the "Green Book," see Guillermo O'Donnell and Philippe C. Schmitter, *Transitions from Authoritarian Rule, Tentative Conclusions About Uncertain Democracies* (Baltimore: Johns Hopkins University Press, 1986); Adam Przeworski, *Democracy and the Market: Political and Economic Reforms in Eastern Europe and Latin America* (Cambridge: Cambridge University Press, 1991).

4. Gabriel Almond and G. Bingham Powell, "Introduction and Overview," in *Comparative Politics: A Developmental Approach*, ed. Gabriel Almond and G. Bingham Powell (Boston: Little Brown, 1966), 1–41. For an example of the application of this theory to the Middle East, see Daniel Lerner, *The Passing of Traditional Society* (Glencoe, Ill.: Free Press, 1958).

5. Seymour Martin Lipset, "Economic Development and Democracy," in his *Political Man: The Social Bases of Politics* (New York: Doubleday, 1960), 46–76.

6. Samuel Huntington, *Political Order in Changing Societies* (New Haven, Conn.: Yale University Press, 1968), 1–92; Clifford Geertz, "The Integrative Revolution: Primordial Sentiments and Civil Politics in the New States," in his *The Interpretation of Cultures* (New York, Basic Books, 1973), 254–310.

7. Michael C. Hudson, *Arab Politics, The Search for Legitimacy* (New Haven, Conn.: Yale University Press, 1977).

8. See, for example, Bernard Lewis, "The Return of Islam," in his *Islam and the West* (New York: Oxford University Press, 1993), 135.

9. See John Esposito and John Voll, *Islam and Democracy* (Oxford: Oxford University Press, 1995).

10. Howard Wiarda, "Toward a Framework for the Study of Political Change in the Iberic-Latin Tradition: The Corporative Model," *World Politics* 25 (January 1973): 250–78.

11. The concept of a second-best solution undergirds *Transitions from Authoritarian Rule*(1986) but was considerably evolved in the work of Adam Przeworski, "Some Problems in the Study of the Transition to Democracy," (1986). See Dankwart Rustow, "Transitions to Democracy: Towards a Dynamic Model," *Comparative Politics*, 2, no. 3 (April 1970): 337–63; and O'Donnell and Schmitter, *Transitions from Authoritarian Rule*, 38.

12. The late and much missed O'Donnell stated on any number of occasions that the transitions paradigm was designed to help opposition leaders forge effective strategies for negotiating with regimes. I return to the importance of this seemingly small observation later.

13. O'Donnell and Schmitter, *Transitions from Authoritarian Rule*, 48–56.

14. While O'Donnell and Schmitter acknowledge that "liberalization can exist without democratization," they nevertheless observe that the "cases studied in these volumes suggest that once some individual and collective rights have been granted, it becomes increasingly difficult to justify withholding these to others." In successful transitions, liberalization and democracy "become securely linked to each other." *Transitions from Authoritarian Rule*, 10.

15. O'Donnell and Schmitter, *Transitions from Authoritarian Rule*, 65–72.

16. Thomas Carothers, "The End of the Transitions Paradigm," *Journal of Democracy*, 13, no. 1 (2002): 5–21; Daniel H. Levine, "Paradigm Lost: Dependency to Democracy," *World Politics*, April 1988, 377–94.

17. O'Donnell and Schmitter, *Transitions from Authoritarian Rule*, 5.

18. John Waterbury, "Democracy Without Democrats? The Potential for Political Liberalization in the Middle East," in *Democracy Without Democrats? The Renewal of Politics in the Muslim World*, ed. Ghassan Salamé (London: I. B. Tauris, 1994), 39 (italics added).

19. Hazem Beblawi and Giacomo Luciani, eds., *The Rentier State* (London: Croom Helm, 1987).

20. Steven Heydemann, "Social Pacts and Persistence of Authoritarianism in the Middle East," in *Debating Arab Authoritarianism, Dynamics of Durability in Non-Democratic Regimes*, ed. Oliver Schlumberger (Stanford, Calif.: Stanford University Press, 2007), 31–38.

21. See Ardeshir Mehrdad and Yassamine Mather, "Political Islam's Relation to Capital and Class," *Critique: Journal of Socialist Theory* 33 (2005): 61–98.

22. Larry Diamond, "Thinking About Hybrid Regimes," *Journal of Democracy* 12 (2002): 27.

23. See Steven Levistky and Lucan A. Way, "Elections Without Democracy: The Rise of Competitive Authoritarianism," *Journal of Democracy* 13 (2003): 52–65.

24. See Stephan Haggard and Robert R. Kaufman, *The Political Economy of Democratic Transitions* (Princeton, N.J.: Princeton University Press, 1995).

25. See Steven Levitksy and Lucan A. Way, "Linkage and Leverage: How Do International Factors Change Domestic Balances of Power?" in *Electoral Authoritarianism:*

The Dynamics of Unfree Competition, ed. Andreas Schedler (Boulder, Colo.: Lynne Rienner, 2006), 199–216.

26. Marc Howard and Philip Roessler, "Liberalizing Electoral Outcomes in Competitive Authoritarian Regimes," *American Journal of Political Science* 50, no. 2 (2006): 365–81.

27. I borrowed this term from Ira Katznelson. See his "Periodization and Preferences: Reflections on Purposive Action in Comparative Historical Social Science," in *Comparative Historical Analysis in the Social Sciences*, ed. James Mahoney and Dietrich Rueschemeyer (Cambridge: Cambridge University Press, 2003), 270–301.

28. Michael Bratton and Nicolas Van de Walle, "Neopatrimonial Regimes and Political Transitions in Africa," *World Politics* 46 (July 1994): 453–89.

29. Jason Brownlee, "Portents of Pluralism: How Hybrid Regimes Affect Democratic Transitions," *American Journal of Political Science* 53 (2009): 528, 530.

30. Howard and Roessler, "Liberalizing Electoral Outcomes," 376.

31. Jason Brownlee, *Authoritarianism in an Age of Democratization* (New York: Cambridge University Press, 2007), 32.

32. Ibid., 33.

33. See Charles Tilly, "War Making and State Making as Organized Crime," in *Bringing the State Back In*, ed. Peter Evans, Dietrich Rueschemeyer, and Theda Skocpol (Cambridge: Cambridge University Press, 1985), 169–86. Tilly used the term "protection racket" in reference to the dynamic by which rulers tried to establish state authority. This involved raising armies to defeat external threats, a goal pursued by providing protection to local populations from those threats in return for their raising revenue for the state. This was a "racket" because to varying degrees it involved producing "both the danger and, at a price, the shield against it" (171). I use the term to refer to domestic dynamics between regimes and oppositions, but war making also fed such domestic rackets. See Steven Heydemann, ed., *War, Institutions, and Social Change in the Middle East* (Berkeley: University of California Press, 2000).

34. Daniel Brumberg, "Liberalization vs. Democracy: Understanding Arab Political Reform" (Washington, D.C.: Carnegie Endowment for International Peace, 2003).

35. This point is nicely illustrated in Sarah Elisabeth Yerkes's PhD thesis, "Pluralism, Co-optation and Capture: Navigating the Civil Society Arena in the Arab World," Georgetown University, 2012.

36. See Holger Albrecht, "How Can Opposition Support Authoritarianism? Lessons from Egypt," *Democratization* 12, no. 3 (2012): 378–97.

37. On Morocco, see Ahmed Benchemsi, "Morocco: Outfoxing the Opposition," *Journal of Democracy* 23, no. 1 (2012): 57–69.

38. See Anna Seleny, "Old Political Rationalities and New Democracies: Compromise and Confrontation in Hungary and Poland," *World Politics* 51, no. 4 (1999): 484–519.

PART I

Regional and
Cross-National Dimensions

3

Diffusion and Demonstration

DAVID PATEL, VALERIE BUNCE, AND
SHARON WOLCHIK

The cross-national spread of popular protests against authoritarian rulers in the Middle East and North Africa (the MENA) caught most analysts by surprise and, for that matter, most of the participants in this wave. In part, this is because constraints on collective action always exist in authoritarian political settings, and diffusion is usually "double" or "interactive."[1] Just as dissatisfied citizens in neighboring countries welcome successful antiregime mobilizations in their neighborhood and try to pattern their behavior on the techniques that were used to achieve these results, so authoritarian leaders are quick to monitor these existential threats and deploy the considerable resources at their disposal to preempt them. For these reasons, intraregional waves of popular mobilizations against authoritarian rulers are rare. Indeed, even when protests succeed, their geographical impact is usually contained. This is precisely what happened in both Southeast and East Asia following the protests that removed authoritarian leaders from office in the Philippines and South Korea in the second half of the 1980s and in Indonesia a decade later.

In this chapter we analyze why and how popular protests against authoritarian rulers spread in the Middle East and North Africa. Because the diffusion is ongoing and the patterns of the dynamic have not yet fully crystallized, we restrict our attention to the following questions. First, why did the dynamic begin in Tunisia? Second, why did ordinary citizens and opposition groups in Egypt then mount their own challenges to their authoritarian ruler, Hosni Mubarak, and why did the protests then spread to so many other countries in the MENA? Finally, not all countries in the region followed in Egypt's footsteps. What, then, explains the contrast in the region between large-scale protests erupting in some countries but not in others?

Our analysis proceeds in three stages. First, we define diffusion and highlight some of its key characteristics. Second, we develop a series of hypotheses about why and how antiregime mobilizations spread among authoritarian regimes located in the same region. These hypotheses are directed to these questions and are derived from a comparison of the only other contemporary examples of the intraregional spread of large-scale popular mobilizations against authoritarian rule. The first is the cross-national diffusion of popular protests against Communist Party rule in the Soviet Union and Eastern Europe from 1987 to 1990. The second, the "color revolutions," was the subsequent wave of ambitious public challenges to authoritarian rule that began in 1996, targeted the hybrid regimes in the same region that followed the Communist regimes, and used sophisticated electoral strategies, often combined with postelection protests, in order to remove authoritarian leaders from office.[2] Finally, we assess the extent to which these hypotheses have been confirmed by recent developments in the MENA.

Diffusion

Diffusion can be defined as the transfer of an innovation—for example, a new product, policy, institution, or repertoire of behavior—across units, such as enterprises, organizations, sociopolitical groups, or governments. Diffusion, therefore, refers to a coincidence between time and space, and it rests on the assumption that the adoption of a change in one locale increases the likelihood of similar changes being implemented in other locales.[3]

Several characteristics distinguish diffusion from other types of change. One is that the spread of the innovation takes place through a horizontal, rather than a vertical, process. The key dynamic, therefore, is not that similar actions are taken by units independent of one another as a result of, say, their common reaction to an external shock or to parallel domestic circumstances but that the clustering of these similar behaviors is prompted by interactions among units and decisions about whether to import or export the innovation. Moreover, it is typical of diffusion processes that the innovation changes as it spreads to new units (because domestic factors always come into play); not all units participate in the process; and the consequences of joining the wave vary as well. In regard to the type of diffusion of interest in this chapter, there always is variation in whether publics join the wave; whether if they join, the demonstrators will succeed in their mission of removing authoritarian leaders from office; and whether if they accomplish that objective, their actions will lead subsequently to the formation of a new government or a new type of regime.

Finally, the drivers of diffusion can be specified in several ways. One distinction is between structural influences—for example, characteristics of the units themselves that support multiple adoptions of the innovation—or behavioral factors—changes in the calculus of players in response to new developments, including new strategies, in neighboring locales. At the same time, diffusion can be deliberate—a result of collaboration among actors in a group of units or the work of a transnational network committed to the spread of the innovation—or it can be the consequence of demonstration effects—the power of the precedent itself (its outcome and the strategies on which it rests) to alter the calculus and behavior of players operating in other units.

Generalizations

Where and why do waves of popular protests begin? In the communist and postcommunist waves, the early risers—that is, those countries in the region where the protests first erupted, succeeded in their mission and thus initiated the wave—present a relatively similar profile. In particular, each of these waves began in regimes that had, in comparison with their neighbors, much more experienced and larger oppositions and that were, at the same time, less authoritarian than other regimes in the region governed by authoritarian leaders. In addition, the trailblazers tended to be distinctive in another way (though the pattern here is less clear-cut), because they featured unusually strong national identities and well-defined states. When combined, these distinctive characteristics lead to a more general point. Waves of antiregime mobilizations seem to start in contexts in which, by regional standards, constraints on collective action are unusually elastic. Also worth mentioning is that in the European and Eurasian waves, economic problems, such as significant downturns and high levels of unemployment, do not do a very good job of distinguishing early risers from other states in the region.

Why did the precedents set by the early risers then travel to other countries in these two waves of antiregime mobilizations? Several mechanisms were in play. First, the initial mobilizations were successful, accomplished their objective relatively quickly and with virtually no loss of life, and provided a transportable model that other actors in the region who also wanted to remove their leaders from office could adopt. For example, in the 1989 case, the strategy was to hold roundtables between oppositions and the regime (often foreshadowed by protests), and in the color revolutions, the strategy was to run a sophisticated electoral campaign that focused, for example, on increasing voter registration and turnout, expanding popular support for the opposition, engaging young people in electoral politics, and making extensive use of vote monitoring. Second, certain characteristics of the region made ordinary citizens and oppositions in other countries unusually receptive to following in the footsteps of the early riser and mounting their own challenges to authoritarian rule, for example, the presence throughout the region of a large number of similar political and economic systems, a history of prior confrontations between the regime and the opposition (which was particularly true for countries that joined the wave in the early stages), and a common regional language that facilitated cross-national interactions among opposition communities and access to the same information.

In addition, as the result of two developments, we also find throughout the region at the time of the protests an unusually malleable political environment. The first was short term, a shift in the policy priorities of the major international actor in the region that signaled the possibility of greater support for political change (Soviet President Mikhail Gorbachev's reforms and increased U.S. support for the Eastern European oppositions in the 1989 case and the U.S. commitment to free and fair elections in the color revolutions). The other was the presence of regionwide succession crises in 1989 (every state was led by either a new leader in the process of consolidating power or an exceptionally long-serving leader) or, for the color revolutions, upcoming elections that allowed for some political competition, albeit on an uneven playing field. Here it is important to recognize that just as succession periods were associated during Communism with the outbreak of popular protests, so elections in mixed regimes more generally have been sites for regime shifts in either a more democratic or a more authoritarian direction.[4]

When combined, these regional factors laid some of the groundwork for diffusion by making it easy for opponents of the regime to attribute similarities between their situation and the circumstances that foreshadowed the events in the early riser; to perceive an expansion in the political opportunities for change; and to be, as a result, more confident, especially if adopting the innovation provided by the early riser, that they also could succeed in removing authoritarian leaders from office. These factors, in turn, made coordination among citizens much easier. Finally, both waves combined demonstration effects with a more deliberate diffusion dynamic. Demonstration effects figured more prominently in the 1989 wave, and transnational networks and cross-national linkages among opposition groups played a more significant role in the color revolutions.

These two waves, however, would not have had such geographical projection if the innovation had not been successfully transferred to a key state in the region (East Germany in the 1989 wave and Serbia in the color revolutions). What made mobilizations against authoritarian rule in these countries critical to the subsequent magnification of the wave was that they demonstrated the portability of the model itself and the fact that it could work in less supportive local contexts, that is, in countries that went much further than the early riser in testing the new commitments of powerful international actors (such as the Soviet Union in 1989 and the United States in the color revolutions); that were powerful states in the region because of, say, size and geopolitical location; and that were in important ways more similar to many other states in the region than was the case for the early risers. Moreover, in these cases the innovation was modified and therefore even more easily transported. Thus East Germany showed that protests could propel regime change (and broke with the model of roundtables used in Hungary and Poland), and Serbia later demonstrated that the opposition's electoral victories could actually lead to regime change if postelection protests were added to the tool kit. As a result, what might have been contained events—that is, the roundtables in Poland and Hungary and the electoral transitions in Slovakia and Croatia—were transformed because these cases turned into a much more far-reaching wave.

Finally, each of the waves followed a similar pattern. First, both waves were sequential, rather than geographically and temporally splattered. In 1989, this reflected cross-national variations in the size and experience of the opposition, their confidence that they could succeed, and constraints on information that placed considerable emphasis on access to knowledge about events taking place "next door." For the color revolutions, the development of the opposition and the electoral calendar generated a similar pattern of protests running their course in one country before they erupted in the next one. Second, whether countries joined the wave depended on whether their leaders were unpopular and the size and experience of their oppositions. For example, in Russia, public support of the president, Vladimir Putin, and the fragmented character and, indeed, unpopularity of the opposition foreclosed the possibility of a color revolution. Finally, as the wave progressed, the demonstrations that did break out became smaller; regimes were more likely to use violence and other measures to demobilize challengers; and the opposition's ability to prevail declined. What is important to recognize here is what "time" meant in these waves. On the one hand, it was a surrogate measure for the fact that the wave moved from more to less hospitable contexts. On the other hand, time carried a Janus-faced lesson. Just as successful precedents in the neighborhood led oppositions to become overly confident and more and more cavalier in how they implemented the strategies developed by their successful counterparts, so the failures of other leaders in the region to withstand popular challenges led authoritarian incumbents to take preemptive actions.

Note that this dynamic is the reverse of what happened in earlier jousting between regimes and oppositions in, say, Poland or Hungary before 1989 and Slovakia, Croatia, and Serbia in the years before the color revolutions. Oppositions in these countries changed their strategies in reaction to their failures, whereas the regimes, flush with success in fending off these challenges, rested on their laurels and later responded to the protests that began the wave by underestimating the threat and trotting out the reactions that had been successful in the past. Ironically, therefore, the contrast between the lessons learned by the opposition and the regime before and during the wave explain both why the wave could start and why it would be limited in its impact and extent.

Tunisia as an Early Riser

The MENA wave began in Tunisia, a country that does not represent a perfect fit with the "low-hanging fruit" explanation of the early risers in the European and Eurasian waves.[5] President Zine al-Abdine Ben Ali's regime had been very repressive for many years (in contrast, for example, to Morocco and Jordan); the opposition was relatively small and certainly fragmented (in contrast to, say, Egypt and Bahrain); and protests were relatively rare during the decades of Ben Ali's rule (though this was less true in the few years leading up to the December 2010 demonstrations).

Under President Habib Bourghiba, Tunisia had experienced popular protests, some experiments with political liberalization, periodic divisions in the political leadership (which occasioned frequent shuffling of the elite), and a large and active labor movement that had played a critical role in freeing Tunisia from French rule and had carried out strikes from time to time. But Tunisia also had some other characteristics that were typi-cal of the early risers in the European and Eurasian waves. These were the national homogeneity of the population and the well-defined borders of the country (which was also true of Egypt), together with a relatively small and depoliticized military (which was rare in the MENA). These three attri-butes were similar to those of Poland under Communism. Indeed, one of the difficulties of analyzing diffusion is identifying where and when the dynamic begins. For example, in the case of 1989, it has often been argued that Communism began to collapse with the rise of Solidarity in Poland nine years earlier.

The protests in Tunisia prompted several other such actions as well as the eruption of small-scale protests in neighboring countries, such as Algeria and Libya. In fact, many of the same regional factors that pro-pelled the European and Eurasian waves also were present in the MENA—for example, striking similarities among political and economic regimes in the region, a common language, and the presence of a large number of long-serving and very corrupt leaders. (At the time the wave began, some of them were in the process of positioning their sons to be their succes-sors.) Also similar as a regional driver of diffusion was the decision by the United States after 9/11 to pursue a two-track policy in the MENA by com-bining its long-term support for authoritarian incumbents with expanded democracy assistance and increased pressures on some of those leaders to introduce democratic reforms. At the same time, while Tunisia was wide-ly viewed in the region as an atypical country, which worked against the transmission of its precedent, at the same time it was unusually influential because the protests had managed to take place and even succeed in such an authoritarian context. While these factors no doubt readied the region's publics to emulate the Tunisian model of removing authoritarian leaders from office, another factor played a more significant role in broadcasting the protest dynamic, the eruption of large-scale and sophisticated demon-strations in Egypt.[6]

Egypt was a logical country to follow in Tunisia's footsteps, in part because these two countries had so much in common. For example, as John Waterbury pointed out, both Egypt and Tunisia were members of the Arab Socialist movement, and as a result they shared a long history of a central-ized, fused, and corporatist political economy. Moreover, both countries experienced a shift in the 1970s and 1980s to a more liberalized economic system (which prompted popular protests in both countries), and their leaders carried out some short-lived and largely halfhearted experiments with political liberalization.[7] In addition, also like Tunisia and unusual for countries in the MENA, Egypt had well-defined state borders, a strong national identity, and, ethnically and religiously, a relatively homogeneous population. Finally, Egypt, far more than Tunisia and, indeed, virtually every other country in the MENA, conformed closely to the profile of an early riser as outlined earlier, given both its rich history of political protests and strikes (especially in the few years leading up to 2011) and the strength of both its civil society and its labor movement.

As in East Germany in 1989 and Serbia in 2000, three developments helped Egypt transform a possible wave into a real one with significant geographical reach. First, without Egypt's participation in the wave, Tunisia would have been a solitary case of a popular uprising that overthrew a dictator. Second, Egypt demonstrated to interested parties throughout the region that the Tunisian precedent could travel and succeed and, what is more, do so in a country that was far more important in regard to size, more similar to other countries in the region, and unusually close to the most influential international power in the region, the United States.

Finally, and also like East Germany and Serbia in the two earlier waves, the Egyptian dynamic built on the model first developed and applied in Tunisia but amended it in ways that made the Egyptian efforts innovative, successful, and highly infectious. In particular, youth played a key role in Egypt as well as Tunisia (as they had in most of the color revolutions), and as the protests continued, they were joined by older or established opposition groups and figures (for instance, the Muslim Brotherhood, the Egyptian Movement for Change [Kefaya], and the Egyptian politician Ayman Nour). Moreover, the eighteen days of Egyptian protests did not start with self-immolation. Instead, from the beginning they targeted large urban areas (as opposed to rural areas in Tunisia) and the establishment of control over central squares. Here, the final two innovations were precisely the same as in East Germany and later in Serbia, and, for that matter, the approach used in Eastern European protests during Communism.[8] Moreover, the protests that took place in Egypt built on past struggles, such as those waged by Kefaya, the April 6 movement, and a large and increasingly active labor movement.[9]

Finally, the Egyptian protests were carefully orchestrated to have maximum impact. For example, organizers chose National Police Day (January 25) to begin their protests; gave specific names to major protest days (for example, "Day of Revolt" followed by "Friday of Anger," with the latter capitalizing on Friday's congregational prayers); used the Internet to send out false rumors about the timing and location of the protests; and prepared for the possibility that rubber bullets and tear gas would be deployed against them.[10] More generally, they used the techniques of nonviolent resistance that had been used by oppositions in other countries.

The tool kit that the Egyptian opposition deployed to take on the Mubarak regime had diverse origins. First, the protesters borrowed some of the practices used in the past by the Muslim Brotherhood. In addition, some protesters devised strategies in collaboration with the Tunisian opposition in the several years leading up to the antiregime mobilizations in Tunisia and Egypt. These linkages helped the oppositions in both countries share their experiences with regime repression and theories about dealing with it, including ways to organize barricades and avoid surveillance. In addition, international actors, as in Tunisia and the color revolutions, provided training sessions, playbooks, and technical assistance in order to help both the oppositions and everyday citizens build sophisticated protest strategies, especially for the younger participants in the demonstrations.[11]

Although external support was important, even more critical, as in the case of the Serbian struggle against Serbia's President Slobodan Milosevic, and the activists in what became the Orange Revolution in Ukraine, were innovations introduced by younger members of the Egyptian opposition. For instance, before the first protest on January 25, leaders of the younger opposition experimented with holding small-scale weekly protests; walking through some of Cairo's slums, yelling out complaints about the regime; and assessing how angry Egyptians of various backgrounds were with the regime and how willing they were to join the procession.[12] As they discovered through their "fieldwork," Egyptians had considerable potential for a Tunisian-like dynamic. This information agreed with other indicators of popular dissatisfaction, as revealed by the rapid and large-scale response of youth and educated people to messages relayed through Facebook and texting.

All this suggests that although the Egyptian model was influenced by deliberate diffusion, which also enhanced its ability to influence publics in other countries, the more important mechanism of diffusion to other countries seems to have been, as in 1989, "demonstration effects." A key insight here is, first, that the Egyptian protesters succeeded in pressuring their military to remove President Hosni Mubarak from office. Second, and much like what happened in East Germany in 1989 and Serbia following Milosevic's refusal to admit electoral defeat, the Egyptian protesters managed to put together techniques that reduced the costs of protest while accomplishing the goal of removing an authoritarian leader from office.

These feats in turn helped people throughout the MENA to overcome fundamental problems of coordination under authoritarianism. Large-scale protests result from thousands of individuals' decisions to participate. Most individuals opposed to a regime can be assumed to be willing to participate in a protest only when they believe that the personal benefit of doing so outweighs the expected personal costs. The number of fellow protesters is an important factor in an individual's decision to join, since the larger the crowd is, the less likely he or she is to be persecuted. One of the main challenges of such collective mobilization, therefore, is identifying whether and when others also will participate in a protest. The concerns are how many others are opposed to the regime, how far they will go to change it, and how costly a failure will be. If an individual correctly expects that enough others will join the group, then she will be willing to participate. But if not enough others participate, the risks of taking such an action increase, and he will decide to stay on the sidelines—at least until he has more information about other citizens' feelings (see chapters 5 and 15).

After the initial "Day of Revolt" in Egypt on January 25, activists developed and circulated detailed plans on how others could join, as well as maps of where to mobilize after Friday prayers and how to move in groups to Cairo's central Tahrir Square. Knowing that large numbers of people would participate, tens of thousands of Egyptians joined the demonstrations on January 28, the "Friday of Rage." Despite the regime's efforts to shut down Internet access, limit texting, and authorize the police to use force against the protesters, mass demonstrations took place. This was the beginning of the Tahrir Square model that was emulated elsewhere: committed activists continuously occupied the central square; crowds of moderates periodically joined and reinforced the activists during organized days of protest, which were named and highly organized; and their demands escalated over time until they became demands for fundamental regime change ("Go!" and "The people want the downfall of the regime."). Although the size of the crowd in Tahrir Square varied over time, a critical mass of several thousand activists remained until Mubarak left office on February 11.

The value of the "square" model was its ability to communicate to citizens about when and how others would protest, for instance, daily and spontaneously, weekly and planned, or constantly. A comparison of Egypt and Yemen brings home this point. In Yemen, a diverse coalition of Islamist and secular opposition groups also were inspired by the Tunisian example and organized mass rallies around the same time that the Egyptian protests began. The Yemeni protests, however, took place in different locations and lacked a geographic focus. On January 27, the day Egyptians were planning their coordinated march on Tahrir Square, Yemenis demonstrated in several far-flung locations in the capital, including outside the house of a prominent Islamist leader and at Sana'a University. Although by February 2, these dispersed Yemeni protests had led President Ali Abdullah Saleh to promise to step down in 2013 and not to position his son Ahmed to succeed him, the protests did not reach a critical mass or tipping point until February 20 when the Yemeni protesters emulated the Egyptians' tactics and began a continuous sit-in in a square near Sana'a University. By that point, pro-Saleh groups had already occupied Sana'a's Tahrir Square to prevent anti-Saleh protesters from moving there.

What made the transfer of these techniques easier, but was missing from the earlier two waves, was that citizens throughout the MENA could watch the protests in Egypt on satellite television and know that others in their country were watching them as well. These reports, moreover, built on al-Jazeera's emphasis over the years on political reforms.[13] The techniques were sufficiently simple that people understood that others understood how something similar could unfold in their own country with similar results. For example, the initial protests in Egypt targeted issues of regionwide concern, such as low wages, police abuses, and the need to lift emergency laws.

The Model Moves

In the days immediately after the fall of Mubarak, protesters in Iran, Libya, and Bahrain tried to seize central squares in their capital cities. But as we noted earlier in our discussion of the European and Eurasian waves, diffusion is usually "double" or "interactive."[14] Accordingly, regimes in the MENA also learned from the Tahrir Square strategy and did not allow protesters to establish a hold on geographically central locations. Iranian security forces blocked off Azadi Square in Tehran, denying it to protesters. This is similar to what happened in Azerbaijan in the 2005 election (but not in Ukraine a year earlier, when the Orange Revolution took place), when the regime cordoned off Baku, forcing the protests to take place far from the city's center and thereby neutralizing their impact.[15] In Libya, Muammar Qaddafi's regime maintained control of Tripoli's Green Square by violently harassing the protesters. Bahraini protesters occupied Manama's Pearl Roundabout, were forced out of it by security officials, reoccupied it, and then were forced out again before the regime demolished the roundabout's primary structure. The Syrian regime squashed several attempts by protesters to demonstrate near the entrances of Damascus's central Suq al-Hamidyya and nearby Martyrs' Square, but protesters in Homs seized that city's Clock Square and renamed it Tahrir Square.

When regimes successfully denied protesters a central square to occupy continuously or did not have a central square, the protests became erratic and were based on designated "days of protest" or relied on mobilizations after Friday prayers in provincial cities. In short, this dynamic is similar to what happened later in the two waves in Europe and Eurasia, that is, a partial implementation of the model as it moved to new places, in part because the protesters were less careful in their preparations and in part because the challenges took place in more daunting political circumstances. Protesters in these situations in the MENA became dependent on the government's blunders and occasionally seemed to be trying to provoke bloodshed to turn people against the regime. For example, protests fizzled in Saudi Arabia after demonstrators were unable to mobilize and occupy a square in Riyadh or Jiddah on their planned "Day of Rage" in March. The Saudi regime showed restraint and periodically released detained activists. Because the violence was minimal, the protesters did not have funerals to try to begin the process anew. Protests in Algeria also declined partly because of the riot police's restraint. In contrast, the violence in Libya, Syria, Yemen, and Bahrain dramatically increased the size of demonstrations against the regime by bringing in fence-sitters or changing people's private preferences regarding the regime's desirability. The deaths of several dozen Yemeni protesters on March 18 increased the size of mass demonstrations and triggered a wave of political and military defections from the regime, as happened in Armenia in the 2008 election.

Some elements of the Tunisian and Egyptian strategy have not diffused. A martyr became a unifying symbol for protesters in Tunisia and Egypt: Mohamed Bouazizi and Khaled Said, respectively. In contrast, no single Yemeni, Bahraini, or Libyan martyr came to symbolize the protests in those countries. Syrian protesters consider the city of Deraa, one of several cities where protests occurred on March 15, as the place where their revolution began. But this was largely because the Syrian regime violently cracked down on protests in that city earlier than in other places. Deraa's Omari Mosque became a symbol of defiance and mobilization, but the names of the city's schoolboys whose detention in February by security forces for writing graffiti stimulated the protests have not been widely circulated. Libyan protesters relied on historic nationalist symbols, such as a Libyan flag used in the 1950s and 1960s and Omar al-Mukhtar, a hero of the early-twentieth-century resistance to the Italian occupation of Libya. The prisoners killed by the Libyan regime in Abu Salim Prison in 1996 or their lawyer, whose arrest in February sparked mass demonstrations in Benghazi, did not become symbols like Bouazizi or Said. Similarly, many Syrian protesters and revolutionaries adopted the old Syrian independence flag— used before the 1963 Baathist coup—as an identifying symbol.

We close our comparison of these three waves by assessing the extent to which the patterns of diffusion in the MENA match the patterns for the European and Eurasian waves. First, rather than sequential, the protests in the MENA have followed a more splattered pattern. By this we mean that after toppling Mubarak, the protests took place in geographically disparate states in the region, not sequentially, and some countries did not have large-scale protests. We hypothesize that this is largely because of the absence of an electoral calendar calibrating the dynamic, as with the color revolutions, and because of much broader access to information about developments throughout the MENA compared with the far more restricted flow of information in the Communist world. Second, while the extent of the opposition's development seems to affect whether countries experience large-scale and continuing mobilizations and whether they join the wave earlier or later—with Bahrain, Egypt, and Yemen contrasting with, say, Saudi Arabia—there nonetheless are some obvious exceptions to this generalization, for example, the absence so far of much protest activity in Algeria and Jordan versus considerable mobilizations in Libya and Syria.

At the same time, however, the other side of the coin, regime capacity, seems to be playing a more important role in the MENA. Even though none of the regimes in 1989 had the economic resources to buy off their challengers and very few in the color revolutions were sufficiently well endowed to use this option (though Kazakhstan, an oil-rich country, did "buy" local support after witnessing the fall of President Askar Akaev in Kyrgyzstan), a number of regimes in the MENA, because of significant oil and natural gas income, were in a position to choose among capitulation, repression, and economic co-optation. Thus, countries with a significant oil or natural gas income have been relatively insulated from the wave. For example, two of the three countries with the highest incomes–Qatar and the United Arab Emirates (UAE)–have not had significant protests, and protests in Kuwait have focused on limited electoral and constitutional reforms and have not called for the overthrow of the monarchy. Saudi Arabia and Oman have had limited protests, with more in the latter than in the former. Libya and Bahrain have significantly lower per capita incomes than the others, and both experienced large regime-threatening protests. Access to a hydro-carbon income allows regimes to preemptively "buy off" potential protest-ers by offering generous stipends, subsidies, and bonuses and announc-ing new job and housing initiatives. For example, as Egyptian protesters became entrenched in Tahrir Square on January 28, the emir of Kuwait announced that all Kuwaiti citizens would receive a grant of 1,000 dinars (approximately $3,559). In late February, the government of Saudi Arabia announced a $38 billion spending package that included pay raises, higher unemployment benefits, and new housing. Another package of $130 billion was announced in mid-March and included the construction of 500,000 homes, two-month stipends to government-funded students, an increase in the minimum wage, and 60,000 new jobs in the Interior Ministry.

These four regimes—Qatar, Kuwait, the UAE, and Saudi Arabia–have used their excessive co-optive capacity to make the Gulf Cooperation Council (GCC) function as a region within the region with regard to its ability to block or limit the extent of the current wave of protests. As pro-tests spread in Oman and Bahrain in early March, the other GCC states pledged $10 billion in aid for each of the embattled regimes. In Oman, the protests declined. But when they continued in Bahrain, Saudi Arabia and the UAE intervened militarily to guarantee the survival of the al-Khalifa regime. In May 2011, the GCC "welcomed" Jordan's fifteen-year-old request to join the group and invited Morocco to "finalize the necessary procedures for joining." If these states join, the GCC would effectively be an exclusive club for the region's monarchies.

It is not obvious, however, why the three MENA states with the lowest oil and natural gas incomes per capita—Lebanon, Jordan, and Morocco—also have had fewer protests than the states with modest (Tunisia, Egypt, Yemen, Syria) or substantial but not overwhelming (Iraq, Algeria, Bahrain, Libya) per capita incomes from hydrocarbon resources. There seems to be an inverted U-shaped relationship between such resources and the size and regularity of protests in the Arab uprisings, though other factors may be at work. It is interesting that in the color revolutions, energy-rich countries like Azerbaijan, Turkmenistan, Kazakhstan, and Russia have either suc-ceeded in putting down protests (in the first case) or not experiencing any major popular challenges to their rule.

More similar to the 1989 wave, however, were the protests in the MENA that initially spread to the countries with the longest-serving de facto chiefs of state. Ben Ali and Mubarak ruled for more than twenty-three and twenty-nine years, respectively. The next two leaders to face sustained protests, Qaddafi and Saleh, ruled for more than forty-one and thirty-two years, respectively. These were four of the five longest-serving rulers in the region; Oman's Sultan Qaboos bin Said al-Said is the other (forty years and counting). Yet they are not the oldest rulers. In 2011, King Abdullah of Saudi Arabia was eighty-seven years old; Emir Sabah of Kuwait eighty-one; and President Abdelaziz Bouteflika of Algeria seventy-four. All three were older than Qaboos, Qaddafi, and Saleh, and who will succeed each of them is uncertain. This suggests that the early diffusion of protests targeted extremely long-serving rulers and that the key issue was this rather than, say, imminent or anticipated succession. Moreover, as the wave has continued, sustained protests in several states, such as Syria and Bahrain, targeted relatively young and healthy rulers with no upcoming succession on the political agenda, although Bahraini protesters focused on the long-serving prime minister. At the same time and unlike the earlier waves, there are few cases in the MENA of recent transitions in which a leader's hold on power was not yet consolidated. Iraq's prime minister, Nouri al-Maliki, and Palestine's president, Mahmoud Abbas, fit in this category. Iraq had protests only intermittently until sectarian protests erupted two years after the Arab uprisings began.

Another factor that appears in the case of the MENA, but not in Europe or Eurasia, is the contrast between republics and monarchies. All the Arab republics except Lebanon have experienced protests in the current wave, whereas the monarchies have been much more stable. It is hard to parse out what this relationship means, because oil incomes confound this relationship. Algeria and Morocco are the two North African states where protests did not escalate to the point of threatening the regime. The most common explanations for their divergence relates to country-specific factors: Algerians might fear a return to civil war, and many analysts claim that the Moroccan monarchy is more entrenched in the sociocultural foundations of the country than other regimes are in theirs. The latter argument, moreover, seems to be supported by the protesters' very modest demands.

Finally, like the European and Eurasian waves, economic and governance deficiencies—for example, corruption, inefficient bureaucracies that fail to meet the expectations of citizens, unemployment, and large numbers of disaffected educated youths—are too widespread throughout the region to play any consistent role in differentiating between the countries that joined the wave and those that did not. At the same time, we do not see the clear pattern, as in the earlier waves, of the most liberalized regimes in the region joining the wave and doing so early in its development. Egypt and Yemen, of course, conform to this argument, but others, such as Jordan and Morocco, do not. In addition, some of the most authoritarian regimes in the MENA have had significant protests (Libya, Syria), but others have not (UAE, Saudi Arabia). This pattern was also the case for the color revolutions.

Conclusions

We can draw several conclusions from this comparison of three waves of popular mobilizations against authoritarian rulers. First, Tunisia only partially fit the profile of the early risers that jump-started the European and Eurasian waves. Second, the drivers of diffusion in the earlier waves were similar to the case of the MENA. For example, the Tunisian precedent moved to Egypt precisely because of these two states' similarities. In many respects, Egypt's qualities were closer to those of an early riser than to Tunisia's qualities; and Egypt was in an ideal position, as were East Germany and Serbia, to modify the innovation and, because of that and the success of the protests, broadcast the dynamic to many other countries in the region. Finally, while the adoption of the innovation was sequential in the European and Eurasian waves, the pattern of adoption in the MENA was more splattered. Moreover, while the principal issue in the first two waves with respect to when and whether countries joined was the size and experience of the opposition, the regime's vulnerability and capacity to defend itself were more important in the case of the MENA—for example, oil incomes, the contrast between republics and monarchies, and the advantages for members of the Gulf Cooperation Council of receiving support from richer, better-armed, and more stable neighbors. In this sense, the regime side of the equation was less important in the European and Eurasian waves because there, regimes in general had much less room for maneuver as a result of severe economic constraints and the absence in virtually every case (except, interestingly enough, Serbia) of a military (at home or in the neighborhood) that could be quickly deployed to defend the regime. In this sense, the opposition played a more pivotal role in the first two waves than it could play in the MENA.

NOTES

1. Dontalla Della Porta and Sidney Tarrow, "Interactive Diffusion: The Coevolution of Police and Protest Behavior with an Application to Transnational Contention," *Comparative Political Studies*, 45, no. 1 (2010): 119–52.

2. On these waves, see, for example, Valerie Bunce, *Subversive Institutions: The Design and the Destruction of Socialism and the State* (New York: Cambridge University Press, 1999); Archie Brown, *The Gorbachev Factor* (Oxford: Oxford University Press, 1996); Archie Brown, "Transnational Influences in the Transition from Communism," *Post-Soviet Affairs* 16, no. 2 (April/June 2000); J. F. Brown, *Surge to Freedom: The End of Communist Rule in Eastern Europe* (Durham, N.C.: Duke University Press, 1991); Gale Stokes, *The Walls Came Tumbling Down: The Collapse of Communism in Eastern Europe.* (Oxford: Oxford University Press, 1993); Joerg Forbrig and Pavol Demes, eds., *Reclaiming Democracy: Civil Society and Electoral Change in Central and Eastern Europe* (Washington, D.C.: German Marshall Fund, 2007); Mark Beissinger, "Structure and Example in Modular Political Phenomena: The Diffusion of Bulldozer/Rose/Orange/Tulip Revolutions," *Perspectives on Politics,* 5, no. 2 (2007): 259–76; Mark Beissinger, "Promoting Democracy: Is Exporting Revolution a Constructive Strategy?" *Dissent,* 53, no. 1 (2006): 18–24; Mark Beissinger, *Nationalist Mobilization and the Collapse of the Soviet State* (New York: Cambridge University Press, 2002); Valerie Bunce and Sharon L. Wolchik, *Defeating Authoritarian Leaders in Postcommunist Countries* (Cambridge: Cambridge University Press, 2012); Valerie Bunce and Sharon L. Wolchik, "A Regional Tradition: The Diffusion of Democratic Change Under Communism and Postcommunism," in *Democracy and Authoritarianism in the Postcommunist World,* ed. Valerie Bunce, Michael McFaul, and Kathryn Stoner-Weiss (Cambridge: Cambridge University Press, 2011), 30–56.

3. See, for example, Beissinger, *Nationalist Mobilization,* 2002; Rebecca Kolins Givan, Sarah A. Soule, and Kenneth M. Roberts, "Introduction: The Dimensions of Diffusion," in *The Diffusion of Social Movements,* ed. Rebecca Kolins Givan, Sarah A. Soule, and Kenneth M. Roberts (Cambridge: Cambridge University Press, 2010), 1–15; Kurt Weyland, "The Diffusion of Regime Contention in European Democratization, 1840–1940," *Comparative Political Studies* 43 (2010): 1148–76; Doug McAdam, "The Cross National Diffusion of Movement Ideas," *Annals of the American Academy of Political and Social Sciences* 528 (1993): 56–74; David Strang, David Soule, and Sarah Soule, "Diffusion in Organizations and Social Movements: From Hybrid Corn to Poison Pills," *Annual Review of Sociology* 24 (1998): 265–90.

4. Valerie Bunce, *Do New Leaders Make a Difference? Executive Succession and Public Policy Under Capitalism and Socialism* (Princeton, N.J.: Princeton University Press, 1981).

5. See, for example, Kenneth Perkins, *A History of Modern Tunisia* (Cambridge: Cambridge University Press, 2004); Christopher Alexander, *Tunisia: Stability and Reform in the Modern Maghreb* (London: Routledge, 2010); Eva Bellin, "Democratization and Its Discontents: Should America Push Reform in the Middle East?" *Foreign Affairs* 87, no. 4 (2008): 112–19; Eva Bellin, *Stalled Democracy: Capital, Labor and the Paradox of State-Sponsored Development* (Ithaca, N.Y.: Cornell University Press, 2002); Eva Bellin, "The Robustness of Authoritarianism in the

Middle East," *Comparative Politics* 36, no. 2 (2004): 139–57; Eva Bellin, "Contingent Democrats: Industrialists, Labor, and Democratization in Late-Developing Countries," *World Politics* 52 (2000): 175–205.

6. David S. Patel and Valerie J. Bunce, "Turning Points and the Cross-National Diffusion of Popular Protest," *APSA Comparative Democratization Newsletter* 10, no. 1 (2012): 1, 10–13.

7. Bruce K. Rutherford, *Egypt After Mubarak: Liberalism, Islam and Democracy in the Arab World* (Princeton, N.J.: Princeton University Press, 2008); Stephen J. King, *The New Authoritarianism in the Middle East and North Africa* (Bloomington: Indiana University Press, 2009).

8. P. Kenney, *Carnival of Revolution: Central Europe, 1989* (Princeton, N.J.: Princeton University Press, 2002).

9. Marsha Pripstein Posusney, "Enduring Authoritarianism: Middle East Lessons for Comparative Theory," *Comparative Politics* 36, no. 2 (January 2004): 127–38; Rabab El-Mahdi, "Enough: Egypt's Quest for Democracy," *Comparative Political Studies* 42 (February 2009): 1011–39.

10. Tina Rosenberg, "Revolution U: What Egyptians Learned from the Students Who Overthrew Milosevic," *Foreign Policy*, February 16, 2011, available at www.foreignpolicy.com/articles/2011/02/16/revolution_u.html; David D. Kirkpatrick, "Wired and Shrewd, Young Egyptians Guide Revolt," *New York Times*, February 9, 2011, available at nytimes.org/2011/102/10/world/middleeast/10youth.html.

11. See, for instance, Rosenberg, "Revolution U"; Courtney Brooks and Milos Teodorovic, "Exporting Nonviolent Revolution, from Eastern Europe to the Middle East," Radio Free Europe/Radio Liberty, February 21, 2011; Bunce interview with Ivan Marovic, Belgrade, 2005; Srdja Popovic, presentation at the School of Advanced International Studies, Washington D.C., April 2011.

12. Kirkpatrick, "Wired and Shrewd."

13. Marc Lynch, *Voices of the New Arab Public: Iraq, Al-Jazeera, and Middle East Politics Today* (New York: Columbia University Press, 2006); Marc Lynch, *The Arab Uprising: The Unfinished Revolutions of the New Middle East* (New York: PublicAffairs, 2012).

14. Also see Karrie Koesel and Valerie J. Bunce, "Diffusion-Proofing: Russian and Chinese Responses to Waves of Popular Mobilizations Against Authoritarian Rulers," *Perspectives on Politics*, 11, no. 3 (September 2013): 753–68.

15. Bunce and Wolchik, "A Regional Tradition."

4

Authoritarian Learning and Counterrevolution

STEVEN HEYDEMANN AND REINOUD LEENDERS

At the outset of the Arab uprisings, it seemed plausible that the era of Arab authoritarianism was nearing an end. Yet as early as May 2011, those possibilities seemed far more remote. Arab regimes in Syria and Bahrain intensified their repression of mass uprisings: in the former case, with backing from Iran, Russia, and Hezbollah; in the latter, through the armed intervention of Saudi Arabia and the United Arab Emirates. Smaller protest movements in Morocco, Algeria, and Jordan failed to achieve the scale or momentum of those in Egypt and Tunisia and gradually dissipated, having evoked only modest commitments for additional political reforms from existing regimes.

Even as postauthoritarian transitions progressed in Egypt and Tunisia, it seemed increasingly clear that the authoritarian pole of the region's political spectrum would continue to be well populated. Unlike earlier episodes of democratic change that produced significant gains in the number of global democracies, the Arab uprisings are far less certain to generate the region-wide transformations that accompanied the Third Wave—notwithstanding the post-Third-Wave backlash that has seen deterioration in the quality of democracy in a wide range of cases.[1] How do we account for the Arab uprising's loss of momentum and the capacity of most other authoritarian regimes in the Arab world to so quickly contain mass protest movements once they had spread beyond Tunisia and Egypt, at least to the extent that they forestalled immediate regime change? Why didn't all the Arab dominoes fall?

Multiple factors might have played a role, not least the willingness of Arab regimes to kill hundreds or even, in the Syrian case, more than one hundred thousand, of their citizens and injure, arrest, and torture many more. The loyalty of the military and security services no doubt mattered as well, preventing splits among the ruling elite that marked critical turning points in the Tunisian and Egyptian uprisings.[2] So did the diffusion of popular uprisings, from the largely homogeneous societies of Egypt and Tunisia to the more heterogeneous and divided societies of Jordan, Bahrain, and Syria where governments and security agencies were disproportionately led by privileged elites or sectarian minorities: East Bankers in the Jordanian case, Sunni Muslims in the Bahraini case, and Alawites in the Syrian case.

Without diminishing the importance of these variables, however, we argue that the capacity of some authoritarian regimes in the Middle East to suppress opposition movements can be explained, at least in part, by their capacity to learn from and adapt to the rapidly emerging challenges that mass uprisings posed for the regime's survival. Moreover, we view this adaptive capacity as a defining and tested attribute of some authoritarian regimes in the Arab world, an attribute we have elsewhere characterized as "recombinant authoritarianism": systems of rule that possess the capacity to reorder and reconfigure instruments and strategies of governance and to reshape and recombine existing institutional, discursive, and regulatory arrangements to create recognizable but nonetheless distinctive solutions to shifting configurations of challenges.[3]

Just as the spread of protests itself was the product of social learning by Arab citizens—a wave effect facilitated by the rapid diffusion of ideas, discourses, and practices from one country to another and their adaptation to local contexts—so too were the counterrevolutionary strategies of regimes shaped by processes of learning and diffusion among regime elites, especially among those in which protests began later in the sequence of events that constitute the Arab uprising. In other words, two parallel processes were at work in the unfolding and potential unraveling of the Arab uprising, one at the level of Arab societies and the other among authoritarian regimes. Initially, these worked to the advantage of protesters. Subsequently, as regimes adapted to the repertoires of contention developed by the protesters and assessed the direction of regional and international trends, the advantage shifted in their direction.

These processes are symmetrical. On the one hand, Arab citizens watched and learned from the experiences of their neighbors, facilitating the spread of uprisings from one country to another. Apart from the use of social media and the Internet, activists across the region emulated Egypt's example, in which the protesters effectively claimed and celebrated key public spaces, turning Tahrir Square in Cairo, Tahrir Square in Sana'a, Pearl Square in Manama, Liberation Square in Benghazi, and Clock Square in

Homs into symbols of popular defiance and podiums of dialogue among a jumble of opposition groups, emergent social movements, and unaffiliated youth.[4] In equally powerful fashion, protesters rallied around human tragedies of regime-inflicted suffering and death, granting iconic status to young victims, first Khaled Said in Egypt, followed by Mohammad Bouazizi in Tunisia, and then Hamza al-Khateeb in Syria.

While initially stunned by events and misreading them through the lens of business as usual,[5] Arab regimes absorbed the lessons from the first wave of protests, adapted to them as they unfolded, and developed new strategies of repression to prove that their countries were not like Egypt, Libya, or Tunisia. Those regimes with significant financial resources, like Saudi Arabia, Kuwait, Oman, the United Arab Emirates, and Qatar, moved quickly to increase public spending in order to deflect potential grievances. Some, such as Jordan, fell back on time-tested tactics such as replacing unpopular prime ministers to present a fresh political face. Syrian President Bashar al-Assad hinted at the learning process this involved by blaming the first wave of uprisings elsewhere in the region on "stagnant water": "You have to upgrade yourself with the upgrading of the society. . . . We have to keep up with this change [in society], as state and institutions."[6]

Yet the literature on the breakdown of authoritarian regimes and transitions to democracy has paid far more attention to the first of these processes, those of democratic contagion,[7] than to the second, the diffusion of authoritarian learning.[8] In general, the diffusion effects associated with social mobilization from below have been well studied in the transitology literature (see chapter 3). More generally, these effects were perhaps best described by Adam Przeworski in *Democracy and The Market*.[9] "I know," Przeworski wrote in reference to the 'Third Wave' of democracy,

> that hundreds of macrohistorical comparative sociologists will write thousands of books and articles correlating background conditions with outcomes in each country, but I think they will be wasting their time, for the entire event was one single snowball. I mean it in a technical sense: As developments took place in one country, people elsewhere were updating their probabilities of success, and as the next country went over the brink, the calculation was becoming increasingly reassuring.

Some twenty years later, this metaphor of a snowball perfectly captures now common descriptions of the diffusion of uprisings from one Arab society to another, beginning in Tunisia in December 2010. In this sense,

Arab protesters clearly disproved the initial assessments by many Middle East pundits and Western officials that no such thing would unfold.[10] What has often been overlooked, however, is that diffusion and learning operate not only from below at the level of social actors but also from above as regime elites update their own sense of probabilities and adapt their own repertoires of suppression in response to developments on the ground, around the region, and at home.

This process of regime learning as the Arab spring unfolded was facilitated by the emergence of distinctive "models" as frameworks that captured and sought to make generalizable the "lessons learned" from how regimes, societies, and international actors responded to mass protests in specific cases. These models served as dissemination constructs and learning frameworks that simplify complex interactions and make them appear broadly applicable and more easily portable, despite the specificities of the cases that gave them their names. They have informed the understandings of surviving autocrats, protesters, and international actors about how to navigate their own circumstances and explicitly shaped regimes' behavior.

The Libyan model, for instance, became a shorthand construct referring to an uprising that reached such an extreme level of violence that it provoked international intervention, causing the military defeat of an authoritarian regime and, eventually, the murder of the fallen autocrat. Thus, as we explain in this chapter, for authoritarian survivors in the region, and most particularly for Syria's Bashar al-Assad, the "Libyan model" is a doomsday tale, a warning of what can befall a dictator whose violence exceeds some ill-defined threshold of international tolerance. For Syria's opposition, in contrast, the Libyan model became an aspiration to be emulated and a benchmark for assessing the adequacy or shortcomings of the international response to the violence unleashed on the country by the Assad regime. For international actors, the Libyan model had enormous, if varied, implications, with significant consequences for how the Syrian uprising has played out. Although Russia and China initially did not object to UN action on Libya, they came to view NATO's intervention as having abused a humanitarian mission for purposes of regime change, in violation of international law and the inalienable sovereignty of states. The experience provided justification for Russia and China to reject any subsequent action by the UN Security Council that seemed remotely comparable to the resolutions that led to intervention in Libya. The Libyan model has forced the United States and its European allies into a defensive posture, compelling them to highlight the differences between Libya and Syria and discourage comparisons that might expose them to charges of hypocrisy and double standards in responding to the mass slaughter of civilians.

In addition to the Libyan model, the "Yemen model" has emerged as a dissemination construct and a learning framework signifying an uprising that induced regional diplomatic intervention, leading to a negotiated transition of power that then paved the way for a slow, evolutionary process of political change. For much of the first two years of the Syrian uprising, the possibility of replicating the Yemen model in Syria influenced regional and international actors' diplomatic activities. Most prominently, it informed a plan put forward by the Arab League in January 2012 for a handover of power in Syria. According to the then Qatari prime minister, Sheikh Hamad Bin Jassim al-Thani, Syria's transition had to resemble the arrangements in Yemen.[11] Although it receded as an option in 2013, the proposed analogy continues to hover above the Syrian conflict as the pathway onto which the international community would like the conflict to move.

The "Bahrain model" serves in similar ways to characterize an uprising in which external intervention by regional allies successfully suppressed mass protests that intersected with deepening sectarian polarization. This model, like its counterparts, has been appropriated and packaged by governments in the Gulf and elsewhere to inform how they perceive and respond to circumstances with characteristics similar to those of Bahrain.

The top-down process of authoritarian learning and adaptation suggested by the appropriation of these models as frameworks for regime behavior is visible in the way that authoritarian incumbents in Saudi Arabia, Bahrain, Kuwait, Jordan, Algeria, and Syria watched how uprisings unfolded in Tunisia, Yemen, Egypt, and Libya; took stock of international reactions to these events; and, in response, developed strategies that they perceived, whether rightly or wrongly, to maximize their probabilities of surviving this wave of popular mobilization and living to rule another day. As indicated in one recent study of the Syrian uprising, for instance, regime elites are described as having taken stock of events in surrounding countries just before the onset of Syria's own uprising, noting their echoes in small-scale events in Syria, and calibrating their own strategic reactions accordingly:

> These [small-scale events in February 2011 in Syria] served as a warning to the regime that Syrian society carried the seeds of explosion, and that the Arab Spring would soon reach Syria. Meanwhile, news was leaked that the President had formed a special committee to examine the possibility of the protests spreading to Syria, and how to avert or respond to them. The committee

reached a conclusion that the reason for the fall of the Tunisian and Egyptian regimes had been the failure to crush the protests at the moment of their inception, a conclusion that was also leaked. This fact indicates that the regime resolved to use the security option even before the protests had begun.[12]

As the Syrian uprising unfolded, however, it was no longer the developments in Egypt and Tunisia that drove the processes of authoritarian learning and adaptation by President Bashar al-Assad and his inner circle. Rather, it was the Libyan experience that gave the Assad regime its most important and most threatening lessons about pathways to regime overthrow that were seen as essential to preempt. The importance of the Libyan model as the basis for learning by the Assad regime is evident in the strategic behavior it has exhibited in responding to a wide range of pressures and how this behavior has shifted over time. These include shifts in how the regime viewed the imperative of maintaining control over territory, the means it has deployed against peaceful protests, the steps it has taken to mitigate possibilities of international intervention, and the rhetoric it uses to characterize the Syrian opposition.

While some in the Syrian opposition viewed the Libyan model as inspiration—combining limited, international military intervention in the guise of a humanitarian mission with the creation of a liberated zone in which a transitional government could be created and supported by the international community—the Syrian regime regarded this scenario as a potential nightmare, one that gained in plausibility as the number of defectors from the Syrian army increased and as the Syrian opposition became more broadly militarized. Only months after the start of the uprising, preventing a "Benghazi scenario" from materializing on Syrian territory emerged as a critical priority of the regime.

Thus, in late September 2011, when a significant force of military defectors organized as the Free Syrian Army (FSA) acted to defend residents of a small city called Rastan from attack by regime security forces, the regime's response was swift, fierce, and disproportionate. To prevent the possibility that Rastan—a city of about 40,000 people located between Homs and Hama and not far from the Lebanese border—might consolidate its independence and provide the basis for some form of international intervention, however unrealistic that scenario might have been at the time, the regime brought massive force to bear against rebel units in the city. By some reports, more than 250 tanks were used in a massive assault that quickly overwhelmed the lightly armed FSA forces.[13] Similarly, regime fears of a Benghazi scenario developing in the southern governorate of Deraa, a city immediately adjacent to Jordan where the uprising began, may explain why, for many months, this area had the largest concentration of regime troops outside Damascus.[14]

This itself may not demonstrate "learning," as any regime will oppose "revolutionary situations," Benghazi style or not.[15] Yet Syrian regime propagandists have not made it a secret that events in Libya weighed heavily in their strategic response to the spread of an armed insurgency. As one commentator for the regime mouthpiece Al-Thawra stated:

> During the Libyan crisis, the biggest city in eastern Libya, Benghazi, was the capital of the opposition and the starting point for attacks on other areas, for the spread of confrontations westward and for NATO's military intervention. But the situation in Syria is different. After more than one and a half year [of fighting], armed opposition gangs could not control any of the Syrian cities. All that these gangs achieved was to temporarily control some neighborhoods in this or that town.[16]

Furthermore, there is little doubt that the Assad regime has consistently calibrated its repression to reflect its assessment not only of what worked and what didn't in other cases of regional uprisings but also of how the international community—in particular the United States and its European allies—would respond to the regime's use of force. In this regard, it is striking that as late as the fall of 2012, the Syrian regime rarely used air power against the opposition, presumably to deflect arguments drawing parallels between Syria and Libya that might be used to justify creating a no-fly zone in the Syrian case.[17] Riyad Hijab, the Syrian prime minister who defected in August 2012, put it as follows:

> Bashar used to be scared of the international community—he was really worried that they would impose a no-fly zone over Syria. . . . But then he tested the waters, and pushed and pushed and nothing happened. Now he can run air strikes and drop cluster bombs on his own population.[18]

Subsequently, as the Assad regime updated its assessment to reflect the West's reluctance to intervene in Syria, it recalibrated its response to such challenges. Asserting its control over every part of Syrian territory declined as a priority for the regime. Indeed, as violence escalated throughout 2012 and the Syrian military came under increasing strain, the regime preemptively withdrew forces from predominantly Kurdish areas in Syria's northeast and from the Golan. Moreover, once it became clear to the regime that the only potential trigger of Western intervention would be to prevent the use or dissemination of chemical and biological weapons (CBWs), it enlisted the assistance of its Russian allies in assuring Western governments that its CBW stockpiles were secure.[19] It also offered assurances that it would not deploy CBWs under any circumstances, and in September 2013 agreed to surrender all of its chemical weapons to avoid international military action.

The Syrian regime has also adapted over time a narrative about the nature of the revolution and the threat it represents, changing its characterization of the opposition to avoid incendiary language that might be used to justify intervention and shifting instead to terminology intended both to legitimate its repression and to elicit sympathy from the West. In a speech on June 20, 2011, for example, Bashar al-Assad likened protesters to "germs" existing "everywhere, on the skin and within the guts."[20] Muammar al-Qaddafi repeatedly used similar rhetoric, routinely describing Libyan rebels as "scumbags, germs and rats." With memories of Rwanda's genocide fresh in U.S. and European policy circles, such terminology was seen as a harbinger of genocide, a clear warning of the Qaddafi regime's intent to unleash massive violence against unarmed civilians and turn Libya into a "problem from Hell" of Rwanda-like proportions.[21] As if recognizing the counterproductive effects of such rhetoric, Assad shifted course.[22] The language of his June speech disappeared. Instead, the Assad regime routinely labeled its opponents as "terrorists" and "al-Qaida," terminology that was intended to legitimate its use of force, demonize its opponents, and communicate to the West that it and the Assad regime shared a common foe—and that the regime should, as a result, be seen by the West as a natural ally in the war against terror.[23]

Libya may have been a formative case in the learning and adaptation of the Assad regime, yet it was only one of many experiences that shaped its struggle to repress the uprising of 2011. Syria also learned from Tunisia and Egypt the importance of preventing at all costs the protesters' celebrating and occupying public squares. The regime's stiff repression in this respect caused Syrian activists to complain that their Egyptian counterparts' success in reclaiming symbolically important public spaces was unfairly used to highlight their failure to do so in Syria.[24]

Similarly, the Syrian regime announced limited reforms and ended the state of emergency. These steps, although widely regarded as being disingenuous and falling short of the opposition's demands, gave opponents of humanitarian intervention, including Russia, grounds to argue that the regime could not be completely written off for not fulfilling its sovereign duties, which was loosely regarded as one precondition for the UN Security Council to activate its "responsibility to protect." In this way, the Syrian regime learned to modulate its violence, repressing just enough to avoid triggering international intervention, but not more.

These regime strategies are not simply defensive or reactive. Rather, they should be seen as complex, multilevel games involving regimes, publics, and external actors, in which regimes develop strategies to affect the strategic calculus of citizens, allies, and adversaries even while constantly updating their own probabilities of successfully suppressing their opponents and, should this become untenable, negotiating the terms of their departure from office. The moves by Morocco's King Mohammed VI, for instance, to offer limited but significant constitutional reforms seemed designed to preempt mass protests that might otherwise have built up momentum, as they did in Egypt and Tunisia.[25]

Regimes also adapted strategies to prevent the emergence of internal splits within ruling coalitions and their key support bases, especially the defection of militaries, which contributed to the overthrow of authoritarian regimes in Tunisia and Egypt. This frequently involved increasing the salaries of armed forces personnel and civil servants and offering financial handouts to regime constituencies generally. During the first months of 2011, from Algeria to the Arab Gulf, governments responded to the spread of popular discontent by spending lavishly on pay rises for the public sector, subsidies, and food handouts.[26] Most strikingly, Kuwait distributed $3,500 to each of its 1.2 million citizens. Despite its dearth of cash, an increasingly beleaguered Syrian government followed suit as it decreed pay rises and upgraded health insurance for public servants and the armed forces, granted full employment status to temporary public workers, expedited loans and grants to the poor and to students, waived fines on farmers not paying their fees for irrigation services, scrapped subsidy cuts on fuel and electricity, and turned a blind eye to illegal construction in poor urban areas.[27] On September 27, 2011, as the effects of economic sanctions on Syria began to be felt, the regime introduced import restrictions designed to preserve foreign exchange. Yet when the local business community signaled its anger with this decision, the regime retreated. Anxious to preserve the loyalty of the business community that it continued to view as essential to the regime's survival, the Assad regime rescinded the new restrictions on October 4, less than a week after imposing them.

In addition, strategies to preserve ruling coalitions included allocating prime responsibility for repression to forces known to be loyal to the regime. Thus, in Syria, state violence against protesters has been mostly the work of the Fourth Armored Division and the Republican Guard, a notoriously ruthless and well-armed force led by Maher al-Assad, the president's brother, together with informal regime thugs known as *shabiha*, who had previously constituted armed criminal gangs. This kind of outsourcing of coercion by governments, whether to mercenaries or to loyal sectarian or ethnic communities, is not unusual. Libya's former leader Muammar al-Qaddafi made ample use of African mercenaries in his efforts to crush the ultimately successful uprising in that country. In Bahrain, Pakistani nationals constitute nearly one-third of the country's police force.[28] Immediately following the onset of the uprising there, the Bahraini National Guard advertised in Pakistani newspapers to recruit hundreds of additional "anti-riot instructors" and security guards.[29] When this proved to be insufficient to quell the demonstrations, the ruling Al Khalifa family invited Saudi and Emirati troops to help restore order. Abu Dhabi seems to have followed suit, as it reportedly contracted foreign mercenaries formerly associated with the U.S. private security firm Blackwater to establish units of elite troops to stave off domestic uprisings and possible Iranian aggression.[30] There are many other examples of using foreign mercenaries to staff security agencies.[31]

In addition, these regimes developed narratives aimed at affecting the strategic calculus of their citizens, stressing the personal costs of participating in protests, as well as the negative consequences that would follow should the regimes be overthrown, including sectarian violence, disorder, and economic decline. The erosion of public order and security in postauthoritarian Egypt and Tunisia has been an important talking point in these efforts. Accordingly, while flipping through issues of the Syrian newspaper *Al-Watan*, owned by President al-Assad's billionaire cousin Rami Makhluf, readers are encouraged to abandon even their faintest hopes for the new Egypt emerging after the January 25 revolution. The country is depicted as facing a general breakdown of law and order (March 6 and 7, April 21, 2011), the threat of a "second revolution" by the Muslim Brotherhood (May 25, 2011), rampant sectarianism (April 6, 2011, May 9–12, 2011), and roaming Israeli spies taking advantage of all the chaos (March 20, 2011). Likewise, Syria's main government-owned daily *Tishreen* described post-Qaddafi Libya as a "fearsome model" while underscoring how drawing in foreign intervention led to Libya's fragmentation, uninhibited tribalism, and a dramatic lack of security.[32] Reminding audiences of Iraq's misfortunes after 2003 and its connotations of chaos and sectarianism serves a similar purpose, particularly in Syria. For instance, the protesters had barely risen up in Deraa before security services displayed on state television a captured truckload of weapons they claimed were smuggled into the country from Iraq to "spread unrest and chaos."[33]

Moreover, regimes developed diplomatic and political strategies for managing the international environment, cultivating support from "counterrevolutionary" allies, and working to deter criticism and punitive measures from adversaries. This is particularly evident in the efforts of the Gulf Cooperation Council (GCC) to bring two non-Gulf monarchies, Jordan and Morocco, into the GCC as a means of shoring up their regimes. Jordan, in turn, provided advice and expertise to the Kuwaiti regime on improving its policing methods.[34] It also stepped up coordination and consultation on "regional issues" with Bahrain, which likely included security and policing.[35] It is evident in Saudi Arabia's financial support of conservative Islamist political parties in Egypt and in the government formed after the overthrow of President Mohamed Morsi in July 2013. It is visible in Syria's efforts to secure commitments from Russia, China, and rising powers like Brazil, Turkey, and India to prevent the imposition of UN Security Council sanctions. For his part, Yemeni leader Ali Abdullah Saleh repeatedly played his international trump card—a track record in repressing homegrown al-Qaida militants jointly with U.S. counterterrorism agencies—to deter U.S. pressures for him to step down, even though this failed to prevent his eventual removal from office.

Authoritarian learning reached new levels as the Syrian regime received counterrevolutionary advice from its allies, primarily Iran and Hezbollah. The head of Iran's Revolutionary Guards, Mohammad Ali Jafari, acknowledged that his force was "giving intellectual and advisory help [to] and exchanging experiences" with the Syrian regime.[36] The Syrian regime's use of para- or nonstate militias to infiltrate and obstruct mass demonstrations showed some similarities with the tactics used by the Iranian Basij militia. Jafari reportedly claimed that the Jaish al-Sha'bi (popular army), grouping together various proregime militias, was modeled after the Basij.[37] Next to offering expertise on Iran's military hardware supplies to Syria,[38] Iran may also have introduced improvised and highly lethal weaponry to the Syrian regime, including "improvised rocket-assisted munitions" (IRAM) or "lob bombs." The Iran-supported Kata'ib Hezbollah, an Iraqi Shiite fighting group, is known to have perfected and used IRAMs and may have initiated their use by the Syrian regime.[39] Syrian government documents, said to be obtained by a cyber hacking group and published by the Israeli newspaper *Haaretz* in February 2012, suggest that visiting Iranian officials gave the Syrian regime advice on how to circumvent international sanctions. A memo repeatedly states that Syria wishes "to learn from the Iranian experience in this area."[40] We also suspect that the Iranian regime's suppression of the Green movement was part of the "experience" that Jafari said he had shared with his Syrian counterparts. Although no solid evidence exists of direct links in this respect, there are some striking echoes in the Syrian regime's tactics of some of the methods used by the Iranian regime against protesters in 2009. The Syrian regime's courting of Christian community leaders and its implicit deal making with Kurdish groups resemble the Iranian regime's taking advantage in 2009 of the disconnect among minority groups in the provinces, including the Kurds, and the Green movement.[41] Furthermore, Syria's "electronic army" is likely to have been modeled on Iran's "Web Crime Unit" set up in 2009 to counter Iranian Internet activists.

Finally, in assessing the probability of negotiating an exit strategy that would provide amnesty from prosecution and the opportunity to retain at least some portion of the rulers' accumulated wealth, there is little question that the region's remaining authoritarian elites have paid close attention to the previous fate of counterparts who were overthrown. In this regard, campaigns to prosecute former Egyptian President Hosni Mubarak and former Tunisian President Zine al-Abdine Ben Ali, in addition to the charges by the International Criminal Court prosecutor Luis Oreno Ocampo against Libyan leader Muammar al-Qaddafi, may well have had an impact on the calculus of a leader like Yemen's President Ali Abdullah Saleh—who until November 2011 refused to accept a negotiated transition of power—concerning the risks of a negotiated exit. Only when he received assurances that his fate would not match those of other Arab leaders—largely thanks to Saudi Arabia—did Saleh resign. Some in the Syrian opposition initially sensed the risks of calling for the prosecution of authoritarian leaders and suggested a truth-and-reconciliation process instead.[42] Yet given the popular demand for retribution for the regime's violence, few officials seemed inclined to place their bets on such a scenario.

In other words, it is important to recognize that along with the social learning and snowball effects at the level of societies to which Przeworski refers, there is also a level of interconnectedness and learning and a process of updating of probabilities and strategies among authoritarian leaders that will be significant in determining the fate of remaining authoritarian regimes of the Arab world and perhaps in the prospects for postauthoritarian transitions to democracy in Egypt, Libya, Yemen, and Tunisia. Indeed, beginning as early as March 2011, this process of authoritarian learning reinforced a perception among authoritarian incumbents about their capacity to survive this wave of uprisings and, at the same time, weakened or eroded perceptions among authoritarian incumbents that credible exit strategies existed that could offer them credible guarantees of their future security—if they were inclined to take advantage of them. In turn, these strategies could be viewed as informing a zero-sum game in which incumbent regimes, exemplified by Syria, are prepared to use maximum force if deemed necessary. Accordingly, as the Syrian regime's doggedness has been matched by the protesters' and insurgents' equal resolve to defy the risks and costs of challenging or fighting the regime, a quasi-permanent and bloody standoff has ensued that has disproved predictions of Assad's imminent demise.

More broadly, however, we argue that by May 2011, adaptive authoritarian regimes in the Arab world began converge around a shared constellation of tactics and practices designed to maximize their probability of survival. Several key elements of this emergent strategy stand out.

First, the regimes that are the target of uprisings recognize that the interests of key regional actors, particularly Saudi Arabia and Iran, either align in ways that favor prolonging the regime's power, as (for now) in the Syrian case, or diverge in ways that conveniently justify the regime's repression, as in the case of Bahrain. Either way, regional factors have tended to expand the regimes' room for maneuver and restricted that of their opponents.

Second, the authoritarian incumbents in the Gulf are well aware that the United States, especially, has modified its posture toward popular uprisings in response to Saudi concerns about U.S. support for regime change in Egypt and Tunisia, constraining its willingness to adopt hard-line measures targeting authoritarian regimes.[43] Similarly, authoritarian incumbents know, too, that in the wake of NATO's military intervention in Libya, additional interventions in far more complex contexts like Syria are not likely enough to seriously affect the regime's calculus concerning its use of coercion.

Third, regimes have converged around the sectarianization of uprisings as well as the use of narratives that frame protests in terms that privilege social order and demonize opposition movements as carriers of *fitna*, a classical Islamic term for strife or disorder, to influence the strategic calculus of citizens as they try to determine the probabilities whether a protest movement will succeed. For example, at an early stage of the uprising in Bahrain, the GCC's League of Muslim Scholars lambasted protesters for instigating "sectarian *fitna*" aimed at the expulsion of Sunni Muslims from the government and the country at large.[44] In Saudi Arabia, too, the state strategy depicted more limited protests as a Shia conspiracy aimed at *fitna*, "pushing the Sunnis to renew their allegiance to the regime."[45] Likewise, Syrian President Bashar al-Assad repeatedly used the term *fitna* in his defiant speech at the Syrian parliament on March 30, 2011.[46] Subsequently, the Syrian regime exaggerated and encouraged sectarianism, helping it reestablish a constituency of sorts by capitalizing on the minorities' existential fears.

Fourth, regimes have been highly strategic in their use of violence, recognizing that they can deploy certain levels of coercion without incurring significant diplomatic costs and that as long as the violence remains below some indeterminate threshold, external constraints on the use of force are likely to remain low. The Syrian case painfully illustrates that this threshold rises when outsiders' stamina for intervention declines. Accordingly, the Syrian regime has resorted to a remarkable gradual dosing of lethal violence, increasing its repression significantly following the botched initiatives of the Arab League in January 2012 and by UN envoy Kofi Annan in August, as if it were capitalizing on outsiders' increased tolerance or indifference.[47]

Fifth, as noted earlier, the possibility of developing acceptable exit strategies for regime elites receded during April and May 2011 as efforts commenced to prosecute regime leaders in Egypt, Tunisia, and Libya and as the international community imposed sanctions on President Bashar al-Assad of Syria, thereby removing any incentive he may have had to seek a negotiated transfer of power.

Collectively, these elements have shaped processes of authoritarian learning and adaptation among the remaining authoritarian elites in the Arab world and have had powerful effects on their calculus of the probabilities of the regimes' survival. As a result, authoritarian incumbents in Syria, Bahrain, Saudi Arabia, and elsewhere in the region became increasingly persuaded that their best bet lay in strategies of repression and, in essence, of hunkering down and doing whatever might be needed to ride out these uprisings, which themselves seemed to confront diminishing probabilities of success. The sharing of "best practices," whether from observation of or direct contact among regimes or security services, constitutes one part of this adaptive survival strategy.

Similarities of regimes' responses, of course, may not be primarily due to "learning effects" but to structural similarities and/or factors inherent in authoritarian rule. When Bahrain and Syria appear to repress demonstrations and activists by targeting medics and hospitals, how can we know whether the Syrian regime "learned" this from Bahrain or whether it is a homegrown tactic inherent in authoritarian rule? While it is difficult to produce decisive evidence to resolve this question, several suggestive trends can be found in common motifs.

Evidence of learning and adaptiveness contrast with common notions that authoritarian incumbents—in the region and beyond—are characterized by inarticulateness, stubbornness, clumsiness, and myopia. In fact, Arab regimes have proved to be more nimble and effective in their responses than is comfortable. It is clearly too soon to claim victory for "civil society" and democratic change over the qualities that were attributed to authoritarian regimes before the uprisings.[48] Just as the Arab uprisings revealed serious limitations on Arab regimes' ability to prevent mass protests, many of the incumbents' responses to these challenges equally reveal their ingrained aptitude to adapt, learn from their own mistakes and those of others, and juggle their resources with the aim of reinventing themselves and prevailing at all costs.

NOTES

1. Lucan Way, "The Lessons of 1989," *Journal of Democracy* 22 (2011): 17.
2. Eva Bellin, "Reconsidering the Robustness of Authoritarianism in the Middle East: Lessons from the Arab Spring," *Comparative Politics* 44, no. 2 (2012): 127–49.
3. Steven Heydemann and Reinoud Leenders, eds., *Middle East Authoritarianisms: Governance and Regime Resilience in Syria and Iran* (Stanford, Calif.: Stanford University Press, 2013).
4. Marc Lynch, *The Arab Uprising: The Unfinished Revolutions of the Middle East* (New York: Public Affairs, 2012).
5. See Frédéric Volpi, " Explaining (and Re-explaining) Political Change in the Middle East During the Arab Spring: Trajectories of Democratization and of Authoritarianism in the Maghreb," *Democratization* 20 (2012): 1–22.
6. Interview in *Wall Street Journal*, January 31, 2011.
7. For example, Samuel P. Huntington, *The Third Wave: Democratization in the Late Twentieth Century* (Norman: University of Oklahoma Press, 1991). Processes of diffusion in the spread of electoral revolutions in postcommunist states are discussed in Valerie Bunce and Sharon Wolchick, "International Diffusion and Postcommunist Electoral Revolutions," *Communist and Postcommunist Studies* 39, no. 3 (2006): 283–304. See also Valerie Bunce and Sharon Wolchik, "Favorable Conditions and Electoral Revolutions," *Journal of Democracy* 17, no. 4 (2006): 5–18.
8. Kristian Skrede Gleditsch, *All International Politics Is Local: The Diffusion of Conflict, Integration, and Democratization* (Michigan: University of Michigan Press, 2002), 52.

9. Adam Przeworski, *Democracy and the Market: Political and Economic Reforms in Eastern Europe and Latin America* (Cambridge: Cambridge University Press, 1991), 3–4.

10. For example, U.S. State Department spokesperson Philip Crowley stated on January 21, 2011: "I'm not sure that I would say . . . that necessarily there will be a snowball effect," Middle East Online, available at http://middle-east-online.com/English/?id=43812.

11. Al-Jazeera, January 23, 2012.

12. Hassan Abbas, "The Dynamics of the Uprising in Syria," Arab Reform Initiative, *Arab Reform Brief* 51, October 2011.

13. Aleppo is also likely to have informed regime fears in this respect. See Amr al-Azm, "Syrian Uprising: Looking In, Looking Out" (Washington, D.C.: U.S. Institute of Peace, October 2011), Peacebrief no. 110, available at http://www.usip.org/publications/syrian-uprising-looking-in-looking-out. As al-Azm notes, the "gravest concern for the regime is the emergence of a 'Benghazi' scenario in a city like Aleppo as a result of Turkish military intervention."

14. Joseph Holliday, *The Asad Regime: From Counterinsurgency to Civil War* (Washington, D.C.: Institute for the Study of War, 2013), 36.

15. "A revolutionary situation begins when a government previously under the control of a single, sovereign polity becomes the object of effective, competing, mutually exclusive claims." Charles Tilly, "From Mobilization to Revolution," CRSO working paper, University of Michigan, 7–5.

16. *Al-Thawra*, August 30, 2012.

17. Human Rights Watch, *Death from the Skies: Deliberate and Indiscriminate Air Strikes on Civilians*, April 11, 2013.

18. Interview in *The Telegraph*, November 8, 2012.

19. "Syria acting to safeguard chemical weapons, says Russia," BBC, December 22, 2012, available at http://www.bbc.co.uk/news/world-middle-east-20825820.

20. Available at ttp://www.presidentAsad.net/SPEECHES/Al_Asad_Speeches_2011/Bashar_Al_Asad_2011_Damascus_University_Speech.htm.

21. Jamie M. Fly, "Libya Is a Problem from Hell," *Foreign Policy*, March 16, 2011, available at http://www.foreignpolicy.com/articles/2011/03/16/libya_is_a_problem_from_hell.

22. The uprising in Syria broke out in the midst of an extensive public relations campaign by the Syrian regime to build support in the West, including the now notorious article in *Vogue* showcasing Asma al-Assad as the "Rose of the Desert." The article can still be found at http://www.ynaija.com/a-rose-in-the-desert-the-vogue-piece-on-syrian-first-lady-that-got-everyone-riled-up/.

23. Anne Barnard, "Syria Plays on Fears to Blunt American Support of Rebels," *New York Times*, April 24, 2013.

24. See Mohammad Al Attar, "The Revolution as a Model and the Image of Tahrir Square . . . Syrians Are Paying a Double Price," *Perspectives—Political Analysis and Commentary from the Middle East*, February 2012, 58–65.

25. Jean-Noël Ferrié and Baudouin Dupret, "La nouvelle architecture constitutionnelle et les trois désamorçages de la vie politique marocaine," *Confluences méditerranée* 3, no. 78 (2011): 25–34.

26. "Throwing Money at the Street," *The Economist*, March 12, 2011.

27. *The Syria Report*, March 28, April 3 and 4, 2011.

28. Alex Delmar-Morgan and Tom Wright, "Bahrain's Foreign Police Add to Tensions," *Wall Street Journal*, March 25, 2011.

29. "Bahrain National Guard to Recruit Former Soldiers from Pak," *Deccan Herald*, March 11, 2011, available at http://www.deccanherald.com/content/144961/bahrain-national-guard-recruit-former.html.

30. Mark Mazzetti and Emily B. Hagen, "Secret Desert Force Set Up by Blackwater's Founder," *New York Times*, May 14, 2011.

31. Ariel Ahram, *Proxy Warriors: The Rise and Fall of State-Sponsored Militias* (Stanford, Calif.: Stanford University Press, 2011).

32. *Tishreen*, March 9, 2012, available at http://tishreen.news.sy/tishreen/public/read/252847.

33. Syrian Arab News Agency (SANA), March 11, 2011. SANA runs a series entitled "The Reality of Events," repeatedly inferring to Iraqi-style chaos and sectarianism, available at http://www.sana.sy/eng/337/index.htm.

34. See *Jordanian Times*, April 11, 2013.

35. See PETRA, April 10, 2013.

36. Cited in the *Financial Times*, September 16, 2012.

37. U.S. Government, "Treasury Sanctions al-Nusrah Front Leaders, Militia Groups in Syria, December 11, 2012, available at http://iipdigital.usembassy.gov/st/english/article/2012/12/20121211139861.html#axzz2GxiqHxql.

38. UN Panel of Experts Established Pursuant to Resolution 1929 (2010), June 12, 2012.

39. The possibility of copycat effects without Iran's or others' involvement cannot, of course, be ruled out. "At War" blog, *New York Times*, October 18, 2012, available at http://atwar.blogs.nytimes.com/2012/10/18/syrian-forces-improvised-arms-desperate-measures-or-deliberate-aid/.

40. Cited in *Haaretz*, February 12, 2012. It is uncertain that the documents are authentic.

41. Güneş Murat Tezcür, "Democratic Struggles and Authoritarian Responses in Iran in Comparative Perspective," in *Middle East Authoritarianisms: Governance and Regime Resilience in Syria and Iran*, ed. Steven Heydemann and Reinoud Leenders (Stanford, Calif.: Stanford University Press, 2013), 219.

42. See, for example, National Initiative for Change, "Syrian Opposition Demand the Army to Protect Civilians and Facilitate a Transitional Period," April 29, 2011, available at http://www.facebook.com/SyrianDayOfRage.

43. Nawaf Obaid, "Amid the Arab Spring, a U.S.-Saudi Split," *Washington Post*, May 16, 2011.

44. Muslim Scholars League, "Bayan bi-Sha'an Ahdath al-Bahrayn," April 18, 2011, available at https://lh5.googleusercontent.com/-QUSbH99EgLk/TYsrLwoi1MI/AAAAAAAAAC4/KbKkP49GqA0/s1600/20110324_MSA+Bahrain.png.

45. Madawi Al-Rasheed, "Sectarianism as Counter-Revolution: Saudi Responses to the Arab Spring," *Studies in Ethnicity and Nationalism* 11, no. 3 (2011): 521.
46. See SANA, March 30, 2011.
47. The number of reported deaths rose to a monthly average of 2,000 from February until July 2012, compared with 600 deaths monthly between August 2011 and January 2012. From August until December 2012, an average of 4,000 people were killed each month. See the website of the Syrian Center for Statistics and Research, http://www.csr-sy.org/index.php?l=1.
48. See Michael Hudson, "Awakening, Cataclysm, or Just a Series of Events? Reflections on the Current Wave of Protest in the Arab World," *Jadaliyya*, May 16, 2011, available at http://www.jadaliyya.com/pages/index/1601/awakening-cataclysm-or-just-a-series-of-events-ref; and F. Gregory Gause III, "The Middle East Academic Community and the 'Winter of Arab Discontent': Why Did We Miss It?" in *Seismic Shift: Understanding Change in the Middle East*, ed. Ellen Laipson (Washington, D.C.: Henry L. Stimson Center, 2011), 11–29.

5

Media, Old and New

MARC LYNCH

The Arab uprisings discussed in this volume took place in a political space uniquely unified by a transnational media environment. Social media such as Facebook and Twitter interacted with traditional broadcast media such as satellite television and, in some cases, the press to create an exceptionally integrated and influential shared media space. The common language (Arabic) and shared set of core political issues had, over decades, created a common sense of identity that gave a distinct meaning to the unfolding protests. The riveting spectacle of protests on al-Jazeera, widely discussed across both the online and off-line Arab public spheres, created a potent sense of shared momentum that drove events across intrinsically very different cases.[1] Across the entire region Arabs found their identities implicated and shaped by a rapid cascade of events. The spectacle of simultaneous Friday protests across dozens of geographically and nationally divided cities, all using similar slogans and protest styles and all televised on al-Jazeera, undermines any attempt to understand these on a case-by-case basis. This media environment imposed a common frame on these protests, making each a chapter in a single ongoing story.

These new media may have reshaped the structure of political opportunity across an increasingly unified political field, but they have had ambiguous effects on the long-term balance of power between state and society or between competing social forces.[2] The new social media and satellite television together offer a powerful tool to the protests' organizers, reducing transaction costs for organization and presenting rapid ways of disseminating messages, images, and frames. They offer transmission routes for reaching international audiences and affecting foreign perceptions of stability or of the normative desirability of particular regimes. At the same time, they do not necessarily translate into enduring movements or robust political parties capable of mounting a sustained challenge to entrenched regimes or becoming governing parties. The Internet-driven youth movements at the core of the Egyptian protest movement lost badly in the parliamentary elections to the better organized and more societally rooted Islamist movements. Furthermore, these same tools can strengthen the surveillance and repression capabilities of authoritarian states.

The Internet's greatest challenge to the state will likely be generational rather than immediate and is likely to work by widening and changing the operation of Arab public spheres rather than by directly changing the Arab state.[3] The rise of networked communication and the transformed competencies of growing numbers of individuals across the region—particularly the young, educated urban elites who have traditionally played an outsized role in driving Arab politics—may be profoundly altering societal norms, religion, the state, and international politics.[4] But such generational changes may be sufficiently slow that Arab states can comfortably absorb them without relinquishing the core of their power. Despite the impressive surge of popular energy, the proposition that these newly empowered and informed citizens will never succumb to dictatorship remains, to this point, untested.

In earlier periods, the regional media were closely unified, most notably during the so-called Arab cold war of the 1950s dominated by the pan-Arab radio broadcasts by Egypt's Gamal Abdel Nasser. The latest transformation of the information environment in the Arab world began more than a decade ago, in the late 1990s, when al-Jazeera and satellite television began to open up new space for political communication, breaking the states' ability to control the flow of information and producing a new kind of Arab public sphere.[5] Satellite television helped unify Arab political space, focusing political discourse on shared Arab concerns such as Palestine, Iraq, and reform. Al-Jazeera, in particular, became a source of the common knowledge of Arab political life, setting the agenda and galvanizing anger over offenses to Arab issues and ideals. It also fueled political protest movements, which used the Qatari television station to spread their message, to break through domestic censorship, and to protect themselves from the worst of regime repression. Just as it did in 2011, the spectacle of simultaneous protests across multiple Arab countries covered on live television within a common narrative frame played out during the 2000–2002 Israeli-Palestinian war and the 2003 American-led invasion of Iraq.

At least in the short term, however, the effects of satellite TV on the immediate core political outcomes proved to be limited. No governments were changed; no major foreign or domestic policies were revised; and no lasting new political coalitions took root. After the initial shock, states started to catch up and respond, setting up their own TV stations and newspapers to compete, harassing journalists, putting diplomatic pressure on Qatar, and, more broadly, blunting the domestic political forces that might have harnessed the new media to mobilize political pressure. Mitigating the challenge of satellite television in the 2000s supported the "authoritarian persistence" hypothesis, as states adapted, rather than surrendered to, these changes.

The rapid growth of the Internet and the penetration of smart phones during the 2000s layered a new dimension onto this rapidly evolving new public sphere. What once could be dismissed as only a narrow slice of a largely English-speaking, cosmopolitan, and youthful elite is now distributed widely across wide swaths of Middle Eastern society. Particularly among educated urban youth and across the wealthy states of the Gulf, Internet access and usage already is, for all practical purposes, universal. By 2011 Facebook had more than 21 million Arab users, more than the estimated total number of newspaper readers in the region, and both Egypt and Tunisia had particularly high levels of membership.[6] The availability of cheap, web-enabled smart phones allowed the uploading of even more sophisticated user-generated videos and content. The new generation of young people communicates differently, interacts differently, and has different expectations of the public sphere than previous generations did. It is difficult to imagine that such a rapid and massive transformation in political communications could not matter in substantive ways.

A strong correlational and environmental case can be made that this new information environment has empowered political and social activism.[7] The decade of the 2000s, when the information environment changed so radically, witnessed massive popular mobilization across the region, with waves of protests over Israel's reoccupation of the West Bank in 2002 and the U.S. invasion of Iraq in 2003, followed by protesters demanding domestic reform across much of the region. In the early 2000s, a generation of Arab bloggers learned to use the Internet as a vehicle for personal expression, political organization, dialogue with the West, and communication with colleagues throughout the Arab world.[8] And then, of course, came Iran's 2009 "Green revolution" and Arab uprisings in the winter of 2010/2011.

In the eyes of enthusiasts, the new social media empower individuals to coordinate, communicate, and circumvent state censorship and repression in order to shift the balance of social power away from authoritarian states or hierarchies of any kind.[9] Networked communication, they argue, fundamentally challenges existing social and political orders, privileging horizontal networks over hierarchical organizations such as the modern nation-state.[10] Clay Shirky contends that the Internet enables individuals to organize outside the state, rendering the traditional nation-state irrelevant and reducing the transaction costs to all sorts of societal-level organization.[11] What such optimists have in common is a sense of the irresistible (if unpredictable) force of broad societal-level changes in the way that information is produced, consumed, and shared. Philip Howard and Muazzam Husain believe that social media were the catalyst that allowed the protests to begin and spread in 2011.[12]

But skeptics respond that these effects will not be directly translated from shifting individual attitudes, competencies, and preferences into political change.[13] The effects will instead be mediated through the existing structures of power and control, which include a massive state capacity and experience in surveillance, repression, infiltration, and control.[14] The wave of protest activity in Egypt between 2003 and 2006 took advantage of the opening of the political opportunity structure around a series of elections and referenda. Facebook helped catch the Egyptian authorities off guard in 2006, for instance, but not in 2007 when the regime was ready and waiting for the second attempt, and the Iranian regime quickly marshaled a daunting array of responses.[15] The robustness of the Arab state can be seen in the "organic, complex . . . contradictory, often oppressive forms of adjustment that are everywhere occurring."[16]

The Arab upheavals do not yet offer complete validation to either side.[17] Facebook seems to have mattered quite a bit in Tunisia, but its existence did not drive the revolution before December 2010.[18] Facebook was crucial to establishing January 25 as the day for Egypt's protesters to emulate Tunisia's protesters, but because it already was an established national holiday, this date was already an obvious focal point. Similarly, the organizers used mosques as the hubs for most of the protests, again using an obvious, but off-line, focal point. Egypt's ability to almost completely shut down its Internet service at the outset of the crisis in 2011 did not noticeably dent the protest momentum, suggesting the limits of the Internet's causal importance. As one youth activist calmly put it, "When the government shut down the web, politics moved on to the street, and that's where it has stayed."[19] Social media seem to be a useful tool in the hands of protest organizers, an accelerant to the impact of specific protest actions, a vital platform for the spread of movement ideas and images, and part of a broad environmental change in the flow of information. But that does not make it the cause of any specific uprising or the essential determinant of their outcomes.

In the following sections, I consider the different ways in which the new media can be seen as challenging the power of Arab states, by (1) promoting contentious collective action, (2) causing diffusion and demonstration effects, (3) limiting or enhancing the mechanisms of state repression, (4) affecting the calculus of violence, (5) affecting international support for the regime, and (6) affecting the overall control of the public sphere. While these changes are distinct, they obviously relate to one another and, depending on the situation, can either reinforce one another or work at cross-purposes.

Contentious Collective Action

The new media can affect the incidence and impact of collective action through a wide range of mechanisms, including lower transaction costs, informational cascades, higher costs of repression, and scale and diffusion effects.[20] Political opportunity structures matter more than technology alone; to quote a widely cited aphorism, "Twitter doesn't cause revolutions, but revolutions are tweeted."[21]

Many studies of social media and collective action have focused on transaction costs. The new media may facilitate protest by lowering the barriers to communication and organization while increasing the visibility of even small-scale protests.[22] Secure and cheap tools of communication lower transaction costs for the organization of collective action, with social media, in particular, allowing like-minded members to find one another across space, gender, and social class and to make their true beliefs known in a semipublic setting. This helps overcome the atomization and social isolation produced by authoritarian regimes, which enforce political conformity and silence. It also allows the small subset of users focused on politics or human rights to organize within this small, semipublic space before taking their campaigns to the wider public. Members of the Egyptian Kefaya movement protesting President Hosni Mubarak's authoritarian rule, for example, initially used the Internet and short message service (SMS, that is, texting) through discussion lists and only later moved to organize their protests creatively and attract international attention. In Bahrain, Internet forums helped galvanize human rights protesters incensed over the manipulation of elections and the clampdown on activists. Tunisian and Egyptian movement leaders privately consulted with one another about how to organize protests in the months before they erupted. Yet examples like these, while suggestive of how the new media can lower the costs of making contact, do not resolve the debate about whether the weak ties generated by Internet relationships are more or less likely to promote contentious political action.[23]

Such public networking could affect the logic of informational cascades. The literature on unexpected revolutions developed by Susanne Lohmann, Timur Kuran, and others suggests that one of the major obstacles to mass protest is ubiquitous preference falsification; that is, individuals who detest the regime refrain from making their views public out of fear of either social or official sanction. According to this view, the increased public incidence of expressing oppositional views online encourage others who privately hold such views also to express them in public.[24]

The Tunisian and Egypt tidal waves certainly hint at "cascade" dynamics, by which the courageous early movers sent a signal to a generally sympathetic public of the value of joining in. Throughout the Egyptian and Tunisian uprisings, participants spoke of "breaking the wall of fear," and most spoke of hearing about the protests or seeing them on al-Jazeera. Generally speaking, the young leaders of the protest movement who gathered in Tahrir Square were not representative of the broader population's political or social views, as they tended to be far more liberal, Western oriented, and secular. In the past, this had limited their ability to spark a broad-based protest, but in 2011 they succeeded in galvanizing the public expression of the shared sentiment of anger at Mubarak and a generic demand for change, particularly when joined on the first day by a wide cross-section of older participants who could be seen by others as "like them."[25] In turn, the regime consistently sought to label the protesters as liberal youth, Islamist extremists, or foreign troublemakers, but with little success in the early days because of the widespread visible evidence to the contrary.

Yet while preference falsification may have been operative in Tunisia, which was one of the most heavily censored states on earth, this does not seem to fit the Egyptian case. As Nathan Brown points out in chapter 15, by the mid-2000s, few Egyptians were not aware of the depth of distaste for Mubarak or feared to express it. The success of the Kefaya movement in the early 2000s was precisely to bring the massive discontent with Mubarak into the public sphere and to alert others to the existence of widespread dissatisfaction. The campaign against the succession of Hosni Mubarak's son Gamal dominated Egyptian politics for half a decade, to the point that few could not have known of its widespread existence. The protest upsurge in Egypt appears to have been due more to altered calculations about the possibility of success after the flight of President Zine al-Abdine Ben Ali from Tunisia; the imitation of specific repertoires of contention; and the successful recruitment of nonactivists into the early protests, which signaled the widespread societal consensus. Therefore, while there may have been information cascades, they seem to have had only secondary importance.

The tension between protest mobilization and political organization has become especially important since the uprisings.[26] The leaderless network structures which can hold together a disparate coalition of millions of protesters around a single, simple demand—"Mubarak must go"—are typically far less effective at articulating specific, nuanced demands in the negotiation process that follows. The Internet may prove to be poor at building warm social networks and trust at the heart of civil society. It even could be depoliticizing, as people remain at home with their computers rather than getting out into the streets or doing the hard work of political organization.[27] Or it could degenerate into constant mobilization against the status quo, outside political institutions and unable to project pragmatic agendas. So far, few workable models for movements fueled by the new media have made the transition to normal politics. This does not mean that it is impossible, only that the literature to date offers us little confidence either way.

Diffusion and Demonstration

Pan-Arab satellite television and social media did create a highly integrated media space that facilitated demonstration effects, if not diffusion (see chapter 3). Al-Jazeera, in particular, explicitly linked together protests across the region into a single narrative, highlighting simultaneous protests on split screens and employing identical language to describe the protagonists in different cases. Moreover, the protesters were watching one another in real time, adopting one another's slogans and chants, and emulating their successful tactics.

In social media, especially, it is possible to see direct evidence of identification and inspiration across cases. Twitter and Facebook users frequently and consistently declared solidarity through the use of hashtags or through their own linking and retweeting patterns. Protesters frequently responded to developments in one country, such as the fall of Mubarak or Qaddafi, with enthusiastic calls for their own struggle to be the next to break through. They appealed for support from abroad and complained bitterly if they felt their own struggle was being slighted or ignored.

Charles Tilly and Sidney Tarrow argue that the media play a vital role in scaling up local protests into broader movements and in localizing broader episodes.[28] The new information technologies have been successful at moving discourse and protest forms across the entire Arab political space, whether protests against the Iraq war in 2003 or mass protests for change in 2011. The even more unified Arab political space also creates distinctive dynamics of diffusion and contagion. Thus the Egyptian revolutionary wave followed the heavy coverage of the Tunisian revolution, which clearly shifted the protesters' beliefs in the possibility of victory, so that the January 25 Facebook protest succeeded where numerous earlier attempts at organizing such a protest had failed. More broadly, in almost every Arab country the protesters adopted similar language and protest methods and competed for the same al-Jazeera cameras. The available evidence suggests, however, that significant majorities of social media content regarding the early uprisings were consumed outside the countries undergoing protests.[29]

The Mechanisms of Repression

At the same time that the new media may empower contentious collective action or inhibit the exercise of brute repression, they also create new resources available to authoritarian states. Along with the activists, authoritarian regimes have learned to use the new powers of the Internet as well (see chapter 4).[30] The states' responses have been technical ones designed to limit or shape access to the Internet, monitoring and surveillance, selective repression, and overt intervention in online communications flows.[31] Cairo responded to the scheduled protest of January 25, 2011, with a globally unprecedented complete shutdown of the Internet and mobile phone network.[32] In many Arab countries, the Internet has become a focus of the *mukhabarat* (military intelligence service, with special units devoted to monitoring, infiltrating, and disrupting online communities).[33] Arab intelligence agencies also use the Internet to identify their adversaries and trace their networks.[34]

What is more, authoritarian states cooperate with one another, trading "best practices" on surveillance and repression, and they have been able to negotiate deals with leading Western companies for further assistance.[35]

From Saudi Arabia's demand that Blackberry allow its messenger service to be screened by state security officials to the use of Facebook and Twitter pages to identify regime opponents to Bahrain's flooding of social media sites with proregime dummy accounts, the authoritarian state can thus benefit as well as suffer from the pervasive effects of the new media. During the years following the failed Facebook protests of the late 2000s, the punch line of a widely circulated grim joke has the then Egyptian President Hosni Mubarak congratulating his intelligence chief, Omar Suleiman, on Facebook, his greatest invention. Facebook, on which individuals proudly list their political affiliations along with their friends and contacts, presented many vulnerabilities, especially since many people did not carefully screen their new friend requests during the heady days of rapid expansion. During the crisis, Vodafone, the mobile phone network in Egypt, collaborated closely with the Egyptian government, providing details on subscribers and sending out proregime text messages.[36] Googling passengers arriving at the airport has become a standard practice, with border police demanding to see supposedly private Facebook pages and other personal information that may reveal political activity.

The Calculus of Violence

In the first two cases of revolt, Tunisia and Egypt, the military opted against unleashing the full power of the army against the protesters. But by February 2011, a series of leaders made a different choice, opting for varying degrees of violent repression to maintain their hold on power. The violence deployed by regime security forces in Libya quickly turned that conflict into a bloody civil war that attracted international intervention. In Bahrain, Gulf Cooperation Council (GCC) troops helped local security forces crush the protest movement and oversee a comprehensive crackdown on all forms of political opposition. In Yemen, the military split, and extreme violence was used at key moments, but escalation to all-out warfare was ultimately avoided. In Syria, violence escalated in a familiar cycle of repression and response, which soon reached crisis proportions.

Media played a distinctive role in these patterns of violence and nonviolence. Activists used social media to capture and disseminate videos and images of the violence, which increased both local and international attention to the atrocities. Facebook pages filled with harrowing images of bloody bodies became a common feature over the spring of 2011. Camera phone videos uploaded to YouTube of violent clashes became a ubiquitous feature of mass media coverage when stations with few reporters on the ground turned to this rich new source of footage. The new media may also increase the prospects of collective action by raising the costs of repression to authoritarian regimes, especially early on, by documenting atrocities and attracting international attention. Social media in the Middle East have developed a robust infrastructure for publicizing videos of police abuse and protest footage. Indeed, al-Jazeera cameras and activists uploading films of police brutality to YouTube did matter, as some regimes shied away from having their worst abuses captured on film.

This publicity does not prevent abuses, obviously, but it is not implausible to suggest that it has raised the costs to would-be repressors, who have had to factor in the possibility of galvanizing international censure or local anger. The televised unleashing of government-backed thugs on Tahrir Square on February 1, 2011, may have ultimately cost the Egyptian regime more in international outrage than it gained in intimidation. The international military intervention against the regime's atrocities against the protesters in Libya reinforced this mechanism, although the less forceful responses to violence in Yemen, Bahrain, and Syria undermined it. One hypothesis to explore is that regimes dependent on and unsure of U.S. support are more sensitive to these costs, as both Egypt and Tunisia largely exercised a restraint not seen in Bahrain or Libya.

The documentation of violence by social media activists served multiple functions. On one level, it simply bore witness to the bloodshed. It forced knowledge of the atrocities into the public sphere, making it impossible to deny their reality. This in turn could drive cascades of defections from the regime by previously apolitical or supportive citizens who withdrew their consent in light of the violence. The genuinely shocking nature of many of the images—dead children, civilians casually gunned down, protesters run over by armored vehicles—put the regimes on the defensive. When brought to regional and international attention, this imposed new costs on regimes for using violence. For some, it likely contributed to their decision to exercise restraint. For others, the failure to show restraint led to major regional and international pressure on them to reform, the loss of legitimacy, and calls for war crimes tribunals.

The manifest impact of the dissemination of these videos and images, however, also led to strategic uses of the media. Protesters hoping to attract domestic or international support had incentives to produce and spread images of regime violence, which could lead to efforts to provoke such violence or to falsify or mislabel the footage. Regimes had incentives either to control the flow of such images (as in the refusal to cover the crackdown in Bahrain on major, Gulf-based satellite television stations) or to fight back with counterpropaganda (as in the Syrian government's efforts to portray their challengers as terrorists, radical Islamists, and armed gangs).

International Attention and Alliances

Arab authoritarian regimes are deeply embedded in a unipolar but rapidly shifting international system, and they depend on international, primarily American, support for their survival. Should the new media somehow undermine that support, it could prove devastating to the regimes' survival.[37] More broadly, al-Jazeera and online social media have played a fascinating, and largely unresearched, role, in shaping how uprisings in different Arab states are covered and understood abroad. Whereas Libya was covered heavily and attracted international response, Bahrain was largely ignored by al-Jazeera but kept in the sights of social media.

This could matter by shaping international responses. During the mid-2000s, activists were able to draw on the public commitments of the George W. Bush administration to promote democracy to compel the United States to pressure Arab regimes to open up political space. During the Iranian protests of 2009, although the United States had no such leverage, Twitter and other social media did help shape American views of events. The swing of international support from the Egyptian regime to the protest movement may be the most dramatic example to date of the new media's actually changing important alliances or regional divisions. Still, the United States understandably seems more interested in uprisings in Libya and Iran than in allies such as Bahrain or Jordan, and its sympathy with Egyptian protesters may prove to have been an aberration.

The shifting American position toward the Mubarak regime was clearly influenced by the powerful images broadcast on al-Jazeera and circulated through social media networks. Crucially, the transmission via social media was generally not from mass public to mass public. Instead, those on the ground—including Western journalists as well as English-speaking local activists—communicated information and opinion from inside the country to an informed and highly focused expert audience abroad. Those specialists then filtered the information and presented it to local media and policy circles, shaping perceptions of what was happening on the ground. The videos and information produced by social media users during these protests controlled television coverage at a time when mainstream journalists faced severe restrictions and al-Jazeera's own bureaus were intermittently shut-tered. Those images helped raise the salience of the issue in American and international politics, while the increased attention generally was channeled through a frame favorable to the protesters rather than to the regimes.[38] To the extent that the information flowing through social media or al-Jazeera did not accurately reflect the realities on the ground, whether by exaggerating the size and scale of protests or violence or by misrepresenting the nature of the protest movements, then this represents an independent causal impact.

The Public Sphere

A final area in which state control might be fundamentally challenged is its ability to control and dominate the public sphere. Here, longer-term shifts in individual competencies and in the broad information environment rather than immediate "tools" of political combat matter the most.[39] Whatever immediate changes result from the 2011 uprisings, the impact of the Internet over the longer term will be to empower and transform the nature of the public sphere in authoritarian Arab societies. This will create the conditions by which demands for accountability and transparency and citizenship can be effectively pressed.[40] A focus on the systemic impact of longer-term transformations of the public sphere shows that the new infor-mation environment is driving massive changes in societal organization, even if it remains frustratingly vague and resistant to empirical testing.

The key to most arguments about the Internet's transformative effects is that new individual competencies and networked forms of communication will aggregate over time into a systemic change. For instance, Manuel Castells argues that the rise of networked communication challenges and transforms the possibilities of power exercised by the territorial nation-state by undermin-ing its ability to legitimate its rule.[41] The confident, wired youth of Tahrir Square embody this vision of new competencies aggregating into political change. By becoming producers of information and circumventing the editorial control of state censors and mass media outlets, these individuals will become new kinds of citizens, better able to stand up to the instruments of state control.[42] Their horizons extend beyond the nation-state, and they demonstrate great impa-tience with the traditional "red lines" of Arab politics. Deborah Wheeler con-tends that the Internet's transformative power lies in these youth, "their sheer weight as a social force, their innovative communication strategies and Inter-net savvy, as well as the fact that youth sub-cultures contain the seeds of future social norms."[43]

One more specific competency is individuals' new ability to evade state surveillance and control, to access information, to communicate and organize, to learn, and to express and engage. One competency is simply Internet fluency, including the ability to access anonymizing software and evade censorship. As many Arab youth learn to evade state firewalls, bans on Bluetooth, and other restrictions, it is not difficult to see those skills transferring to a more fundamental ability to evade state controls over communication and information.

The rise of such new citizens and a transformed public sphere could have ambiguous and contradictory effects, however. Slow, long-term changes offer ample opportunities for authoritarian regimes to adapt and absorb the challenge. The uneven distribution of such new competencies may create an intense digital divide, widening the gap between cosmopolitan, wired urban elites and the mass populations lacking such skills. The tension between restless, expressive protest politics and the mundane business of political organization and governance could pose a serious challenge to the stability of regimes even if they do become more democratic, transparent, and accountable. A new public sphere will fundamentally change the conditions of political possibility, but in what direction remains uncertain.

NOTES

1. Marc Lynch, *Voices of the New Arab Public: Al-Jazeera, Iraq and Arab Politics Today* (New York: Columbia University Press, 2006); Marc Lynch, "Blogging the New Arab Public," *Arab Media and Society* 1, no. 1 (2007); Dina Matar, "Contextualizing the Media and the Uprisings: A Return to History," *Middle East Journal of Culture and Communication* 5 (2012): 75–79.

2. On political opportunity structure, see Doug McAdam, Sidney Tarrow, and Charles Tilly, *Dynamics of Contention* (New York: Cambridge University Press, 2001).

3. On the Arab public sphere, see Lynch, *Voices of the New Arab Public*; Dale Eickelman and Jon W. Anderson, *New Media in the Middle East: The Emerging Public Sphere*, 2nd ed. (Bloomington: Indiana University Press, 2003); Armando Salvatore, *The Public Sphere: Liberal Modernity, Catholicism, Islam* (New York: Palgrave Macmillan, 2010); Armando Salvatore, "New Media, the 'Arab Spring,' and the Metamorphosis of the Public Sphere: Beyond Western Assumptions on Collective Agency and Democratic Politics," *Constellations* 20 (2013): 1–12.

4. Deborah Wheeler, *The Internet in the Middle East* (Albany: State University of New York Press, 2006); Navtej Dhillon and Tarik Yousef, eds., *Generation in Waiting: The Unfulfilled Promise of Young People in the Middle East* (Washington, D.C.: Brookings Institution Press, 2009); Eickelman and Anderson, *New Media in the*

Middle East; Gary Bunt, *iMuslims: Rewiring the House of Islam* (Chapel Hill: University of North Carolina Press, 2009).

5. Kai Hafez, ed., *Arab Media: Power and Weakness* (New York: Continuum, 2008); Naomi Sakr, *Arab Television Today* (New York: I. B. Tauris, 2007).

6. *Arab Social Media Report* (Dubai School of Government, February 2011), available at http://www.dsg.ae/NEWSANDEVENTS/UpcomingEvents/ASMRHome.aspx.

7. Marc Lynch, "After Egypt: The Limits and Promise of Online Challenges to the Authoritarian Arab State," *Perspectives on Politics* 9, no. 2 (2011): 301–10; Craig McGarty, Emma F. Thomas, Girish Lala, Laura G. E. Smith, and Ana-Maria Bliuc, "New Technologies, New Identities and the Growth of Mass Opposition in the 'Arab Spring,'" *Political Psychology*, August 19, 2013; Mohamed Nanabhay and Roxane Farmanfarmaian, "From Spectacle to Spectacular: How Physical Space, Social Media and Mainstream Broadcast Amplified the Public Sphere in Egypt's 'Revolution,'" *Journal of North African Studies* 16, no. 4 (2011): 573–605; Nadav Samin, "Saudi Arabia, Egypt, and the Social Media Moment," *Arab Media & Society* 15 (2012), available online only at http://www.arabmediasociety.com/?article=785.

8. Lynch, "Blogging the New Arab Public"; Wheeler, *The Internet in the Middle East*.

9. Mona Eltahawy, "Facebook, YouTube and Twitter Are the New Tools of Protest in the Arab World," *Washington Post*, August 7, 2010.

10. Manuel Castells, *Communication Power* (Stanford, Calif.: Stanford University Press, 2008); Yochai Benkler, *The Wealth of Networks: How Social Production Transforms Markets and Freedom* (New Haven, Conn.: Yale University Press, 2007); and Clay Shirky, "The Political Power of Social Media: Technology, the Public Sphere, and Political Change," *Foreign Affairs* 90, no. 1 (January/February 2011): 28–41.

11. Clay Shirky, *Here Comes Everybody! The Power of Organizing Without Organizations* (New York: Penguin, 2008); Shirky, "The Political Power of Social Media."

12. Philip Howard and Muazzam Hussain, *Democracy's Fourth Wave* (Stanford, Calif.: Stanford University Press, 2013).

13. Evgeny Morozov, *The Net Delusion: The Dark Side of Internet Freedom* (New York: PublicAffairs, 2011); Larry Diamond, "Liberation Technology," *Journal of Democracy* 21, no. 3 (July 2010): 69–83.

14. Golnaz Esfandiari, "The Twitter Devolution," *Foreign Policy*, June 7, 2010, available at http://www.foreignpolicy.com/articles/2010/06/07/the_twitter_revolution _that_wasnt; Sean Aday, Henry Farrell, Marc Lynch, and John Sides, *Blogs and Bullets: New Media in Contentious Politics* (Washington, D.C.: U.S. Institute of Peace Press, 2010).

15. Samantha Shapiro, "Revolution, Facebook-Style," *New York Times Magazine*, January 22, 2009, available at http://www.nytimes.com/2009/01/25/magazine/25bloggers-t.html?pagewanted=all; Rob Faris and Rebekah Heacock, "Cracking Down on Digital Communication, Political Organizing in Iran," *Open Net Initiative*, June 15, 2009, available at http://opennet.net/blog/2009/06/cracking-down-digital-communication-and-political-organizing-iran ; Aday et al., *Blogs and Bullets*; Merlyana Lim,

"Clicks, Cabs and Coffee Houses: Social Media And Oppositional Movements in Egypt, 2004–2011," *Journal of Communication* 62, no. 2 (2012): 231–48.

16. Emma C. Murphy, "Theorizing ICTs in the Arab World: Informational Capitalism and the Public Sphere," *International Studies Quarterly* 53, no. 4 (December 2009): 1131–53.

17. Gilad Lotan, Erhardt Graeff, Mike Ananny, Devin Gaffney, Ian Pearce, and Danah Boyd, "The Arab Spring The Revolutions Were Tweeted: Information Flows During the 2011 Tunisian and Egyptian Revolutions," *International Journal of Communication* 5 (2011), available at http://ijoc.org/ojs/index.php/ijoc/article/view/1246/643; Phil Howard and Muazzam Hussain, *Democracy's Fourth Wave* (Stanford, Calif.: Stanford University Press 2013); Charles Levinson and Margaret Croker, "The Secret Rally That Sparked an Uprising," *Wall Street Journal*, February 11, 2011; Gadi Wolfsfeld, Elad Segev, and Tamir Sheafer, "Social Media and the Arab Spring: Politics Comes First," *International Journal of Press/Politics* 18, no. 2 (2013): 115–37.

18. Ethan Zuckerman, "The First Twitter Revolution?" *Foreign Policy*, January 14, 2011, available at http://www.foreignpolicy.com/articles/2011/01/14/the_first_twitter_revolution.

19. Quoted in Jack Schenker, "Cairo's Biggest Protest Yet Demands Mubarak's Immediate Departure," *The Guardian*, February 5, 2011.

20. Zeynep Tufekcip and Christopher Wilson, "Social Media and the Decision to Participate in Political Protest: Observations from Tahrir Square," *Journal of Communication* 62, no. 2 (2012): 363–79; Nabil Dajani, "Technology Cannot a Revolution Make: Nas-book Not Facebook," *Arab Media & Society* 15 (2012), available online only at http://www.arabmediasociety.com/?article=782; Magdalena Wojcieszak and Briar Smith, "Will Politics Be Tweeted? New Media Use by Iranian Youth in 2011," *New Media and Society*, published online March 25, 2013, available at http://nms.sagepub.com/content/early/2013/03/23/1461444813479594; Sahar Khamis and Katherine Vaughn, "Cyberactivism in the Egyptian Revolution: How Civic Engagement and Citizen Journalism Tilted the Balance," *Arab Media & Society* 13 (2011), available online only at http://www.arabmediasociety.com/?article=769; Sahar Khamis and Katherine Vaughn, "We Are All Khaled Said: The Potentials and Limitations of Cyberactivism in Triggering Public Mobilization and Promoting Political Change," *Journal of Arab & Muslim Media Research* 4 (2012): 145–63; Philip N. Howard and Muzammil M. Hussain, "The Role of Digital Media," *Journal of Democracy* 22, no. 3 (2011): 35–48; Sahar Khamis, Paul B. Gold, and Katherine Vaughn, "Beyond Egypt's 'Facebook Revolution' and Syria's 'YouTube Uprising': Comparing Political Contexts, Actors and Communication Strategies," *Arab Media and Society* 15 (2012), available online only at http://www.arabmediasociety.com/?article=791.

21. On "political opportunity structures," see McAdam, Tarrow, and Tilly, *Dynamics of Contention*; Sidney Tarrow and Charles Tilly, *Contentious Politics* (New York: Paradigm Publishing, 1996).

22. McAdam, Tarrow, and Tilly, *Dynamics of Contention*; Sidney Tarrow, *The New Transnational Activism* (New York: Cambridge University Press, 2005).

23. Malcolm Gladwell, "Small Change: Why the Revolution Will Not Be Tweeted," *New Yorker* (October 4, 2010), available online at http://www.newyorker.com/reporting/2010/10/04/101004fa_fact_gladwell.

24. Timur Kuran, "Now Out of Never: The Element of Surprise in the East European Revolution of 1989," *World Politics* 44, no. 1 (October 1991): 7–48; Susanne Lohmann, "The Dynamics of Informational Cascades: The Monday Demonstrations in Leipzig, East Germany, 1989–91," *World Politics* 47, no. 1 (October 1994): 42–101.

25. Lohmann, in particular, emphasizes the importance of the protesters being seen as "like us" rather than as outsiders or marginal youth ("The Dynamics of Informational Cascades").

26. Maha Abdalrahman, "In Praise of Organization: Egypt Between Activism and Revolution," *Development and Change* 44, no.3 (2013), 569–85.

27. Vickie Langohr, "Too Much Civil Society, Too Little Politics: The Case of Egypt and Arab Liberalizers," *Comparative Politics* 36, no. 2 (January 2004): 181–204.

28. McAdam, Tarrow, and Tilly, *Dynamics of Contention*.

29. Sean Aday, Henry Farrell, Dean Freelon, and Marc Lynch, "Watching from Afar: Media Consumption Patterns Around the Arab Spring," *American Behavioral Scientist* 57, no. 4 (2013): 899–919.

30. Morozov, *The Net Delusion*.

31. Ronald Deibert, John Palfrey, Rafal Rohozinski, and Jonathan Zittrain, eds., *Access Denied: The Practice and Policy of Global Internet Filtering* (Cambridge, Mass.: MIT Press, 2008).

32. For a graphic on this shutdown, see Ian Schafer, "Egypt's Internet Traffic, Visualized," January 28, 2011, available at http://www.ianschafer.com/2011/01/28/egypts-internet-traffic-visualized/.

33. Morozov, *The Net Delusion*.

34. Ian Gallagher, "Egyptian Police Use Facebook and Twitter to Track Down Protesters' Names Before 'Rounding Them Up,'" *Daily Mail U.K.* (February 5, 2011), available at http://www.dailymail.co.uk/news/article-1354096/Egypt-protests-Police-use-Facebook-Twitter-track-protesters.html.

35. Abbas Milani, "Iran's Hidden Cyberjihad," *Foreign Policy*, July/August 2010, available online at http://www.foreignpolicy.com/articles/2010/06/07/irans_hidden_cyberjihad; and Noam Latar, Gregory Asmolov, and Alex Gekker, "State Cyber Advocacy," paper presented at the tenth annual Herzliya Conference, Herzliya, Israel, January/February 2010.

36. Andy Greenberg, "As Egyptians Reconnect, Their Government Will Be Watching," *Forbes Online* (February 4, 2011), available at http://blogs.forbes.com/andygreenberg/2011/02/04/as-egyptians-reconnect-their-government-will-be-watching/.

37. On the international sources of regime survival, see Eva Bellin, "Arab Authoritarianism in Comparative Perspective," *Comparative Politics* 36, no. 2 (2004): 139–57.

38. See Aday et al., *Blogs and Bullets*; Aday et al. "Watching from Afar."

39. Shirky, "The Political Power of Social Media."

40. Jon Anderson, "New Media, New Publics: Reconfiguring the Public Sphere of Islam," *Social Research* 70, no. 3 (summer 2003): 887–906; Eickelman and Anderson, *New Media in the Middle East*; Dale Eickelman, "New Media in the Arab Middle East and the Emergence of Open Societies," in *Remaking Muslim Politics*, ed. Robert Hefner (Princeton, N.J.: Princeton University Press, 2005), 37–59; Bunt, *iMuslims*.

41. Castells, *Communication Power*.

42. Rania Al-Malky, "Blogging for Reform: The Case of Egypt," *Arab Media and Society* 1 (spring 2007), available online only at http://www.arabmediasociety.com/?article=12.

43. Deborah Wheeler, "The Internet and Youth Subculture in Kuwait," *Journal of Computer-Mediated Communication* 8, no. 2 (January 2003), available at http://onlinelibrary.wiley.com/doi/10.1111/j.1083-6101.2003.tb00207.x/abstract.

6

Inter-Arab Relations and the Regional System

CURTIS R. RYAN

This chapter focuses on the international relations of the Arab regional system and especially the interaction of internal and external dynamics, that is, how internal changes have had external effects on the region itself and how external regional politics has, in turn, affected the outcomes of the Arab uprisings. The chapter first looks at three waves of change, each of which has transformed the regional system. Next it examines the dynamics of the regime security dilemmas that have dominated regional politics and have, until recently, hampered hopes for greater reform and change. Finally, the chapter turns to several key areas of change in the regional system, each of which has affected outcomes in the evolving "Arab spring." These changes include the shifts in the regional balance of power, changing meanings of Pan-Arab identity politics, and the resurgence of a new Arab cold war.

A great paradox of Middle East politics is that the region with the oldest civilizations and deepest cultural roots is also home to some of the world's youngest countries, in the sense of modern Westphalian nation-states. The modern regional system is not short of real causes of external conflict and wars, from the Arab-Israeli conflict to the various Persian Gulf wars. It is these external security concerns, coupled with the Cold War era of superpower support for regional militaries and arms races, that helped lead to the hypermilitarization of the entire region. Although Arab regimes have emerged in different forms, including both authoritarian republics and monarchies, most share the theme of being what I have referred to elsewhere as "security states."[1] They remain the products of a security environment in which "security" refers not so much to countries as to ruling regimes.[2] Regime security has remained the principal job of

Arab governments, and many regard internal security threats as even more pressing than those emanating from across national borders.

In international relations, the classic concept of the security dilemma refers to an external dynamic in which the state's attempts to ensure security through arms and military buildups unintentionally undermine the security of the state itself.[3] The Arab states system also has a domestic or internal security dilemma, in which the militarization of the state—and the creation of large militaries, paramilitaries, police forces, and multiple intelligence services (*mukhabarat*)—has actually undermined regime security across the Arab world. Massive spending on state security has shifted limited resources away from domestic economic development, perpetuating and even deepening economic and social stratification in Arab societies.[4] In the context of the 2011 revolutions, it is important to remember that many of the grievances were economic. As regimes became garrison or fortress states, they resisted even small reforms, instead perpetuating their own domestic regime security dilemma.[5]

In shifting resources toward their own security apparatus, Arab states were supporting their own militarized ruling coalitions. The gamble was that this same army, police, or intelligence service would continue to preserve the regime against its own society. But there also was always the chance that some part of the security apparatus would turn on the regime. In the case of Tunisia, the country's small but fairly professionalized army turned against the regime's paramilitary police, backing the Tunisian people against the regime of deposed leader Zine al-Abdine Ben Ali. Similarly, the top commanders of Egypt's vast army ousted their own president in order to save the regime from a more comprehensive revolution by sacrificing the ruling family. In doing so, the Egyptian military secured its own institutional interests in the Egyptian economy along with the political order. In Yemen, President Ali Abdullah Saleh survived for almost a year owing mainly to the control of his extended family over numerous military, police, and intelligence commands. In Libya, before the revolution, Muammar al-Qaddafi systematically weakened his own armed forces so as to neutralize them as a threat, relying instead on smaller elite units commanded by family members and augmented by foreign mercenaries. And in Syria, President Bashar al-Assad, like his father before him, relied on heavily Alawite intelligence services and forward combat units against largely Sunni rebel forces.

Many of the oil-producing Arab states have attempted to ensure regime security by extensively relying on oil wealth, providing a heavily subsidized existence to their citizens and often substituting economic well-being for political participation. The precise dynamics, of course, differ from country to country. But many Arab regimes benefited for decades from the politics of the global Cold War by obtaining arms and military aid from the super-powers. To be clear, local security dynamics may indeed be local, with profound costs to domestic reform, but they have long been fed and facilitated by broader regional and global security dynamics. In short, the arms and security-obsessed addictions of many Arab dictatorships were aided and abetted by alliances with global powers such as the United States.

The development of authoritarian regimes with their concomitant internal security dilemmas has resulted in both domestic and regional politics that have, until recently, dampened prospects for meaningful reform and change. Yet for the last several decades there has been no shortage of dissent or opposition and no shortage of calls for change across the Arab world. Recently, however, the severe economic hardship suffered by most Arab peoples, faced with indifferent, incompetent, and even predatory governments, sowed the seeds for the Arab revolutions.

It may have been the pervasive presence of the new Arab media revolution across the region that made this possible.[6] In fact, the new media acted as the main accelerant to the Arab revolutions, allowing revolutionary ideas and inspiration to spill over from one Arab country to the next (see chapter 5). The new media have created a broader Arab public sphere, not only within but also across all Arab states, creating a more genuine form of pan-Arab solidarity and sympathy than perhaps had ever existed in the more explicitly political and governmental version of the 1950s and 1960s. This is, in a sense, a new more cultural and social pan-Arab level of identity alongside that of national identities. Accordingly, Arabs in Egypt and throughout the region became aware of the fate of one disconsolate vegetable vendor in Tunisia, aware of the violent state repression against this young man, and aware of his final act of taking his own life. That event sparked the already deep level of anger and outrage across Tunisia as youths eschewed traditional state and opposition channels of action and instead took directly to the streets—and to the Internet, social media, and satellite television.

The new media revolution eliminated the state monopoly on information and helped break through the ceiling of fear of the Arab security states. New media and the pervasive awareness of a far broader Arab public sphere also encouraged activists to create virtual as well as real transnational connections between movements. These factors also allowed activists elsewhere, even in states without revolutions, to mobilize under a kind of cover. They could organize, not necessarily against their own regime but in support of revolutions in Tunisia, Egypt, or Syria. From Morocco to Jordan in the course of these demonstrations, activists also were able to shift their focus back to the home front, calling at minimum for reform and, in other cases, for the overthrow of their regime, too.

These mobilizations of Arab publics across the region were clearly influenced by media representations of the revolutions and government repression, reaching every corner of the Arab world and creating a demonstration effect from one revolution to the next (see chapter 3). It also is clear that people across the region—Arabs and Kurds, Armenians and Berbers, Muslims and Christians—felt emotionally connected to these revolutionary events in the region because they had had similar experiences of repression. Yet for the Arab peoples in particular, a large part of this pervasive revolutionary feeling (appearing as a virtual contagion to the Arab regimes themselves) was rooted in a solidarity born of a broader sense of not only national identity but also pan-Arab identity. This renewed Pan-Arabism proved to be very different from that of its forebears in the pan-Arabist "era" of the 1950s and 1960s.

Waves of Change in the Regional System

The first Arab revolt refers to the wave of Arab nationalism of the latter days of the Ottoman Turkish Empire. That wave of change included resurgent Arab nationalism and identity politics, which was based largely in northern Arab urban areas—Beirut, Damascus, Baghdad—but also included an actual armed revolt from southern and decidedly nonurban sources, with armed tribes allied with Britain rebelling against the Ottoman Turks. This, in turn, helped hasten the collapse of the empire, creating a regionwide Arab uprising and also leading to Western imperial control over much of the region. The first Arab revolt established the foundation of the modern regional system and brought competing claims over Arab nationalism, identity, and citizen loyalty. The first revolt also sowed the seeds for the next wave of regional change.[7]

Most Arab peoples did not achieve independence following the first Arab revolt but instead exchanged control by one local empire for that of several European imperial powers when Britain and France divided much of the region between themselves. But after World War II, the weakened European empires gradually relinquished their colonies, mandates, and protectorates. This created another transformation of the regional system in the mid-twentieth century: the wave of independence of Arab states. This wave transferred power and sovereignty to local regimes, reinforced the often European-drawn border divisions (with many remaining contested today), and set the stage for postindependence Arab politics. But during this postindependence era, a new wave of political change challenged the Western-backed regimes and Western-drawn borders in the region, creating the basis for the second Arab revolt. This one was led not by tribal leaders but by heads of independent states.

The second Arab revolt was a very ideological challenge and came mainly in the form of Pan-Arabism and leftist and populist ideologies, from Nasserism to Baathism to communism. Structurally, these ideas came to pervade key institutions, such as the armed forces, which often toppled Western-backed monarchies or even civilian republics and replaced them with ideologically charged military juntas. This wave of change swept away and transformed the regimes in Egypt, Syria, Iraq, Libya, and Yemen. At the same time, Algerian guerrilla fighters fought a long and bloody independence war against France (1954–1962), leading to Algeria's independence under a new nationalist party, the FLN, backed by the military. In its struggle against French colonialism, the FLN drew support from the pan-Arab nationalist regimes, which presented themselves as revolutionary republics, poised to sweep away the last vestiges of European colonialism as well as the more conservative regimes still backed by the Western imperial powers.

Yet much like the 2011 wave of change, regime change during the second Arab revolt came to some, but not all, of the region's states. Conservative monarchies in particular resisted the wave of change. Although several had already fallen, others tried to hold the line, bolstering their regimes against the internal and external threats to their regime security, even when these threats emanated from the newer pan-Arabist military regimes. The Hashemite monarchy in Iraq, for example, was overthrown and massacred by nationalist military officers led by General Abd al-Karim al-Qasim. The neighboring Hashemite monarchy in Jordan, in contrast, thwarted a military coup and managed to survive repeated challenges to its rule.

These regionwide domestic changes emerging from the second Arab revolt, however, led to a transformation in inter-Arab relations and regional politics in the form of the rise of the Arab cold war. That ideological struggle dominated the politics of the 1950s and 1960s and centered on two levels of inter-Arab conflict: between Egypt's President Gamal Abdel Nasser and his sometime allies (Iraq, Syria, Libya, and Yemen) against the conservative

Western-backed monarchies (Jordan, Morocco, Saudi Arabia, Kuwait, and the other emerging Gulf monarchies), and also an intra-ideological rift between Nasser and his Baathist rivals. The Arab cold war was both a struggle over ideas, especially for the heart and soul of Pan-Arabism, and a more material power struggle for hegemony in Arab regional politics.

Most of the attempts at Pan-Arab unity and unification in the 1950s and 1960s failed, and with the devastating Arab defeat by Israel in the 1967 Six-Day War, Nasser and Arabism had plummeted in regional esteem and influence. By the 1970s, the once-revolutionary Arab states did not seem all that revolutionary anymore. Most had created single-party, military-backed regimes, with vast secret police forces, bloated bureaucracies, and large, state-controlled industries dominating domestic economies.

Neither the populist nor the reactionary regimes seemed to inspire the Arab public sphere, and all were challenged by Islamist movements across the region, creating a new populist politics of opposition against largely secular regimes. Yet despite the pervasive nature of the Islamist opposition to Arab regimes, the Islamist challenge resulted in no Arab regime change whatsoever. Only in a non-Arab country, Iran, did a successful revolutionary coalition (including Islamists) emerge, overthrowing the shah of Iran in 1979 and creating the region's first "Islamic republic" in the form of a largely theocratic state.

The current era represents a third wave of change across the region, one equally embedded in international and domestic forces. Both Islamist and secular political currents have challenged and even toppled incumbent regimes. In many ways, the third Arab revolt mirrors elements of the second, especially the return of Arab cold war politics. Regional political dynamics has seen transformations specifically in regional norms, identities, alliances, and the regional balance of power.

Changes in the Regional Balance of Power

As the Arab uprisings have challenged the security, stability, and existence of Arab regimes, they also have transformed the regional balance of power, and in turn, that has affected outcomes, especially in later Arab revolts such as the one in Syria. What is most striking about the changing balance, however, is the reemergence of Arab powers in the regional system, after years of dominance by non-Arab states such as Iran and Israel. Domestically, Arab publics mobilized and tried to retake their own destinies from ossified dictatorships. But just as important, the uprisings have triggered a resurgence of Arab roles in the Middle East regional system, whereas previously there had been almost a vacuum of Arab leadership.

Claimants to regional leadership and sometimes even hegemony have tended to emerge from capitals like Cairo, Damascus, and Baghdad. Yet even before the uprisings, the traditional power centers had declined, each in different ways and each concentrating on domestic politics rather than elusive claims to regional dominance. Iraq's government remained mired in rebuilding in the wake of the U.S. invasion and occupation. The collapse of Iraq in 2003 caused the regional power balance to shift toward an Iranian-led bloc, perceived by many in Arab politics as a Shia crescent ranging from Hezbollah in Lebanon, to Alawite Syria, to a largely Shia led coalition of Islamist parties governing Iraq, and, finally, to the Islamic Republic of Iran itself. After the fall of the Mubarak regime and amid continuing revolutionary struggles to transform Egypt, Egypt's government too had no choice but to focus internally. In Syria, the regime was locked in an internal conflict with a mobilized, if diffuse, opposition in a scenario so violent and repressive that it quickly descended into a full-scale civil war.

In short, between 2003 and 2011, there seemed to be no Arab power playing a significant regional role. With Iran playing a larger regional role than perhaps ever before, the other two non-Arab states, Israel and Turkey, played assertive but inconsistent roles in the regional balance. Israel remained in conflict with the Palestinians, with Hezbollah in Lebanon, in a standoff with Baathist Syria, and in a cold war of its own with Iran. Iran, meanwhile, hailed the revolutions against mainly pro-U.S. Arab dictators and likened them to its own revolution of 1979 against the last shah of Iran. But for prodemocracy activists across the Arab region, the relevant comparison was to the youth movement and the prodemocracy demonstrations in Iran in 2009, demonstrations that were crushed by Iran's theocratic regime. Despite pretensions to regional "revolutionary" leadership, Iran in many ways has been marginalized once again in regional politics. As revolution swept across its closest ally, Syria, Iran backed the Syrian dictatorship, weakening its credibility still further.

Only a few years before the Arab revolutions, any attempt at a more assertive Turkish foreign policy in the region would have been read as neo-Ottoman imperialism. But by the time of the uprisings themselves, Turkey's domestic politics, foreign policy, and regional image all had changed dramatically. Previously, Turkish governments had focused on hopes of acceptance into the European Union while maintaining a "zero problems" nonconfrontational policy with its Middle Eastern neighbors. But by the time of the Arab usprisings, Turkey's moderate Islamist Justice and Development Party (AKP) had won several rounds of elections, and Prime Minister Recep Tayyip Erdogan had led Turkey toward a kind of reentry into regional politics. Unlike the era of the second Arab revolt, when Nasser enjoyed considerably popularity among Arab publics, the current era seemed to feature no equivalent among Arab leaders. Rather, it was a Turkish Islamist who filled that long-empty role. Erdogan's support of the Arab uprisings and his calls for democracy in the Arab world had earned him the regional status of a pop star. Erdogan's Turkey also seemed to appeal for a variety of reasons: it seemed to balance Islamist activism with pluralist democracy, good relations with the West but with an independent foreign policy, and civilian rule despite having a powerful (and, in the past, interventionist) armed forces. With both Israel and Iran increasingly isolated (even as they waged their own cold war against each other), Turkey appeared resurgent and engaged actively in Arab affairs to a greater degree than ever before in the postindependence period. Top Turkish officials even began attending meetings of the Arab League, something that would have been unthinkable before the 2011 revolutions. Turkey's luster began to diminish, however, after Egypt's Muslim Brotherhood government (which Erdogan's AKP had supported) was overthrown in a coup in July 2013.

In Arab politics, meanwhile, the temporary absence of the traditional power centers—Cairo, Baghdad, and Damascus—left much of the regional stage to Riyadh (Saudi Arabia) and even Doha (Qatar). With the Western powers supporting the ouster of regimes that had been allies to both the Western powers and the Gulf states, countries like Saudi Arabia and Qatar moved to use their wealth and influence to affect the Arab uprisings, in some cases to support them (as in Libya and Syria) and in others to act as a counterrevolutionary bloc supporting monarchies against their challengers (as in Bahrain). The Arab Gulf monarchies felt that they were too late to preserve allies like the Ben Ali and Mubarak regimes, in Tunisia and Egypt, respectively, and they no longer trusted the Western powers to support them or other Arab allies. Rather, the Gulf monarchies themselves would have to act, often in concert, as a transnational alliance of reactionary regimes, countering the latest wave of change but also riding that wave when it served their interests.

Although the states of the Gulf Cooperation Council (GCC) therefore backed military intervention by NATO against the Qaddafi regime in Libya, they also intervened militarily themselves to secure the regime and the counterrevolution in Bahrain. The Saudis and other GCC regimes were so worried about the implications of the Arab revolutions (at least against monarchies) that they even reached out to non-Gulf monarchies, in Morocco and Jordan, inviting them to join the GCC. While not inviting Yemen to join, the GCC attempted to dampen the fires of the Arab spring by brokering deals to trade partial regime change in Yemen for an end to domestic unrest there.[8] Yet the GCC was by no means a unitary actor in foreign policy. Its two most active members, Saudi Arabia and Qatar, were actively engaged in a competitive politics of intervention, backing different social forces around the region. While Saudi Arabia backed Salafi groups across the Maghreb and Mashreq, Qatar supported the Muslim Brotherhood and its offshoots, from al-Nahda in Tunisia to Hamas in Gaza.

In sum, the Arab uprisings had rearranged both the regional balance of power and inter-Arab relations. Amid very different levels of domestic change, Egypt, Iraq, and Syria were temporarily absent as significant players in the international relations of the region. In their stead, Saudi Arabia, Qatar, and the states of the GCC—whether successful or not—had asserted themselves as major players in inter-Arab relations and regional politics. New regimes in Libya and Tunisia, joined sometimes by newly assertive non-Arab Turkey, attempted to support efforts at democracy and regime change elsewhere.

When the Syrian revolution shifted to an increasingly bloody civil war, Saudi Arabia and Qatar called for intervention, hoping to bring down the Assad regime once and for all and to complete the shift in the regional balance away from the Shia axis they feared and toward a GCC-led Arab regional system. But this struggle over Syria and beyond was not only a material struggle in the regional balance of power; it was also a struggle over ideas and identity in regional politics and the front line of a new Arab cold war. It evolved in an increasingly sectarian direction as the war intensified, transforming the regional image of Hezbollah and Iran while intensifying the scrutiny on Shia-ruled Iraq. It also brought Saudi and Qatari competition into the open in unflattering ways.

The Changing Meanings of Arabism

The contemporary Arab system is characterized by a third Arab revolt and wave of change, as well as by a new Arab and regional cold war. This time the revolt is not that of tribes or of states but of mobilized populations against their own ruling regimes. In addition, the new cold war, like the old one, has multiple levels, once again including conservative hereditary monarchies engaged in regime survival politics but this time without a countervailing coalition of revolutionary Arab republics. As in the earlier periods, nationalism and identity politics matter.

Like the earlier Arab cold war, the current version includes intervention in the domestic affairs of other Arab states as well as alliances of conservative and even reactionary monarchies attempting to resist revolutionary change. Unlike the earlier cold war, however, the current version includes divisions along sectarian Sunni-Shia lines. Today's Arab cold war also includes new dynamics and norms emerging from the Arab uprisings themselves. The contemporary Arab cold war is therefore marked by state-state rivalries as well as state-society conflicts characterized by reemergent Arab identity politics and demands for greater participation in public life.[9]

Arabism, therefore, remains alive, but not at all in its earlier form, when it was too often used like a bludgeon to undermine the legitimacy and internal regime security of rival states. Today's Arabism is more deeply rooted in domestic politics, emphasizing the social and cultural links of a pan-Arab regional identity. Today's Arabism has been deeply impacted by the new media revolution, including social media. In the context of the Arab uprisings especially, there appears to be a greater sense among Arab publics of being connected to one another, often in mutual struggle against their own regimes.

During the period of the second Arab revolt and the original Arab cold war, Arabism came to be associated with the idea of pan-Arab unity and even unification. Perhaps ironically, in actual practice Pan-Arabism led to disunity as much as to unity. In the 1950s and 1960s inter-Arab relations shifted regularly between attempts at formal unification and overt conflict, and regional politics was marked mainly by the fractious politics of the Arab cold war. Indeed, in the Arab cold war of the 1950s and 1960s, Pan-Arabism was associated mainly with one side of the conflict as the ideology of revolutionary republics, led by military officers who aimed to change both the regimes and the political map of the region. While it had a great deal of influence across Arab societies at the time, Pan-Arabism increasingly became an ideology of states, which is not at all the type of pan-Arab identity and solidarity found in the Arab revolutions today.

Today's calls for unity are calls for transnational cooperation, not national unification. Today's Pan-Arabism is not the ideology of largely secular and leftist military juntas but a more societal and cultural Pan-Arabism. If Arabist discourse dominated the 1950s and 1960s and Islamist discourse dominated the decades afterward, today we see more of an overlap between previously polarized ideas, with Arabism and Islamism overlapping at times, if not actually merging. This amounts, in the words of Andre Bank and Morten Valbjorn, to a "new societal Islamic Political Arabism."[10] Failure to grasp the continuing nature of Arabism and Arab identity dynamics has led many outside observers to miss key dynamics in regional politics.[11]

This has implications for multiple levels of meaning in inter-Arab political struggles as different groups attempt to harness pan-Arab identity and turn it to their own ends. New regimes in Tunisia and Libya, for example, called for the support of fellow Arabs in their struggles against the old regimes. Even conservative monarchies, historically the least pan-Arabist entities in regional politics, seem to have rediscovered the importance of Arab unity and even tried to reenergize the Arab League as a more influential actor in regional politics, favoring regime change in the more radical states like Libya and Syria and also using the same institution as a mutual support group against regime change elsewhere. Finally, beyond governments, when social activists use the new media to communicate with one another other via blogs, Twitter, and Facebook, they are speaking a common written Arabic language, with no dialects and no accents, just pan-Arab revolutionary solidarity, the very pan-Arabist feature that the conservative monarchies seek to avoid. But it is this dilemma, this state-society struggle over Pan-Arabism and its meaning, that has also become a key part of the new Arab cold war.

Even before the Arab revolutions, the Arab Gulf monarchies were focused on the threat of Iran's rising power and, more broadly, on perceived ideological challenges from Shiism in general. The GCC states therefore increasingly viewed conflicts from Iraq to Lebanon in both power politics and sectarian terms as proxy struggles between Saudi- and Iranian-led blocs in the regional balance of power and also as struggles between Sunni and Shia alliances within regional politics.[12] That sense of sectarian power struggles only deepened with the Arab uprisings. In 2011 during the Bahrain uprising, instead of GCC military intervention being used to counter a foreign power (notwithstanding the rhetoric of Iranian conspiracies), it was used to counter a state's own population (for the Bahraini monarchy) and also to curb the power of ideas deemed too subversive for regime security (for Bahrain and all other GCC monarchies). That is, GCC forces crossed the bridge to Bahrain to support an allied monarchy and, even more important, to stop the contagion of ideas that GCC states feared might undermine their own regimes. Still, echoing the ideological lines of a new Arab cold war, the GCC's intervention in Bahrain was reframed as

Sunni solidarity against Shia (and allegedly Iranian) subversion instead of as an authoritarian reaction against democratic change.

These moves by the GCC can best be read in three distinct, but equally important, ways: (1) as the material power politics moves of a Saudi-led alliance bloc attempting to counter perceived Iranian-led incursions against the regional balance of power; (2) as an authoritarian alliance of monarchical regimes crushing and preventing the spread of prodemocracy movements; and (3) as part of the increasingly sectarian ideological rhetoric of Sunni and Shia alignments immersed in a new version of the Arab cold war. On top of this, clear differences emerged regarding views of the Muslim Brotherhood, with some regimes (such as Qatar's) appearing to welcome and even promote new Islamist governments and others (such as Saudi Arabia's and the United Arab Emirates') fiercely opposing them and seeking ways to support their domestic rivals.

Conclusions

The Syrian imbroglio brought together, in the worst ways, every theme discussed in this chapter. During the Syrian civil war, the regime was essentially living own its internal security dilemma and turning its militarized might on its own people. Both the use of new media by besieged prodemocracy activists in the country and the global response demonstrated the radical changes in the Arab public sphere and the inability of even a police state to monopolize information. It is tragic as well as ironic that the Baathist regime, which saw itself as the last standard bearer of the Pan-Arabism of the earlier Arab cold war, would be in confrontation simultaneously with its own Arab people and most of the Arab world, all of whom asserted a very different societal vision of pan-Arab identity and solidarity.

But the Syrian crisis also bore all the hallmarks of the new Arab cold war and the shifting regional balance of power, including domestic struggle between a regime and an opposition, each with outside patrons, attempts to fan the flames of sectarianism, and dueling ideological narratives regarding who was really the aggressor in the conflict.[13] Like the earlier Arab and even global cold wars, the conflict was awash in propaganda, disinformation, and attempts to manipulate regional and global media.

In contrast to the promising beginnings and democratic aspirations associated with, particularly, the early days of the Tunisian and Egyptian revolutions, the Syrian crisis threatened to become a broader regional conflict. Iran, Hezbollah, Russia, and China supported the Syrian regime, while

Turkey, Saudi Arabia, Qatar, France, Britain, and the United States backed the opposition, creating multiple levels of resurgent regional and global cold war dynamics that threatened to crush the hopes of Syria's people even while they already were being victimized by their own brutal regime.

Syria, in fact, was declining almost to its state in the 1940s and 1950s: no longer a major regional power itself but instead an arena for regional conflict and ideological struggles. Saudi Arabia, Qatar, and Turkey all supported the rebel movement against the Assad regime, and Iran strongly backed the Alawite-dominated state against a mainly Sunni rebel movement. The Syrian conflict began in March 2011 as a peaceful prodemocracy movement. The regime responded with violence, and as of October 2013, the Syria's largely sectarian civil war had claimed the lives of more than 100,000 Syrians. More than a million have been displaced, with more than 500,000 Syrian refugees flowing to Jordan alone. By May 2013, the sectarian dimensions had widened still further and, with them, the regionalization and internationalization of the Syrian war as Hezbollah fighters openly joined Assad's forces, while foreign Sunni jihadists, including groups such as Jabha al-Nusra (affiliated with al-Qaida), supported the rebels; these forces then met in battle over the city of Qusayr near the Lebanese border. The Sunni and Shia jihadists engaged each other in Syria, with regional and global powers backing opposite sides with money and arms. In other words, Syria's fate will be determined by both Syrians for or against the regime and by outside forces. In Syria, as elsewhere in the Arab world, outcomes of the Arab uprisings will be determined by internal political factors, as well as the international relations of the region.

NOTES

1. Curtis R. Ryan, *Inter-Arab Alliances: Regime Security and Jordanian Foreign Policy* (Gainesville: University Press of Florida, 2009).

2. Caroline Thomas, *In Search of Security: The Third World in International Relations* (Boulder, Colo.: Lynne Rienner, 1987); Edward E. Azar and Chung-in Moon, eds., *National Security in the Third World: The Management of Internal and External Threats* (College Park: Center for International Development and Conflict Management, University of Maryland Press, 1988); Nicole Ball, *Security and Economy in the Third World* (Princeton, N.J.: Princeton University Press, 1988); Brian L. Job, ed., *The Insecurity Dilemma: National Security of Third World States* (Boulder, Colo.: Lynne Rienner, 1992). For several reassessments of security specifically in the Arab regional context, see Bahgat Korany, Paul Noble, and Rex Brynen, eds.,

The Many Faces of National Security in the Arab World (New York: St. Martin's Press, 1993).

3. Robert Jervis, "Cooperation Under the Security Dilemma," *World Politics* 30, no. 2 (January 1978): 167–214; John Herz, *Political Realism and Political Idealism* (Chicago: University of Chicago Press, 1951); Glenn H. Snyder, "The Security Dilemma in Alliance Politics," *World Politics* 36, no. 4 (July 1984): 461–95.

4. Fred Lawson argues that several factors add to the security dilemma in the Arab world: the continuous process of state building, contradictions within ruling regime coalitions, the late development of industrialization, and, finally, asymmetrical interdependence in the world political economy. See Fred H. Lawson, "Neglected Aspects of the Security Dilemma," in *The Many Faces of National Security in the Arab World*, ed. Bahgat Korany, Paul Noble, and Rex Brynen (New York: St. Martin's Press, 1993), 100–126.

5. For a more detailed analysis, see Ryan, *Inter-Arab Alliances*, chap. 2, "Security Dilemmas in Arab Politics."

6. Marc Lynch, *Voices of the New Arab Public: Iraq, al-Jazeera, and Middle East Politics Today* (New York: Columbia University Press, 2006).

7. Bruce Maddy-Weitzman, *The Crystallization of the Arab State System, 1945–1954* (Syracuse, N.Y.: Syracuse University Press, 1993); David Fromkin, *A Peace to End All Peace: The Fall of the Ottoman Empire and the Creation of the Modern Middle East* (New York: Avon, 1989).

8. Despite Saudi efforts to use the GCC as its main tool in a regional counterrevolution, other GCC states often break with Riyadh and maintain defiantly independent foreign policies. Even in the midst of the bilateral Saudi-Iranian cold war, for example, the United Arab Emirates, Oman, and Qatar each challenged Saudi primacy, and the latter two states even maintained cordial and sometimes even warm relations with Teheran. Mehran Kamrava, "The Arab Spring and the Saudi-Led Counterrevolution," *Orbis*, winter 2012, 96–104.

9. Curtis R. Ryan, "The New Arab Cold War and the Struggle for Syria," *Middle East Report*, no. 262 (spring 2012): 28–31.

10. Andre Bank and Morton Valbjorn, "Bringing the Arab Regional Level Back in . . . Jordan in the New Arab Cold War," *Middle East Critique*, 19, no. 3 (fall 2010): 312.

11. F. Gregory Gause III, "Why Middle East Studies Missed the Arab Spring," *Foreign Affairs* 90, no. 4 (July/August 2011): 81–90.

12. Morton Valbjorn and Andre Bank, "Signs of a New Arab Cold War: The 2006 Lebanon War and the Sunni-Shi'i Divide," *Middle East Report* 242 (spring 2007): 6–11.

13. Curtis R. Ryan, "The New Arab Cold War and the Struggle for Syria," *Middle East Report*, no. 262 (spring 2012): 28–31.

PART II

Key Actors

7

States and Bankers

CLEMENT M. HENRY

The pattern of the Arab uprisings cannot be separated from the nature of the states and their intermediary associations.[1] Egypt, Morocco, and Tunisia are the only ones in the region having relatively autonomous precolonial histories as state entities. Algeria's rupture with France was so great that state building began virtually anew in 1962. Likewise Libya, conquered and integrated by Italy, was reinvented in 1951. Syria, Lebanon, and Iraq evolved from the 1919 Treaty of Versailles, followed by Transjordan, while the Saudi dynasty emerged more than a century after Morocco's, as did its evolution into a modern state. The British occupation of Aden in 1839 shattered Yemen's evolution, which in 1990 resumed in fits and starts.

These less developed states have little civil society: the state, to borrow the expression of French political scientist Jean Leca, is "folded in" on the society and is directly managed by clans, tribes, or personal networks, not developed bureaucracies.[2] None of their regimes, whether monarchy or republic, allows relatively autonomous bureaucracies, much less credible intermediary bodies capable of making "pacted" transitions. These regimes have no principals capable of representing critical constituencies other than the primary groups of family, clan, tribe, sect, or clientele. By contrast, the more developed states of Egypt, Morocco, and Tunisia have maintained the appearance of intermediary bodies in supposedly vibrant civil societies, even if the reality was tighter police control.

Less noticeable but equally vital is that underpinning these intermediary bodies are financial intermediaries, the commercial banking systems that allocate credit, the lifeblood of public and private enterprises. These are the command and control systems of their respective political economies.

While the International Monetary Fund (IMF) and the World Bank had pressured most of the Arab countries to engage in neoliberal reform during the two or three decades before the Arab spring, private-sector development varied significantly. Tunisia, like Egypt, had generated a substantial, if politically subordinate, private sector from a restructured socialist economy. Syria, Libya, and Yemen, had consigned their private sectors, by either design or lack of financial capacity, to the shadows of the informal economy. By contrast, Morocco, the other more developed state, had never engaged in state socialism but, even so, surpassed Tunisia and Egypt in structural adjustment and privatization initiatives.

This chapter argues that these variations better explain variations in the mobilization of Arab protest movements, incumbent regime responses, and potential outcomes than do the broader causal factors raised in traditional political economy literature, such as youth bulges and unemployment (especially of university-educated youth), rising prices of food, growing inequalities in income distribution, and the alienation of previously protected sectors such as public-sector labor and management.[3] Even global warming, an undiscriminating background variable that helps explain rising food prices in 2010/2011, has been introduced to help explain the Arab uprisings.[4] But such factors, broadly affecting the southern Mediterranean, cannot explain why the rising discontent and widespread perceptions of regime illegitimacy took the different forms and timing that they did on the various types of regimes across the region after December 2010.

Only agents, not structures, determine timing, but private-sector enterprise is the bedrock of potential collective action in civil society. It is the material infrastructure that offers resources for the intermediary associations of civil society. Structures do not create active agents, but they do offer opportunities for agents of social change. Business communities enable other forms of association—be they trade unions, charities, or human rights associations—usually without direct subventions. The material infrastructures may also amplify the effects of food prices and even global warming, as the case studies suggest.

Typologies of Political Economies

Relatively developed states go roughly hand in hand with the relatively dense private sectors in the Arab region, possibly because property rights are a key indicator of "stateness" as well as a guarantor of economic enterprise.[5] The more developed states of Egypt, Morocco, and Tunisia also have

TABLE 7.1

REGIME TYPES, CREDIT, AND COMMERCIAL BANKING STRUCTURES

COUNTRY NAME	REGIME TYPE	PRIVATE CREDIT AS % GDP 2010	BANKING STRUCTURE	
Lebanon	Democracy	85.5	Private	Less concentrated
Bahrain	Monarchy	75.9	Private	Less
Kuwait	Family	73.6	Private	Concentrated
Jordan	Monarchy	73.2	Private	Less
UAE	Families	72.5	Private	Less
Tunisia	Bully	68.8	Public	Less
Morocco	Monarchy	68.6	Private	Concentrated
Saudi Arabia	Monarchy	45.9	Private	Concentrated
Qatar	Family	43.9	Private	Concentrated
Oman	Monarchy	42.9	Private	Concentrated
Egypt	Bully	33.1	Public	Less
Syria	Bunker	22.5	Public	Concentrated
Algeria	Bunker	15.6	Public	Concentrated
Sudan	Bunker	12.0	Destroyed	
Libya (2009)	Bunker	10.9	Public	Concentrated
Iraq	Bunker	9.2	Destroyed	
Yemen	Bunker	6.3	Public	Concentrated

Sources: World Bank, World Development Indicators 2012; Clement Henry and Robert Springborg, *Globalization and the Politics of Development in the Middle East*, 2nd ed. (New York: Cambridge University Press, 2010), 80, 95.

the most extensive private sectors, as indicated by their access to bank credit. Table 7.1 shows that the political typology correlates closely with commercial banking structures. The countries are ranked by credit to the private sector as a percentage of gross domestic product.[6] The "bunker" regimes rule the predominantly cashed-based informal economies with low private-sector credit ratios.

Commercial banking systems tend to be the mirror image of the real economy and thus reflect its structure. The banks may be publicly or privately owned, and their market shares may be concentrated in a small number of banks or less concentrated, and therefore potentially more competitive, in structure. Table 7.1 indicates the four possibilities. All the least developed "bunker" states fall into the category of concentrated public ownership, whereas the more developed "bullies," Egypt and Tunisia, retain predominantly public ownership but display more diversified banking systems as well as consistently greater credit allocations to the private sector. The monarchies display predominantly privately owned banks but with the relatively high degrees of concentration characteristic of bunker states. Arguably there is less distinction between public and private sectors in monarchies, given the businesses of royal families. Still, the more developed state of Morocco also displays proportionately greater credit to the private sector than does the less developed Saudi Arabia, for instance, despite the latter's great oil wealth. Especially in Morocco, the concentrated control of the banking system offers the same tight control as do bunker regimes over the private sector, but the monarchy enjoys greater leverage, since its private sector is more extensive. Consequently, Morocco is better able to fine-tune its patronage network than any bunker regime, such as neighboring Algeria, can. In resource-poor Morocco and Jordan, such capabilities seem essential to their regimes' survival.

Of special interest for understanding the origins of the Arab uprising, however, are the differences among the more authoritarian republics. Egypt and Tunisia, the *bully* police states depicted in table 7.1, have stronger states than the *bunkers* do. They deploy power through relatively autonomous administrative structures and other controlled intermediary bodies interacting with them. Egypt's Muhammad Ali and Tunisia's Ahmad Bey engaged in modern state building in the nineteenth century and, unlike the other Arab republics, enjoyed previous legacies as political entities living off their respective sedentary tax bases.[7] They also substantially altered the commanding heights of their respective economies in the 1970s. To open up their economies to foreign investment, they encouraged private ownership in their commercial banking systems, even though these still remained under the heavy influence of state-owned banks. The bullies allocated substantially more credit to the private sector than did those in the bunkers, who usually continued, as in the heady days of state socialism, to be state officials, not real bankers, doling out off-budget patronage.[8] Note in table 7.1 that Iraq, bunkered in its Green Zone after being "liberated" from Saddam Hussein, offered even less credit to the private sector than Syria did in 2010.

The more progressive monarchies, especially Morocco, also nurtured a variety of intermediaries that served as shock absorbers and might perform "pacted" transitions to democracy. On a smaller scale, Bahrain, which, like Kuwait, had occasionally experimented with parliamentary representation, might have experienced genuine reform had Saudi Arabia not intervened. The other family-run municipalities and larger members of the GCC seem more akin to the bunker regimes of the Janissary republics, however, for their prime intermediaries, too, are families, tribes, and patron-client networks, not political parties or other forms of secondary associations. But because they are much wealthier than the other bunkers, they have preempted, with substantial social spending programs, any revolt by their potentially restive populations. Their bunkers, then, are more akin to bank vaults than to underground military fortresses.

It seems no coincidence that the bully regimes were the first to experience the Arab uprisings. After practicing state socialism in the 1960s, they also developed dense webs of private-sector interests, as indicated by outstanding credits to the economy, which could support civil society. Monarchies, which also harbor significant private sectors, usually manipulated them more astutely. The Moroccan *makhzan*, for instance, used the concentrated banking system to leverage new forms of royal patronage. The bullies were less skilled in not only political but also financial arts. Their patronage generated substantially larger proportions of nonperforming loans, as both regime sycophants and public enterprises simply neglected to repay their debts. Politically, too, the presidents who relied on ruling parties appeared less able than monarchs to stay above politics. Bullying their civil societies required ever larger security forces, up to one police person (including plainclothes and thugs) for every fifty Egyptians or seventy Tunisians.

A cross-sectional view of commercial banking structures in the mid-1990s can be interpreted as the march of civil society across the broader region. In the 1930s and 1940s, before the advent of a multiparty system, the region's banks were largely government owned and dominated by three or four big ones. By the 1990s more of them were privately owned and the structure was less concentrated. Figure 7.1 is a scatter plot of the region's commercial banking structures, indicating the degree of state ownership along the horizontal x axis and the degree of concentration of their respective markets along the vertical y axis.[9] Our praetorian bunker states all are lined up in the upper-right-hand quadrant of highly concentrated state-owned banking systems. Farther down, still largely state owned, are Egypt and Tunisia, marching in a path toward Turkish and Lebanese democracy, as reflected in their diversified, predominantly privately owned commercial banks. The monarchies—and Israel, for that matter—tend to have more

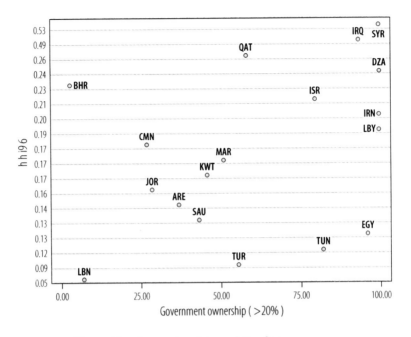

FIGURE 7.1 Human Development and Armed Conflict.

Map by kind permission of Project Ploughshares (www.ploughshares.ca)

concentrated banking systems, reflecting the oligopolistic control of their ruling families, who are also heavily steeped in commerce and in controlling the working capital provided by the banks.

Tunisia and Egypt

Among the republics, Tunisia has marched slightly farther down the line than Egypt, and both of them are clearly much closer to Turkey than to Libya, Algeria, Iraq, and Syria—or Iran, for that matter. By the mid-1990s the two bullies had clearly emerged from the bunkers of state socialism. In the heyday of Arab socialism, Egypt, with its four state-owned banks, would have clustered with Algeria, Syria, and Iraq at the extremities of concentration and state ownership, extremes that Tunisia's more prudent leadership had avoided. The two bully regimes had progressed the furthest in structural adjustment by the 1990s and had steady 5 percent growth rates in much of the following decade, as well as many of the social and political strains accompanying the new dynamic.

Before 2011 Tunisia already seemed the ripest candidate in the region for political change.[10] As table 7.1 indicates, credit to its private sector exceeded that of every other non-GCC state in the region except Jordan and Lebanon. Of the non-oil states, its per capita income was second only to Lebanon's. Prudent economic management had generated the highest average per capita wealth growth rate since 1987, the year that General Zine al-Abdine Ben Ali succeeded Habib Bourguiba as president. The regime boasted that the home ownership of 80 percent of its population was a sign of its growing middle and lower middle classes. Tunisia's carefully crafted policies of export-led growth had fostered a light manufacturing base with as much value added as neighboring Algeria's, which had triple Tunisia's population.

After 2007 the invasion of the Ben Ali and Trabelsi clans into lucrative slices of the Tunisian economy accelerated. The credit offered to this web of some 114 individuals reached 3 billion dinars by 2011 ($2.2 billion). Even more serious, in the opinion of Dr. Mustapha Nabli—Tunisia's highly respected new governor of its central bank who was brought in to clean up the mess—was that this credit had doubled in 2009 and again in 2010, revealing how ravenous the ruling thieves' appetites were becoming.[11] Family members had gained control of two of country's principal private-sector banks.

Ben Ali's crude dictatorship became a political anomaly to Tunisia's growing middle class. His police regime tortured dissidents, mugged investigative journalists, imprisoned youth for circumventing Internet filters, and destroyed any semblance of judicial autonomy. But he could not insulate its largely literate population from constant interaction with its European neighbors, the closest of which was only ninety miles across the Mediterranean. By 2010 the government's injustice was just as apparent to rural folk as to Tunis's upscale chattering classes. Wikileaks confirmed much of the gossip about Leila Trabelsi, Ben Ali's wife, and other members of her notorious family, as well as other Ben Ali in-laws, thanks to judicious reporting by U.S. Ambassador Robert F. Godec.[12] Information about their predations traveled rapidly across the country via Facebook as well as word of mouth, but mobilizing the population required intermediaries on the ground as well.

The profile of the bully police state does not quite explain why it was Tunisia rather than Egypt that started the Arab chain reaction, but its private sector, as measured by bank credit, was more extensive than Egypt's, possibly offering greater opportunities for collective action. Tunisia also may have been better positioned than Egypt because it was smaller, with an eighth of Egypt's 83 million people. It was wealthier as well and had less geopolitical weight. Tunisia's greater wealth also was correlated with greater associational activity, Internet connectivity, and, proportionate to population, greater Facebook membership.[13] Perhaps equally important, its very success in building up an export- and services-led economy may have contributed to the dictator's downfall. The contrast between a relatively dynamic economy, blocked only by visible, top-heavy centralized corruption, became too great for Tunisia's marginalized elites. Tunisia's economic growth could not keep pace with an ever expanding education system. While Tunisia's overall unemployment rates were similar to those of Algeria and Morocco, officially a bit below 15 percent, more than 50 percent of its secondary school– and university-educated citizens were unemployed in 2005, substantially exceeding its neighbors' respective rates of 34 and 44 percent. Possibly the aftershocks of world recession, coupled with high food prices, also affected Tunisia more adversely than its neighbors because trade constituted a substantially larger proportion of its GDP.[14]

The catalyst for Tunisia's revolution of January 14 mirrored the country's economic predicaments and acted out earlier visions of political change. Manfred Halpern identified the "New Middle Class" as the agent of change in the early 1960s, and he defined it primarily by its aspirations rather than its educational attainments.[15] Likewise in 2010, Tunisia's self-immolated high school dropout, Mohamed Bouazizi, had wanted to go to university. But unlike Halpern's putative urban revolutionaries, the dropout who became Tunisia's revolutionary icon represented an angry rural periphery. In Tunisia, the revolution of January 14 swept in from the country's western and central provinces to Sfax, Tunisia's second-largest city, and finally up the coast through the Sahel, the ruling party's heartland, to Tunis.

The contrast with Egypt could not be sharper. In Egypt, which is significantly poorer and less urbanized than Tunisia, the revolution was mostly confined to major cities, not the rural peripheries that had grounded Tunisia's urban protest. While Egyptians may view their revolution as emerging bottom-up from the people rather than top-down like previous mobilization efforts, the people in question were still drawn primarily across urban rather than rural strata.[16] Even climate change may help to explain the differences. Even though revolutionaries in both countries waved their baguettes and called for bread as well as freedom and dignity, periodic droughts had dislocated Tunisians living in the rural periphery more than they had the peasants of the irrigated Nile Valley.

Each of these relatively developed states had a professional military that projected the appearance, once the police repression became violent, of taking sides with the people against the security forces. There were major differences, however, between the two armed forces.

In Tunisia the military blocked a police crackdown in the early days of the revolution and subsequently preserved law and order while Ben Ali fled the country. It had no particular interests to articulate other than maintaining professional integrity, defending the state, and staying out of politics. Bourguiba and, subsequently, Ben Ali had marginalized the military, preferring to invest in police and presidential security forces, whereas in Egypt the military gained great prestige when Gamal Abdel Nasser took power, and it had accumulated substantial economic interests, encouraged as a means of keeping it loyal to the president. As a state within the state, the Egyptian armed forces crowded out the private sector in a variety of nonstrategic domains, possibly helping explain why civilian businesses occupied a smaller financial surface than in Tunisia. The Supreme Council of the Armed Forces (SCAF) removed President Hosni Mubarak and others associated with the ancien régime in part to preserve its economic interests. As Robert Springborg explains in chapter 8, these interests went well beyond the state's military factories, constituting a veritable military-industrial octopus extending into the civilian economy, with capital accumulated in part by the United States' annual military injections of $1.3 billion since the late 1970s.

The business networks of the two bully regimes also displayed other significant differences. Corruption in Tunisia was highly centralized and top-heavy.[17] Prosecuting a few members of the extended ruling family could clean up the business environment.[18] Indeed, if Tunisia had continued its prudent export-oriented economic policies, the new political climate would have been able to attract the substantial local as well as foreign investment that the Ben Ali and Trabelsi families had scared off. In Egypt, by contrast, the corruption was more widespread, and consequently SCAF, committed to protecting its extensive economic interests, could only scrape the surface. SCAF and the Tunisian transitional authorities might have competed with each other in exposing the financial misdemeanors of their former presidential families, but they faced different problems.

Each country, however, enjoyed the advantage of a state with a functioning bureaucracy detached from social forces. As Yossi Shain and Juan J. Linz argued, "One of the most important elements for ensuring a democratic outcome by any interim government is for the state to retain sufficient bureaucratic apparatus and minimal respect for the rule of law of law."[19] The two bully regimes had relatively autonomous bureaucracies, grounded in centuries of state development. The other Arab regimes governed more problematic states with weaker administrative and civil infrastructures. The clans that occupied the bunkers of Syria, Yemen, and Libya viciously lashed out at insurgent populations, one family, clan, tribe, or sect against another, without the insulation of either a bureaucracy or a professional military.

In Tunis, many might also, as in Egypt, have welcomed provisional military rule, but General Rachid Ammar wisely determined to preserve Bourguiba's legacy of civilian rule. The provisional president's choice of his former patron, eighty-five-year-old Beji Caid el-Sebsi, as prime minister was a stroke of luck, for as a former interior and defense minister under Bourguiba, he had the requisite political as well as technical skills. Identifying the revolutionary enemies was a daunting task in a country where many technically competent people had been obliged, like their counterparts in Baathist Iraq, to join the ruling party. Civil society nevertheless reemerged in the form of a self-co-opted Higher Instance for the Preservation of the Objectives of the Revolution, Political Reform, and Democratic Transition. This body, originally a commission of jurists to study constitutional reform, expanded into a sort of transitional parliament to devise an electoral law and procedures leading to the October 2011 elections of a relatively representative constituent assembly. In Egypt, by contrast, the army, not civil society, took the lead. The Supreme Council of the Armed Forces dominated the transition process until August 2012, when the newly elected president, Mohamed Morsi, managed to retire its top leaders and, in a controversial power grab, ensure passage of a new constitution. Backed and perhaps propelled by the conservative leadership of the Muslim Brotherhood, Morsi polarized Egypt's civil society between its Islamist and secular components.

In Tunisia too, civil society became polarized despite the efforts of al-Nahda and two smaller, more secular parties to maintain their alliance. The balance of political forces appeared to be similar in the two countries, with al-Nahda and the Muslim Brotherhood each winning some 40 percent of the vote in legislative elections conducted in 2011. But the Salafists won an additional 23 percent in Egypt, whereas in Tunisia much smaller numbers made headlines with their violent activities. Islamists may have been the popular majority in Tunisia, as Rachid Ghannouchi claimed, but he also admitted that the majority of the elite opposed his al-Nahda Party.[20]

As of October 2013, indeed, Tunisian civil society seemed more capable than its Egyptian counterpart of sustaining the transition launched by their respective revolutions. Not only did it rest, as already noted, on a stronger material base of private sector credit.[21] It also continued in the form of a quartet headed by the powerful trade union to supervise talks between the governing al-Nahda Party and the principal opposition parties.[22] Oppositions in both Tunisia and Egypt had viewed with increasing misgivings the maneuvers of their ruling Islamists to place their followers in key government positions. Shocked also by two political assassinations, opponents of al-Nahda went so far as to blame it for tolerating criminal Salafist behavior. After the second murder, fifty-nine opposition members of Tunisia's Constituent Assembly (out of 217) walked out in July, and its constitutional deliberations were suspended until their return. Meanwhile, however, the quartet managed to keep negotiations with al-Nahda on track.[23]

In Egypt, by contrast, the massive uprising of June 30 and removal from office of President Morsi on July 3, 2013, ended any tacit alliance between the armed forces and the Muslim Brotherhood and led to the latter's dissolution and a drastic reorientation of any possible transition. Bitter distrust between Islamists and more secular elements jeopardized the political transition in both countries and threatened to ruin any economic recovery, especially in Egypt, despite the latter's richer history of parliamentary government and political contestation.

The Moroccan Monarchy

By contrast, the monarchy had perfected a style of divide-and-rule for the intermediary bodies, coupled with periodic promises of reform that postponed any frontal mass assaults of the type waged in Egypt and Tunisia. The underlying political economy offers a partial insight into tactics of survival.

The financial command-and-control structures of the Arab monarchies are mostly clustered in the center of figure 7.1 and offer a fascinating clue. To the extent that banking concentration reflects royal control of the political economy, as in Morocco, there are ways of controlling businesses and civil society organizations while giving up some formal levers of power. Morocco effectively deregulated parts of the economy and moved toward a market economy in the early 1990s, but only after the *makhzan* had first established effective control of the banking system and some associated conglomerates. In effect, King Hassan II reconstructed and expanded his system of royal patronage by commanding many of the spaces of private enterprise. Two decades later under a new king, the *makhzan*'s portfolio, concentrated in a holding company SIDER ("of the king," in Latin, spelled backward) has been rationalized. Although centralizing control and leveraging assets may carry some financial risks, they also offer cushions for further political and financial engineering.[24]

To contain the awakening of his people, articulated in the February 20 movement, King Mohammed VI promised on March 9 to delegate substantial powers to an elected prime minister. Drafted by experts supervised by the palace, the new constitution offers greater powers to an elected prime minister but "reserves for the king three areas as his exclusive domain: religion, security issues, and strategic major policy choices."[25] It was adopted by referendum on July 1 by an overwhelming 98.6 percent majority but was contested by the February 20 movement. It may in reality extend King Hassan II's political opening in 1997, when he appointed a prime minister from a leading opposition party and allowed him to form a government but reserved key domains for royal appointees. The extensive royal patronage machine serviced by the political economy ensures royal control while offering an appearance of big changes toward constitutional monarchy that sufficed to divide the February 20 movement.

The region's other monarchies and family regimes rest on state foundations less well established than Morocco's. There are fewer intermediary bodies, in the sense of private-sector enterprises or civil society or professional associations that might transcend primary cleavages. The small wealthy Arab states, with the exception of Bahrain, field few nongovernmental organizations, as most public matters are discussed in ruling family circles, such as Kuwait's *diwaniya*.[26]

Not even Jordan, much less the GCC members, has Morocco's rich assortment of political parties and civil society associations. Relatively large private sectors, however, point to a potential development of civil society. The GCC countries, with the exception of Oman, also are at the forefront of Islamic finance in the region, raising the eventual possibility of an Islamic bourgeoisie emerging in competition with the ruling families. Meanwhile, though, the tragedy of Bahrain reflects the Saudis' determination to block any significant reform. Nonetheless, Bahrain may finally be the catalyst that ignites the rest of the GCC, including its larger neighbor, where young, rapidly growing, educated populations remain underemployed and the private sector is largely under expatriate management.

Relatively strong states, such as Egypt, Morocco, and Tunisia, offered more hospitable environments for mobilization than did the bunkers or most of the family-run regimes. The Moroccan monarchy could contain protest through adept preemptive maneuvers, whereas bully presidents had to be sacrificed. The commanding heights of the political economy helped explain why both bullies and the monarchy had adequate protection in the form of viable civil societies, heavily policed, to be sure, but available, too, to engage populations in new political experiences once they gained greater freedom. Each aroused citizenry was grounded in a particular political economy. It is no accident that Tunisians were the first to awaken, as the country's blatantly distorted political economy made it the prime candidate for a regime change. Nor, after the fact, is it so surprising that Egypt followed suit, for its structures resembled Tunisia's more than those of any other Arab state. Finally, the more politically experienced Moroccan regime could offer modest reforms without limiting the capacity of its pervasive patronage networks to manipulate civil society. In sum, these distinct patterns of political economy help explain the nature of civil society and the ability of regimes to respond to their challengers during the Arab uprisings.

NOTES

1. An earlier version of this chapter, "Political Economies of Transition," was published in *The Arab Spring: Will It Lead to Democratic Transitions?* ed. Clement M. Henry and Ji-Hyang Jang (Seoul: Asian Institute of Policy Studies, November 15, 2012).

2. Andrea Liverani, *Civil Society in Algeria: The Political Functions of Associational Life*, Routledge Studies in Middle Eastern Politics (New York: Routledge, 2008), xii.

3. For an excellent overview, see Omar S. Dahi, "Understanding the Political Economy of the Arab Revolts," *Middle East Report* 259 (summer 2011): 2–6.

4. Caitlin E. Werrell and Francesco Femia, eds., *The Arab Spring and Climate Change* (Washington, D.C.: Henry L. Stimson Center, February 2013).

5. Robert P. Parks, "Local-National Relations and the Politics of Property Rights in Algeria and Tunisia," PhD diss., University of Texas at Austin, 2011.

6. Private credit is also closely correlated with "contract-intensive money," the percentage of money (M2) held in banks rather than in cash. The term is borrowed from Lewis W. Snider, *Growth, Debt, and Politics: Economic Adjustment and the Political Performance of Developing Countries* (Boulder, Colo.: Westview Press, 1996), and is used by Clement M. Henry and Robert Springborg, *Globalization and the Politics of Development in the Middle East* (New York: Cambridge University Press, 2010), 80–81, as a proxy for the credibility of institutions and property

rights. The bunker regimes scored substantially lower on this measure than did other types of authoritarian regimes or democracies in the region.

7. Karl A. Wittfogel, *Oriental Despotism: the Comparative Study of Total Power* (New Haven, Conn.: Yale University Press, 1957). Although Wittfogel presents the classic argument relating taxation to hydraulic engineering, the extended coastal Sahel of Tunisia was also, like the Nile Valley, a relatively rich tax base.

8. On clandestine Syrian "networks" relating the state to the business community, for instance, see Bassam Haddad, *Business Networks in Syria: The Political Economy of Authoritarian Resilience* (Stanford, Calif.: Stanford University Press, 2012). One chapter's subtitle, "The Bottom Line: Economic Power Bereft of Political Power," summarizes the story of the networks that keep the private sector—and any formal civil society—at bay.

9. HHI, the Herfindahl-Hirschman Index of concentration, is simply the sum of the squares of commercial banks' market shares, ranging from 1, a monopoly, to very small numbers, as in Lebanon.

10. Clement M. Henry, "Tunisia's 'Sweet Little' Regime," in *Worst of the Worst: Dealing with Repressive and Rogue Nations*, ed. Robert Rotberg (Washington, D.C.: Brookings Institution Press, 2007), 300–323.

11. Interview with Dr. Mustapha Nabli, governor, Central Bank of Tunisia, June 20, 2011. For a summary of the family and its holdings, see "Ali Baba Gone, but What About the 40 Thieves?" *The Economist*, January 20, 2011, available at http://www.economist.com/node/17959620?story_id=17959620.

12. See Alan McLean, Scott Shane, and Archie Tse, "Wikileaks: A Selection from the Cache of Diplomatic Dispatches," *New York Times*, November 28, 2011, available at http://www.nytimes.com/interactive/2010/11/28/world/20101128-cables-viewer.html#report/tunisia-09TUNIS492.

13. In 2001 there were seventy-seven NGOs for every 100,000 Tunisians, compared with only twenty-five for the same number of Egyptians. Twenty-one percent of Egyptians used the Internet in 2010, compared with 34 percent of the Tunisians, and 15 percent of the Tunisian population had Facebook, compared with only 4.3 percent of Egyptians. Data sources are Salim Nasr, "Arab Civil Societies and Public Governance Reform," United Nations Development Program, January 2005, available at http://chenry.webhost.utexas.edu/public_html/AUC/civil%20society/salim-nasr-arab-civilsociety.pdf, www.internetworldstats.com; and MENA Facebook Digest online at http://logicks.com/pdf/2010-05-22-MENA_Facebook_Digest.pdf.

14. Note, however, that food prices had skyrocketed in Egypt, too, as documented by Holger Albrecht, "Authoritarian Transformation or Transition from Authoritarianism? Insights on Regime Change in Egypt," in *Arab Spring in Egypt: Revolution and Beyond*, ed. Baghat Korany and Rabab El-Mahdi (Cairo: American University in Cairo Press, 2012), 254.

15. Manfred Halpern, *The Politics of Social Change in the Middle East and North Africa* (Princeton, N.J.: Princeton University Press, 1963).

16. In "The Protesting Middle East," in *Arab Spring in Egypt: Revolution and Beyond*, ed. Baghat Korany and Rabab El-Mahdi (Cairo: American University in Cairo Press, 2012), 7–15, Baghat Korany and Rabab El-Mahdi argue for a "paradigm shift" toward informal politics from below to understand the Arab spring.

17. In "Demystifying the Arab Spring," *Foreign Affairs* 90 (2011): 2–7, Lisa Anderson also compared Tunisia's top-heavy corruption with that of Egypt and Libya and observed that "Tunisia's government institutions were relatively healthy, raising the prospects for a clean, efficient, and technocratic government to replace Ben Ali" (3).

18. Just seizing the assets of the presidential family turned out to be more complex than beheading a snake, however. Ben Ali's three daughters by his first marriage, for instance, had parked their assets with their mother, who was not under investigation. See Slim Bagga, "Indiscretions sur le clan Ben Ali," *L'Audace*, March 17–30, 2011, as reported online, available at http://www.paperblog.fr/4302914/indiscretions-sur-le-clan-ben-ali-source-le-journal-l-audace/.

19. Yossi Shain and Juan J. Linz, eds., *Between States: Interim Governments and Democratic Transitions* (New York: Cambridge University Press, 1995), 94.

20. Interview with Rached Ghannoushi, Tunis, May 24, 2012.

21. On the rise of domestic government debt since 1993, see Samer Soliman, *The Autumn of Dictatorship: Fiscal Crisis and Political Change in Egypt Under Mubarak* (Stanford, Calif.: Stanford University Press, 2011), fig. 4.5, kindle location 2036. Private-sector credit reached 68.4 percent of Tunisia's GDP in 2009 while plummeting to 32 percent of Egypt's, according to the World Bank's World Development Indicators.

22. In Turkey the Special (Islamic) Finance Houses also increased their market share to about 5 percent by 2009.

23. Daria Solovieva, "What Morsi Means for Islamic Banking," *Business Today—Egypt*, March 15, 2012, citing Mohamed Gouda, economics and finance spokesperson for the Muslim Brotherhood.

24. In a recent study of *makhzan* finances, Catherine Graciet and Eric Laurent, *Le roi prédateur: Main basse sur le Maroc* (Paris: Editions du Seuil, 2012), concludes that Mohammed VI has concentrated even more wealth than his father, Hassan II.

25. For the details, see Marina Ottaway, "The New Moroccan Constitution: Real Change or More of the Same?" (Washington, D.C.: Carnegie Endowment for International Peace, June 20, 2011), available at http://carnegieendowment.org/publications/index.cfm?fa=view&id=44731&solr_hilite=Morocco.

26. Bahrain had forty-six NGOs per 100,000 inhabitants, compared with Kuwait's four, the UAE's three, Saudi Arabia's one, Jordan's seventeen, and Morocco's 103, according to Nasr, "Arab Civil Societies and Public Governance Reform."

8

Arab Militaries

ROBERT SPRINGBORG

The decisions by Arab militaries played a crucial role in determining the outcomes of their countries' protest movements. In some cases, such as Egypt and Tunisia, military leaders decided to refrain from using their violent power to crush protesters and instead to jettison the regime's leadership. In others, such as Libya and Syria, despite widespread defections, the militaries remained largely loyal and willing to fight to the end. In Yemen, the military fractured, creating an overlay of armed conflict atop the dynamic of protester-regime. Explaining the variation in the responses of militaries to the outbreak of protest therefore is vital to understanding the overall course of the Arab uprisings.

Unfortunately, the political science literature is poorly equipped to address this pivotal question. The Arab world was a key region for investigating civil-military relations for some two decades following the coup d'état that brought Gamal Abdel Nasser and his Free Officer colleagues to power in Egypt in July 1952.[1] But as military rule continued, analysts of the Arab world increasingly shunned that institution as a subject of study. Research access became increasingly difficult as Arab militaries burrowed further down into their respective political economies, obscuring their continued, powerful role of "ruling, but not governing."[2] In the meantime, the focus of political science literature on civil-military relations shifted from how militaries seize and exercise power to the role of militaries and security services in democratic transitions. Arab states, profoundly nondemocratic, were irrelevant to this new interest in "transitology," so they essentially disappeared from the academic field of civil-military relations and its new concern with civilian oversight and control.[3] Even studies of

Arab authoritarian rule typically tended not to focus on the military.[4] And where academic analysts feared to tread, the U.S. government was equally reticent. Although the Arab world received a disproportionate amount of U.S. funding to promote democracy, it received virtually no support to enhance civilian control of the militaries. The one study of Arab civil-military relations financed before the Arab spring by the United States Agency for International Development (USAID) noted the politically important role of Arab militaries and their absorption of record shares of public budgets but questioned "the ripeness of many countries in the region for major programs in civil-military relations."[5]

Although the study of Arab militaries and their relationship with civilian political orders atrophied after the mid-1970s, investigations of Arab authoritarianism proliferated. One strand of this literature did make the case that a distinctive feature of Middle Eastern authoritarianism was the profound, enduring centralization of power by the military and associated security/intelligence organizations, coupled with the covert penetration of the rest of the state and the society and economy as well. The terms "shadow" and "deep" state," coined to describe this phenomenon with regard to Iraq and Turkey, respectively, refer to this extension into other institutions and arenas by armed forces through informal, clandestine means.[6] So Middle Eastern and especially Arab exceptionalism was a reference not just to its authoritarianism but, at least for some analysts, also to the pervasiveness of subterranean networks of power emanating from coercive agencies.

Despite their concern with shadow or deep states, most analysts shied away from labeling Arab politics as "sultanistic," a concept that incorporates the primary attributes of such states. Max Weber appropriated the term "sultanism" from his reading of Ottoman history to describe personalized, concentrated power heavily dependent on coercion, wherever it might be found.[7] Those studying the Middle East have been less inclined to draw on and elaborate Weber's characterization of sultanism than have specialists in other areas. This understandable reaction has, however, had costs for theorizing about Arab authoritarianism and the role of armed forces in it.

The first book-length effort by contemporary political scientists to develop the concept of sultanism and utilize it to compare contemporary political systems was that by H. E. Chehabi and Juan Linz, published in 1998. Of the six countries they investigated, only one, Iran, was Middle Eastern.[8] According to Chehabi and Linz, the key characteristics of sultanism are blurring the distinction between regime and state, personalism, constitutional hypocrisy, narrow social bases, distorted capitalism, and particularly problematic transitions to democracy. This last criterion is especially germane to the role of militaries in sultanistic regimes. Because of personalistic, top-down control, sultanistic militaries are said to be less likely to harbor reformers than are militaries in other types of authoritarian systems, so the prospects for alliances between reformers within and outside the state are limited.[9] In the preceding year, Latin American specialist Alfred Stepan argued that of the different forms of authoritarian rule, sultanism was the least likely to undergo democratization, but he used only one Middle Eastern example.[10] Linz's 2000 monograph does discuss some Middle Eastern countries, particularly those of the Maghreb, but not in the section on sultanistic regimes, in which he focuses on regimes in South and Central America.[11] Over the past decade, a sprinkling of publications drawing on sultanism appeared, but the only Middle Eastern country that has been consistently analyzed in the monographs and journals in the conceptual framework of sultanism is Iran.[12] In his thoughtful review of Chehabi and Linz's book, M. Crawford Young speculates on the applicability of sultanism, noting several countries in Africa to which it may have or might now apply, though only one of those mentioned, Libya, is Arab.[13] In sum, Middle Eastern scholars stand out among area specialists for paying so little attention to Weber's concept of sultanism.

Paradoxically, if Weber had chosen a term with no Middle Eastern association, it is likely that his analysis of arbitrary, capricious, coercion-based authoritarian rule would have resonated with Middle East specialists. Linz's and Stepan's concentration on the particular challenges facing democratic transitions in sultanistic regimes and the potential for the "capture" of revolutions seems especially apposite in light of the Arab spring:

> The extreme personalism and despotism of a [sultanistic] regime . . . facilitates
> the "capture" of a revolution by groups very close to the old regime . . . [as]
> new leaders, even if they had close links to the regime . . . advance the claim
> that the sultan was responsible for all of the evil.[14]

Egypt after President Hosni Mubarak illustrates both the potential and the limits for such capture. The military high command under Minister of Defense Mohamed Hussein Tantawi constituted itself as the Supreme Council of the Armed Forces (SCAF) and withdrew support from President Mubarak, thus sealing his fate.[15] It then sought to distance itself from the negative aspects of the regime, of which it had been a vital component, while preserving the military's privileged role and even much of the essence of the regime itself. But the Tantawi-led SCAF proved to be so politically maladroit that its continued exercise of power began to threaten the military's institutional interests. This in turn made possible a coalition of "military reformers"—in the sense that their strategy to preserve the status and power of the military was to form a coalition with the most powerful element of the opposition rather than seek to subdue it—led by General Abd al-Fattah al-Sisi and the Muslim Brotherhood. Together they purged Tantawi and the SCAF in August 2012, before going on to impose a new constitution intended to perpetuate their joint rule. On July 3, 2013, Sisi turned on the Brotherhood and seized power for the military anew. General Tantawi's capture strategy had failed because of diminished political capacities due to the longevity of Mubarak's rule, the advanced age, and the political ineptitude of those pursuing the strategy. But younger officers within two years would preserve, even expand, the military's powers.

Other Arab uprisings may not have witnessed such manifest attempts at capture by ancien régime elements, nor have they given rise to strong reformers able and willing to forge coalitions with revolutionaries. Defectors from the Libyan and Syrian officer corps, for example, may have wanted to be reformers, but shorn of command over their units by entrenched despots, they had little leverage. No visible, empowered reform elements have emerged in Bahrain. Those that did in Yemen resulted primarily from external pressure and support orchestrated by Saudi Arabia and the United States. Arab sultanistic regimes have clearly provided little space for reformist coalitions, an attribute inherent in the sultanism model.

The literature on sultanism thus provides suggestive hypotheses to guide research on the role of coercive forces in Arab politics.[16] Narrowly focused on the mode by which power is exercised by a particular type of authoritarian leader, however, it ignores other important and determining political, economic, and even social factors. A comparison of responses by militaries to Arab uprisings, for example, suggests that a political system's degree of institutionalization is a crucial variable. Accordingly, those in Tunisia and Egypt, the two most institutionalized of the republics, behaved markedly differently than did those in the other republics under threat from newly mobilized oppositions. In Tunisia, the military in fact sought to serve as a midwife of democracy, siding with the demonstrators against the security services loyal to President Zine al-Abdine Ben Ali and ultimately moving against the president himself. Then, having power in its hands, the Tunisian

military stood aside to enable the protesters to commence the task of building a new political order. This exemplary behavior resulted from both the
relatively high degree of institutional coherence in Tunisia generally and in
the army specifically, as well as a particular quirk of Ben Ali's brand of sultanism. Neither he nor his predecessor trusted the military, so they based
their coercive power on security and intelligence organizations, ensuring
that the strikingly professionalized military remained small, underequipped,
and under rather distant U.S. tutelage. In contrast, the security and intelligence forces were French trained and equipped, with Ben Ali much more
confident of that country's abiding support for his rule, as indeed turned
out to be the case, as signaled by the French foreign minister's offer in late
December 2010 to beef up those forces against popular protests.[17]

Similar to Ben Ali, Mubarak came to depend more heavily on the security and intelligence services within the Ministry of Interior to subdue
political opposition, but unlike Ben Ali he controlled his military not by
marginalizing it but by showering its officers with direct and indirect economic rewards. So as in Tunisia, the military had institutional interests
apart from those of the president. Security and intelligence organizations
served as the real "sword" of the sultan president and remained loyal to
him to the end, indeed, maybe even past the end.[18] The leadership of the
Muslim Brotherhood appears to believe, for example, that the *fulul*, or remnants of those forces from the Mubarak era, not only provided the organizational resources for the June 2012 presidential campaign of Mubarak
loyalist Ahmed Mohamed Shafik, but then in November and December of
2012 purposefully withdrew their protection of President Mohamed Morsi,
newly ensconced in the presidential palace in Heliopolis, so as to allow the
coalition of secular forces grouped into the National Salvation Front to
bring more direct pressure on him.

Whether true or not, this interpretation suggests that like the military,
the Egyptian security and intelligence forces have institutional interests
in their own right. Because Mubarak had served those interests well, they
stood by him. Unlike the military, which is a much stronger actor, the
Brothers were required to strike a deal with it, and so the security and intelligence forces are now more vulnerable. They feared that the Brothers were
less interested in a deal than in subduing them, so a covert struggle raged.
Whatever the outcome, the very existence of this conflict is suggestive of
the comparative institutionalization of intraregime politics in Egypt.[19]

The coercive forces in other Arab republics were held together by personal loyalties anchored in social forces of tribe, ethnicity, and religion, not

by institutional interests reinforced by professional norms. Those loyalties nevertheless proved to be quite resilient. Yemen's and Libya's armies, much less cohesive and institutionalized than Tunisia's and Egypt's, ultimately did split to some degree under the pressure of demonstrations and then all-out attacks. But the bulk of forces remained loyal to President Ali Abdullah Saleh and Colonel Muammar al-Qaddafi until the former was forced into a compromise and the latter out of his Tripoli bunker and then out of a drainpipe. Essentially extensions of their rulers' households, as reflected in the fact that the rulers' close kin were in key command positions, these militaries at their core were inseparable from the regime and the social force on which it was based. This was the source of both their strength and their weakness, as the Syrian case also demonstrates. President Bashar al-Assad, facing uprisings throughout the length and breadth of his country, could count on his Alawite compatriots but not on regular army units in which Sunni conscripts predominated, even though most officers were Alawites. Such units were typically assigned garrison duties. Increasingly President Assad came to rely for strike forces on the Alawite-dominated air force and elite Alawite brigades, as well as on gangs headed by Alawites, the *shabiha*, in his desperate attempt to subdue the uprising. Sultanic powers, constrained in Egypt and Tunisia by institutionalization, are limited in the other republics by the narrow base of the regime, resting as it does on a particular social force.

Thus far, none of the sultanic kings has faced divisions within his military or security services. The one case of sustained popular pressure on a ruling family, that of Bahrain, did result in conflict between the soft-line crown prince and the hard-line prime minister, but any possibility that the family or military might fracture was preempted by the Saudis' military intervention. The subsequent declared intent to expand the Gulf Cooperation Council (GCC) to include Jordan and Morocco seemed to suggest, among other things, that the Saudis and their Gulf allies were eager to add the substantial weight of those two countries' armed forces to bolster Arab monarchial rule generally. In November 2012, for example, Kuwait reportedly had turned to Jordan for 3,500 security troops to stiffen its own coercive capacities in the face of ongoing protests.[20] Apparently unwilling to place all his trust in Arab military forces, whether his own or others, Sheikh Mohammed bin Zayed al-Nahyan, crown prince of Abu Dhabi, was reported in May 2011 to have paid Erik Prince, founder of the infamous Blackwater Worldwide security firm, $529 million for a battalion of American-led mercenaries.[21] Long a feature of sultanistic militaries, mercenaries are particularly prevalent in the GCC states. The only known use of them in contemporary Arab republics was that by Qaddafi, whose African mercenaries' tenacity may inspire other Arab heads of state, whether presidents or kings, to add foreign mercenaries to their armed forces as means of additional security against coups and control of oppositions.

In sum, the impact of sultanism on Arab civil-military relations was made evident by the Arab uprisings. With the partial exception of Tunisia, nowhere have reformers emerged from within the military or security services to forge coalitions with democratizers. In Egypt, the military and security services moved to secure their own positions. In the other republics challenged by uprisings, the sultanistic control of elite units drawn from the president's own social force remained intact until the bitter end. In the monarchies, the sultanistic methods of control have been strengthened. The proposition that transitions to democracy from sultanism are particularly difficult has been confirmed. Nevertheless, the focus on methods of authoritarian control and their consequences, which is the essence of sultanism, is too narrow to account for the widely varying reactions by military and security forces to the challenges of the Arab uprisings. Other, systemic, factors also need to be taken into account.[22]

Context and Character of Arab Militaries

It may also be useful for "retheorizing" Arab militaries and informing speculation about where they are headed to examine the particular contexts in which they operate and the special features that differentiate the various Arab militaries. The crudest distinction—between monarchies and republics—does differentiate military type, means of control, and political and economic roles to some degree, as reflected by the events of the Arab uprisings. That no monarchial military or security service has turned on its ruler indicates that monarchs are politically stronger than presidents, that their societies are less mobilized, or that the monarchs are better able to control their armed forces.

Leaving aside the first two explanations, the third begs the question of what the differences are in the mechanisms of political control of armed forces. In reality they seem not to be systematic. Even though the GCC monarchies rely more heavily on mercenaries than do republics, neither Morocco nor Jordan do, and Qaddafi's Libya did. Restricting the size of the military as a means of controlling it was true of Tunisia's Ben Ali but is also the case in Morocco and, to a lesser extent, the statelets of the GCC.

That Morocco's and Tunisia's militaries have been comparatively small may reflect their Maghribi location as much as it does a means of control. Counterbalancing strategies are characteristic of both monarchs and presidents, as shown in the parallel structures of military and national guard in Saudi Arabia and in the oversized presidential security forces—the Republican Guards in Egypt and in Saddam Hussein's Iraq. The use of security and intelligence forces as counterbalances to militaries does, however, seem to be more common and important in the republics, as demonstrated by the examples of Tunisia and Egypt, whose forces under Ben Ali and Mubarak came to substantially outnumber military personnel. But the security and intelligence forces of, say, Saudi Arabia, Jordan, and Bahrain also are substantial, suggesting that the difference is a matter of degree. Control through direct command by members of ruling families is exercised in all the monarchies except Morocco and Oman but also has been a feature of the Syrian, Yemeni, and Libyan regimes.

The extensive involvement of foreign militaries in procurement, training, logistics, and maintenance has been true of both regime types, whether the Soviets earlier in Egypt, Syria, Algeria, Iraq, Yemen, and Libya or the United States currently in various monarchies and republics from Morocco to the Gulf. But there is a difference of degree in this area as well, for while the republics, including Egypt, rely on foreign military patrons, they tend to restrict their politically relevant access more than do the monarchies. U.S. military personnel in the GCC states and Jordan, for example, can interact with their local counterparts and visit military installations more or less at will, whereas in Egypt they may not do so without prior notification and clearance from the high command, which is rarely forthcoming, even after Mubarak's removal. The monarchial militaries also tend to have much greater interoperability with U.S. forces than do the republics. The more open embrace of foreign and especially U.S. military patrons in the monarchies reflects their profound dependence for regime survival on those forces, as well as the republics' comparatively greater autonomy and true sovereignty.

Another difference between the monarchial and republican militaries is the latter's greater propensity to be engaged directly in the productive economy, as either a corporate institution or in the form of individual officers (see chapter 7).[23] Egypt's military economy is the largest in the Arab world, but smaller equivalents have also existed in Syria, Sudan, and Iraq. Algerian officers acting individually or in cabals lurk behind their country's hydrocarbon economy. Among the monarchies it is only in Jordan where an institutionalized military economy is emerging along with the networks of economic penetration and influence of the officer corps. The relative absence of militaries from monarchial economies, except in comparatively poor Jordan, reflects both the greater wealth of the monarchies—hence their ability to reward militaries directly rather than through side payments in the broader economy—and their comparatively weaker military institutionalization.

This differentiation of monarchies and republics into subtypes thus reveals some systematic variation in militaries and their control, suggesting that sultanism is shaped by context, whose key element is institutionalization, especially of the military. Praetorian "bunker" republics, "ruled physically or metaphorically from bunkers" because their states "have little if any autonomy from the traditional social forces" that seized control of them at the end of colonial rule, include Algeria, Libya, Syria, Iraq, Yemen, and Sudan.[24] Authority in these states is highly sultanistic in that loyalties are based primarily on family, clan, tribe, and/or sect, rather than on broad horizontal alliances or institutional affiliations. Personalistic control by rulers operates through these primordial loyalties, so shadow states lurk behind institutions, which exercise only nominal authority.

The means of coercion, being the most vital components of these states, are particularly enmeshed in networks of primordial loyalties extending down from president sultans. Typically, their close relatives, preferably sons who are being groomed to inherit power, command key military units, while much of the officer corps is recruited from the dominant vital social force. The professionalization and institutionalization of militaries and intelligence services are limited, so even though those armed forces do not pose threats to the sultan, neither can they as a whole be trusted to implement his orders without attrition due to desertion by those officers and men not members of the dominant social force. But as the Libyan, Syrian, and Yemeni cases attest, the "shadow state" core of those militaries can be expected to remain loyal even when the peripheral components collapse. Because these president sultans anticipate that their narrowly based rule may be challenged by force, they rely more heavily on militaries than on intelligence services, thereby elevating the role and capacities of the former over the latter. So, for example, in Libya, Yemen, and Syria, the three bunker republics that, beginning in 2011, confronted the uprisings, military units commanded by sons or, in the case of Syria, both brother Maher al-Assad and brother-in-law Assef Shawkat, played the most important role in attempting to subdue the opposition. Security and intelligence forces have been virtually absent from those battlefields. In all three cases, desertions have been commonplace by officers and soldiers who are not members of the state's key social force or enmeshed in the president's personal network of control. In Yemen, the highly factionalized tribal system underpinning the military was too fragile to sustain the challenge to Ali Abdullah Saleh, so parts of it broke off, taking their components of the military into opposition with them. These, then, are states that purposely obstruct the growth of institutions in order to preserve the ascriptive norms, personalism, and deep states on which political power rests and through which their sultan presidents rule.

Tunisia and Egypt are "bully" praetorian states in which presidents have based their rule "on the institutional power of the military/security/party apparatus" because these leaders are not drawn from a clearly identified social formation and are not, therefore, "unrepresentative of their relatively homogeneous political communities."[25] Thus the armed forces in Tunisia and Egypt are more institutionalized and have stronger professional commitments and loyalties than do those in the bunker republics. Security and intelligence services have also played relatively greater political roles in Tunisia and Egypt, precisely because their presidents did not anticipate the violent reaction to their rule based on widespread countermobilization within tribally, ethnically, or religiously based social solidarities. These regimes foresaw the potential opposition in these states to be conducted by individuals and groups that did not have preexisting constituencies based in quasi-autonomous social formations that they could mobilize. The means of control exercised by security services were deemed to be adequate to such challenges not underpinned by "organic" social solidarities.

The monarchies are more similar in nature than the republics, so their armed forces also are more alike. But the monarchies can be thought of as being subdivided into two main groups, along with one outlier. Morocco, Jordan, and Kuwait are more liberal, tolerating greater degrees of political expression and competition and possessing more sophisticated political infrastructures than the remaining GCC monarchies, although Oman is a somewhat special case, not being ruled by an extended family, as is the case with the others. The relative institutionalization of the respective militaries varies according to these categories, with those in Morocco and Jordan and, to a substantially lesser extent, Kuwait, being more institutionalized than those in Saudi Arabia, Bahrain, the United Arab Emirates, and Qatar. The Omani military is closer to those of Jordan and Morocco than to those in neighboring GCC countries, in that the ruling family does not control key command positions in the officer corps. Unlike the liberal monarchies, however, Oman has a long and continuing tradition of foreign involvement. The militaries in the four most authoritarian GCC states are, as the sultanistic model would suggest, the most directly subordinate to family rule and have the least developed separate, corporate identity. The officer corps in Morocco and Jordan is both relatively professional and unrelated to the ruling family, whereas in Kuwait the ruling Sabah family controls the military largely through the Ministry of Defense rather than through the officer corps itself and by ensuring that the army remains small.

The Moroccan, and especially the Jordanian, military plays a key role in projecting the identities of their states, such as by participating in peace support activities worldwide, as does the Omani military, though to a lesser extent. Militaries in the more authoritarian monarchies are not used to project national images, a privilege that is reserved for the ruling families.[26] In the event of major challenges to the monarchies, the militaries in Morocco and Jordan would likely seek to save their states if they were in danger of going down along with their monarchs, whereas those in the more authoritarian GCC monarchies might replicate the behavior of militaries in the bunker republics, with the officer relatives of the ruling sultans choosing regime over state, or at least some royals in the regime, thus inviting fragmentation or at least debilitation of the military institution. Kuwait is probably closer to its GCC neighbors in this regard, and the Omani military might be more like those in Morocco and Jordan, choosing to save the state, in part because there is not a sprawling, extended monarchial family to defend.

In sum then, sultanism's impact on the military is attenuated considerably in the bully republics and at least two of the liberal monarchies, in which institutionalization of the military and professionalism of the officer corps is relatively greater than in the bunker republics or the more authoritarian monarchies.

Prospects for Civilian Control of Arab Militaries

Tight and highly personalized control of militaries by executives, whether presidential or monarchial, is ubiquitous in the Arab world. Control based on law and exercised by civilian institutions of the state and civil society is nowhere to be found. *A*, if not *the*, challenge facing the movements that brought about the Arab spring is to establish such control. The relevance of the literature on civil-military relations that focuses primarily on control, especially during democratic transitions, seems limited.[27] Much of it was

based on the experience of Latin America, where the militaries were comparatively highly corporatized and polities had previous experiences with
at least quasi constitutionalism and rule of law, if not established democracy. In most cases, civil societies were considerably more robust than they
have been in the Arab world. Sultanism is conspicuous by its near total
absence in Latin America, as it is in Eastern Europe, the region that, after
Latin America, has contributed most to the literature.

Finally, regional and global effects have been much more favorable for
civilian control of militaries and broader democratization in areas other
than the Arab world. It is the least democratized region and therefore,
by definition, the one with the least civilian control of its militaries. The
regional effect, to the extent that there is one, has been to support authoritarianism and the subordination of civilian politics to the armed forces.
Regional effects in Europe and Latin America, in contrast, were conducive
to the democratic control of armed forces. Various countries on both continents were established democracies or passed through democratic transitions, accompanied by the establishment or reestablishment of civilian
control of militaries. There were, in short, positive models to emulate, to
say nothing of supportive regional norms and institutions, not the least of
which was the European Union in the case of Europe. In Latin America
an energized nongovernmental organization, RESDAL, supported by the
Open Society Foundations and the U.S. Department of Defense's Center for Civil-Military Relations, has played a vital role in raising political
consciousness and providing the necessary information for effective civilian control of the armed forces.[28] As for global effects, the Middle East is
the world's most highly securitized region, as indicated by the amount and
intensity of inter- and intrastate conflict, the existence of terrorism and
counterterrorism, the spending on arms, the presence of external forces,
and the size and roles of armed forces. The most powerful external actors
since World War II, the United Kingdom, the Soviet Union, and the United
States, all emphasized the security dimension in their relations with the
region, as reflected by their greater concern with armed forces than with
civilian political institutions. The United States, the only such external
actor remaining, persists with this approach.

Those who brought about the Arab uprisings cannot, therefore, readily find road maps for the democratic control of armed forces in the existing literature, nor is their task of establishing such control going to be easy.
Regional and global forces are not favorable. Sultanism remains pervasive.
Where institutionalization of the armed forces has occurred and sultanism

constrained, if not transformed, the military institution itself may defend its prerogatives and independence from civilian control, as it seems intent on doing in Egypt and would probably do so in Jordan, Morocco, and Oman if it came to power in any of those countries. Tunisia looks to be the one possible short-term exception, but evidence of the military's behind-the-scenes influence on the emerging political order, combined with the popularity of the institution and tensions between Islamists and secularists, suggests that any bet on a successful transition in Tunisia should at least be hedged. Increasing speculation about the relevance of the Turkish model to civil-military relations, including speculation about the Egyptian military, which is seeking to preserve a guardian role for itself, is not encouraging. It is presented as an alternative to immediate, substantial civilian oversight and control and is projected into the indefinite future, not as a short-term, transitional stage.[29]

Be that as it may, those Arab militaries less penetrated by sultanistic networks may at least entertain ways and means of further enhancing institutionalization and professionalization, which are in turn associated with civilian control, if not necessarily guarantees of it. Ultimately, however, effective control of the armed forces requires civilian authorities to fight for its establishment, no matter how professional the officer corps may be. Whether or not the Arab streets that rose up in 2011 against ruling regimes are ultimately able to accomplish this remains to be seen. The apparent preference of Islamist movements to instrumentalize armed forces to serve their own political interests, as opposed to seeking to subordinate them to institutionalized civilian control, does not bode well. Indeed, Islamists seem to be offering a reprieve to the nondemocratic armed forces just recently threatened by popular uprisings. So the most positive observation possible at this stage is that at least in some countries, including Libya, Tunisia, and Egypt, secular civilian activists are contemplating how to oversee and, indeed, control their militaries. They too, however, are tempted to instrumentalize the armed forces as a tactic in their struggle against Islamists. The Arab world may, therefore, ultimately contribute an interesting, new chapter to the literature on civil military relations.

NOTES

1. See, for example, Amos Perlmutter, *Egypt: The Praetorian State* (New Brunswick, N.J.: Transaction Books, 1974); Anouar Abdel-Malek, *Egypt: Military Society: The Army Regime, the Left, and Social Change Under Nasser* (New York: Vintage Books, 1968); P. J. Vatikiotis, *The Egyptian Army in Politics: Pattern for New Nations?*

(Bloomington: Indiana University Press, 1961); Elizier Be'eri, *Army Officers in Arab Politics and Society* (Jerusalem: Israel Universities Press, 1969); and J. C. Hurewitz, *Middle East Politics: The Military Dimension* (New York: Praeger, 1969).

2. Steven A. Cook, *Ruling but Not Governing: The Military and Political Development in Egypt, Algeria and Turkey* (Baltimore: Johns Hopkins University Press, 2007).

3. Recent anthologies of civilian control of militaries that do not include chapters on the Arab world include Thomas C. Bruneau and Harold Trinkunas, eds., *Global Politics of Defense Reform* (New York: Palgrave Macmillan, 2008); Thomas C. Bruneau and Scott D. Tollefson, eds., *Who Guards the Guardians and How: Democratic Civil-Military Relations* (Austin: University of Texas Press, 2006); Larry Diamond and Marc F. Plattner, eds., *Civil-Military Relations and Democracy* (Baltimore: Johns Hopkins University Press, 1996); and Constantine P. Danopoulos, ed., *The Decline of Military Regimes: The Civilian Influence* (Boulder, Colo.: Westview Press, 1988). Works that do have chapters on the Arab world (Egypt, Sudan, and Algeria) include Constantine P. Danopoulos, ed., *Military Disengagement from Politics* (New York: Routledge, 1988); Constantine P. Danopoulos and Cynthia Watson, *The Political Role of the Military: An International Handbook* (Westport, Conn.: Greenwood Press, 1996); and Gavin Cawthra and Robin Luckham, eds., *Governing Insecurity: Democratic Control of Military and Security Establishments in Transitional Democracies* (London: Zed Books, 2003). Some of the exceptions to the general rule of little academic focus on Arab militaries before 2011 include Cook, *Ruling but Not Governing*; and, in chronological order, Erik B. Riker-Coleman, *Middle Eastern Civil-Military Relations in Global Perspective: Antecedents and Implications of Militarization,* available at http://www.unc.edu/-chaos1/mideast.pdf (1999); Norvell B. De Atkine, "Why Arabs Lose Wars," *Middle East Quarterly* 4, no. 4 (December 1999), available at http://www.meforum.org/441/why-arabs-lose-wars; Mehran Kamrava, "Military Professionalization and Civil-Military Relations in the Middle East," *Political Science Quarterly* 115, no. 1 (2000): 67–92; Barry Rubin, "The Military in Contemporary Middle East Politics," *Middle East Review of International Affairs* 5, no. 1 (2001), available at http://www.gloria-center.org/2001/03/rubin-2001-03-04/; Michael Eisenstadt and Kenneth M. Pollack, "Armies of Snow and Armies of Sand: The Impact of Soviet Military Doctrine on Arab Militaries," *Middle East Journal* 55, no. 4 (2001): 549–78; Kenneth M. Pollack, *Arabs at War: Military Effectiveness, 1948–1991* (Lincoln: University of Nebraska Press, 2002); Risa A. Brooks, "Making Military Might: Why Do States Fail and Succeed?" *International Security* 28, no. 2 (2003): 149–91; Ahmed Hashem, "Saddam Husayn and Civil-Military Relations in Iraq: The Quest for Legitimacy and Power," *Middle East Journal* 57, no. 1 (2003): 9–41; Assaf David and Oren Barak, "How the New Arab Media Challenges the Arab Militaries: The Case of the War Between Israel and Hizbullah in 2006," Policy Brief no. 20 (Washington, D.C.: Middle East Institute, October 2008); and David S. Sorenson, "Civil-Military Relations," in *Interpreting the Middle East,* ed. David S. Sorenson (Boulder, Colo.: Westview Press, 2010),

125–56. The one exception to the rule of little analysis of Arab militaries before 2011 was in the area of security-sector reform, a subfield stimulated in large measure by direct Western involvement with the security sectors in Iraq, Lebanon, and Palestine. See, for example, Yezid Sayigh, "Security Sector Reform in the Arab Region: Challenges to Developing an Indigenous Agenda," ARI Thematic Paper no. 2 (Arab Reform Initiative, December 2007); Yezid Sayigh, "Fixing Broken Windows: Security Sector Reform in Palestine, Lebanon and Yemen," Carnegie Papers no. 17 (Washington, D.C.: Carnegie Endowment for International Peace, October 2009); Ellen Laipson, "Prospects for Security-Sector Reform," *Survival* 49, no. 2 (summer 2007): 99–110; Oren Barak and Assaf David, "The Arab Security Sector: A New Research Agenda for a Neglected Topic," *Armed Forces and Society* 36, no. 5 (November 2009): 804–24; and Basma Kodmani and May Chartouni-Dubarry, "The Security Sector in Arab Countries: Can It Be Reformed?" *IDS Bulletin* 40, no. 2 (January 2009): 96–104.

4. The editor of one such collected work on Arab authoritarianism, for example, writing in its introduction, observed that "although repression . . . may help autocrats survive critical moments, it does not in itself enable them to hold power indefinitely, let alone ensure regime stability. Therefore in this volume we chiefly look at factors 'beyond coercion' to capture the ongoing political dynamics." Oliver Schlumberger, ed., *Debating Arab Authoritarianism: Dynamics and Durability in Nondemocratic Regimes* (Stanford, Calif.: Stanford University Press, 2007).

5. Claude E. Welch Jr. and Johanna Mendelson, "USAID Programs in Civil-Military Relations," prepared for the USAID Center for Democracy and Governance of the Global Bureau, April 1998, 15.

6. Charles Tripp coined the term "shadow state" and has used it extensively in his analyses of Iraq. See, for example, Charles Tripp, *The History of Iraq*, 3rd ed. (Cambridge: Cambridge University Press, 2007); and Charles Tripp, "Militias, Vigilantes, Death Squads," *London Review of Books*, January 25, 2007, 30–33. The literature on the Turkish *derin devlet*, or "deep state," is vast and was recently further augmented as a result of the so-called Ergenekon conspiracy. For analyses that link traditional analyses of the deep state (which in some accounts can be traced back to the Ottomans) to this most recent manifestation, see Maureen Freely, "Why They Killed Hrant Dink," *Index on Censorship* 36, no. 2 (May 2007): 15–29; and Serdar Kaya, "The Rise and Decline of the Turkish 'Deep State': The Ergenekon Case," *Insight Turkey* 11, no. 4 (2009): 99–113.

7. Max Weber, *Economy and Society: An Outline of Interpretive Sociology*, ed. Guenther Roth and Claus Witich (Berkeley: University of California Press, 1978), part 1. For Weber's description of sultanism, which is most succinctly defined as existing "where patrimonial authority lays primary stress on the sphere of arbitrary will free of traditional limitations," see 231–32.

8. H. E. Chehabi and Juan J. Linz, eds., *Sultanistic Regimes* (Baltimore: Johns Hopkins University Press, 1998).

9. Of the Arab upheavals that commenced in December 2010, none resulted in such an alliance that succeeded in gaining power. The militaries in Tunisia and Egypt acted as institutions in removing their respective presidents, while "reformers," maybe more accurately described as defectors, were not decisive in tipping the balance of power away from the state in Libya, Syria, or Yemen.

10. Alfred Stepan, "Democratic Opposition and Democratization Theory," *Government and Opposition* 32, no. 4 (October 1997): 657–78.

11. Juan J. Linz, *Totalitarian and Authoritarian Regimes* (Boulder, Colo.: Lynne Rienner, 2000), especially 144–55.

12. Alexander J. Motyl, "The New Political Regime in Ukraine—Toward Sultanism Yanukovych-Style?" Great Debate Paper no. 10/06 (Maastricht: Cicero Foundation, July 2010); Steven M. Eke and Taras Kuzio, "Sultanism in Eastern Europe: The Socio-Political Roots of Authoritarian Populism in Belarus," *Europe-Asia Studies* 52, no. 3 (May 2000): 523–47; Farid Guliyev, "Post-Soviet Azerbaijan: Transition to Sultanistic Semiauthoritarianism? An Attempt at Conceptualization," *Demokratizatsiya* 13, no. 3 (summer 2005): 393–435; Sara Bjerg Moller, "Backsliding into History: Regime Type and 'Third Wave' Reversals," paper presented at the Mini-APSA conference, New York, April 30, 2010; Gary Dean, "Indonesia's Economic Development in Comparison to South Korea and Taiwan," Okusi Associates, September 1999, available at http://okusi.net/garydean/works/IndEcDev.html; Javier Diez Canseco, "Fujimori: Neo-Liberalism, Neo-Sultanism, and Corruption," Latin American Program Working Paper (Washington, D.C.: Woodrow Wilson International Center for Scholars, spring 2008); Juan Jose Lopez, *Democracy Delayed: The Case of Castro's Cuba* (Baltimore: Johns Hopkins University Press, 2002); Akbar Ganji, "The Struggle Against Sultanism," *Journal of Democracy* 16, no. 4 (October 2005): 38–51; Akbar Ganji, "Rise of the Sultans," *Foreign Affairs*, June 24, 2009, available at http://www.foreignaffairs.com/print/65137.

13. M. Crawford Young, "Resurrecting Sultanism," *Journal of Democracy* 10, no. 3 (July 1999): 165–68.

14. Juan J. Linz and Alfred Stepan, *Problems of Democratic Transition and Consolidation: Southern Europe, South America, and Post-Communist Europe* (Baltimore: Johns Hopkins University Press), 358.

15. This behavior can be seen as an example of the "paradox of the sultan" described by Max Weber. That paradox is that as the sultan relies ever more heavily on the military to subdue his opponents, he steadily empowers the military at his own expense. Weber, *Economy and Society*, 231–32. See also Bryan S. Turner, *Weber and Islam: A Critical Study* (London: Routledge & Kegan Paul, 1974), 80–81, 172–73.

16. The one noteworthy analysis of the Arab spring that draws on the concept is by Jack A. Goldstone, a general theorist of sociopolitical change. See Jack A. Goldstone, "Understanding the Revolutions of 2011: Weakness and Resilience in Middle Eastern Autocracies," *Foreign Affairs* 90, no. 3 (May/June 2011): 8–16. He confidently concludes that "the rule of the sultans is coming to an end" (16).

17. The real "sword" of the sultan president, the security services, thus did remain loyal to him to the end. See Robert Springborg and Clement M. Henry, "Army Guys," *The American Interest* 6, no. 5 (May/June 2011): 14–21.

18. Springborg and Henry, "Army Guys."

19. For a discussion of the relationship between the military and security services in the wake of the uprising, see Tewfick Aclimandos, "Reforming the Egyptian Security Services: A Review of the Press, Conventional Wisdom and Rumours," ARI Thematic Study: Security Sector Reform (Arab Reform Initiative, June 2011), available at http://www.arab-reform.net/spip.php?article4933.

20. Habib Toumi, "Kuwaiti Emir Trashes Talk of Qatari Interference," *Gulfnews.com*, November 7, 2012, available at http://gulfnews.com/news/gulf/kuwait/kuwait-emir-trashes-talk-of-qatari-interference-1.1100777.

21. Mark Mazzetti and Emily B. Hager, "Secret Desert Force Set Up by Blackwater's Founder," *New York Times*, May 14, 2011, 1, available at http://www.nytimes.com/2011/05/15/world/middleeast/15prince.html.

22. Robert Springborg, "Learning from Failure: Egypt," in *The Routledge Handbook of Civil-Military Relations*, ed. Thomas C. Bruneau and Florina Cristiana Matei (London: Routledge, 2013), 93–109.

23. For a brief discussion of what are termed military and officer economies in various Arab countries, see Robert Springborg, "Economic Involvement of Militaries," *International Journal of Middle East Studies* 43, no. 3 (August 2011): 397–99.

24. Clement Moore Henry and Robert Springborg, *Globalization and the Politics of Development in the Middle East* (Cambridge: Cambridge University Press, 2010), 113.

25. Ibid., p. 162.

26. Qatar deployed several hundred special forces troops to Libya to assist in operations against Qaddafi loyalists, an operation for which the ruling al-Thani family claimed primary credit, although it did permit the military's chief of staff, Major General Hamad bin Ali al-Attiya, to make an announcement about Qatar's role in the wake of Qaddafi's demise. See Ian Black, "Qatar Admits Sending Hundreds of Troops to Support Libya Rebels," *The Guardian*, October 26, 2011, available at http://www.guardian.co.uk/world/2011/oct/26/qatar-troops-libya-rebels-support.

27. For an assessment of the causes and consequences of that focus, see Thomas Bruneau and Harold Trinkunas, "Democratization as a Global Phenomenon and Its Impact on Civil-Military Relations," *Democratization* 13, no. 5 (December 2006): 776–90.

28. The RESDAL acronym stands for Red de seguridad y defensa de America Latina, founded in Argentina in the 1990s and now serving as a continentwide coordinator for NGOs working on civil-military relations. See http://www.resdal.org.

29. The Egyptian Supreme Council of the Armed Forces initially put forward a demand for such a guardianship role based on the Turkish model in June 2011, in response to increasing attacks on its continuing political role. See, for example, "Presidential

Candidate Vows to Grant Military Greater Power," *al Masry al Youm*, June 16, 2011, available at http://www.almasryalyoum.com/en/node/468631. It then incorporated into its declaration of constitutional principles, issued in October 2011, clauses that in effect elevated the military above elected authorities and ensured that there could be no effective civilian oversight of the military budget or its operations. These clauses were in turn incorporated into the constitution ratified by a referendum in December 2012.

9

Political Geography

JILLIAN SCHWEDLER AND RYAN KING

The Arab uprisings have spatial dimensions that have not been systematically explored in the flurry of analyses that have emerged since 2011. For example, protest mobilization and police activity are frequently structured by spatial considerations, including the accessibility and visibility of certain locations, the layout of prominent public squares, and the quotidian uses of those spaces. In Cairo, protesters launched the January 25 demonstrations in Tahrir Square in part because of its symbolism as a former site of revolution. But Tahrir Square is also among the most easily accessible spaces in the city, with its wide streets and easy access from multiple directions. Its vast size created, however, challenges for protesters: a gathering of a few thousand could be offset by an even larger expanse of empty space, thus deflating the impact of the protest. Indeed, the revolution gained a toehold that day because more than 75,000 protesters unexpectedly turned out, creating a spectacle of a massive movement that could not be easily denied or repressed. Nonetheless, the impact of these spatial dynamics on the uprisings has received little attention.

Introducing questions of space into analyses of the Arab uprisings also illustrates how massive gatherings of bodies can restructure existing topographies of power and eradicate even the most entrenched symbols and practices of repression and compliance. Although many analyses focus on the arc of the uprisings—their beginning, how they develop, whether mobilization escalates, and when and whether the regime fragments—in this chapter we look instead at the spatial dynamics in order to unpack the revolutionary potential of who is visible (and to whom) and what particular capacities are enabled or foreclosed (for both protesters and state security agencies) as a result of spatial dimensions. We highlight the intersection of the physical characteristics of a space and how space is represented though its meaning and social context. Politics of contention affect, and are affected by, built space, which in turn teaches populations about ordinary realities of representation, inclusivity, and engagement. In this sense, space is not a passive container or set of constraints but an active player in the production of knowledge about politics and its possibilities. Significantly, each of the countries affected by the uprisings had recently adopted massive urban projects catering to global capital and not the needs of the people.[1] The uprisings have attempted, sometimes successfully, a radical reclaiming of public spaces by citizens insisting that their countries belong to them rather than to corrupt and repressive regimes or foreign corporations. Yet scholarly inquiry has largely ignored the effects of a changing urban fabric, instead focusing on the expected stories of democratization and elections.

This chapter first elaborates on the significance of thinking theoretically through the lens of political geography and then examines the spatial dimensions of political contention in broad terms, invoking historical cases from both inside and outside the Middle East. We then turn to empirical cases from the Arab uprisings and conclude by identifying broad patterns in changing global infrastructure throughout the Middle East and related possibilities for future research.

Space and Politics

Until recently, space was treated by scholars as "the dead, the fixed, the undialectical, the immobile." By comparison, time has long has been treated as saturated with "richness, fecundity, life, dialectic."[2] Space has been often treated as an inert container for human activity or a stage on which activities take place. Yet since at least the early 1970s, the work of the Marxist thinker Henri Lefebvre, among others, has demonstrated that space is socially produced through networks of flow among goods, information, and bodies.[3] These insights were not embraced by mainstream social science until recently, even though thinking theoretically about the interplay of space and time helps us draw more compelling narratives about history.[4] Rather than being fixed in physicality, spatial characteristics are constituted by their social context. How can we use these insights in our analyses of the Arab uprisings?

To start, we recognize that the Middle Eastern cityscapes of today are changing to meet the global competition for speed, efficiency, foreign investment, and cosmopolitan tourism. A focus on political geography draws our attention to the spatial and material organizations of international and domestic economic institutions and bureaucracies, the identification of a wide range of constructed boundaries, regulators of flow and exchange, and the patterns of movement in everyday life. Political crises such as the Arab uprisings emerge within and against these topographies of power, yet seldom is attention paid to the ways in which a cityscape invokes and evokes power relations. Examining political geography brings to light enclaves of political and economic privilege and exclusion instead of the more familiar focus on revolutionary master narratives, teleologies of democratic transition, and "life-cycle" stories of the rise and decline of individual movements. If we consider how space and power are interconnected, we will immediately recognize why some spaces are extremely provocative sites for protest and others are not.

Tunisia's Boulevard Bourguiba, for example, is a wide thoroughfare in the heart of Tunis, with one end stretching toward the old casbah district. The boulevard has a wide pedestrian path down the middle, with cafés, stores, benches, and rows of lush trees. It passes in front of the Ministry of the Interior, an institution popularly known as the site of state repression and the headquarters of the secret police. Before the revolution, pedestrians passing in front of that ministry were forbidden to even look at the building.[5] In the days before the regime of President Zine al-Abdine Ben Ali fell on January 14, 2011, protesters packed the streets in front of the building, facing it directly and chanting, "Dégagez!" meaning that the regime should "Go!" Symbolically, the ministry *was* the regime, and tens of thousands of Tunisians packed that boulevard as the central space in the capital from which they demanded that the people reclaim their own country. This simple example illustrates how thinking about space in episodes of contentious politics points to the intertwining of embodied experiences (here, of repression) and power, whether compliance while the regime remained strong or defiance as citizens gathered to urge it to fall.

As Salwa Ismail wrote, "Practices, action, and movement make space lived and, as such, social. Through practices, place is attributed meaning, is rendered social, and at the same time becomes inhabited by power relations."[6] Just as fascist architecture played a central role in rendering the individual minuscule and powerless in the face of a massive and dominating state, some public spaces are intimidating precisely (and perhaps only) because citizens view them as such. Repression and silent forms of violence emanating through space often are not declared, perhaps unnoticed by scholars but well understood by the citizens who move through and across those spaces.

Through space we can also think about the political economy of security and surveillance paradigms and how they are connected to foreign aid, notions of modernity and cosmopolitanism, neoliberal economic projects, and which states (or nonstate groups) are training which security agencies in which countries.[7] Behind the mask of the market, private powers join different aspects of the states in ways that make it virtually impossible to determine who is in charge. As Christopher Parker argued, "State agencies become 'entrepreneurial' in these arrangements by joining forces with, rather than acting as an external source of regulation upon, the private sector."[8] Therefore, rather than thinking of cities as merely spaces in which a concentration of citizens reside (and sometimes protest), we can think of them as assemblages of social, economic, political, geographic, and infrastructural entities that structure everyday practices even as those practices give meaning to those very spaces.[9] Urban spaces include planned and unplanned environments, both of which are marked by locally produced configurations of practice. Indeed, the former is frequently transformed by the latter, for example, when people use spaces in ways not intended by planners. Sometimes the question is not *how* the space is being used but *who* is using it. As Keller Easterling put it, "Some of the most radical changes to the globalizing world are not being written in the language of international law and diplomacy, [but] rather in the spaces of architecture and urbanism. These spaces are creating forms of polity faster than official channels can legislate them."[10]

Globalization has further propelled spatial typologies that are determined in large part by their capacity to conduct flow:

> The capacity for buildings to handle large flows of transient populations and goods is one of the mechanisms of spatial displacement[11] that global capitalism has created as one of its basic infrastructures. Their ability to host crowds, enclose public space and control flow in an artificially controlled environment, as well as their conflictive relationship with the local, qualifies [them] as highly politically charged.[12]

The enclaves of wealth that are formatting cityscapes in the Middle East can be qualified as transformations of the free-trade zone, a sort of meta-infrastructure, that merge park, resort, campus, and corporate headquarters. Corporations that choose to locate branches or headquarters inside such zones "might help their various zone hosts to forge relationships with the International Monetary Fund and the World Bank, and they might provide expertise and support for developing transportation and communication infrastructure."[13] They also necessarily exclude anyone who is "not invited." Even more, these spaces—including free-trade zones and qualified industrial zones—create spaces where "normal" legal codes are not applicable.[14] The widespread adoption of such "free" zones creates new spaces where environmental laws do not apply, taxation is reduced, and manufacturing processes are exempt from the demands of organized labor. For example, King Abdullah Economic City in Saudi Arabia on the Red Sea contains an industrial zone, seaport, residential area, resort, educational zone, and central business district, but the flow of individual bodies into its spaces is not free and open to all comers.[15] These dimensions of space and power have received little consideration in analyses of the Arab uprisings.

Spaces of Protest, Spaces for Repression

Most analyses of the Arab uprisings understandably have emphasized mobilization, but the uprisings themselves also have brought to light the ongoing impact of colonial rule on urban form. Historically, public space in Middle Eastern cities could be found in front of mosques, but urban redevelopment that considered Western-dominated forms brought straight lines and wide streets to cities and new built communities. Strict laws were placed on public gatherings in order to prevent the sorts of popular mobilizations that emerged globally during the late eighteenth and nineteenth centuries.

How else has the "modernization" of cities affected the protest dynamics? Under the commission of Napoleon III, Baron Georges-Eugene Haussmann famously led a massive renovation of Paris in the mid-nineteenth century, eradicating many of the dense and irregular medieval streets and transforming some 60 percent of the city's buildings. His modern Paris consisted of long, straight, and widened boulevards, with new thoroughfares radiating like spokes from massive squares and roundabout traffic circles, such as Charles de Gaulle Square. The renovation also included major infrastructure improvements, including comprehensive sewer systems, gardens (to replace smaller gardens destroyed to widen boulevards), cafés, and shopping districts.[16]

Haussmann also gave the state more ability to quell protests. Broad boulevards enabled the army to easily reach sites of protest, while protesters lost the advantage of their intimate knowledge of dense neighborhoods and mazes of streets and thus their ability to shut down large portions of the city. This spatially imagined modernity—to which Haussmann was only one contributor—was replicated in cities around the world, including those in many colonies.[17] Baghdad's Sadr City, for example, was built with wide roads under Haussmann's brutal axis-cutting principle. Today it is a vast slum for 1.2 million Shia and is effectively off-limits to the army and national government. Paid for by American and European funds in the 1950s, it was one of the largest top-down modernist plans ever to be executed in the Middle East.[18]

During a visit to France in 1867, Egypt's Ismail Pasha greatly admired the changes made to Paris under Haussmann and wanted to remake Cairo in its image. He imagined a "Paris on the Nile," with wide boulevards, palaces, and gardens, and he lavishly spent revenue from Egypt's flourishing cotton industry to finance "parks, open squares, roads, bridges, villas, an opera house, theater, a library, and residential palaces for his European guests."[19] This was the city that foreigners would see, along with scattered monuments of a distant past, sometimes confusingly mixed with contemporary projects.[20] As Nasser Rabbat described it,

> Tahrir Square was not planned as a central square in the city: It grew out of the accumulation of leftover spaces that coalesced over time to form its huge trapezoidal contours. An urban planning failure of sorts, Tahrir Square holds in its unwieldy open span and its hodgepodge of built edges a key to understanding the modern history of Cairo—and, by extension, Egypt.[21]

Clearly, topographies embody power and create possibilities and constraints for both mobilization and policing. By 2011, after all of Tahrir's renovations over the years, some twenty-three streets and two bridges led to the square. But control of public spaces is not a problem that begins only when protesters attempt to congregate there; indeed, spaces are too often considered mere objects (or volumes that can be filled) rather than "actors with agency or temperament."[22] In practice, spaces are never empty of power. Practical access is crucial, but as Easterling explained, "Each topology [of space] possesses a quotient of aggression, submission, violence, resilience or exclusivity immanent in its arrangement."[23] These topographies are learned by populations, whose activities within and across these spaces sometimes challenge and sometimes reinforce power dynamics. Wakalat Street in western Amman, for example, was envisioned as an open-air pedestrian shopping mall where citizens would stroll, relax, and shop. But when the "wrong sort" of Amman residents—working class and youths rather than upscale cosmopolitan elites—began to congregate along the street and relax on benches, those benches and other places to sit were quickly removed.[24]

The uprisings in Tunisia showed that spatial dimensions and their symbolic power were not limited to urban centers. The protests that led to Ben Ali's departure began weeks before the regime's overthrow as protesters gathered in a small town south of the capital and, for several weeks, spread to other towns where economic grievances were acute. The Tunisian police struggled to put down protests in multiple locales for more than two weeks before crowds in Tunis even mobilized.[25] In those peripheral towns, the demonstrations often centered on public squares or main intersections, where a single pile of burning tires could shut down traffic in all directions. Policing in smaller towns might at first seem to be a simpler affair than in major urban centers, given the smaller size of crowds and area to be policed. But the protesters' deep local knowledge—and their personal connections and network ties within the community as a whole—can create significant obstacles for police when faced with repressing protesters who are personally known to the whole community. Even minor instances of repression can outrage an entire community and send multitudes into the streets. The scholarly focus on large-scale uprisings in major urban centers, therefore, can sometimes overlook crucial dynamics in early or spatially peripheral protests. As James Holston noted, "Insurgent citizenships may utilize central civic space and even overrun the center," but they are typically manifestations of outrage that began in peripheries of populations excluded from spaces or from access to state power.[26] As important as the center is to a gathering of citizens to gain national (and international) attention, simmering issues frequently occur in the peripheries—in urban peripheries, small towns, and rural areas.

One common tactic of protest policing is to deploy police who come from other regions so that they will not be known to the protesters and thus will be less hesitant to use severe force if ordered to do so. The Royal Guard in Jordan, for example, is made up of Bedouins loyal to the monarchy who also hail from outside the locales where they need to be the most repressive.[27] Many urban centers typically have less tightly knit communities than do small towns and rural areas, and police frequently portray protesters as outside agitators who have come from elsewhere to bring unrest to local neighborhoods. These charges serve to keep citizens or, more specifically, the middle class aspiring to elite status, from sympathizing with the dissenters.

Spatial dimensions of protest policing often entail a strong class dimension. In affluent neighborhoods, where embassies, foreigners, and upper classes reside in grand apartment buildings and villas, police strive to prevent protesters from mobilizing at all. In poorer neighborhoods, repression is less visible to anyone outside the community. Many planned protests, particularly those in visible locales or wealthier neighborhoods, have a higher obstacle to mobilization because they will need not only to get people out and onto the streets but also to arrive at the same location at around the same time. But when these mobilizations do take place, they can be more threatening to the regime. For example, Bahrain's mobilization in Pearl Square, a roundabout in the capital of Manama, was the site of a major uprising in 2011 that continued into 2012. Although the protesters were able to occupy the grassy parklike lands surrounding the huge monument at the square's center, they also were severely exposed. While the repression was rapid once the regime made that decision, it was also highly visible. Criticism flowed in internationally, including a firm but constrained rebuke by U.S. President Barak Obama during his May 19, 2011, address on the Arab uprisings. The decision by the regime in Bahrain to disassemble the Pearl Square monument in late 2011 was a drastic attempt to control the representation of space. Pearl Square had become a symbol for the mobilization, and even coins bearing its image were removed from circulation, with protesters stenciling the image on walls in acts of defiance. Indeed, destroying the monument itself seems only to have enhanced its symbolic weight.

The Arab uprisings overall have been unprecedented in their national and international visibility, due to the presence of al-Jazeera and other media and the ubiquitous use of cell phone cameras to record events. With these media immediately accessible to many protesters, participants have become narrators operating in a new social space, a networked space with a broad reach beyond physical space. Through these media, they can also "alter, instantiate and disrupt geographies of power" and share those efforts with networked communities.[28] The ability to make images widely accessible through the Internet allows them to obtain currency as they rapidly circulate.[29] This newfound visibility enables the protesters to convey their experiences and perceptions to a national audience outside the protest site, and it can also affect how the police respond. The local becomes national, but both are visible and accessible internationally. That is, Egyptians across the nation were watching what was happening in Tahrir Square, even when their own local (and often substantial) mobilizations received scant media attention. Instant communication outpaced the regime's administration of fear, with atrocities and triumphs shared in a way that transcended spatial limitations before the technological revolution.[30] This complex conception of space and connectivity allows us to sidestep the narrative that social media served only to facilitate the coordination of the uprisings and instead consider how technology mediated the protesters' experiences and how it facilitated the disruptions of existing topographies of power.

Egypt

The organizers of Egypt's January 25 protest knew they had to outmaneuver the Ministry of Interior. "We had to find a way to prevent security from making their cordon and stopping us," said Basem Kamel, an architect and core planner of the initial protest. Although they have received little attention, the organizers' spatial strategies played a great role in the initial protests. The organizers chose twenty protest sites, mostly near mosques and in working-class neighborhoods, and announced them via social media to others who would facilitate the organization on the ground. The protests were planned for January 25, a national holiday celebrating Egypt's police force. The planners hoped that multiple protests would overextend the police, enabling at least some protesters to reach Tahrir Square. They also planned, however, a twenty-first protest that was not announced on the Internet. This protest was to begin in front of the Hayiss Sweet Shop in the Bulaq al-Dakrour neighborhood, a poor area where Internet connectivity is extremely low. With its unpaved winding roads and muddy alleyways, it was a surprising location for a protest and a difficult place to police. Although each of the twenty announced protests was, unsurprisingly, confronted by thousands of police, the crowd of roughly three hundred that formed in front of the sweet shop in Bulaq encountered no police resistance. Years of neglect by the regime and virtually no police presence "prompted neighborhood residents to stream by the hundreds out of the neighborhood's cramped alleys, swelling the crowd into the thousands."[31] As the crowd began to march toward Tahrir, they were powerful enough to deter the few police they encountered. The spatial organization of Tahrir then facilitated their arrival. "They poured into the square from the various boulevards connecting it to its venerable surrounding neighborhoods—thus repurposing the Haussmannian axes as a network of active linkages."[32]

The Bulaq group was the only one of the original protests to arrive in Tahrir. Others later joined them in smaller groups, and together they were able to occupy the space until midnight.

Compared with Tahrir and with many wealthy, planned neighborhoods, Bulaq al-Dakrour is a very different space in terms of structure, class, global connections, and residents' daily movements. Since the 1990s, central Cairo has undergone extreme "reordering" to generate good business climates, tourist attractions, and neat and ordered apartments for wealthy Egyptians.[33] Not all of central Cairo has undergone such reconstruction, of course, but Tahrir has certainly been a site of control and transformation, as the seemingly endless renovation of the square (and the subway station underneath) illustrates. While the area is largely a lower-middle-class neighborhood of coffee shops, low-end clothing stores, book stores, and fast-food restaurants, it is also the site of major government buildings, foreign embassies, the (now burned) headquarters of the National Democratic Party, and the Egyptian National Museum, which houses the King Tut treasures, among others. Even before the January 25 demonstrations, Tahrir was a place of contestation between the regime's desired image of a vibrant modern square, on the one hand, and the practical space in which working-class Cairenes moved daily, on the other. At various times the "public" spaces surrounding the square were surrounded by fences designed to keep out the public—or, at least, the kind of public that the state deemed as either a nuisance or threatening. In this sense, one of the most remarkable outcomes of the Arab uprisings has been the attempt to reclaim public spaces throughout the region as spaces that the public controls, owns, reshapes, and utilizes as they wish. These attempts have not always been successful, but they illustrate citizens' efforts to wrench control from local police (and the drug and extortion rackets they frequently operate). The spread of revolutionary graffiti and artwork in Tunisia and Egypt after their uprisings, for example, illustrates a further reclaiming of public space from repressive state control.

Tahrir (Liberation) Square was named by President Gamal Abdel Nasser to commemorate the 1952 liberation of Egypt from the monarchy that was propped up by Great Britain. It is surrounded by structures that present a narrative of Egyptian history supporting the legitimacy of the regime:

> To the south of the square stands the Mugamma', a bulky, Soviet-style structure that has long been a symbol of Egypt's monumental bureaucracy. Overlooking Tahrir Square on the west are the headquarters of the Arab League, with

its Islamic architectural motifs, and the former Hilton, the city's first modern hotel. Just north of the hotel lies the salmon-colored Egyptian Museum and, behind it, the headquarters for Mr. Mubarak's National Democratic Party, with its monotonous Modernist facade left charred by a fire set during this year's protests. . . . The square's geography and structures embody the shifting political currents of modern Egypt as it encountered colonialism, modernism, Pan Arabism, Socialism and Neoliberalism.[34]

Tahrir thus narrates a multilayered history of renewal and triumph at the same time that it embodies the oppressive script of the Mubarak regime. Its planned central square and wide boulevards stand in stark contrast to neighborhoods like Bulaq, which were created by local needs and practices and neglected by the central state. Bulaq is adjacent to the affluent neighborhoods of Doqqi to the east and Muhandissin to the north. Neighborhoods like Bulaq are described as *ashwa'iyyat*, meaning "haphazard," for its miscellaneous urban forms, compared with the "modern" wide boulevards of central Cairo. Indeed, "certain spatial and social characteristics of the quarter, as well as their symbolic investment, produced the effects of separation and division" from wealthy but adjacent neighborhoods.[35] Railroad tracks sever it from surrounding neighborhoods, with the waste-filled Zumor canal also running parallel to the railroad on the eastern border. Three narrow bridges cross the canal, all of which are in need of repair. The borders of the area are under police surveillance to monitor "crossings to the other side" and execute "stop-and-question policies" that seriously "inhibit the mobility of a considerable segment of the population."[36] A high fence along portions of its eastern border further ensures its exclusion from affluent Doqqi. Such deliberate spatial divisions make it unlikely that wealthier Egyptians or even the most curious tourists would wander into its streets. Taxi drivers are reluctant to accept fares into Bulaq; as one resident put it, "Here, the train line separates two worlds, here is one world [Bulaq] and there is another [the outside]."[37] Only one boulevard is paved. Water, electricity, and sewage systems are unevenly distributed; there are no public high schools; and most residents participate in the informal economy. In practice, Bulaq functions as an internment camp.

Neighborhoods like Bulaq are common globally as transitory arrival spaces, often described as slums, shantytowns, urban villages, or ethnic districts. Such labels symbolically construct the enclaves as "static appendages, cancerous growths on an otherwise healthy city" and deny them the vibrancy of the lived and practiced spaces that they are.[38] They are peripheral to the regime and its sanctioned economy, even though they may be centrally located. *Ashwa'iyyat* also are aspirational neighborhoods filled with people looking to improve their lives but frustrated with a state that appears distant and inaccessible except in its practices of surveillance. If the "modern" representation of space emphasizes the open and visible, lacking secrets and mysteries, then the *ashwa'iyyat* are the sites of crime, backwardness, drugs, and decay—shadowy and "undeveloped" spaces in need of isolation and harsh control. Internationally, such neighborhoods have been portrayed as "inhuman, problematic, concentrations of immigrants, unemployed, archaic behavior, tribal conflict, religious backwardness, and so on."[39] Residents are treated uniformly as a plague to be contained and controlled.

The spatial dynamics of the January 25 protests that started Egypt's revolution demonstrate that development priorities and their articulation in spatial and class terms are fundamental to questions of the exclusion and isolation of citizens from a regime, a formal economy, or other nodes of power. Most analyses of the Arab uprisings neglect these issues. Particularly surprising is the lack of attention to spatial dynamics in the social movement analyses, as certain of the dynamics discussed earlier would fit easily into analyses of political opportunity structures and resource mobilization. Despite the flood of commentary that followed the January 25 revolution focused on the role of personal technology and social networks as central to the success of the protests—specifically, smart phones that connected protesters to Facebook, Twitter, and YouTube—the economic underpinnings of the protests received little attention. Scholars, however, had been documenting the escalating labor protests and the ways in which spatial divisions among classes were deepening.[40] For example, in early 2011 Egypt was experiencing a severe water crisis, with reserves well below the UN water poverty line of one thousand cubic meters of water per person a year.[41] While neighborhoods like Bulaq suffered from severe shortages, water flowed uninterrupted to the paying customers of the gated communities and elite neighborhoods, with names like Dreamland, Utopia, and Beverly Hills, that stretched far into the desert.

To be sure, numerous plans to advance a radical respatialization of Cairo that exacerbate exclusions have been adopted repeatedly over the decades.[42] In 2008, the Egyptian government began promoting the "Cairo 2050" plan designed collaboratively by the General Organization for Physical Planning, the Ministry of Housing Planning, the United Nations Development Program, the United Nations Human Settlement Program, the World Bank, the German Society for International Cooperation, and the Japan International Cooperation Agency.[43] The plan called for the enormous privatization of spaces and services to make Cairo

> a city of international standards, . . . [w]ith skyscrapers and luxury developments replacing all the informal neighborhoods, and their working class residents shunted to the desert. The busy, historic heart of Cairo, home to plenty of crumbling, informal housing of its own, would be remade as a sanitized tourist park.[44]

Postrevolutionary Egypt needed a reimagining of the protesters' demands in order to retain these plans for a new Cairo while also embracing the spirit of the revolution. Recognizing that the protesters largely suffered from such megaprojects, the new narrative portrayed the January 25 protesters as romantic and brave patriots but treated ongoing protesters as foreign-supported thugs and hoodlums intent on threatening Egypt's stability.[45] This reframing of the protesters—many of whom maintained the early demands that their economic grievances be redressed—enabled the emerging political elite to carry the mantle of the revolution while assuaging the fears of the business elite and foreign investors that their projects were in peril. Construction on many major projects resumed within months, if not weeks, signaling to many lower-class Cairenes that the "revolution" would not redraw the lines of access to economic privilege. The Khufu Plaza Parks Project, for example, planned for the site of the critical twenty-first protest, "aims to create a wide boulevard of parks and multilane avenues that would cut through the informal [neighborhood] of Boulaq el Dakrour."[46]

Jordan

Many analyses of the Arab uprisings describe Jordan's regime as having largely evaded the Arab uprisings because it has not been threatened by massive, nationwide demonstrations. While protesters have not coalesced into a unified movement, the regime nevertheless has felt considerable pressure from a diverse range of domestic groups and from the conflict in Syria to the north, particularly the massive flow of refugees into Jordan. But Jordan has not been untouched by the uprisings. While its trajectory does not neatly parallel that of Egypt, Jordan has nevertheless experienced a set of substantive reforms that provide a richer context for understanding certain dimensions of the protests that have escalated since 2011.

The most significant developments in the capital city of Amman have emerged since the late 1990s, as the Hashemite Kingdom has moved toward neoliberalism and the reconstruction of the city that such economic reforms require.[47] Vast parts of western Amman are hardly recognizable from year to year, while most of eastern Amman (as well as the more working-class neighborhoods of western Amman) remains characterized by winding streets on steep hills, pedestrian staircases, and few wide boulevards. Economic reform is being applied spatially through the creation of new sites of production and consumption that generate new patterns of work and leisure, while the city "is being remade and presented to investors as a new city that conforms to [the] globalized benchmarks" of speed and high technology.[48] Networks of highways, tunnels, and bridges have been restructured in a way that advances global connections.

A narrative of the inevitability of Hashemite rule has been built directly into the cityscape of Amman in projects such as the Abdali urban regeneration project and the King Hussein Gardens, which aggressively promote the idea that the regime is the forebear of modernization. Meanwhile, cities and towns in the periphery are largely excluded from this modernization and have seen the emergence of new forms of personal rule.[49] Gated communities, expensive restaurants, and tourist attractions are creating enclaves that bypass large swaths of Amman itself, bringing with them a new type of citizen: the global Jordanian. These enclaves operate explicitly on the basis of inclusion and exclusion and appeal to certain utopian sentiments in their advertising as a lifestyle and available for purchase. Gated communities with names like Royal Village and Greenland offer an idealized vision for living, while office space and high-rise residences operate on a plane that is spatially well above the street. The cosmopolitan can "live 'above' the city in gated realities."[50]

Yet this cosmopolitan, global, and neoliberal Amman is presented as merely the present moment in a seamless history. Inside the King Hussein Gardens is a half-kilometer monument of panels created by artists from Jordan, Syria, and Iraq that depict various eras of Jordan's history, from its pre-Islamic heritage of the Neolithic Age and the Iron Age to the present. The monument concludes in "a lesson of Hashemite inevitability featuring portraits of the monarchs and scenes of a diverse, yet united citizenry bound by the prosperity and stability it has enjoyed under the kings' leadership."[51] Jordan's history has unfolded exactly as it should have. Heritage tourism in Amman has been funded and encouraged by organizations such as the World Bank, USAID, and the Japanese International Cooperation

Agency, which have identified urban heritage as important to the generation of tourism.[52]

As did the Egyptian regime, Jordan's regime has prioritized the reshaping of certain spaces but neglected others while facilitating narratives of
national glory and regime accomplishments. But these spaces provide
more than a mere background or set of physical locations (or containers)
in which protests might be organized. Protests in certain spaces are tolerated more than in others not because they are more or less disruptive
but largely because not all are equally threatening to the regime. To understand why this is the case—how a few hundred protesters can be far more
threatening than a massive gathering of ten thousand or more—we look at
the differential value of particular spaces to the regime and to its image of
its own historical inevitability. Compared with that of other Arab states,
Jordan has a long history of protest activities characterized by relatively
few violent clashes with security agencies. Protests increased throughout
Jordan with the outbreak of the uprisings elsewhere in 2011, but the protesters largely failed to cohere into a single movement.[53] In March 2011,
however, the Darak (gendarmarie) police turned violent against a peaceful protest of no more than a few hundred. How can this uncharacteristic
response be explained?

The events in question took place on March 25, when a few hundred
protesters clashed with police on the second day of a planned sit-in outside the Ministry of the Interior. The protesters, who called themselves the
March 24 Youth (marking the first day of the protest), had been holding
Jordanian flags and donning the red-and-white kaffiyehs that signified
Jordanian national identity. They hoped that their expressed patriotism
might deflate the police response and allow them to establish an indefinite
camp, Tahrir style, at this major traffic circle. The first day was relatively
peaceful, although a "loyalty march" had arrived and began chanting and
signing patriotic songs while expressing support for the king. Overnight
the two camps remained relatively calm, though by morning the tension
began to escalate. The loyalty march participants began to broadcast music
while the March 24 Youth were performing their morning prayers, an
extreme provocation because playing music during prayer is forbidden. By
lunchtime the second day, the Darak forces, along with plainclothes thugs
(*baltajiyya*) used batons, pipes, and other hard objects against the protesters, violently dispersing them. While attempting to flee, many protesters
were trapped by the barricades and fences that had been rapidly assembled
to constrain them. Images and videos of the police response were widely

circulated on the Internet. In the melee, hundreds were injured and one Jordanian was killed.[54]

Compared with Tunisia, Libya, Syria, and even Egypt, Jordan is unquestionably far more liberal and tolerant of political dissent and far less prone to the excessive use of force in repressing political protests. But describing Jordan as relatively open compared with those states fails to explain the variation in why some protests are tolerated and contained and others are quickly repressed. The March 24 Youth had called for an indefinite sit-in, Tahrir style, and had arrived with tents along with placards. The regime routinely tolerated demonstrations of limited duration, but it rejected an ongoing occupation. The sit-in clearly crossed a line. In addition, the Jordanian regime appears to prefer protests organized by known groups, such as the Muslim Brotherhood, political parties, professional associations, legal nongovernmental organizations, and so on. The March 24 Youth, however, were largely unaffiliated activists, hardly the usual suspects and thus unfamiliar to the security services.

But space proved to be among the most significant factors. The Ministry of the Interior had never been a common site for political protest, so holding an event there departed significantly from early practice. Common locations over the years (as well as since the outbreak of the Arab uprisings) have included the parliament, the prime minister's office, and the professional associations complex, as well as refugee camps and university campuses. The protesters were few enough in number that it is not even clear that they would have disrupted traffic significantly if the police had not cordoned off the square by the second day. The protesters were not calling for the overthrow of the regime; indeed, they waved Jordanian flags and framed their claims around love of the country, avoiding direct criticism of the monarchy.

The location of the Ministry of the Interior also may have been highly provocative, given that its sister institution in Tunisia had been a central location for the mobilization just two months earlier. While the Jordanian regime cherished the image of its friendly police passing out water to protesters who chatted idly with officers, a protest in front of Jordan's Ministry of the Interior was too provocative for the regime to tolerate.

Conclusion

As Max Page pointed out, "A protest can succeed only . . . if it defies the regime by occupying space usually denied it, or occupies it in a way that transforms the place's meaning."[55] Egypt's January 25 revolution accomplished precisely such a repurposing of Tahrir Square, even if only temporarily: struggles over the future of that space and its meaning continue to this day. Jordan's March 24 protest did not.

In this chapter, we tried to demonstrate that exploring various spatial dynamics of the Arab uprisings brings to light interesting variations within cases while offering a richer framework for understanding why and how the uprisings emerged where and when they did, as well as why the regimes responded in such a wide variety of ways. Incorporating political geography into analyses does not answer all questions, but it helps explore a variety of questions salient to the Arab uprisings: Why do some mobilizations begin in the periphery before moving toward the center? How to economic development programs set the stage for dislocations, exclusions, and other sorts of divisions between segments of the population that might otherwise interact directly? How do social media or other new technologies create new spaces for mobilization, reduce distances between physical spaces, and forge entirely new notions of solidarity, coexistence, or citizenship? How are the formations of new subjectivities connected to space? And how do all these processes and practices help explain the specific dynamics of protest in diverse settings?

New technologies, for example, have enlarged the potential of a space beyond its physical capacity. The space of Tahrir could be understood in new ways, as the people standing in it wanted to understand it, connecting and communicating with other people but always returning to the physicality of those individuals putting aligning bodies in a particular space with the attendant risks of doing so.[56] As the world watched the uprisings in real time, we understood that our sense of space was altered: we could share the tensions and elations of those on the ground, and we understood that the massive gathering of Egyptians in Tahrir Square (and elsewhere) represented a seminal moment in the politics of the Middle East. Attention to political geography, we argue, will enrich our understanding of these varied uprisings while also expanding our understanding of the dynamics of politics.

NOTES

1. These projects, variously described as structural adjustment programs, the Washington Consensus, or (more recently) neoliberalism, have been carefully studied for their impact on national economies, but seldom has attention been given to the ways in which they often fundamentally restructure urban and even peripheral

spaces. For exceptions, see Diane Singerman and Paul Amar, *Cairo Cosmopolitan: Politics, Culture, and Urban Space in the New Globalized Middle East* (Cairo: American University of Cairo Press, 2009); Christopher Parker, "Tunnel-Bypasses and Minarets of Capitalism: Amman as Neoliberal Assemblage," *Political Geography* 28, no. 2 (2009): 110–20; Jillian Schwedler, "The Political Geography of Protest in Neoliberal Jordan," *Middle East Critique* 21, no. 3 (2012): 259–70.

2. Michel Foucault and Paul Rabinow, *The Foucault Reader* (New York: Pantheon, 1984), 70.

3. Henri Lefebvre, *The Production of Space* (Oxford: Basic Blackwell, 1991).

4. Edward W. Soja, *Postmodern Geographies: The Reassertion of Space in Critical Social Theory* (London: Verso, 1989).

5. Laryssa Chomiak, "The Making of a Revolution in Tunisia," *Middle East Law and Governance* 3, no. 2 (2011): 68–83.

6. Salwa Ismail, *Political Life in Cairo's New Quarters: Encountering the Everyday State* (Minneapolis: University of Minnesota Press, 2006), xxxvi.

7. Jillian Schwedler, "Spatial Dynamics of the Arab Uprisings," *PS* 46, no. 2 (2013): 230–34.

8. Parker, "Tunnel-Bypasses and Minarets of Capitalism," 114.

9. Stan Allen, "Urbanism in the Plural: The Information Thread," in *Fast-Forward Urbanism: Rethinking Architecture's Engagement with the City*, ed. Dana Cuff and Roger Sherman (Princeton, N.J.: Princeton Architectural Press, 2011), 36–61.

10. Keller Easterling, "Active Forms," in *Fast-Forward Urbanism: Rethinking Architecture's Engagement with the City*, ed. Dana Cuff and Roger Sherman (Princeton, N.J.: Princeton Architectural Press, 2011), 210.

11. The phrase "spatial displacement" is borrowed from David Harvey, *The History of Postmodernity: An Inquiry into the Origins of Cultural Change* (London: Blackwell, 1989).

12. Alejandro Zaera Polo, "The Politics of the Envelope: A Political Critique of Materialism," *Volume* 17 (2008): 82.

13. Keller Easterling, "Zone: The Spatial Softwares of Extrastatecraft," *Places Design Observer*, June 6, 2012, 9.

14. Pete Moore, *Doing Business with the State: Politics and Economic Crisis in Jordan and Kuwait* (New York: Cambridge University Press, 2005); also Aihwa Ong, *Neoliberalism as Exception: Mutations in Citizenship and Sovereignty* (Durham, N.C.: Duke University Press, 2006).

15. Todd Reisz, "Pipe Dreams and Real Deals," *Volume* 34 (2012): 46–51.

16. David H. Pinkney, *Napoleon III and the Rebuilding of Paris* (Princeton, N.J.: Princeton University Press, 1958).

17. Timothy Mitchell, *Colonizing Egypt* (Cambridge: Cambridge University Press, 1991).

18. Wouter Vanstiphout, "People vs Planners," lecture. 2067: The Indesem Explores the Future of Architecture. (Amsterdam: Archis, 2007), 130–41, available at http://

find.lib.uts.edu.au/;jsessionid=4293CB9D7F692482A8572151ECB9DAF5?R=OPAC_b2712843.

19. Farha Ghannam, *Remaking the Modern: Space, Relocation, and the Politics of Identity in a Global Cairo* (Berkeley: University of California Press, 2002), 27.

20. Janet Abu-Lughod, *Cairo: 1001 Years of the City Victorious* (Princeton, N.J.: Princeton University Press, 1971), 98–111.

21. Nasser Rabbat, "Circling the Square: Architecture and Revolution in Cairo," *Artforum* 49 (April 2011): 184.

22. Easterling, "Active Forms," 211.

23. Ibid., 210–25.

24. Jillian Schwedler, "Amman Cosmopolitan: Spaces and Practices of Aspiration and Consumption," *Comparative Studies of South Asia, Africa and the Middle East* 30, no. 3 (2010): 947–62.

25. Laryssa Chomiak and Jillian Schwedler, "Le Kef Is Still on Fire: A Mountaintop View of the Anniversary of the Tunisian Revolution," *Jadaliyya*, January 19, 2012, available at http://www.jadaliyya.com/pages/index/4067/le-kef-is-still-on-fire_a-mountaintop-view-of-the.

26. James Holston, *Insurgent Citizenship: Disjunctions of Democracy and Insurgency in Brazil* (Princeton, N.J.: Princeton University Press, 2007).

27. Joseph Massad, *Colonial Effects: The Making of National Identity in Jordan* (New York: Columbia University Press, 2001).

28. Julie Cohen, "Cyberspace as/and Space," *Columbia Law Review* 107, no. 1 (2007): 210–56.

29. David Joselit, *After Art* (Princeton, N.J.: Princeton University Press, 2012).

30. Paul Virilio, *The Administration of Fear*, trans. Ames Hodges, Semiotext(e)/Interventions (Cambridge, Mass.: MIT Press, 2012).

31. Charles Levinson and Margaret Corker, "The Secret Rally That Sparked an Uprising," *Wall Street Journal*, February 11, 2011.

32. Rabbat, "Circling the Square," 191.

33. Singerman and Amar, *Cairo Cosmopolitan*.

34. Nezar Al Sayyad, "Cairo's Roundabout Revolution," *New York Times*, April 13, 2011.

35. Ismail, *Political Life in Cairo's New Quarters*, 7.

36. Ibid., 24.

37. Ibid., 18.

38. Doug Saunders, *Arrival City: How the Largest Migration in History Is Reshaping Our World* (New York: Vintage Books, 2010), 19.

39. Vanstiphout, "People vs Planners," 140.

40. Joel Beinin and Hossam Hamalawy, "Egyptian Textile Workers Confront the New Economic Order," Middle East Report online, March 25, 2007, available at http://www.merip.org/mero/mero032507; Singerman and Amar, *Cairo Cosmopolitan*.

41. Karin Piper, "Revolution of the Thirsty," *Egypt's Arab Spring: Places: Design Observer*, July 12, 2012, available at http://places.designobserve.com/feature/egypt-revolution-of-the-thirsty/34318/.

42. Timothy Mitchell, *Rule of Experts: Egypt, Techno-Politics, Modernity* (Berkeley: University of California Press, 2002).

43. Nada Tarboush, "Cairo 2050: Urban Dream or Modernist Delusion?" *Journal of International Affairs* 65, no. 2 (spring 2012): 171–86.

44. Frederick Dekantel, "2050 or Bust: On Urban Planning in the Egyptian Desert," *LA Review of Books*, November 16, 2011.

45. Paul Amar, "Egypt After Mubarak," *The Nation*, May 23, 2011, available at http://www.thenation.com/article/160439/egypt-after-mubarak.

46. Tarboush, "Cairo 2050," 176.

47. Nabil I. Abu-Dayyeh, "Persisting Visions: Plans for a Modern Arab Capital, Amman 1955–2002," *Planning Perspectives* 19 (2004): 79–110.

48. Parker, "Tunnel-Bypasses and Minarets of Capitalism," 110; Schwedler, "Amman Cosmopolitan."

49. Malika Bouziane, "The State from Below: Local Governance Practices in Jordan," *Journal of Economic and Social Research* 12, no. 1 (2010): 33–61.

50. Rami Daher, "Amman: Disguised Genealogy and Recent Urban Restructuring and Neoliberal Threats," in *The Evolving Arab City : Tradition, Modernity and Urban Development*, ed. Yasser Elshweshtawy (New York: Routledge, 2008), 65.

51. Elena Corbett, "Hashemite Antiquity and Modernity: Iconography in Neoliberal Jordan," *Studies in Ethnicity and Nationalism* 11, no. 2 (October 2011): 163–93, 164.

52. Daher, "Amman," 44.

53. This is largely because the protesters in Jordan do not share the objective of ousting the regime from power. Some would like to see an end to the monarchy, but many more—particularly among the tribal communities of the south—desire a return to earlier levels of regime patronage that have been eroded by the neoliberal reform projects. That is, some want an end to the monarchy, but others want the old-style monarchy to return.

54. Jillian Schwedler, "Jordan," in *Dispatches from the Arab Revolts*, ed. Paul Amar and Vijay Prashad (Minneapolis: University of Minnesota Press, 2013), 243–65.

55. Max Page, "Urban Design and Civil Protest," *Places* 30, no. 1 (2008): 84–87.

56. Judith Butler, "Bodies in Alliance and the Politics of the Street," September 2011, available at http://eipcp.net/transversal/1011/butler/en (accessed March 16, 2013).

10

████████

Labor Movements and Organizations
VICKIE LANGOHR

Since the "Third Wave" of democratization across the globe began in 1974, those studying these regime changes have often argued that workers were central to many democratic transitions. Ruth Collier and James Mahoney suggested that mobilizing the working class was key to five of eleven Latin American and southern European transitions in the 1970s and 1980s. They then used these cases to critique the near-canonical transitions paradigm developed by Guillermo O'Donnell and Philippe Schmitter, arguing that "the [transitions] literature as a whole has erred . . . in portraying transitions as primarily an elite project, a conversation among gentlemen, with labor protest having relatively little consequence."[1] Studies of the early 1990s wave of regime change in sub-Saharan Africa similarly found that trade union activism was essential to many of these transitions.[2]

The event that started the Arab spring—the self-immolation of Tunisian Mohamed Bouazizi after the police took away his job as a fruit seller—was a workplace grievance. But the role of workers organized as workers—as opposed to citizens who also happen to be workers—varies widely across the Arab spring, in ways that differ from other regions and sometimes appear counterintuitive. Michael Bratton and Nicolas van de Walle, for instance, found that the single biggest factor explaining the variation in protests in African countries during the "African wave" of democratization between 1989 and 1994 was the number of legally registered trade unions in a country in 1989. High scores on this variable, which were strongly associated with high degrees of protest, presume some form of union pluralism in which unions were allowed to organize outside a single umbrella confederation.[3] But during the Arab spring, unions in Morocco, the country with the region's highest degree of union pluralism, participated relatively little in the February 20 democratization movement. Similarly, there has been little worker support for Arab spring protest in Algeria, where many unions function outside the single official confederation and labor activism was central to the introduction of a multiparty system in 1989. In contrast, in all three of the cases in which workers agitated for regime change in the Arab spring—Egypt, Tunisia, and Bahrain—more than 99 percent of all workers were organized through a single national confederation.[4]

This chapter begins with a detailed examination of the Tunisian, Bahraini, and Egyptian cases and then briefly addresses the limited or, in some cases, nonexistent role of workers in protests in the other countries that saw significant protest. during the Arab spring: Morocco, Syria, Libya, Algeria, and Yemen. I examine the role of labor movements in the African wave of democratization, highlighting some differences and one similarity with the Arab uprisings cases. I conclude by looking at how workers' situations have, and have not, changed in the two Arab uprisings that overthrew their leaders—Egypt and Tunisia—and what this may mean in the near future.

Worker Activism in the Arab Uprisings

The central role of workers in the uprising against President Zine al-Abdine Ben Ali in Tunisia is not surprising. In a society in which almost all independent civil society organizations had been stifled, seven months of strikes by mine workers in Gafsa in 2008 represented "a mass mobilization unprecedented in the 23 years" of Ben Ali's regime.[5] Although the leadership of Tunisia's single union confederation, the Union generale tunisienne du travail (UGTT), did not support the unrest in Gafsa, dissidents within the UGTT did.[6] Similarly, UGTT members were involved with Mohamed Bouazizi's case in December 2010 from the beginning. Teachers from the national secondary education syndicate took him to the hospital,[7] and Michele Angrist, citing an International Crisis Group report, noted that "local members from UGTT education, health, and postal unions were active in framing what had happened to Bouazizi not as a suicide . . . but rather as a political assassination; they cast Bouazizi as a victim of [the] regime."[8]

On December 24, protests against unemployment in front of the UGTT headquarters led to clashes with government forces in al Ragab and Miknassi.[9] Three days later, six unions called for a protest across from the

UGTT headquarters in Tunis, using slogans like "No, no to tyranny."[10] The UGTT's national leadership was unwilling to back such activism. Secretary-General Abdessalam Jrad stated that the executive did not support the Tunis protest, and a UGTT board member explained that the "'political' slogans chanted by the Tunis protesters do not reflect the union's position."[11] Only after two weeks of protest did the UGTT national body take a more explicitly political position, demanding the prosecution of those responsible for the protesters' deaths and calling for the first time for "political reforms . . . to deepen democracy."[12] This more critical stance may have been prompted by police violence against the unionists, as the statement condemned the encirclement of UGTT offices and violence against union members.

As the violence escalated, UGTT locals continued to mobilize dissenters. On January 8 and 9, the largest number of protesters to date were killed, amid claims that many of them, including those in Kasserine, had been murdered by government snipers. The UGTT in Kasserine may have participated in the protests or been expected to do so, as a statement from the UGTT national body again condemned the police invasion and destruction of property in the Kasserine office.[13] On January 8, the first protest was held inside the UGTT's Tunis headquarters, amid a heavy police presence.[14] Assistant Secretary-General Abaid al-Bariqi told the attendees that "it is impossible for the UGTT to do anything other than to be with this movement,"[15] and a statement by the UGTT administrative committee supported the "promotion of democracy and strengthening of freedoms."[16]

The UGTT leadership, however, was still not uniformly behind the protests. A heated struggle broke out at the regional UGTT headquarters in Gafsa on January 10 between activists trying to get the local union to support the movement and a regional UGTT secretary who, on orders from the national leadership, refused.[17] It was only on January 10 or 11, more than three weeks into the uprising, that the UGTT authorized regional unions in Sfax and other cities to call for a general strike.[18] The UGTT's participation was central to the success of a demonstration by thirty thousand people in Sfax on January 12,[19] the largest protest before Ben Ali left the country, while in Sousse, hospital workers organized a huge march.[20] But the position of the national leadership seemed to waver until the end. On January 13, the day before the UGTT called for a general strike and the last day of Ben Ali's rule, state television reported that Ben Ali had met with the UGTT president, Abdessalam Jrad, and quoted him as calling for calm to "enable everyone to focus on implementing measures taken by the president."[21]

The UGTT's participation in the protests against Ben Ali was central to its success in two ways. The first was its initial framing of Bouazizi's self-immolation. It was hardly foreordained that a poor youth setting himself on fire in a remote Tunisian town would spark nationwide protests, and it was important that activists reframed his personal hardship in terms of larger political issues.[22] But by far the most important role of the UGTT offices and activists was spreading the protests across the country, from Kasserine and Gafsa in the interior to Sfax and Sousse on the eastern coast to Tunis in the north.[23]

As in Tunisia, workers in Egypt were a main source of protest in the years before the Arab spring. In 2007 Joel Beinin and Hossam Hamalawy noted that "the longest and strongest wave of worker protest since the end of World War II is rolling through Egypt,"[24] and more than 1.7 million workers participated in more than 1,900 strikes or protests between 2004 and 2008.[25] These strikes often resulted in meeting the workers' demands. Many protests targeted the privatization of state-owned factories, which was in fact suspended temporarily in June 2010. Political economist Ragui Asad noted that "I am surprised they announced [the suspension] openly . . . that . . . seems an attempt to make a concession to all the protesting workers."[26] Some workers also attempted to form unions outside the Egyptian Trade Union Federation (ETUF), the only legal confederation since 1957. In 2009, real estate tax workers were licensed as Egypt's first independent union, followed by a second one month before the uprising.[27]

Despite the similar prominence of worker agitation in the pre–Arab spring years in Egypt and Tunisia, the role of workers in the Egyptian uprising is strikingly different from that in Tunisia. While some workers and labor leaders joined the protests from the beginning, large-scale worker action came only four days before President Hosni Mubarak stepped down, and it took the form not of antiregime protests but of factory strikes that were held outside the framework of the ETUF and that largely advanced economic, not political, demands. In the first week of the uprising, some workers participated as individuals in the protests. On January 25, the first day, large protests, including many workers, headed from the working-class Cairo neighborhood of Shubra toward Tahrir Square,[28] and protests also were held in industry-heavy areas such as Mahalla and Kafr al Dawwar. One long-time activist in the movement to create independent labor unions noted that he met "not fewer than sixty to seventy worker leaders in the protests on January 25."[29] On January 30, the leaders of that movement announced the creation of the Egyptian Federation of

Independent Trade Unions, emphasizing "the support [of the labor move-
ment] for the . . . requirements . . . demanded by the . . . revolution."[30]

Although Tunisia's UGTT leadership did not support the protests
against Ben Ali until late in the uprising, the ETUF acted aggressively, even
violently, to prevent activism. From the second day of the uprising, the
ETUF's president, Hussein Megawer, was reported to have instructed the
union presidents to solve any problems that workers were facing on the job
and to abort attempts to "drag" workers into the protests.[31] A fact-finding
committee reported that Megawer "received orders from high-ranking
[government] leaders . . . to gather a large number of progovernment workers and NDP [National Democratic Party] supporters and to pay them to
attack" protesters on February 2, the "Day of the Camel," when thugs on
horses and camels beat protesters in Tahrir Square with clubs and knives.[32]
Kamal Abu Aita, head of the independent real estate tax collectors' union,
remarked that on the Day of the Camel he met in Tahrir Square the head of
the government real estate tax collectors' union parallel to his own and that
he said "in front of the cameras that they were going to punish the protesters and break the revolution."[33]

In the second week of the uprising, an evening curfew imposed in order
to hamper protesters necessitated shutting the factories, most of which
operated on twenty-four-hour shifts.[34] The factories reopened on February
6. On February 7, the prominent newspaper al Masri al Yom gave a sense of
the changed atmosphere with its headline, "A Different Day for the Demonstrations in the Governorates," noting strikes and workplace protests
in eight of Egypt's twenty-seven governorates. Workers at Trast for Weav-
ing Industries protested the nonpayment of January's salary by blocking
a major road for two hours, leading to a backup of freight trucks headed
for ports. Workers left the road only when leaders of the Third Army were
sent in and it was agreed that the company president would pay the salaries.[35] Six thousand workers at the Suez Canal company also began a sit-
in.[36] Kamal Abbas, head of the Center for Trade Union and Workers Services, noted that "this day in the revolution [February 9] could be named
for the labor unions," with more than twenty thousand workers on strike.[37]
With few exceptions,[38] the workers' demands did not include the removal
of Mubarak from office, but they added two new noneconomic demands:
that corruption cease and that the heads of their factories step down. One
veteran labor leader suggested that striking workers focused their anger on
their factory presidents rather than on Mubarak because "people thought
the revolution will not be achieved from the top only. . . . In reality it wasn't

Mubarak who beat me in the street. It wasn't Mubarak who would lower my wages . . . so for [a hypothetical worker], getting rid of Mubarak [*isqat Mubarak*] was getting rid of my factory president [*isqat rayyis shirkati*].[39]

Unlike the Tunisian case, in which workers were active mainly in protests against the regime, the workers' most influential activism in Egypt was in the factory strikes, which threatened to paralyze economic activity. Since the widespread mobilization of workers did not begin until four days before Mubarak stepped down, it is difficult to assess how central it was to his departure. It certainly is possible that the strikes represented a significant escalation of the ongoing protest and a "last straw" that convinced the military to intervene. Indeed, the actions of the generals who replaced Mubarak demonstrated that they were deeply concerned about the strikes. On February 16, five days after Mubarak's departure, the generals sent text messages to cell phones calling on workers to stop the strikes, which they said were "delaying our progression,"[40] and on March 23 the cabinet outlawed any protest that would "interrupt . . . businesses or affect the economy in any way."[41]

As in Tunisia, Bahraini workers participated actively in the Arab spring protest through their single union confederation, the General Federation of Bahrain Trade Unions (GFBTU). Demands for political change, including the creation of a fully elected parliament headed by an elected prime minister, as well as socioeconomic grievances, led to demonstrations beginning on February 14.[42] After the protests were violently dispersed, the GFBTU called for a general strike beginning on February 20, partly in protest against the government's preventing medical workers from caring for the injured. On February 28 the union issued a statement supporting the protesters' demands, and on March 13 it called another general strike to protest violence and express socioeconomic concerns affecting workers.[43] Soon afterward, more than two thousand workers were fired from government ministries and private companies with large government ownership stakes, generally on the grounds that they had been absent from work (during the protests), involved in the demonstrations, or participated in "union activity related to the demonstrations."[44] Among the fired were fifteen members of the GFBTU executive and thirty-six other union leaders.[45]

Trends of Labor Participation in the Arab Uprisings

Tunisia and Bahrain, the only countries in which unions played a key role in Arab spring protests, share two key features of worker organization: a single union confederation that represented almost all workers, and some degree of independence for that confederation from the government *before* December 2010. When high-ranking UGTT members attempted to break away to form the Tunisian General Labor Confederation in 2007, they were thwarted, and the government rapidly engineered a takeover of the board of the first legally recognized independent union, the National Syndicate of Tunisian Journalists,[46] leaving the UGTT as the only game in town. Similarly, all unions in Bahrain are required to join the General Federation of Bahrain Trade Unions (GFBTU). Both groups are quite independent of the regime.[47] Even before independence, the UGTT was a major force in politics: it had enough influence over the nationalist Neo-Destour Party that its support for party leader Habib Bourguiba over his challenger in the 1950s ensured his success, and Bourguiba went on to become the country's first president. The union later openly confronted the government, calling a general strike in 1978 to protest the arrest of union activists, which resulted in a ten-year jail sentence for the UGTT's leader.[48] After this, the UGTT *leadership* generally refrained from opposing the government, but dissidents *within* the UGTT continued to support antigovernment activities, most notably the 2008 strikes in Gafsa. The GFBTU was even more independent of the regime. Active trade unionism had characterized the British rule of Bahrain, and when unions were outlawed and replaced in the 1980s with labor-management committees, workers' elections of representatives to these committees were generally free and fair.[49] After 2000, and during talks to establish a free-trade agreement with the United States, unions were legalized and labor laws liberalized.[50] Melani Cammett and Marsha Posusney pointed out that in both Bahrain and Jordan, the "absence of ruling parties affords greater potential for unions to defy government pressures."[51]

Egypt also had a trade union confederation, which included workers in all but two independent unions, formed only in 2009 and 2010. In the past the ETUF sometimes openly opposed the regime's policies, strongly condemning President Anwar Sadat's removal of subsidies in 1977, which led to widespread "bread riots," and publicly defending imprisoned workers.[52] In 1991, however, increasing pressure by the state led the ETUF to reverse its earlier stance and agree to the privatization of state-owned factories,[53] arguably the economic policy issue with the single most detrimental effect on workers. Subsequent amendments to the trade union law significantly eased the reelection of ruling party incumbents,[54] and the great distance between the ETUF and the workers' concerns in the years immediately preceding the uprising was underlined by the fact that one of the work-ers' main demands of the last several years—an increase in the minimum wage to 1,200 Egyptian pounds, three times the prevailing minimum[55]—was pursued without the ETUF's participation but with the assistance of a prominent nongovernmental organization, the Egyptian Center for Eco-nomic and Social Rights.[56] Similarly, the previously noted wave of strikes beginning in 2004—many of which opposed the ETUF-supported privati-zation—was held without the confederation's support.

In sum, in Tunisia, Bahrain, and Egypt the workers had some degree of freedom to work for their goals *before* the Arab spring. Where the unions had some level of independence from the regime, the workers protested through them in the Arab spring; where they did not, the workers mobi-lized in an uncoordinated fashion, factory to factory. If the workers' autono-my from the regime is central to labor protest, then how can we explain the relative quiescence of workers in the Moroccan and Algerian cases? Melani Cammett and Marsha Posusney argue that "Moroccan workers [have] the greatest freedom in the region,"[57] largely owing to a tradition of competi-tive unionism unique in the Arab world. Morocco is the only Arab coun-try whose unions are linked to parties, a common phenomenon in Latin American countries, in which labor actively pursued democratization. Workers largely stayed away, however, from protests called by the February 20 movement, which initially called for dissolving the parliament and the government and creating a transitional government focused on reforms.[58] Some sections of the union movement did support the February 20 move-ment, particularly the Democratic Labor Confederation, affiliated with the Socialist Union of Popular Forces party, and some parts of the politi-cally unaffiliated Moroccan Union of Labor, the country's largest union. But much of the labor movement failed to join the February 20 cause, and the protests may not have been widely popular even among unions osten-sibly supporting it. Labor Day protests on May 1, 2011, "marked the first time that some of Morocco's trade unions have joined protests driven by the youth-led February 20 Movement," and when the same movement organized a sit-in on May 1 in Casablanca, only about 1,500 UMT members "explicitly supported the sit-in and the UMT's leading figures were absent," while other unions, including the banking employees' union, protested separately.[59] As one banking worker at the protest noted, "We are marching because we want to push for a social agenda that has nothing to do with the political agenda of the February 20 Movement."[60] Since the constitutional referendum in July 2011 pledging reforms that slightly decreased the king's power and augmented the role of elected officials in the government, protest in Morocco has largely fizzled out.

Algeria, like Morocco, has significant union pluralism and arguably the region's most militant labor movement. The General Union of Algerian Workers (UGTA) is the only legally permitted national confederation, but unions are allowed to form outside it, and confederations without legal recognition still organize, such as the Autonomous Union of Public Sector Workers (SNAPAP).[61] In 1989, strikes initiated an antigovernment protest that led the regime, for the first time since independence, to allow a multiparty system, and in the years before the Arab spring, "public-sector strikes occur[red] almost daily in a wide variety of professions, from medical personnel to schoolteachers to oil and gas workers."[62] In early January 2011, unrest over rising food prices quickly escalated into slogans such as "No to the police state" and "[President] Boutef [lika] out."[63] But the unions have usually stayed away from Arab uprising protests. Some of the independent unions are part of the National Coordination for Democratic Change coalition,[64] but the UGTA has largely been absent.[65] Lahcen Achy wrote that since January 2011, "associations of petroleum workers, public health employees, telecommunications professionals, fire fighters, [and others] . . . protested separately to defend their own . . . interests. Protests . . . [such as] an open-ended strike by physicians in public hospitals, were able to mobilize more people compared to anti-regime protests."[66]

The refusal of workers to oppose a regime suggests that they might be content with their current state of affairs. Eva Bellin contends that many late-developing countries with state-sponsored industrialization offered organized labor benefits that tied it closely to the state. Workers, then, would be willing to oppose a regime if there was a lack, or a removal, of state sponsorship or if they did not enjoy an aristocratic position in which organized labor benefited more from the state than other lower-class groups did.[67] Before and during the Arab spring, the Algerian government used its oil revenues to try to buy workers' quiescence through measures such as canceling price increases and raising wages, but both the frequency of strikes in the country before January 2011 and the continuation of labor mobilization around sectoral economic grievances during the Arab spring indicate the workers' dissatisfaction. Several analysts contend instead that the fear of violence was more decisive in limiting antiregime protests by workers and others. Azzedine Layachi noted that "an important reason why the 2011 mobilization is small thus far may be the decade-long national trauma starting in 1992," in which at least 100,000 people died during the civil war between the government and the Islamists.[68] That violence could be repeated, as the military's power is deeply entrenched and Algerians fear that it would readily use violence to defend itself.

The Syrian regime, like that of Algeria, carefully attended to workers' concerns before the Arab spring. The minimum wage in the public sector more than doubled between 2001 and 2006,[69] and in 2008, public-sector wages increased again by 25 percent.[70] The workers' dissatisfaction with economic policy, however, was clear. The tightly government-controlled General Federation of Trade Unions (GFTU) sharply criticized the government in 2010, noting that prices had risen by much more than wage increases, with a GFTU leader saying that state economic plans had "exhausted" laborers.[71] GFTU leaders also criticized a new labor law passed in June 2010, which allowed employers to fire workers without cause.[72] It is more likely, then, that the GFTU has abstained from participating in the Syrian uprising not because it was happy with the regime but because it wanted to avoid attacks by the government. The U.S. State Department attributed the paucity of strikes in the recent past—with no mention of any strike in 2008 or 2009 and only one in 2010[73]—to "fear of repercussions,"[74] and the barbaric state attacks on protesters now have prevented *any* preexisting civil society organization from openly supporting regime change. In Libya, as in Syria, workers were organized into a single confederation tightly controlled by the regime, and the amount of state violence during the uprisings against the ruler, Muammar al-Qaddafi, may well have prevented the workers from participating through their union.

The relative lack of labor participation in the one other country with significant Arab uprising protests, Yemen, is more puzzling. Sheila Carapico observed that during colonialism, Aden had "the Arab world's most militant labor union," made up largely of port and oil workers,[75] but it shriveled when traffic through the Aden port shrank after 1967, which may explain both why labor protest has been limited in the Arab spring and why the few instances of it were protests by some public-sector workers and professional associations. Certainly the proportion of Yemenis in the General Federation of Trade Unions of Yemen (GFTUY)—only 1.4 percent of the population[76]—is small compared with the 5.7 percent of Tunisians and 5.4 percent of Egyptians in their country's union confederations.[77] But Jon Krause's comparative study of the role of trade unions in African democratization found that

relative or absolute trade union size was not directly related to a major strike/protest role in democratization. Our cases include union movements with the largest and smallest size in Africa: South Africa with . . . five union federations . . . and smaller union movements in Senegal, Namibia, and Niger.[78]

In fact, the proportion of Bahrainis in the GFBTU—1.7 percent—is almost exactly the same as that in Yemen.[79] Bahrain has by far the highest percentage of its labor force working in industry, 79 percent,[80] of all the countries experiencing Arab uprising protest, while fewer than one-quarter of Yemenis are employed in industry, trade, or other nonagricultural fields.[81] However, Benin, the first country to democratize in the "African wave," looks much like Yemen, and union protest was key to its transition. Like Yemen, Benin is one of the poorest countries on earth, and its union movement was composed almost entirely of public-service, not industrial, unions.[82] In light of the relatively large space for political and social organization in Yemen, which made it one of the freer countries in the region before the Arab spring, the relative lack of activism by Yemeni workers in the uprising against President Ali Abdullah Saleh remains a puzzle.

Insights from Comparative Cases: Africa, Latin America, and Southern Europe

Before the Arab spring, the last region to experience a "wave" of protest leading to significant regime change was sub-Saharan Africa. Michael Bratton and Nicolas van de Walle calculated that the number of protests in 1990 in sub-Saharan Africa represented a fourfold increase over the average across the 1980s,[83] with thirty-five of a total of forty-seven countries experiencing regime change by the end of 1994.[84] Labor activism was key to many of these transitions. Bratton and van de Walle found that the single biggest factor explaining variations in protests in African countries between 1989 and 1994 was the number of a country's legally registered trade unions in 1989, with each trade union "increasing the incidence of protest by 0.25."[85] Similarly, Jon Krause concluded that worker or union protests were central to democratization in fourteen of thirty-eight sub-Saharan African countries.[86]

One similarity between labor protests in the African cases and the Arab spring is in the relationship between levels of competition in the preexisting authoritarian regime and the outcome of labor protests. Krause showed that in those cases in which union activism led to regime change, protracted strike and protest resistance led authoritarian regimes to initiate negotiations over a transition, and the prominence of unions in the unrest then gave them important roles in these negotiations. This typically occurred in one of two types of cases: in white-minority ruled regimes like South Africa or Namibia, which had traditions of freedom of association (although these were largely restricted to whites), and in countries like Zambia, which had experienced some level of democratic rule or political competition. Where worker protest was central to regime change in more deeply authoritarian African countries, it led to outright regime collapse, as in Benin, Congo Republic, Niger, and Mali. Similarly, the only Arab countries where large levels of worker protest facilitated regime change were deeply authoritarian, Tunisia and Egypt.[87] Moreover, regime collapse, rather than negotiated transitions, was the result.

Levels of worker protest in the Arab uprisings differ more sharply from the African cases on two other dimensions, the connection between union pluralism and levels of worker protest and the frequency with which labor protest was initially prompted by the rejection of structural adjustment programs. Bratton and van de Walle's finding that the number of unions was the most important factor explaining variations in protests between 1989 and 1994 suggests that the lack of union pluralism correlates with lower levels of protest, since they coded countries with only a single union confederation as having one union. Indeed, they noted that "in countries with pluralistic labor movements like South Africa, Niger and Zambia, industrial action was at the center of mass uprisings and the trade unions helped to provide an organizational infrastructure for opposition movements."[88] By contrast, the two Arab countries in which "unions helped to provide an organizational structure for opposition movements" were Tunisia and Bahrain, but workers in both countries were organized in single union confederations. And as previously noted, Moroccan and Algerian workers largely failed to join protests, despite their relatively high levels of union pluralism.

In several of the African transitions in which unions played a key role, workers were moved to action initially by their resistance to International Monetary Fund (IMF) or World Bank austerity programs. The Zambian Congress of Trade Unions (ZCTU) "started a series of strikes and protests in the 1980s to combat austerity measures, six stabilization and SAPs [structural adjustment programs], and losses of income and jobs."[89] The ZCTU went on to help form the Movement for Multiparty Democracy (MMD), and a former ZCTU head first became the head of the MMD and then was elected president of Zambia. In Niger, high school and university students protesting a World Bank education program that would reduce student benefits were shot and killed while crossing the John F. Kennedy

Bridge in the capital, leading the already dissatisfied labor unions to form a coordinating committee calling for democratization and, later, to spearhead a general strike that paralyzed the government.[90] There is a close parallel between these and other similar African cases and the situation in Arab countries like Jordan[91] and Algeria in 1989, in which protests against austerity produced political liberalization. By contrast, the union protests in Tunisia and Bahrain were prompted by an explicit desire for democratizing reforms, not by the response to structural adjustment.

Worker Activism in Tunisia and Egypt After the Overthrow of Their Leaders

Not surprisingly, one of the first tangible effects of the overthrow of Ben Ali and Mubarak was a formal democratization of labor organization. By May 2011, two union confederations in addition to the UGTT were legally recognized in Tunisia, and Egypt also now has two additional confederations: the Egyptian Federation of Independent Trade Unions (EFITU), formed during the uprising, and the Egyptian Democratic Labor Congress, which split from the EFITU in October 2011.[92] In both Tunisia and Egypt, the new confederations face significant obstacles in challenging the UGTT and ETUF for members. In Tunisia, most important labor negotiations take place through tripartite negotiations among a union, the government, and the country's strongest business association; the latter two continue to include only the UGTT in collective bargaining procedures.[93] Five months into his term as president in Egypt, Mohamed Morsi had met only with ETUF representatives, not those of the independent labor movement.[94]

The role of the central union movement in Tunisia and Egypt continues largely to be the same as it was during the uprisings: the UGTT has emerged as a major opponent of the elected al-Nahda Party–led government, while in Egypt the Muslim Brotherhood's Freedom and Justice Party extended its control over the ETUF during the tenure of President Mohamed Morsi, continuing the Mubarak-era tradition of state domination of the federation. In December 2012, protests by the UGTT for jobs and the removal of the local al-Nahda governor in Siliana were met with government repression, including victims blinded by birdshot. The protests escalated, with hundreds of UGTT members around the UGTT headquarters in Tunisia chanting for the downfall of the national al-Nahda government being attacked by knife-wielding Islamists.[95] This led to the UGTT's calls for a general strike on December 13,[96] which was averted at the last minute.

Independent labor unionists initially seemed as if they would have significant influence over a democratized ETUF; in the month after Mubarak's departure, their demand that the Supreme Council of the Armed Forces (SCAF) rescind its appointment of the ETUF treasurer as the minister of manpower and migration was met, and he was replaced by Ahmed el-Borai, the minister suggested by the unionists. In November 2011, however, el-Borai was pressured into bringing back all the Mubarak-era ETUF leaders except the imprisoned president.[97] In November 2012, President Morsi amended Egypt's labor law to remove ETUF board members over the age of sixty, a reform long championed by independent unionists, but the amendments vested the power to replace most of them in the Freedom and Justice Party (FJP)'s minister of manpower.[98] The fact that the FJP chose to take the Ministry of Manpower as one of only five ministerial portfolios it assumed, out of a total of thirty-six[99] in Morsi's first cabinet, attests to the importance the party accorded to labor policy. After Morsi's ouster, EFITU president Kamal Abu Eita was named minister of manpower, and his appointment could lead to improvements in workers' rights. The SCAF already had increased the minimum wage for government workers to LE (Egyptian pounds) 700, with the promise that it would rise to LE 1,200 within five years, and the government of Prime Minister Hazem el-Beblawi said that the LE 1,200 public-sector minimum wage will take effect in 2014. The workers' right to strike, however, remained unprotected. After Morsi was deposed, Abu Eita wrote (before being appointed minister) that "workers who were champions of the strike under the previous regime should now become champions of production," and during the summer of 2013, several strikes were crushed by security forces.[100]

In a more politically competitive Egypt and Tunisia, an effective way for workers to influence labor policy would be through joining labor-friendly parties. There was little evidence of this in the first elections. The long-banned Tunisian Workers' Party won only three of 217 seats in the constituent assembly elections, subsequently forming a popular front joining many left-wing parties. Some contend that unionists see the UGTT itself, rather than the parties, as the most appropriate framework through which to engage in politics. Hela Yousfi suggested that "the UGTT is taking the place of the opposition political parties. . . . It has decided to stand 'alongside civil society and the Tunisian people in all their diversity, to defend not only the working masses but, above all, the republic and its institutions.'" She observed that "the actions called by the UGTT to defend individual liberties and denounce the violence of small Salafist groups or the police occasionally take precedence over strikes and demonstrations over pay and conditions."[101] Labor also had little impact in the Egyptian parliament, regarding which Joel Beinin estimated that approximately twenty-five of the 508 seats were won by pro-labor MPs in different parties.

What does the Egyptian and Tunisian pattern of weak linkages between unions and parties and increasing union pluralism portend for the success of labor demands? In a study of post-transition labor mobilization in eastern Europe, Spain, and Latin America, Graeme Robertson argues that the levels and success of labor protest are determined by the level of competition between national labor union confederations and the strength of confederation alliances with parties.[102] Strong competition among confederations for members and weak confederation-party coalitions produced "a higher level of militancy overall, rising waves of mobilization, and government vulnerability, as unions try to outflank one another and maintain leadership of workers," as in 1990s Bulgaria.[103] Lower levels of confederation competition and weak union links with parties led to what Robertson calls "isolated, weak labor movement[s]," as in post-1991 Russia and post-1989 Argentina. Confederations in both Egypt and Tunisia are linked weakly, if at all, with parties, suggesting that if earlier precedents hold, levels of competition between the UGTT and the ETUF, on the one hand, and the new confederations, on the other, will determine the level of strength and militancy of the labor movements in the future.

Conclusion

As was the case in several Latin American, eastern European, and African transitions, workers played central roles in the Tunisian and Bahraini uprisings and mobilized powerfully in the final days of the Egyptian revolt. The cases of Morocco and Algeria, however, demonstrate that the labor unions' strength and independence does not automatically predispose them to mobilize for democratization. Morocco strongly resembles cases such as South Africa and Zambia, where union pluralism and relatively high levels of associational freedom or political competition allowed unions to provide the framework for prodemocracy protest. It may be the case, however, that both the king's early allowance of significant political competition—Morocco had its first opposition-led parliament in 1998—and the additional liberalizing reforms during the Arab uprisings are sufficient for most Moroccan workers now. In some ways, the cases of Tunisia and Bahrain, where workers organized in a single union confederation struck out powerfully at the regime, seem more logical than the opposite findings in Africa of a strong connection between union pluralism and antigovernment mobilization, because of the obvious strength and ease of decision making derived from a single organization representing all workers. With the UGTT continuing to represent arguably the major oppositional force in post-Ben Ali Tunisia, and with already-high levels of strikes certain to accelerate in Egypt if the proposed $4.8 billion IMF loan and corresponding austerity provisions go through, labor protest will clearly continue even where authoritarian regimes have already been overthrown.

NOTES

1. Ruth Berins Collier and James Mahoney, "Adding Collective Actors to Collective Outcomes: Labor and Recent Democratization in South America and Southern Europe," *Comparative Politics*, April 1997, 299.
2. See, for example, Michael Bratton and Nicolas van de Walle, *Democratic Experiments in Africa: Regime Transitions in Comparative Perspective* (New York: Cambridge University Press, 1997); and Jon Krause, ed., *Trade Unions and the Coming of Democracy in Africa* (New York: Palgrave Macmillan, 2007).
3. Countries where no unions were allowed were coded as "0," and countries with only one official umbrella confederation were coded as "1," while systems with more than one allowed confederation and large numbers of unions measured as high as 66. Personal communication, Michael Bratton, March 4, 2013.
4. For example, in 2010, Egypt had only two independent unions (licensed only in 2009 and 2010), compared with 1,751 in the national confederation. See Joel Beinin, "Justice for All: The Struggle for Workers' Rights in Egypt, a Report by the Solidarity Center" (Washington, D.C.: Solidarity Center, February 2010). Before Ben Ali's fall, Tunisia had only one union outside the national confederation.
5. Rasha Moumneh, "Tunisia: Where Solidarity Brings Sanctions," Human Rights Watch, November 9, 2010, available at http://www.hrw.org/news/2010/11/09/tunisia-where-solidarity-brings-sanctions (accessed November 18, 2013).
6. Borzou Daragahi, "Tunisia's Uprising Was Three Years in the Making," *Los Angeles Times*, January 27, 2011.
7. Michele Penner Angrist, "Understanding the Success of Mass Civic Protest in Tunisia," paper presented at the annual meeting of the Middle East Studies Association, Washington, D.C., 2011.
8. Ibid.
9. Ryan Rifai, "Timeline: Tunisia's Uprising," al Jazeera.net, January 23, 2011.

10. BBC Monitoring, Middle East, December 29, 2010, quoting Munji Saedani, "Protests Continue for Tenth Day in Sidi Bouzid, and Unions Express Solidarity with Region," *al Sharq al Awsat*, December 28, 2010.

11. BBC Monitoring, Middle East, December 30, 2010.

12. "Bayan al Hay'a al Idariya al Wataniya lil-Ittihad al Aam al Tunisi lil-Shogl" (Statement of the National Administrative Body of the UGTT), January 4, 2011.

13. "Bayan" (Statement), January 11, 2011.

14. "Akbar Niqaba Tunisiyya Tad'hum Harakat al-Ihtijaj wa Amrika Qaliqa ala al-Hurriyat" (The Largest Union in Tunisia Supports the Protest Movement and America Is Worried About Freedoms), *Dar al Hayat*, January 9, 2011.

15. Ibid.

16. Ibid.

17. Olivier Piot, "Tunisia: Diary of a Revolution," *Le monde diplomatique*, February 2011, 4–5.

18. In "Tunisia: Diary of a Revolution," Piot says that hours after Ben Ali closed educational institutions, on January 10, the UGTT leadership authorized Sfax and other UGTT regional sections to call a general strike the next day. This suggests that the strike was on January 11, but the only other press reports of UGTT protests in Sfax in this period put it on January 12.

19. Angrist, "Understanding the Success," 17.

20. Piot, "Tunisia: Diary of a Revolution."

21. "Tunisian Leader, Trade Union Boss Discuss Developments in Country," BBC Monitoring Middle East, January 13, 2011.

22. This "framing" process also occurred in Egypt. The January 18 YouTube video in which Egyptian April 6 activist Asmaa Mahmoud calls on citizens to protest on January 25, watched by almost half a million people, begins by rejecting the government's description of these self-immolations as the acts of "psychopaths" and embedding them in an explicitly antigovernment narrative.

23. Amr Hamzawy, "Tunisian Unions Eclipsing Parties as Democratizing Force?" *Democracy Digest*, January 24, 2011, available at http://www.demdigest.net/blob/2011/01/tunisian-unions-eclipsing-parties-as-democratizing-force-2/ (accessed November 18, 2013).

24. Joel Beinin and Hossam Hamalawy, "Strikes in Egypt Spread from Center of Gravity," *Middle East Report Online*, May 9, 2007.

25. Beinin, "Justice for All."

26. Michael Slackman, "Egypt Concedes to Resistance on Privatization Push," *New York Times*, June 27, 2010.

27. Joel Beinin, "Egypt at the Tipping Point," *Foreign Policy.com*, January 31, 2011.

28. Interview with a worker and leader in the independent union movement, Cairo, June 8, 2011.

29. Ibid.

30. Press Release, Center for Trade Union and Worker Services, January 30, 2011, text available at http://www.solidaritycenter.org/Files/egypt_ctuws013011_english.pdf.

31. Mohammed Azzouz, "'Ittihad al Ummal' Yutalib Ru'asa al Niqabat bil Ta'ahub li-Ijhad Ayy Mutharat Ummaliya" (The 'ETUF' Calls on Union Heads to Be Prepared to Abort Any Worker Protests), *al Masri al Yowm*, January 26, 2011.

32. "Habs Hussein Mugawer wa Ihab al Umda 15 Yowman fii 'Mawqa'at al Jamal' . . . wa Masadir Tu'akkid Tawarut Qiyyadat bi Television" (Incarceration of Hussein Mugawer and Ihab al Umda for 15 Days in the "Camel Incident" and Sources Confirm the Involvement of the Leadership in Television), *al Shaab*, April 22, 2011.

33. Interview with Kamal Abou Aita, president of the Real Estate Tax Authority Union, March 7, 2011, on the website of the International Trade Union Confederation, available at http://www.ituc-csi.org/spotlight-interview-with-kamal.html.

34. The Egyptian workweek is Sunday through Thursday. Factories were closed from Sunday, January 31, until Thursday, February 3, followed by the normal weekend (Friday and Saturday) holiday, returning to work on Sunday, February 6.

35. "Yowm Mukhtalif lil-Muthaharat fii al Muhafathat: Ummal 'Trast' Bil Suez Yehtajun ala Ta'akhur al Ratib . . . wa l'itisam in 'Silk Kafr al Dawwar' Bi-sabab al Hawafiz" (A Different Day for the Demonstrations in the Governorates: Workers at "Trast" in Suez Protest over Delay in Their Wages . . . and a Sit-In in "Silk Kafr al Dawwar" over Incentive Pay), *al Masri al Youm*, February 8, 2011.

36. Kareem Fahim and David Kirkpatrick, "Labor Actions in Egypt Boost Protests," *New York Times*, February 9, 2011.

37. "Egypt: Today Strikers Took Center Stage," Jane Slaughter interview with Kamal Abbas, *Labor Notes*, February 9, 2011.

38. On February 9, public transportation workers organized a strike in many Cairo garages and distributed a statement in Tahrir Square that supported the demands of the protesters there and called for Mubarak to step down. Mohammed al Kholy, "Bayann li Ummal al Naql al Aam Bi Midaan al Tahrir Yu'ayyid al Thowra wa Yu'akkid Dukhulihum Fii Idrab Shamil on al Amal" (Statement by the Public Transportation Workers in Tahrir Supports the Revolution and Confirms Their Entry into a Complete Work Stoppage), *al Destour*, February 9, 2011. I learned of this article from Hossam Hamalawy's *al Masrawy* website.

39. Interview with leader in the independent union movement, Cairo, June 8, 2011.

40. Kareem Fahim, "Freed by Egypt's Revolt, Workers Press Demands," *New York Times*, February 16, 2011.

41. "Egypt Cabinet Criminalises Strikes That Affect Economy, Enraging Activists," *al-Ahram* (English) online, March 23, 2011.

42. Mahmoud Cherif Bassiouni, Nigel Rodley, Badria al-Awadhi, Philippe Kirsch, and Mahnoush Arsanjani, Report of the Bahrain Independent Commission of Inquiry (BICI), November 23, 2011, 65–68.

43. Ibid., 331–32.

44. Ibid., 331.

45. International Trade Union Confederation, "Spotlight on Ebrahim H. Abdulla and Abdulla M. Hussain (GFBTU-Bahrain)," July 5, 2011.

46. Human Rights Watch, "The Price of Independence: Silencing Labor and Student Unions in Tunisia," October 2010.

47. On the GFBTU, see "U.S. State Department Human Rights Report, 2011: Bahrain."

48. Lisa Anderson, *The State and Social Transformation in Tunisia and Libya, 1830–1980* (Princeton, N.J.: Princeton University Press, 1986), 242.

49. Melani Cammett and Marsha Pripstein Posusney, "Labor Standards and Labor Market Flexibility in the Middle East: Free Trade and Freer Unions?" *Studies in Comparative Economic Development* 45, no. 2 (2010): 250–79.

50. Ibid., 264.

51. Ibid., 276.

52. Marsha Pripstein Posusney, *Labor and State in Egypt: Workers, Unions, and Economic Restructuring* (New York: Columbia University Press, 1997), 196–97.

53. Ibid., 209.

54. Vickie Langohr, "Too Much Civil Society, Too Little Politics: Egypt and Liberalizing Arab Regimes," *Comparative Politics*, 36, no. 2 (January 2004): 187.

55. Joel Beinin, "Egypt at the Tipping Point," *Foreign Policy.com*, January 31, 2011.

56. Joel Beinin, "Egyptian Workers Demand a Living Wage," *Foreign Policy.com*, May 12, 2010.

57. Cammett and Posusney, "Labor Standards and Labor Market Flexibility," 256.

58. Press Kit, link available at http://arabist.net/blog/2011/6/13/for-journalists-covering-morocco.html.

59. "Trade Unions Join Reform Protests for May Day Marches," France 24, May 1, 2011.

60. Ibid.

61. U.S. State Department Human Rights Report 2011, "Algeria."

62. Laryssa Chomiak and John Entelis, "The Making of North Africa's Intifadas," *Middle East Report* 259 (2011): 8–15.

63. Ibid.

64. Lahcen Achy, "Why Did Protests in Algeria Fail to Gain Momentum?" *Foreign Policy.com*, March 31, 2011, available at http://mideast.foreignpolicy.com/posts/2011/03/31/why_did_protests_in_algeria_fail_to_gain_momentum.

65. Azzedine Layachi, "Algeria's Rebellion by Installments," *Middle East Report Online*, March 12, 2011.

66. Achy, "Why Did Protests in Algeria Fail?"

67. Eva Bellin, *Stalled Democracy: Capital, Labor, and the Paradox of State-Sponsored Development* (Ithaca, N.Y.: Cornell University Press, 2002).

68. Layachi, "Algeria's Rebellion by Installments."

69. Nader Kabbani, "Why Young Syrians Prefer Public Sector Jobs," Middle East Youth Initiative Policy Outlook, Wolfensohn Center for Development at Brookings / Dubai School of Government, March 2009, 5.

70. Kabbani, "Why Young Syrians Prefer Public Sector Jobs," 5. The private sector also was required to raise salaries.

71. "Wages Fail to Keep Up with Inflation, Union Group Warns," *Syria Today*, December 2010, no longer available online.

72. Muhammed Atef Fares, "Labouring Under the Law," *Syria Today*, June 2010, no longer available online.

73. U.S. Department of State Human Rights Reports, 2008–10: Syria. In a June 2010 feature on a new labor law, *Syria Today* ("Labouring Under the Law") also notes that "strikes in Syria are rare, but not unheard of," citing a 2003 strike in the petroleum and gas sector.

74. U.S. Department of State, 2010 Country Reports on Human Rights Practices, "Syria."

75. Sheila Carapico, *Civil Society in Yemen: The Political Economy of Activism in Modern Arabia*, Cambridge Middle East Studies no. 9 (Cambridge: Cambridge University Press, 1998), 91.

76. The GFTUY reports having 350,000 members. *Arab Political Systems: Baseline Information and Reforms—Yemen* (Washington, D.C.: Carnegie Endowment for International Peace, 2008),18. The population of Yemen in 2012 was almost 25 million. CIA World Factbook, Yemen, available at https://www.cia.gov/library/publications/the-world-factbook/geos/ym.html (accessed March 15, 2013).

77. In "Justice for All," Beinin says that "the ETUF claims 4,431,290 members organized in 1,751 local unions" (11). The CIA World Factbook lists the current Egyptian population as 82,079,636.

78. Krause, *Trade Unions*, 271.

79. The Solidarity Center report on Bahrain reports that the 2008 membership of the GFBTU was approximately 22,000, while the CIA World Factbook estimates the Bahraini population at 1,248,348.

80. CIA World Factbook.

81. CIA World Factbook, Yemen (accessed February 16, 2012).

82. See Thomas Beirschenk, "Democratization Without Development: Benin 1989–2009," Working Paper no. 100 (Mainz: University of Mainz, Department of Anthropology and African Studies).

83. Bratton and van de Walle, *Democratic Experiments in Africa*, 3.

84. Ibid., 4.

85. Ibid., 150–51.

86. Krause, *Trade Unions*, 257.

87. Egypt did have a more competitive system earlier in the 2000s, as exemplified by the independents affiliated with the Muslim Brotherhood winning 20 percent of the seats in the 2005 parliament. The November 2010 election, however, was one of the most fraudulent in Egypt's history, with the Brotherhood's share falling from eighty-eight seats in 2005 to only one in 2010.

88. Bratton and van de Walle, *Democratic Experiments in Africa*, 148.

89. Emmanuel Akwetey and Jon Krause, "Trade Unions, Development and Democratization in Zambia: The Continuing Struggle," in *Trade Unions and the Coming of Democracy in Africa*, ed. Jon Krause (New York: Palgrave Macmillan, 2007), 263.

90. Robert Charlick, "Labor Unions and 'Democratic Forces' in Niger," in *Trade Unions and the Coming of Democracy in Africa*, ed. Jon Krause (New York: Palgrave Macmillan, 2007), 61–82.

91. On the close connection between economic austerity and the introduction of political liberalization in Jordan, see Malik Mufti, "Elite Bargains and the Onset of Political Liberalization in Jordan," *Comparative Political Studies* 32, no. 1 (1999): 100–129.

92. Joel Beinin, "The Rise of Egypt's Workers," Carnegie Paper, June 28, 2012, 16.

93. U.S. Department of State Human Rights Report 2011: Tunisia.

94. Dina Bishara, "Who Speaks for Egypt's Workers?" Foreign Policy.com, September 6, 2012.

95. "Tunisian Islamists, Leftists Clash in Tunis After Job Protests," Reuters, December 4, 2012.

96. "Strikes Raise Tensions Between Unions, Islamist Government in Tunisia," *al Arabiya* (English), December 6, 2012.

97. Beinin, "The Rise of Egypt's Workers," 8–14.

98. Dina Bishara, "Egyptian Labor Between Morsi and Mubarak," Foreign Policy.com, November 28, 2012.

99. Bishara, "Egyptian Labor Between Morsi and Mubarak." The figures on the number of ministries come from "The Brothers of the Cabinet," *Egypt Independent*, August 10, 2012.

100. Jano Charbel, "And Where Do the Workers Stand?" *Mada Masr*, July 15, 2013.

101. Hela Yousfi, "Tunisia's New Opposition," *Le monde diplomatique* (English), November 3, 2012.

102. Graeme Robertson, "Leading Labor: Unions, Politics, and Protest in New Democracies," *Comparative Politics* 36, no. 3 (April 2004): 253–72.

103. Ibid., 255.

11

Islamist Movements

QUINN MECHAM

Islamist groups lagged behind in mobilizing their supporters to call for revolutionary change in authoritarian regimes. Indeed, prominent Islamist groups like the Egyptian Muslim Brotherhood engaged the protest movement cautiously and in a way that revealed internal divisions in their position with respect to the popular protests. This finding contrasts with some of the predictions of the scholarship on Islamism, which suggests that Islamist groups are likely to be uniquely effective in mobilizing protest against political and economic injustice. In many countries, though, Islamists appeared uncharacteristically slow and generationally divided in their support of the widespread popular protest in those countries where it has occurred.

This does not mean, however, that Islamist groups missed their opportunity to reshape regimes in key Arab countries undergoing political transformation. Indeed, Islamist groups have played major roles as the opposition to authoritarian regimes evolved, and especially in the political processes of emerging regime transitions. In this chapter, I address the strategic behavior of Islamist groups in the protest environment of 2011, the conditions under which Islamist militancy emerged, and why visible popular support for Islamist groups increased dramatically in some countries during the process of electoral competition.

The chapter begins with a brief examination of the patterns of Islamist behavior during and after protest cycles in countries with historically strong Islamist oppositions. I then turn to patterns of Islamist militancy in the cases of Libya, Syria, and Yemen. Finally, I assess Islamist electoral strategies and outcomes in three cases that held elections in 2011, Tunisia, Morocco, and Egypt. I argue that the muted Islamist responses during popular protests reflect both the risk management strategies and the strategic divisions in Islamist groups. I also argue that Islamist groups were well positioned to play a larger role in shaping the aftermath of protest and were often better positioned to shape the postprotest environment than they were to shape the protests themselves. I highlight the comparatively low levels of Islamist militancy but contend that Islamist violence and sectarian conflict has increased over time in contexts of heavy state repression and state failure. I conclude by discussing the political polarization around Islam and the emerging intra-Islamist competition, particularly some of the main issues for Islamist movements in the aftermath of the initial uprisings.

Islamists in the Initial Uprisings

Islamist groups are political organizations that use Islamic religious narratives to make political claims on the state. These political claims often concern social and cultural norms, resource allocation, and models of governance. Existing scholarship on Islamist organizations focuses on the strength of these organizations as possible loci for opposition against authoritarian regimes.[1] This potential for political mobilization is due to several factors that make Islamist organizations somewhat different from their more secular rivals. Islamists often have access to rich social networks in religious, educational, and charitable circles that can be used for recruitment and communication. Their position as religious as well as political actors also can shield them from the full repressive apparatus of the state, as many Arab regimes try to maintain a semblance of Islamic legitimacy. This leaves Islamist organizations both institutionally stronger and with a wider range of resources for social mobilization than their nonreligious rivals. Combined with strong symbolic capital that creates a framing narrative rejecting unjust and corrupt rulers, Islamists appear well positioned to lead popular opposition against authoritarian leaders.

In the early popular uprisings in Tunisia and Egypt, however, Islamists either remained on the sidelines or joined the popular protests late, and when they did participate it was often as secondary or even subordinate opposition actors. Why? One answer is that the perceived costs of visibly participating in the popular protests appeared higher than the perceived costs of not participating. This calculation of the relative costs of participating or staying on the sidelines shifted over time in countries like Egypt, Jordan, and Yemen and eventually led Islamist groups into the fray, but in deliberately secondary positions to those of other opposition actors. In addition, the leaders of Islamist groups faced important calculations regarding internal group politics (such as the difficulty of maintaining control in the face of challenges from a younger generation of activists), which led to caution in assuming leadership of the protests.

In each of the countries experiencing mass popular mobilization, including Tunisia, Egypt, Bahrain, and Yemen, the levels of uncertainty regarding the ultimate outcome were very high throughout the early days of the protest and remained painfully uncertain in many places for some time. While opposition protesters deliberately used nonviolent resistance, regime leaders looked for any opportunity to repress in the name of containing a security threat. Islamists have historically been the first to be rounded up as the "usual suspects," and Arab leaders have been quick to blame Islamists (depicted by the state as religious radicals or terrorists) as the instigators. By blaming religious radicals for popular unrest, leaders thus try to deflect criticism of state repression both at home and from abroad.

This means that Islamist groups face a high risk of repression at the beginning of a new protest cycle but see few perceptible benefits that would encourage them to claim leadership of the protests. Likewise, non-Islamist protesters also have an interest in keeping Islamists on the sidelines in order to clearly demonstrate the mass popular character of the protests, to reduce the chances of repression, and to expose the fallacy of the security threat narrative that the regimes try to impose on the protests. In both Egypt and Libya, for example, state leaders openly (and falsely) accused radical Islamists of leading the protests as a way of justifying state repression. Both Islamists and non-Islamist protesters thus have similar interests in framing these protests explicitly outside an Islamist framework when a protest cycle begins. In Tunisia, Egypt, and Yemen, although members of Islamist groups participated in popular protests reasonably early, they did so within a broader and explicitly non-Islamist narrative, with little attempt to shift that narrative toward an Islamist one. In Bahrain, where most of the traditional opposition actors are Shia Islamists, religious and sectarian identities were likewise subordinated early on to a broader, non-Islamist narrative of political injustice.

Also in countries where Islamists have historically been the backbone of the organized opposition, Islamist groups may see themselves as the natural beneficiaries of democratic regime change, regardless of its source. That is, Islamists sense the possibility of "free riding" on the protests, thereby receiving the likely benefits of democratic reform but allowing others to pay the high costs. Because they are likely to pay higher costs from repression than other groups who engage in protest, free riding on regime change can be very attractive. Free riding is not an option for the non-Islamist opposition, however. Both because the Islamists have proven unwilling or unable to force regime change in the past and because the non-Islamist opposition has a smaller institutional and resource base, its objectives can be met only by taking active leadership, including paying the costs of mobilization during the early and most uncertain periods of challenge. This creates a situation in which the non-Islamist opposition is willing to lead protests, and the Islamist opposition is willing to wait on the sidelines to see how the protests unfold.

There is another, organizational, reason why some Islamist groups were cautious about taking a visible leadership position in the initial protests. From the perspective of the Islamist groups' internal politics, older leaders who sense a possible threat from their younger rivals may be wary of joining popular protests dominated by a broader youth movement. If they do so, they may unwittingly create new leadership opportunities for their younger internal rivals (who resonate more with the youthful protesters) and gradually cede control over the direction of the movement. In Egypt, for example, significant divisions across generational lines emerged within the Brotherhood about when to call its members to protest in Tahrir Square and when to refrain, with the youth wing unsuccessfully pushing for more aggressive protest leadership from the broader organization.[2]

Despite these initial pressures for Islamist groups to cede protest leadership to others, however, there are costs to remaining on the sidelines for too long. As protests in Egypt and Tunisia increasingly looked like they would succeed in meeting their objectives, Islamists became more comfortable and visible in calling for political change. They began to realize that they risked creating internal generational splits unless they joined the protests, as the younger members (of the Egyptian Muslim Brotherhood, for example) were actively pressuring their organizations to participate. In addition, the longer they remained on the sidelines, the more they ran the risk of losing control of the regime change narrative or of being perceived to be out of touch with popular sentiment. Moreover, as popular mobilization becomes more widespread over time, the anticipated costs of targeted repression decline, and the political costs of remaining on the sidelines rise. Under these circumstances, Islamist groups become more likely to participate in protest, and thus "coming late to the revolution" may be an optimal strategy for these groups. By coming late, they can free ride by not paying the full costs of challenging the regime but still anticipate the future benefits of regime change for their organization.

And the future benefits of regime change for Islamists may be large indeed. As the 2011 elections in Tunisia and Egypt demonstrated, Islamist organizations can reasonably assume significant support in the context of democratic transitions to governance through free and fair elections. In contexts of diverse and divided political opposition, Islamist organizations have institutional resources and social networks that allow them to channel popular discontent in politically effective ways; these organizational benefits have yielded rich, but fragile, rewards at the ballot box in the majority of Arab countries that have recently held elections.

Despite their initial hesitancy, therefore, Islamists understandably emerged as major political players in the period following the initial popular mobilization. Prominent Islamist figures returned from exile to countries such as Tunisia and Bahrain in an effort to capture new opportunities to provide leadership and shape the narratives of potential regime change.[3] Likewise, as constitutional changes occur that increase the potential for Islamist groups to play an active part in political competition, these groups have shown that they can use their existing institutional advantages to outcompete their fragmented rivals in notable ways. While Islamist groups conceded some of the early protest mobilization to more secular rivals, they became institutionally well positioned to serve as focal points for voters' convergence in the face of highly fragmented, diverse, and untested alternatives. In cases in which political mobilization has taken more violent forms, Islamist militancy was initially low but also grew in proportion to other forms of militancy over time. I discuss several cases that illustrate the growth of both militant and electoral Islam as the political uprisings evolved. I argue that in both types of Islamist mobilization, the evolution of political conditions (either greater state repression or new electoral opportunities) led Islamists into positions of greater prominence in the period after the initial uprisings.

Militancy

Although most of the protests associated with the Arab uprisings explicitly sought to challenge existing regimes without resorting to violence, uprisings did become violent in several cases, most notably in Libya and Syria, and to a lesser extent in Yemen, Egypt, and Bahrain. Protests have been actively and violently repressed in a number of countries, which in some cases led to the protesters' capitulation and, in other cases, to the transformation of nonviolent protest into violent rebellion. In none of these cases was the initial violence associated with the uprisings explicitly or exclusively led by Islamist groups, although members of Islamist groups have participated in violent rebellion where it occurred. Islamist militancy should be seen in the context of increasing militancy by rebels more broadly, as one of several responses to heightened state repression. Islamist militancy in these countries also is affected by transnational developments, as militants from Iraq and around the region traveled to participate in armed incursions against localized states, particularly in Syria. The cases of Libya, Syria, and Yemen are most instructive in understanding the role of Islamic militancy in the uprisings.

A rich, though controversial, strain in Islamist thought argues that under specific conditions, religion justifies militant actions against rulers. This could be because rulers have ruled unjustly (using corruption or repression, for example) or have failed to sufficiently defend and support the principles of Islam in the societies they govern. The Islamic principle of *jihad*, or a religiously mandated struggle to defend Islam, has been invoked on occasion by militants against Muslim rulers for perceived violations of Islamic principles. Islamist militants have a history of violence against governing regimes across much of the Arab world, including those in the countries at the center of the Arab uprisings, such as Egypt, Syria, Yemen, and Libya. Despite this history, however, explicitly Islamist militancy was not a defining feature of any of the early uprisings. But the context of the uprisings provided new opportunities for militants to play a role in consolidating their minority positions in society. Likewise, the ongoing state weakness in countries like Libya, Yemen, and Syria created the conditions for Islamist militants to intensify their influence and strength over time.

Libya provided the most fertile ground initially for the expression of Islamist militancy, as militants played an important role in the rebel movement that led to the collapse of Muammar Qaddafi's regime. Qaddafi's heterodox interpretations of Islamic thought and his aggressive repression of Islamist groups, including the Libyan Muslim Brotherhood, led to long-standing resentment of the regime by Islamist groups, whose members had been killed or imprisoned for long periods before the beginning of the rebellion. Islamists in Libya thus had an interest in participating in the Libyan rebellion and provided leadership at key moments, with Abdel Hakim Belhaj, the former emir of the Libyan Islamic Fighting Group, leading a final rebel surge to capture Qaddafi's compound in Tripoli. Despite some concerns from outsiders that the rebellion would be increasingly defined as an Islamist one, the range of actors who participated in the rebellion was very diverse, including a number of defectors from the Libyan army and Qaddafi's government, effectively diluting the number of rebels who defined their rebellion in Islamist terms. Although the Libyan National Transitional Council, a broad coalition representing the challengers to Qaddafi's regime, incorporated some Islamist leaders and general Islamic language and discourse in articulating its vision and justifying its actions, it was far from a militant Islamist group in its composition. Indeed, the results of the July 2012 elections for the Libyan General National Congress demonstrate that religiously conservative actors, such as the Muslim Brotherhood's Adala wa al-Bina (Justice and Construction Party, which came in second place) still lag non-Islamist groups in popular support.[4] As post-Qaddafi Libya transitions to a period of competing militias operating in parallel with electoral politics, however, it is likely that Islamic identity will be important to defining the framework for political participation, both militant and democratic, owing to the population's strong identification with Islam and the long, challenging period of state building ahead.[5]

The Syrian case has intriguing parallels with Libya, including historical militant challenges to the regime by Islamist groups (especially the Muslim Brotherhood), the active repression of those groups, and the reemergence of militancy in the wake of widespread government repression in 2011. As in Libya, the popular uprising in Syria has incorporated a wide range of groups, including many who explicitly reject an Islamist narrative of rebellion in favor of a narrative of democracy and human rights. As sustained state repression tipped the opposition toward militancy and sent Syria into civil war, however, opportunities for Islamist militancy grew, particularly in the industrial towns of central Syria (Hama, Homs), which have a history of Islamist organization. In 2012 the Islamist component of the Syrian rebellion grew in strength and used increasingly visible and violent tactics against state targets. Initially the largest of the Islamist militant groups in Syria, the al-Nusra Front, evolved to become one of the most visible actors in the rebellion, with several thousand fighters articulating an allegiance to al-Qaida and an aspiration to lead Syria to a model of Islamist governance. Al-Nusra was heavily influenced by ideology and strategies coming out of the Iraq conflict and claimed dozens of major suicide attacks in the Syrian conflict. As the conflict continued, Islamist militants in Iraq and Syria joined forces to create a movement known as the Islamic State of Iraq and Syria, which took control of a number of towns in the north and east of

Syria. As a result, these Islamist militant groups helped internationalize the conflict and made other members of the Syrian opposition increasingly wary of their intentions and role in a future Syria. As the Syrian civil war has continued and the rebellion has struggled to topple the Syrian state, Islamist militants have found opportunities and support for increasingly radical and violent actions.

In Yemen, in parallel to the formal Islamist political opposition represented by the Islah Party, Islamist militancy grew in the waning years of Ali Abdullah Saleh's presidency and expanded rapidly in the context of ongoing state weakness since his departure. Al-Qaida in the Arabian Peninsula (AQAP), a small but explicitly militant group that depended initially on fighters and ideologues coming from Saudi Arabia, openly challenged Saleh's regime through much of the last decade and extended its territorial reach in the wake of infighting between state security forces, beginning in 2011. Though marginal to both the formal opposition groups (under the banner of the Joint Meeting Parties) and the mass popular street protests, al-Qaida has a history of consolidating its resources in rugged and unpoliced parts of the Yemeni countryside, and it took advantage of the greater freedom of movement and operations as central state control declined since the uprising and subsequent political stalemate. Ansar al-Sharia, an al-Qaida affiliate, seized control over large swaths of territory in Abyan Province during 2012, which led to significant fighting with state security forces. Owing to the Yemeni state's inability to meet its citizens' basic needs and to control its territory, militant Islam is likely to find additional opportunities to challenge state control over time. As in Libya and in Syria, the primary drivers of militancy's growth in Yemen since the Arab uprisings include initial state repression followed by growing state weakness that creates new opportunities for rebellion.

Electoral Success

Despite the influence of Islamist militants in several important cases, and the possibility that militancy will increase over time, Islamist militancy has so far been comparatively marginal to the story of Islamist participation in the Arab uprisings, with the possible exception of Syria. The real story to date has been the widespread and successful Islamist electoral mobilization in the countries experimenting with political transitions. The Islamists' success in new elections has varied but has been strong enough across transitional countries to have profound implications on the future of governance in the Arab world. Indeed, the Islamists' success at the ballot box has been a polarizing issue in many countries, as political divisions have increasingly centered on the role of Islam in government. As Mark Tessler and Michael Robbins observe in chapter 13, public opinion suggests that a large, if not dominant, portion of societies in much of the Arab world would prefer a democratic-secular government to either a democratic or an authoritarian Islamic regime. This finding problematizes the success of Islamist parties and helps explain some of the political polarization that has resulted from the Islamists' electoral victories, as exemplified by Egypt (see chapter 13). Michael Hoffman and Amaney Jamal's findings on political attitudes of Arab youth, however, suggest that despite being overall less religious than their older counterparts, the young people who played such a significant role in leading the opposition to their governments are substantially more supportive of experiments with political Islam (see chapter 14). This willingness to give Islamist groups a chance to see if they can govern effectively enabled Islamists to do particularly well in the elections of 2011 and 2012.

In the three countries of North Africa (Tunisia, Egypt, and Morocco) where constitutive assembly and legislative elections were first held after the Arab uprisings, Islamist political parties scored dramatic successes at the ballot box. The popular support for the parties of al-Nahda (Renaissance) in Tunisia, al-Hurriya wa al-Adala (Freedom and Justice) and al-Nour (Light) in Egypt, and al-Adala wa al-Tanmiya (Justice and Development) in Morocco was higher than might have been expected simply by looking at the relative levels of Islamist participation in these countries' street protests. Although the Justice and Development Party in Morocco and the Muslim Brotherhood in Egypt (which formed the Freedom and Justice Party) had a recent track record of competing in elections and mobilizing their constituents to vote, immediately before the elections both Tunisia's al-Nahda Party and Egypt's al-Nour Party had to newly form or reconstitute themselves after a long absence. In all cases, the parties performed better in the elections than their recent political experience may have indicated.

Why have Islamist parties done so well at the polls? At least three plausible explanations are consistent with recent research on Islamism. First, as the result of political reform, Islamists have had a clear institutional advantage over their rivals. In most cases, Islamists have a track record of social and political mobilization based on a wide range of institutions that operated under the previous regime, especially in the religious, charitable, educational, media, and professional sectors. These organizational foundations provide a readymade network that can be used for political mobilization and communication, which are less likely to be readily available to their competitors.

A second, related explanation is the high degree of fragmentation among the Islamist parties' competitors, which amplifies the impact of organizational discipline among the Islamist parties. Liberal, left-wing, and new competitors emerging after the popular protests have had a hard time coalescing around a unified leadership and have usually not had the advantage of a strict party hierarchy that can call for party discipline at the polls.

A third, more idea-based explanation, is that the Islamist narrative is particularly compelling to voters in the face of widespread uncertainty and insecurity, both economically and politically. Amid the political uncertainty, the Islamist parties are a known quantity, with a simple, identity-focused message largely untarnished by association with the previous regime. Their narrative is focused on both a return to authenticity and greater social and economic equality, with attention to the most vulnerable. This message is particularly appealing to those who are worried about their future under the new regime and seek security in a more extensive moral social order. In all cases, Islamists have long been perceived as unjustly treated under the old regimes, making much of the electorate particularly interested in observing how well they could do at the polls without artificial competitive restraints. These three explanations, focused on Islamist organization, fragmentation in the competitive landscape, and ideological appeal are not mutually exclusive; rather, all likely explain a portion of these parties' success. As Michelle Pace and Francesco Cavatorta observed, Islamist parties have done well in the aftermath of the uprisings largely because they are the strongest parties in their emerging systems, with an agenda that covers a broad spectrum of voters' concerns.[6]

As the first Arab country to hold an election for a constitutive assembly in 2011, Tunisia's election was highly anticipated and the results particularly uncertain. Because the mass protests in Tunisia were predominantly led by existing labor and youth groups, Tunisia's revolution was described as explicitly un-Islamist, and the historic opposition movement of al-Nahda had long been driven underground, with its leaders in exile. By the time elections were held in October 2011, however, al-Nahda had reconstituted itself as a powerful political force in Tunisia, with a clear political ideology that articulated respect for the democratic process and pluralistic points of view, in parallel with its message of religious revival. The veteran Islamist intellectual and al-Nahda's leader, Rachid al-Ghannouchi, returned to Tunisia to help craft the narrative of transition and to carve out a meaningful role of his Islamist group within it. The movement swiftly outflanked its wide range of competitors, winning 37 percent of the vote and eighty-nine of 217 seats in the assembly elections by appealing to religious identity and articulating a platform of social justice, respect for pluralism, and clean government.

Although Morocco's political reforms have been less revolutionary, widespread popular protest throughout 2011 led King Mohammed VI to make important changes to the Moroccan constitution in an attempt to pacify demands for regime change. A series of constitutional amendments were passed by a popular referendum before the elections in November 2011, which required, among other things, that the king appoint a prime minister from the party winning the most seats in parliament. The Justice and Development Party (PJD), an established Islamist competitor committed to working within the monarchical framework, led the fragmented political field with 23 percent of the vote, leading to 107 out of 395 legislative seats. In a dramatic first for Morocco, the king then invited the PJD's leader, Abdeliliah Benkirane, as prime minister, to form a government. Although significant calls for more meaningful political reform remain, an established Islamist party was able to benefit from the reform environment to expand its voter base and increase its political power within the Moroccan system.

The multistage Egyptian elections of 2011/2012 proved particularly interesting from the perspective of Islamist electoral success. Although all observers agreed that the Muslim Brotherhood's newly created Freedom and Justice Party would be very competitive as the best-known quantity in Egyptian politics, the extent of its success, as well as the level of success of its Islamist (Salafist) competitors, was uncertain before the elections. At the conclusion of the three-month electoral process for Egypt's constitutive assembly, the Freedom and Justice Party and associated parties dominated the assembly with a large plurality of 37 percent of the vote and 235 of 498 seats, followed by the more conservative Salafist party, al-Nour, and associated religious parties, with 28 percent of the vote and 123 of the 498 seats.[7] This meant that the Islamist groups, which had appeared comparatively marginal throughout the eighteen-day mass uprising that ousted President Hosni Mubarak in February 2011, were suddenly anything but marginal in determining the future direction of the Egyptian regime, holding the dominant majority of seats in the constitutive assembly. A dramatic shift had taken place in Egyptian politics, which put comparatively untested Islamist groups in the position of negotiating a transition with an increasingly intransigent and forceful Egyptian military. The Brotherhood's presidential candidate, Mohamed Morsi, subsequently won the presidency and began to push through a constitution that favored the interests of Islamist groups. The presidency became increasingly important after the elected assembly was temporarily dissolved by the courts, and the president sought to consolidate power amid ongoing opposition in the streets and subsequent hostility by the military establishment, which would ultimately depose President Morsi in the summer of 2013.

Islamists also scored a major success at the polls in the February 2012 Kuwaiti elections, winning twenty-three of fifty seats, thus becoming newly relevant after a period when the Islamist opposition appeared to wane in the face of renewed tribal and family identity politics. In Yemen, Islamist groups also are well positioned to play a role in the country's uncertain democratic transitions and also, though to a lesser extent, in Libya. The Libyan elections scheduled for late 2013 and future Yemeni legislative elections may see significant electoral support for Islamist groups because of the established electoral record of Islah in Yemen and the fragmentation of other types of identity groups in Libya.[8]

The Egyptian elections showcase one of the most interesting developments in Islamist politics since the Arab uprisings, which is the rise of Salafist groups into the realm of negotiated and electoral politics. Salafism is a broad category based on the Arabic term *salaf* (ancestors of the Islamic community), which is used to describe very religiously conservative groups that argue for the creation of an Islamic state inspired by the original Islamic community under the leadership of the Prophet Muhammad. Multiple Salafist groups competed in the Egyptian elections, with most Salafi votes going to the al-Nour Party. Although observers of Egypt were previously aware of the importance of Salafi movements at the social level, the degree of electoral support that the al-Nour Party received was a surprise, despite the party's own predictions of its success. Salafi groups also rose to heightened prominence in other countries, leading violent protests in Tunisia against a broadcast station and later against the American embassy and security forces,[9] as well as increasing their political profile in Yemen, among other countries. Their success in Egypt indicates a strong desire among a minority segment of the population for more dramatic forms of regime and policy change than the Muslim Brotherhood pledged to provide.

The increasing prominence of the Salafists has led to an important new political dynamic, that of intra-Islamist competition, which emerged as a major theme by the end of 2011. As Islamist groups differ substantively over both their end objective (how Islamic should state and society be?) and their strategies in achieving those objectives (how accommodative or militant should they be?), the prospect of power has led to ideological and organizational battles over the direction of Islamist movements. Indeed, the future political fault lines of much of the Arab world may lie as much in the diverse Islamist movements themselves as across Islamist-secular lines.

Emerging Trends

In addition to the rise of intra-Islamist competition, which has become evident in both elections and popular mobilization, several trends have emerged that make the future direction of Islamist movements both dynamic and uncertain in the medium term. First, as Islamists succeed in securing pluralities in inaugural elections under the new regimes, they will be pressured to build political coalitions across ideological lines in order to govern their societies. Second, as Islamist groups develop opportunities to govern, they will be required to use new skills and make a wide range of difficult political choices, which they have historically been able to avoid making while in the opposition. How well they are able to secure the necessary alliances to maintain their governance of transitional societies has been called into question since President Morsi's forceful removal from power in Egypt and since al-Nahda's agreement to form a technocratic government in Tunisia following the anti-Islamist protests in 2013. Finally, as transitioning Arab states inevitably struggle with poor performance and as tensions across identity groups become heightened through government repression or the discriminatory policies of emerging organizations, sectarian conflict and Islamist militancy by marginal groups has the potential to become much more prominent.

After the Tunisian, Moroccan, and Egyptian elections of 2011, individual Islamist parties secured a plurality, but not a majority, of seats in their respective assemblies. This requires these parties to form a coalition with others in order to govern and therefore requires a measure of compromise and pragmatism not necessary while they were operating in opposition. Much of the scholarship on Islamist parties has suggested that the political compromises associated with deal making and coalition building can lead to more moderation in both ideology and behavior by Islamist groups, although the direction of causality around successful coalition building is not always clear.[10] In Tunisia, for example, al-Nahda led a government composed of members of multiple rival parties, including the center-left

Congress for the Republic and Ettakatol Parties.[11] Being in such a position in which governance depends on other parties has surely encouraged al-Nahda to collaborate with less Islamist parties, although al-Nahda's interests in Islamist centrism came earlier than its participation in government.

This tendency toward political compromise is likely to be magnified when a failure to secure coalition partners may prevent the party from governing, but it may not apply as well to minority parties (like Egypt's al-Nour) that do not participate in the governing coalition or to individual actors who have substantive powers directly associated with their office (like the Egyptian president). However, when governance requires coalitions, the stakes for building effective coalitions rise, and the failure to build them can have starkly negative consequences for the Islamist parties in power. Forming these coalitions will necessitate more pragmatism, and that pragmatism has the potential to speed up the evolution of Islamist parties to be more normalized political actors. For this process to occur, the rules of the game must be reasonably clear and institutionalized to enable political learning. In weakly institutionalized contexts in which the rules of the game always are changing, as has been the case in Egypt, the normalizing effects of electoral participation are less predictable because there are fewer constraints to shape strategic behavior.

The extent to which diverse movements like the Muslim Brotherhood will act more pragmatically or more ideologically once in power is often difficult to predict, but in a genuinely competitive political system, parties that can capture centrist voters have strong incentives to act pragmatically to cater to their concerns, particularly on economic and rule-of-law issues. Actors that have little chance of capturing the center, however, such as newly mobilized Salafist political actors, may actually find that ideological rigidity is politically useful and can be used to diminish the reputation of more centrist actors that are forced by the realities of governance to compromise on political positions that were easier to maintain in opposition.

As Islamists participate in governance, the process of governing will force elected Islamist parties to make difficult decisions that have the potential to complicate their Islamic identity and lead to dissatisfaction among the parties' traditional constituents. Ambiguities in political platforms, in which specific policy-based solutions to social and political problems are often glossed over in favor of religious values or slogans, may both compromise the quality of governance and make it difficult to manage the diverse set of expectations held by supporters. Likewise, many members of Islamist groups with no practical experience in governing have been elevated to positions of authority for which their previous professional and political experiences leave them essentially unqualified. This raises the risk of the Islamist parties being unable to meet the high expectations for their behavior in office as well as for their ability to remedy political, economic, and social ills in their respective countries.[12] Indeed, two years after the January revolution in Egypt, that country's experience with its first Islamist-led government left much cause for popular dissatisfaction.

On a different, and even more worrisome, note, the rise of Islamist groups in the context of the Arab revolts, particularly in cases that have involved significant societal violence, raises the very real possibility of greater sectarian conflict and militancy that could take a long time to fully dissipate. Sectarian conflict has the potential to intensify under conditions of increased resource competition, due to either more scarcity or new opportunities. Likewise, as more marginal political players (for example, the Salafis or threatened religious groups) seek to consolidate their communities or influence evolving political outcomes, ideological attacks can be one of the most rapid and effective ways to do so. As more mainstream Islamist groups discover new avenues to strengthen their social influence and political power, minority groups fear marginalization or exclusion from access to resources, both material and symbolic. Tensions between Muslims and Christians in Egypt, already high before the revolutionary uprising, rose and led to substantial violence in 2011 as militant Islamists increased their profile and Coptic Christians led protests over religious discrimination. In Bahrain, where a long history of sectarian tensions between the Sunni ruling minority and the poorer Shia majority framed the February 2011 uprising, the regime sought to discredit the protesters by heightening Sunni fears of Shia radicalism and trying to implicate the uprising's leaders as having ties to Iran. The bloody civil conflict in Syria saw sharply increasing sectarian violence over time as well, as the Sunni majority framed the state repression as repression by an Alawite minority, a development that fueled more militant Islamist discourse. Militant groups that incorporate strident sectarian preferences as a point of ideology are finding an opportunity for much greater autonomy as a result of persistent state frailty since the uprisings and regime transitions.

Conclusion

Although Islamist groups came late to some of the more prominent mass uprisings in the Arab world during 2011, they did so for sound strategic reasons and benefited significantly since the political reforms and regime transitions. By not publicly leading the uprisings, Islamist groups allowed political mobilization to be defined in broad national terms, which made the popular revolts in Tunisia, Egypt, Libya, and Yemen more successful in achieving their objectives. By gradually increasing their participation within a diverse set of identity groups, Islamist groups also initially managed to escape the targeted repression that has historically plagued their relationship with these regimes. Despite heightened political uncertainty and the fragmentation of an underinstitutionalized opposition, Islamist groups emerged as prominent leaders in shaping political outcomes during regime transitions. This has been especially true for the founding elections, in which Islamist groups demonstrated both their organizational discipline and their substantial electoral appeal.

Whether or not the initial popular enthusiasm for Islamist groups can be maintained over time is open to question, and events in Egypt during 2013 suggest that the Muslim Brotherhood's early popularity did fade quite quickly. In their role as leaders of uncertain political transitions and in their untested governing responsibilities, Islamist parties have many opportunities to disappoint their supporters. The reasons are their inexperience with governance, the enormous structural obstacles to their success, and the unrealistic popular expectations about the level of ideological purity that can be maintained in coalition politics. As the number of opportunities for militants to challenge the new order grows and as religious and nonreligious minorities begin to fear for their status in the context of shifting power relations, Islamist groups have already begun to find that their political honeymoon is shorter than anticipated. Likewise, as the pluralism of Islamist political views puts the divisions in the Islamist movements into the political spotlight, multiple contested Islamisms will emerge. In the end, the newly politicized publics of the Arab world are likely to find in Islam only one of many possible solutions that will be called for if any meaningful political reform is to be consolidated in the new Middle East.

NOTES

1. See, for example, Mohammed Hafez, *Why Muslims Rebel: Repression and Resistance in the Islamic World* (Boulder, Colo.: Lynne Rienner, 2003); Quintan Wiktorowicz, ed., *Islamic Activism: A Social Movement Theory Approach* (Bloomington: Indiana University Press, 2003); Carrie Rosefsky Wickham, *Mobilizing Islam: Religion, Activism, and Political Change in Egypt* (New York: Columbia University Press, 2002).

2. David D. Kirkpatrick, "Muslim Brotherhood Struggles to Find Its Balance in Egypt's Whirlwind," *New York Times*, November 23, 2011.

3. Note that although the political opportunities for Islamists in Tunisia have increased, those in Bahrain have become more restricted over time.

4. A large organization encompassing a diverse set of political tendencies known as the National Forces Alliance dominated in the elections to the National Congress, with 48 percent of the vote, with the Brotherhood-affiliated party coming in much lower, at just over 10 percent of the vote. For full results, see the Libyan High National Commission report, available at http://www.hnec.ly/en/.

5. The overwhelmingly dominant identity highlighted by respondents in the National Survey of Libya opinion poll, conducted by the University of Oxford and the University of Benghazi, was Islam, with those claiming a Libyan identity being a small minority. See www.oxfordresearch.com/1.html.

6. Michelle Pace and Francesco Cavatorta, "The Arab Uprisings in Theoretical Perspective—An Introduction," *Mediterranean Politics* 17, no. 2 (2012): 133.

7. The Freedom and Justice Party won 213 of the 235 seats won by its broader coalition of parties, the Democratic Alliance for Egypt. Al-Nour won 107 of the 123 seats won by the Islamist bloc, which it led.

8. As suggested in the first National Survey of Libya opinion poll, conducted by the University of Oxford and the University of Benghazi, Libya; see www.oxfordresearch.com/1.html.

9. Ben Child, "Islamist Protestors Attack Tunisian TV Station over Animated Film Persepolis," *The Guardian*, October 10, 2011.

10. See, for example, Jillian Schwedler, *Faith in Moderation: Islamist Parties in Jordan and Yemen.* (New York: Cambridge University Press, 2007); Janine A. Clark, "The Conditions of Islamist Moderation: Unpacking Cross-Ideological Cooperation in Jordan," *International Journal of Middle East Studies* 38 (2006): 539–60.

11. Sana Ajmi, "The Composition of the New Tunisian Government," November 21, 2011, availableatTunisialive.http://www.tunisia-live.net/2011/11/21/the-composition-of-the-new-tunisian-government/.

12. See Nathan J. Brown, "When Victory Becomes an Option: Egypt's Muslim Brotherhood Confronts Success" (Washington, D.C.: Carnegie Endowment for International Peace, January 2012).

12

Elections

ELLEN LUST

Egypt's parliamentary election in November 2010 was a dour affair. Widespread repression marked the months leading up to the election; few voters came out on polling day as military trucks lined up near voting stations; and the Egyptian opposition heavily contested the results. The election may have been aimed in part to prepare the ground for Gamal Mubarak to succeed his father, President Hosni Mubarak, but many would argue that this election—like others before it here and elsewhere in the Arab world—was meaningless. Only one year later, following dramatic uprisings across Egypt and Mubarak's ouster, elections were held once again. Arguably, the air was equally tense, but this time it was filled with energy. Campaigning was boisterous; voters streamed to the polls, most for the first time ever; and the results, although contested, were unprecedented and largely seen as legitimate. The elections left open many questions about Egypt's future, but one thing seemed certain: *these* elections mattered.

This dichotomous portrayal of elections before and after the Arab uprisings—viewed, respectively, as irrelevant and significant—is widespread, but is it accurate? Were elections meaningless before the uprisings of 2011 and transformative following them? Did elections contribute to the long-standing authoritarian regimes, as scholars have often argued,[1] or to the instability that led to a regionwide crisis, as they did during color revolutions of eastern Europe?

Elections neither wholly determined regimes' abilities to withstand pressures nor caused the uprisings of 2011, but they did play a role. They affected the maintenance and breakdown of authoritarian regimes, were an instrumental part of the regimes' responses to the regionwide crises that erupted in January 2011, and ultimately were part of the transition process after the regimes fell. Moreover, the role of elections depends on how elections fit within the regime's logic and power structure. In regimes in which elections are integrally tied to the regime's legitimacy (primarily one-party regimes), elections contribute most to instability and are least useful in shoring up incumbents during crises. When a regime's legitimacy is insulated from electoral politics (primarily monarchies), elections are least likely to contribute to instability.

Analyzing how elections affect the breakdown, process, and ultimate outcomes of the instability following January 2011 yields important lessons not just for understanding politics in the Arab world but also for understanding electoral politics, authoritarianism, and transitions more generally. Such an analysis underscores how the underlying logic of the political regime affects the roles of elections. My analysis in this chapter highlights the variation in the roles of elections held in monarchies and one-party states. As Daniel Brumberg argued in chapter 2, however, what is at stake is not whether a king or president is at the helm but the relationship between elections and the regime's power structure and legitimacy. Seemingly contradictory arguments about whether elections are stabilizing or destabilizing, intended to co-opt opposition or signal regime strength, can often be reconciled by recognizing how different types of elections (for example, executive or legislative) or elections in different contexts (dominant-party regimes, monarchies, military juntas) fit within the regimes' power structure. So, too, debates over the relationship of regime type, the breakdown of authoritarianism, and the consolidation of democracy can be illuminated by focusing on how the logic of different regimes affects when and how elections contribute to stability. In short, scholars of elections, authoritarianism, and transitions would do well to look more closely at differences in regimes' fundamental power structures.

This chapter explores the multiple roles of elections and their impact on political stability. The first section discusses how elections helped stabilize authoritarian regimes before 2011. The second section explores why this role diminished over time and why one-party regimes experienced greater instability than others in the Arab world. The third examines the role of elections in regimes that were shaken by the political crisis of 2011, considering their roles when incumbents were still trying to hold onto power as well as how the elections varied in postrupture regimes. The fourth section looks at the relationship between electoral politics and outcomes of the

Arab uprisings. The chapter concludes with lessons learned and insights for the future.

Elections Under Authoritarianism: Mechanisms of Regime Maintenance

It goes almost without saying that elections under authoritarian regimes have little influence on the selection of ruling elites or policymaking. Presidential elections have often been rubber-stamping referenda or minimally contested multicandidate contests,[2] with little expectation that they will bring to power new parties and personalities. Local and national legislatures have little influence over important policies.[3] Nevertheless, just as in other regions, elections have been used to shore up authoritarian regimes in the Arab world.[4] They have provided a venue to co-opt opposition,[5] to deter defection from the ruling coalition,[6] and to efficiently distribute patronage and access to state resources.[7] The extent to which elections served these roles depended in large part on regime type (for example, one-party[8] versus monarchical regimes).

In all regimes, elections provide a venue for elite contestation, helping co-opt and divide the opposition. In the face of heightened opposition and widespread unrest, ruling elites often reopened legislatures or expanded them, often with promises of democracy to come.[9] King Hassan II played this card in Morocco, restoring parliament in 1976 following two attempted coups and heightened dissatisfaction;[10] Egypt's President Anwar Sadat broadened the playing field in 1977,[11] responding to discontent over economic liberalization and Egypt's overtures toward peace with Israel; Hosni Mubarak expanded to multiparty elections in 1984, following Sadat's assassination; Algeria's President Chadli Benjedid called for the first multiparty elections in 1988, after bread riots shook the country; Jordan's King Hussein followed suit in 1989; and even Syria's President Hafez al-Assad expanded the number of independent seats in the Syrian legislature in 1991, attempting to appease business elites chafing under economic reforms.[12] The list goes on.

Notably absent are most of the Gulf monarchies. There, extraordinarily high levels of state resources and, with the exception of Saudi Arabia, small populations outnumbered by expatriates have, until recently, stifled demands for reform. Elections are not entirely absent, but they are dispensable. Elections have been held in Kuwait since independence in 1961, when the monarchy inherited an elected national assembly from the British, and in Bahrain since 1973.[13] In both cases, however, the elections were suspend-

TABLE 12.1

OVERVIEW OF REGIMES AND ELECTIONS IN THE MENA,
AS OF DECEMBER 2010

	TYPE OF REGIME/ ELECTIONS	ELECTED HEAD OF STATE	LEGISLATURE SUSPENDED	AGE OF LEADER
Algeria	Competitive	Yes	1992–1997	73
Bahrain	Monarchy	No	1975–2002	60
Egypt	One party	Yes (Referenda until 2005)	None	82
Iraq	Competitive	Yes	None under current regime	60
Jordan	Monarchy-Elections	No	1967–1989, 2001–2003 elections postponed	48
Kuwait	Monarchy-Elections	No	1976–1981; 1986–1990; 1990–1992; dissolved in 1999, 2006, 2010	81
Lebanon	Competitive	Yes	Legislature remained seated, but elections not held during the 1975–1990 civil war	62
Libya	No elections	No	—	68
Morocco	Monarchy-Elections	No	1965–1970; 1972–1977; 1990–1993 elections postponed	47
Oman	Monarchy	No	—	62
Palestine	Competitive	No	—	Haniyeh 47; Abbas 75
Qatar	Monarchy	No	—	58
Saudi Arabia	Monarehy	No	—	87
Syria	One party	Referenda	None	45
Tunisia	One party	Yes	None	74
UAE	Monarchy	No	—	62
Yemen	One party	Yes	TBD	68

ed for long periods in response to political tensions (see table 12.1). Indeed, far from integral to the regime, elections in the Gulf have been themselves a tool—extended in the face of medium pressures but withdrawn if the pressures exerted through them are too great. The Gulf is thus the exception that proves the rule: elections gave rulers a means to hold onto power in the face of escalating opposition, at least in the short run. But where such pressures were muted or elected institutions have proved unruly, regimes have been happy to do without them.

National and local[14] legislative elections also provide opportunities for contestation over access to patronage. Legislatures are primarily a space in which limited demands can be voiced and through which elites and their constituents can gain access to state resources. From the voters' perspective, elections are for "service parliamentarians" who can help ease transactions with the state with limited bureaucratic capacity and rule of law.[15] From the candidates' perspective, they are an opportunity to vie for privilege, status, and the ability to aid their constituents in a regime in which the weak rule of law and lack of transparency severely restrict paths to power.[16]

Indeed, elections offer the regime a tool to bring some elites closer to the regime, sideline others, and hold out hope to many more that their turn in the outer rooms of power will come. In contrast to the widespread conventional wisdom of elections as predetermined contests in which only the handpicked are chosen, there often are large numbers of entrants into legislative electoral races, even in one-party regimes. Certainly the regime intervenes in some races, ensuring the success of favorite sons and preventing potentially strong opponents from winning. But in general, the races are competitive and highly contested. With high numbers of candidates for each seat, winners often gain their seats through pluralities; large numbers of votes are wasted and up for grabs in subsequent elections; and the turnover rate in legislatures is strikingly high, with less than 25 percent incumbency rates across the Arab world.[17] As a result, elections provide hope to elites and would-be elites that they can win tomorrow, if not today.

Elections can also help legitimize the regime and signal its strength to the would-be opposition. In all authoritarian regimes, they do so in part by providing state-sanctioned venues for "legitimate" competition, limiting the opposition's access to this arena and demonstrating the state's ability to yield acceptable outcomes. To maintain legitimacy, incumbents seek high turnout, although the level of "acceptable" turnout varies across states and the level of elections (for example, executive, national legislative, and local). When turnout remains stable and elections proceed relatively smoothly, regimes send strong signals to the would-be opposition that they remain in control.[18]

Elections take on additional meaning in one-party regimes. There, legitimacy is based in large part on popular support for the leading party, whereas in monarchies, legitimacy centers on personalized, hereditary rule. Thus, to maintain legitimacy, rulers in one-party regimes need to limit the representation of nonruling parties in the legislature, and they have a difficult time disbanding the legislature in the face of political crises. Monarchies, in contrast, benefit from diverse legislatures, since no single party then emerges as a challenger and the king can claim to have a critical role in mediating among competing factions in society. Moreover, in the face of political crises, monarchies (even less wealthy ones outside the Gulf) can—and have—easily disbanded parliaments, sometimes for long periods at a time. This is simply not a viable, long-term option in one-party regimes.

In one-party states, strong support in presidential elections is important to signaling the regime's strength. As Barbara Geddes pointed out, presidents in dominant party states used relatively uncontested elections and referenda—with astoundingly high (reported) turnout rates and overwhelming majorities voting in incumbents' support—to show the military and other potential opposition the futility of attempting to unseat them.[19] The election results may raise eyebrows and become the butt of countless jokes, but they also demonstrate that the regime can get away with the spectacle. That too, Lisa Wedeen reminded us, reinforces their power.[20]

Change and Limitations: When Elections Fail to Stabilize

Elections do not inevitably contribute to a regime's stability. Indeed, as many scholars have found, elections can become moments of real contestation, with the regime's survival at stake, when the incumbent's inability to stand for reelection generates divisions in the ruling elite.[21] Even when opposition elections do not take on such heightened meaning or when parties lose, stolen elections (or credible claims of them) can spark moral outrage, foster opposition coordination, and mount new, and sometimes definitive, challenges to regimes,[22] ushering in new possibilities for democracy. Nowhere were such effects more evident than in the color revolutions of Eastern Europe.

Although the Arab world has not witnessed the emergence of color rev-olutions[23] around electoral moments, in the past two decades three main factors came together that weakened the stabilizing role of elections. First, economic crises and reforms limiting the state's control over the economy limited its ability to distribute patronage through elected institutions; second, the passage of time led to increased frustration, as promises of democratiza-tion became stale and the Arab world was left behind the global trend toward democracy; and third, the divide between secularist and Islamist, which had once served to stifle secularists' demands for immediate reform, narrowed through cooperation both inside and outside the electoral sphere. Across the Arab world the heightened discontent and limitations in the electoral sphere undermined the regimes' stability. The problem was exacerbated in one-party regimes, in which attempts to consolidate personalistic power and shore up the regime in the face of declining resources undermined electoral institu-tions that were linked to the very core of the regime's legitimacy.

As in other regions, declining state resources and neoliberal reforms weakened the links between patronage and parliament.[24] Constituents con-tinued to expect services, seeking representatives' help in obtaining jobs, education, and assistance. However, their representatives were increasingly unable to meet their demands. This heightened the frustration with rep-resentatives, and the skepticism toward the electoral process contributed to unrest,[25] resulting in a lower turnout.[26] Regimes recognized this as a problem and at times tried to breathe new life into elections, but cynicism toward the process continued to grow.

The passage of time contributed to this problem as well. After promises of "gradual democratization" following the once widely heralded opening of multiparty elections, Arabs experienced decades of disappointment.[27] Rather than a gradual blossoming of democracy, many countries endured notable de-liberalization. The vast majority of citizens became disinterested in elections, repudiating participants and processes alike. Some continued to go to the polls in the hopes that they could elect someone they could count on to help them access state resources; others did so to garner gifts and cash payments; and many chose to stay home. Nearly all had concluded that elections would not deliver democracy.[28]

This was particularly grating for opposition elites, who found their promises unmet and their access to power and resources restricted. They turned to boycotts and protests to pressure the regime for change.[29] They also formed cross-party, and even cross-ideological, alliances in attempts to press their demands. These alliances often dissolved; demands went unmet;

and the public often dismissed party leaders as ineffective at best and as regime lackeys at worst. Far from effectively co-opting opposition elites, elections were prompting the opposition to develop skills and cross-ideological alliances that could embolden broader political challenge.[30]

Indeed, in the Arab world, the stabilizing role of elections was further eroded by the gradual inclusion of Islamist forces, which weakened the barriers that had previously divided secularist and Islamist forces. Secularist demands for democratization in the Arab world had long been muted by the fear of Islamist forces, a fear reinforced by what Daniel Brumberg (chapter 2) argued was the regime's manipulation of identity politics in order to create a "protection racket."[31] In the early 1990s, secularist opposition forces feared that Islamists would come to power through elections, only to undermine democracy (what U.S. Ambassador Edward Djerejian famously called "one-person, one-vote, one-time"),[32] or that the democratization process would collapse into civil war, as it had in Algeria. Their fears were exacerbated by the fact that Islamists and secularists had almost no experience cooperating with each other, a fact proved in many states by electoral rules that banned Islamist forces (Egypt, Morocco).

By the mid-2000s, the situation began to change. In countries like Morocco and Egypt, the regimes had responded to growing Islamist support in the population to allow Islamists a greater role in parliament. In Morocco, the Islamist-oriented Democratic and Constitutional Popular Movement Party (MPDC), which later became the Party of Justice and Development (PJD), was allowed to run as a legal party for the first time in the 1997 elections, when the king reversed his long-standing position that Morocco did not need an Islamist party. In Egypt, the Muslim Brotherhood remained illegal, but it was allowed to win nearly 20 percent of parliamentary seats in the 2005 elections.[33] Such participation did not serve to allay secularists' fears entirely, but it did lead at times to joint secularist-Islamist efforts. In the face of increasingly repressive regimes, this helped shift many secularists from their initial stance that "the devil you know (the regime) is better than the devil you don't" to one in which mutual collaboration and trust was conceivable.[34]

In one-party regimes, the role of elections was further undermined by the contradiction between the impulse to consolidate a personalistic regime and the need to maintain participatory institutions that would legitimize and strengthen the regime. This impulse was evident across the Arab world, particularly as ruling elites sought to maintain their allies' support in the face of diminishing resources. Yet in monarchies, there is no tension between shoring up personal power and strengthening a regime based on hereditary (that is, personalized) legitimacy. On the contrary, in one-party states, in which legitimacy is closely tied to electoral institutions, the personalization of power hurt the very institutions on which the regime relied.

Consolidating personalistic power required presidents in one-party states to weaken the very ruling parties that were once developed to help settle conflict among elites or mobilize support against the opposition.[35] Indeed, by 2005, Egypt's ruling National Democratic Party (NDP) had lost its ability to control its slate of candidates in parliamentary elections,[36] and when unrest escalated in January 2011, it did not play a clear organizational role in defending the regime against protesters. The same was largely true in Tunisia, where the ruling Constitutional Democratic Rally (RCD) had become so weakened that it was dissolved in 2011, even before the opposition fully removed former regime loyalists from power. In Syria and Yemen, too, ruling parties became largely impotent, as evidenced by the fact that even though they helped rubber-stamp reforms in the wake of political crises, the primary defense for the regime was not found in the ruling party but among key elites in the regime's inner circle. The contradiction between personalized power and strong political institutions, combined with the need to restrict the electoral playing field, left dominant-party states with a narrow political support base.

The problem was particularly acute in regimes in which aged rulers faced succession crises. In part, this is because age raised the specter of succession, making palpable a vision of the regime without its leader. Internal disputes also arose over potential contenders, creating moments in which critical elite defections were likely.[37] Finally, regimes refitted the electoral arena to bide time to shepherd succession processes and, in many cases, to tilt the balance of power toward their progeny. They rewrote constitutions,[38] manipulated electoral rules, stepped up electoral repression, and constrained opposition representation in legislatures in an effort to maintain elite cohesion and smooth transition processes. Such efforts were often counterproductive, however, as constraining the playing field led to declining participation, limited the reach of patronage distribution, prompted disaffection of political elites and, at times, the formation of broad boycott coalitions, and eroded legitimacy.[39] It is thus not surprising that one-party regimes with elderly presidents—Zine al-Abdine Ben Ali in Tunisia, Hosni Mubarak in Egypt, Ali Abdullah Saleh in Yemen, Muammar al-Qaddafi in Libya—were among the first to come under attack in 2011.

Under such conditions, as Egypt demonstrates, parliamentary elections not only fail to shore up the regime, but they also arguably contribute to its downfall. Anticipating the 2011 presidential elections, for which it was widely rumored that Gamal Mubarak would be his father's favored contender, eighty-two-year-old Hosni Mubarak sought to ensure that legislative elections returned a docile parliament. The ruling circle was taking no chances that the Muslim Brotherhood would win a substantial number of seats, as it had in the 2005 elections. It thus harshly repressed the Brotherhood, manipulated first-round elections to effectively shut out the opposition, and then ridiculed the opposition as it united first to boycott second-round elections and then to form a shadow parliament.[40] This ultimately undermined Mubarak's regime in four ways: (1) manipulating the elections heightened antipathy toward the regime; (2) eliminating the Muslim Brotherhood from parliament made it more willing to join the opposition forces that mobilized in January; (3) repressing the opposition prompted coordination that served as a dress rehearsal for the uprising; and (4) responding flippantly to their efforts only escalated opposition to the regime.[41]

So, too, in Yemen, sixty-nine-year-old Ali Abdullah Saleh's determination to manipulate elections destabilized the regime. Reportedly determined to buy time to groom his son Ahmed for power, he reneged on a 2006 promise that he would not seek reelection, pushed for constitutional revision to remove the two-term limit for the presidency, and sidelined and denigrated the opposition Joint Meeting Parties (JMP).[42] Yemeni forces were locked in a political crisis over the upcoming elections. Elections had been postponed since February 2009, and no progress had been made on the electoral reforms promised in the February agreement of that year. In December 2010, the General People's Congress (GPC) unilaterally announced elections would be held in April 2011; the JMP called for a boycott; and the GPC ridiculed their efforts.[43] Elections were not held, but as in Egypt, the conflict over elections heightened opposition to the regime, failed to co-opt opposition forces, and strengthened opposition alliances across the ideological spectrum.

In short, economic crises and reforms increased frustration over stalled democratization, and the diminished divide between Islamist and secularist forces weakened the ability of limited elections to stabilize the regime. However, the extent to which they did so depended in part on the structure

TABLE 12.2

RELATIONSHIP BETWEEN ELECTORAL POLITICS AND THE PROCESSES
IN 2011 ARAB UPRISINGS AS OF DECEMBER 2012

	LITTLE MOBILIZATION	PARTIAL MOBILIZATION	MASS MOBILIZATION	VIOLENT UNREST
No or heavily restricted elections	Qatar Saudi Arabia UAE	Oman		Libya
Elections: one party			Egypt Tunisia Syria Yemen	Syria
Elections: monarchy		Jordan Kuwait Morocco	Bahrain	
Elections: competitive	Algeria/Lebanon Iraq/Palestine			

of power underlying the regime. My analysis adds support to those who
argue that regime type affects the possibility of breakdown, but it does so
differently than the prevailing literature would suggest. The Achilles heel
in one-party states (and hybrid regimes) is elite incentives and institutional structures and also the inability of elites to shore up personal power and
maintain electoral institutions that strengthen their regime.[44] In monarchies in which elections either were not held (because resources cushioned
the regime from demands) or, if held, were more competitive, the opposition's demands appear to have been weaker, and mobilization was limited.
In monarchies holding more significant elections, the demands for reform
were stronger, with the public often taking to the streets to call for reform.
(The one exception was in Bahrain, where the minority Sunni rule over
the majority Shia population led the opposition to take to the streets in
greater numbers.) In one-party regimes that held elections, in which the
stabilizing effects of elections had diminished most significantly, incumbents came under earlier and harsher attacks. This relationship is shown
in table 12.2.[45]

Elections After 2011: Business as Usual or a Radical Transformation?

To what extent did the 2011 Arab uprisings fundamentally alter electoral politics across the region? Certainly, the uprisings have reconfigured relations between citizen-subjects and their states; even where regimes have remained intact, their citizens demand more, and do so more forcefully, than ever before. Elections are an important arena through which these struggles are carried out and a tool that authoritarian regimes can use in various ways to try to maintain its hold on power. As Steven Heydemann and Reinoud Leenders (chapter 4) noted, authoritarian leaders can adjust their strategies, learning from the experiences of others in the region. Yet their options also depend on the structure of power within the regime and the extent of the crisis that the regime faces.

In many cases, authoritarian regimes holding onto power use elections to pump new energy into the political sphere and to control the pace of reform. This has been used extensively since January 2011 (see table 12.3). In the Gulf, where oppositions have been weaker, electoral reforms are less threatening to the regime, and even limited electoral reforms are heralded as a significant step forward. Thus, for instance, Saudi Arabia's decision to hold the second-ever municipal elections (after a two-year delay) in September 2011 while announcing that it would allow women to participate in 2015; the UAE's September 2011 elections with an expanded electorate (from 6,000 to 129,000 voters) for the forty-member, half-appointed Federal National Council (with extremely limited legislative powers); and Oman's October 2011 vote for the eighty-four-member Consultative Assembly after announcing—but not defining—"significant powers" that the assembly would enjoy all were deemed "significant reforms." In Kuwait, the parliament has more power and the electoral sphere is more vibrant; however, one election in three years highlights the fact that the monarchy, not parliament, calls the shots.

Outside the Gulf, electoral reform is used also to preempt escalating opposition. In Morocco, Mohammed VI responded to demonstrations spearheaded by the February 20 movement by instituting constitutional reforms, calling voters to endorse them in the July 1, 2011, referendum and then to return to the polls for parliamentary elections on November 25 of that year. The elections brought to power, for the first time, a coalition government including the Islamist PJD, and the constitutional reforms theoretically enhanced the parliament's power. Similarly, King Abdullah II of

TABLE 12.3

ELECTIONS SINCE JANUARY 2011

	LAST ELECTION HELD BEFORE JANUARY 2011	ELECTIONS SCHEDULED SINCE JANUARY 2011	ELECTIONS HELD SINCE JANUARY 2011?
Algeria	Parliamentary: May 17, 2007; presidential: April 9, 2009	Parliamentary: May 10, 2012 Presidential: April 16, 2014	Yes
Bahrain	Parliamentary: October 23, 2010	Parliamentary: September 24, 2011 (by-election); October 2014	Yes
Egypt	Shura council (1st and 2nd rounds); June 1 and 8, 2010; parliament (1st and 2nd rounds); November 28 and December 5, 2010	Constitutional referendum: March 19, 2011: parliamentary: phase 1 (1st round); November 28–29, 2011, phase 2 (1st round); December 14 15, 2011, and phase 3 (1st round) January 3–4, 2012; Shura council: January 29, 2012, through February 22nd, 2012; presidential elections (1st round); May 23, 2012, and (2nd round): June 16, 2012; May 26, 2014	Yes
Iraq	Parliamentary: March 7, 2010	April 26, 2014	Yes
Jordan	Parliamentary: November 9, 2010	January 23, 2013	Yes
Kuwait	Parliamentary: May 16, 2009	Parliamentary: February 2, 2012, and December 1, 2012 (February elections declared null and void)	Yes
Lebanon	Parliamentary (subnational phases 1–4); May 2, 9, 23, and 30, 2010	Parliamentary: June 2013	No
Libya	Parliamentary: March 2010	Legislative: July 7, 2012	Yes
Morocco	Parliamentary: September 7, 2007	Constitutional referendum: July 1, 2011; parliamentary: November 25, 2011	Yes
Oman	Legislative: October 27, 2007	Legislative: October 15, 2011	Yes
Palestine	Parliamentary: July 17, 2010 (canceled); January 25, 2006	Parliamentary (tentative): October 2014	No

TABLE 12.3 *(continued)*

ELECTIONS SINCE JANUARY 2011

	LAST ELECTION HELD BEFORE JANUARY 2011	ELECTIONS SCHEDULED SINCE JANUARY 2011	ELECTIONS HELD SINCE JANUARY 2011?
Qatar	Legislative: April 2007 (postponed)	Parliamentary: June 2013 (tentative)	No
Saudi Arabia	Municipal: February 10–April 21, 2005	Subnational legislative: September 29, 2011	Yes
Syria	Parliamentary: April 22, 2007; referendum: May 27, 2007	Subnational legislative: December 22, 2011; constitutional referendum: February 26, 2012; parliamentary: May 7, 2012; Presidential: June 2014	Yes
Tunisia	Parliamentary: October 25, 2009; presidential: October 25, 2009	Parliamentary: October 23, 2011; legislative and presidential: June 23, 2013	Yes
UAE	Parliamentary (1st, 2nd, and 3rd stages); December 16, 18, and 20, 2006	Legislative: September 24, 2011	Yes
Yemen	Presidential: September 20, 2006; legislative: April 27, 2003	Legislative: April 27, 2011 (postponed); presidential: February 21, 2012	Yes

Sources: IFES Election Guide, available at http://www.elecionguide.org (accessed April 22, 2012); Reuters.

Jordan responded to increased unrest and demands for political reforms that included eliminating the unpopular, one-person, one-vote electoral law; expanding parliamentary powers; and electing the prime minister by establishing a commission to devise a slate of reforms. The promise of reforms convinced many Jordanians to wait and see, and the steady stream of new electoral commissions, political party laws, and other changes captured Jordanians' attention as many turned to debating and evaluating rumored and proposed reforms. Algeria, too, called elections and instituted reforms, including invitations to international observers, the newly created National Elections Observation Commission (CNSEL), and an expanded National Assembly from 389 to 462 seats.[46] The elections were not without the familiar problems, but they did demonstrate that the regime continued to see elections as a tool to appease opposition and mobilize support. And at least in the short run, such elections alleviated tensions.

Elections are used to promise reform and downplay the extent of the crisis, portray a sense of "normalcy," and demonstrate a regime's resolve against the opposition. In June 2011, as air strikes pounded Tripoli to fight what the regime referred to as "rats" and "terrorists" supported abroad, Saif-al-Islam Qaddafi announced that his father would stand for first-ever presidential elections, promising to step aside if defeated. This seemingly odd announcement in a country without elected institutions was intended to bolster the conviction that the majority of Libyans stood with the regime. Similarly, Bahrain's decision to hold by-elections on September 24, 2011, owing to vacancies left when eighteen parliamentary members of the al-Wefaq opposition walked out, was an effort to draw lines in the sand. Held as thousands of protesters marched toward Pearl Roundabout to demonstrate their opposition, the elections underscored the regime's determination that they would continue with "politics as normal" and "punish" those who chose to defect.

Bashar al-Asad's decision to hold elections as violence escalated in Syria is also better understood as an attempt to signal control than as a step in the reform process. Local elections were held on December 12, 2011, following reforms intended to increase the power of local councils. Reportedly, 43,000 candidates competed for 12,000 local council seats, despite an opposition boycott, and as fierce fighting continued across the country (reportedly killing twenty on polling day alone). Similarly, in March 2011, as Kofi Annan, former secretary-general of the United Nations, met with members of the Syrian regime to establish a cease-fire, the international community stepped up pressure on the regime, and fighting escalated throughout the country. Asad announced that parliamentary elections would be held on May 7, 2012, as the next step in a reform process that included the promulgation of a new constitution in February of that year. The international community and Syrian opposition quickly objected, but the regime resolutely continued its plans. The Syrian regime, alone, was to control the political process.

It may seem farcical for regimes under siege to call for elections, but they may also benefit from doing so. It reinforces the notion that the regime remains firmly in control and that the political conflict can be resolved through "reform as normal." The strategy may not always succeed; low-turnout rates can undermine confidence in the regime, and as Bahrain demonstrated, the elections themselves may provide a focal point around which protests are mobilized. Nevertheless, elections can also send an important message to fence-sitters. It tells those who would support the opposition only if they believe it will win, or those who believe there is no other path to reform, that the regime is in control and intent on "peaceful" reform. If fence-sitters believe this is the case, they will continue to sit it out.

Finally, elections can be used as a concession, presenting a proposed exit strategy to protesters. This was the case in Egypt, Tunisia, and Yemen, although they did not appease publics embittered by broken promises of past reforms and (in Egypt and Yemen) emboldened by the images of Ben Ali's abrupt departure from Tunisia. Ben Ali's declaration on January 13 that he would not run for reelection, coming amid orders to the police to stop firing live ammunition at protesters and followed the next day by the dissolution of parliament and calls for new elections within six months, did nothing to end the protests. By evening on January 14, Ben Ali had fled the country, leaving his prime minister, Mohamed Ghannouchi, and the military in charge. Protesters in Tahrir Square also rejected Mubarak's February 1 promise not to run for reelection in the presidential polls scheduled for September that year. Arguably, the announcement may have divided the Egyptian public—at least the initial discussions suggested some were willing to accept what could have been a peaceful, electoral transfer of power, but the "Night of the Camels"—when regime-backed thugs running roughshod over protesters in Tahrir Square were televised across the world—turned the tide against the regime. In Yemen, President Saleh's attempt to follow suit with an announcement on February 2 that he would postpone the much criticized April parliamentary elections and not run for the next presidential elections, followed by a promise on May 21 for early presidential and parliamentary elections, also was roundly rejected. Such promises only raised the ire of the opposition, which wanted long-standing leaders to step down, and potentially signaled the regime's weakness. Certainly, they did not slow their demise.

In short, and as summarized in table 12.4, incumbents have used elections in various ways to respond to the crises that emerged in 2011. In some cases, electoral reforms were part of a broader package of political reforms, intended to alleviate opposition by signaling the possibilities of further change, co-opting some opposition elites, and providing a mechanism to distribute patronage more broadly. This strategy was particularly prominent in regimes in which minor reforms could be heralded as significant change and the upper echelons of power were relatively insulated from electoral politics (for example, in monarchies and, given the military's guardianship role, Algeria). Incumbents have also used elections to

TABLE 12.4

ELECTIONS IN RESPONSE TO THE 2011 ARAB UPRISINGS
AS OF FEBRUARY 2013

	ELECTIONS AS PROMISED EXIT	ELECTIONS AS REFORM	ELECTIONS AS SIGNALING STRENGTH	LITTLE OR NO CHANGE IN ELECTIONS
No or restricted elections		Oman, UAE Qatar, Saudi Arabia	Libya	
Elections: one party	Egypt, Tunisia, Yemen		Syria	
Elections: monarchy		Morocco, Jordan, Kuwait[a]	Bahrain	
Elections: competitive		Algeria		Lebanon, Iraq/Palestine

[a] Kuwait could be coded as either little change or reform. The emir routinely responds to crises by dissolving parliament and calling for new elections, just as he did in December 2011. There were no major institutional changes before the new election, but the new parliament did include more opposition voices than previous ones had.

demonstrate resolve. This was the case in Bahrain, Libya and Syria, where minority regimes expected that reforms would undo the regime. Finally, incumbents offered elections as an exit strategy in Egypt and Yemen. This occurred in one-party regimes, which came under the greatest pressure and when calling new elections could have prevented the regime's institutional structure from unraveling, giving the dominant party a chance to remain in control, and, some would argue, may even have eventually allowed the leader to bide his time and regain power.

The Future of the Arab World and the Role of Elections

The depth of the crises that incumbents face, their capacity to respond, and the oppositions' ability to push back determine whether or not regimes change and the possible replacements that emerge. The processes at hand are stochastic, highly uncertain, and contentious, and they are influenced by myriad factors at home (for example, regime type, social cleavages, economic conditions) and abroad (geostrategic concerns and regional instability especially in neighboring countries, and international coalitions). Elections are one part of a multifaceted strategy that incumbents and oppositions use to press their case, but they nevertheless play an important role in the depth of the crisis that each regime faces, the regime's ability to appease the opposition, and the final outcome. The role of elections and the final outcome achieved depend in part on how they fit within the regime's power structure.

In some countries, elections may contribute to stabilizing authoritarian regimes, much as they did in the past. Limited electoral openings may appease opposition voices, and the crisis may pass with little real change. This is most likely in small oil monarchies with large expatriate populations, in which elections are not a key to the regime's legitimacy or the distribution of power and in which allegiance (or at least acquiescence) is maintained through other means. This outcome is more likely still if the fall of regimes elsewhere leads to massive instability or civil war, and if international forces—perhaps spurred by the rise of anti-Western forces through elections elsewhere—step up efforts to limit change in geostrategically important areas.

In other cases, the elections may be a key to gradual regime change. This outcome may seem unlikely, given that more than two decades of promised reform in most of the region helped create a cynical, impatient public. As happened in Egypt, Tunisia, and Yemen, many people are satisfied with nothing less than their leader's removal. Yet the option should not be entirely dismissed. As Arabs across the region observe the violence and instability in regimes where rapid change has occurred, they may increasingly prefer a less dramatic path. Emboldened by the changes across the region but not intent on an immediate, all-or-nothing outcome, they may push institutional openings toward more fundamental openings. Such possibilities appear greater in monarchies like Jordan, Kuwait, and Morocco. Problems still exist, however: the dynastic nature of the Kuwaiti regime makes such an outcome difficult, and in Jordan, tensions between the minority but privileged Jordanians of East Bank background and those of Palestinian origin are likely to prevent greater power sharing. Nevertheless, in these cases, the regime's institutional structure allows a process that would shepherd a constitutional monarchy and continue to allow some privilege, at least to the ruling family. The outcome also is possible in Algeria, where the negotiations following the civil war have already eliminated a ruling party's hold on power, and the guardianship role of the military can help ensure privileges for those at the apex of power. It also is possible in Yemen, where thus far limited but significant changes following Saleh's departure have provided the basis for further reform. In these cases, regime change would not develop overnight but rather through a medium-term push-and-pull process that gradually opened the playing field to new actors, fostered new contestation, and reshaped the political institutions.

Finally, elections can become a key arena for the struggle over the country's future. This is particularly true when old leaders fall and *ancien regimes* are swept away. Such elections pose enormous challenges and opportunities.[47] Playing fields are opened more widely than ever before; debates focus on political platforms, ideologies, and the country's future; and voter participation is high.[48] Indeed, as we saw in Egypt and Tunisia, voters rushed to the polls—often for the first time ever—and previously unthinkable results were realized.

Yet even elections that follow regime ruptures can take on varied meanings and lead to different ultimate outcomes. The significance of elections depends in part on how completely the old regime was removed and on the strength of electoral institutions under authoritarianism. In both Tunisia and Egypt, for instance, electoral institutions were well established. But in Tunisia the *ancien régime* was largely swept aside before new elections to the Constituent Assembly were held, and the elections were the focus of contestation over the country's future. In Egypt, the removal of the old regime was much less complete, and in the continued struggle over power, the electoral institutions were undermined. The first elected parliament was disbanded, and much of the struggle over the country's future is taking place through extraelectoral politics (demonstrations, protests).

Where electoral institutions are less developed, postrupture elections are important but not the nexus of contestation over the country's future (see table 12.5). Thus, both Libya (which saw the former regime removed) and Yemen (where elements of the former regime remain) saw dissolution into conflict when political forces used extraelectoral means to fight their battles. In the lead-up to the June 2012 parliamentary elections in Libya, intensifying armed conflict threatened to make elections untenable, and in Yemen, President Abd al-Rabbu al-Hadi's attempts to remove figures close to Saleh were resisted on the basis of pro- and antireform figures, as well by mobilizing tribes in resistance. This is somewhat consistent with the large literature that finds countries with more experience with elections and higher contestation under an authoritarian regime are more likely to consolidate democracies after transition.[49] But as the case of Yemen

TABLE 12.5

RELATIONSHIP BETWEEN ELECTORAL POLITICS AND
OUTCOMES AS OF APRIL 2013

	FALL OF LEADER	REPRESSION	INSTITUTIONAL REFORMS	NO CHANGE OR LIMITED REFORMS
No or restricted elections	Libya	(Libya)		Oman, UAE, Qatar, Saudi Arabia
Elections: one party	Egypt,[a], Tunisia Yemen[a]	Syria	Syria	(Egypt), (Tunisia), (Yemen)
Elections: monarchy		Bahrain	Morocco, Jordan[a]	Kuwait
Elections: competitive			Algeria	Lebanon, Iraq, Palestine

[a] Before removed from power, presidents promised not to stand in upcoming elections.

suggests, the main factor may not be the electoral history and contestation alone, but the relative strength of state institutions versus extrastate politics more broadly.

In sum, elections play different roles in outcomes, from helping maintain authoritarian regimes (likely in small Gulf States), to providing an arena of reform (Algeria, Morocco, and Jordan), and to being an important venue in the postrupture transitions. The extent to which elections are critical to the struggle over the state after its leaders fall depends on the extent of the break and how well developed the electoral institutions were under authoritarian regimes. That is, electoral politics—and their place in the broader political structure—will influence the possibility of transition and also will likely affect the nature of the regimes to follow.

Conclusion

In the Arab world as elsewhere, elections have influenced the consolidation, breakdown, and transition processes of authoritarian regimes. In contrast to the conventional wisdom—that elections were "meaningless" before the Arab uprisings and significant following them, we find that elections played important, but different, roles before the political crises that emerged with the Arab uprisings, in the regimes' responses to these crises, and likely in the outcomes that follow. In contrast to the dominant scholarship, which seeks to understand the role of elections and elected institutions under authoritarian regimes, as well as in processes of regime breakdown and democratization, this chapter pointed out the multiple roles that elections play before, during, and following regime ruptures. In doing so, it sheds new light on both electoral politics and the relationship of regime types, stability, and democratization. I argue not that electoral politics is the only factor affecting these processes but that it is an important one and the broader political context (including regime type) has an important influence on the roles of elections.

Indeed, the roles of elections before 2011 and their ability to help stabilize regimes depended in part on the regime's structure of power. Elections were a means of co-opting the opposition and deterring defection from the ruling coalition, distributing patronage, and signaling the regime's strength. The regime's strength was particularly important in one-party regimes, in which majority control in legislatures, high turnout, and support rates for incumbents in presidential elections signal to would-be opponents that the regime remained firmly in place.

Nonetheless, in the last two decades, social, political, and economic changes have eroded the stabilizing role of elections. Economic crises and reforms limited the state's ability to distribute patronage; the continued delay of promises of democratization increased popular cynicism and discontent; and a decline (though certainly not elimination) of secularist-Islamist antagonisms fostered cooperation across opposition groups. Moreover, the impulse to consolidate personalistic regimes undermined electoral institutions, particularly in one-party states, in which establishing personalistic rule conflicted with the internal political contestation needed to strengthen ruling parties and elected institutions. Across the Arab world, popular discontent escalated; opposition forces became stronger (often under the radar); and regimes grew more fragile. Changes in elections did not cause the Arab uprisings, but they did contribute to regimes' inability to withstand political crises, most notably in the one-party regimes.

Incumbents have also used elections as a tool in responding to the regional political crises following January 2011. As part of a broader package of responses, the role of elections depends in part on the nature of the political regime. First, some regimes (and especially monarchies) have called elections and, at times, revised electoral laws in order to appease the public, co-opt the opposition, and signal that broader political reforms are forthcoming. Others—and here the one-party regimes of Egypt, Tunisia, and Yemen stand out—have used elections as a proposed exit strategy, hoping that by calling elections and promising not to run in them, they can stifle the opposition, cushion the shock of change, and minimize the losses for regime elites. Finally, and perhaps most notably, in regimes under siege, leaders have called new elections "as usual," arguing that the returns would demonstrate the widespread, unshaken support of the "silent majority." It is in this way that we can best understand why Qaddafi called for elections in Libya even while bombs were falling on Tripoli, and Assad continued with plans to hold elections in Syria even while the military was fighting opposition forces across the country.

Finally, elections also play an important role in establishing outcomes of the political crises that swept the region. Elections are not the sole factor influencing the outcome, and processes of breakdown and transition are inherently stochastic and indeterminate. Yet the logic of elections in different political circumstances suggests we are likely to find that elections will help maintain authoritarian regimes in small, wealthy Gulf states; foster small (perhaps nearly imperceptible and reversible) reform in Algeria, Morocco, and Jordan, where a third-party guardianship role eases reforms; and be an arena of contestation in the postrupture transitions of Egypt, Libya, Tunisia, and Yemen. In these cases, the extent to which elections contribute to the struggle over the state after leaders fall—and the possibility that they will help usher in democracy—depends on how greatly the transitional regime has broken with the former elites and on how developed multiparty elections were in the past. That is, electoral politics—and their place in the broader political structure—both influence the possibility of transition and affect which regimes will emerge in the future.

NOTES

1. For a more detailed review of the following arguments and the challenges remaining in ascertaining the role of elections, see Jennifer Gandhi and Ellen Lust-Okar, "Elections Under Authoritarianism, *Annual Review of Political Science* 12 (2009): 403–22.
2. Multicandidate presidential elections are rare in the Arab world but have been held in Egypt and Algeria.
3. Jennifer Gandhi and Adam Przeworski argue that elected institutions (e.g., parliaments) can provide an arena for elites to contest policies. See Jennifer Gandhi and

Adam Przeworski, "Cooperation, Cooptation, and Rebellion Under Dictatorship," *Economics and Politics* 18, no. 1 (2006):1–26; and Jennifer Gandhi, *Political Institutions Under Dictatorship* (New York: Cambridge University Press, 2008). There is little evidence of this in most of the Arab world, and few citizens see the parliament in this light.

4. Empirically, authoritarian regimes with elections are more durable than their non-electoral counterparts. See Barbara Geddes, "Authoritarian Breakdown: Empirical Test of a Game Theoretic Argument," paper presented at the annual meeting of the American Political Science Association, Atlanta, 1999. Opposing this argument, see Jason Brownlee, "Portents of Pluralism: How Hybrid Regimes Affect Democratic Transitions," *American Journal of Political Science* 53, no. 3 (July 2009): 515–32; and Axel Hadenius and Jan Teorell, "Pathways from Authoritarianism," *Journal of Democracy* 18, no. 1 (2007): 143–56.

5. See Carles Boix and Milan Svolik, "The Foundation of Limited Authoritarian Government: Institutions and Power-Sharing in Dictatorships," paper presented at Dictatorships: Their Governance and Social Consequences Conference, Princeton University, Princeton, N.J., 2009; Gandhi, *Political Institutions Under Dictatorship*; Gandhi and Przeworski, "Cooperation, Cooptation, And Rebellion Under Dictatorship"; Joseph Wright, "Do Authoritarian Institutions Constrain? How Legislatures Affect Economic Growth and Investment," *American Journal of Political Science* 52, no. 2 (2008): 322–43; Beatrice Magaloni, *Voting for Autocracy: Hegemonic Party Survival and Its Demise in Mexico* (New York: Cambridge University Press, 2006); Ellen Lust-Okar, *Structuring Conflict in the Arab World: Incumbents, Opponents, and Institutions* (New York: Cambridge University Press, 2005); Emily Beaulieu, "Protesting the Contest: Election Boycotts Around the World 1990–2002," PhD diss., University of California, San Diego, 2006; Jennifer Gandhi and Ora John Reuter, "Opposition Coordination in Legislative Elections Under Authoritarianism," paper presented at the annual meeting of the American Political Science Association, Boston, 2008.

6. Barbara Geddes, "Why Parties and Elections in Authoritarian Regimes?" paper presented at the annual meeting of the American Political Science Association, Washington, D.C., 2005; Alberto Simpser, "Making Votes Not Count: Strategic Incentives for Electoral Corruption," PhD diss., Stanford University, 2005; Magaloni, *Voting for Autocracy*; Beatrice Magaloni, "Credible Power-Sharing and the Longevity of Authoritarian Rule," *Comparative Political Studies* 41 (2008): 715–41; and Edmund Malesky and Paul Schuler, "Why Do Single-Party Regimes Hold Elections? An Analysis of Candidate-Level Data in Vietnam's 2007 National Assembly Contest," paper presented at the annual meeting of the American Political Science Association, Boston, 2008.

7. Ellen Lust-Okar, "Elections Under Authoritarianism: Preliminary Lessons from Jordan,"" *Democratization* 13, no. 3 (May 2006): 455–70; Lisa Blaydes, *Elections and*

Distributive Politics in Mubarak's Egypt (Cambridge: Cambridge University Press, 2011).

8. I use "one-party" here to refer to both strictly one-party regimes and dominant-party authoritarian regimes.

9. Even in monarchies, legitimized through hereditary rule and not political parties, elections were not entirely new; colonial powers had left behind elected institutions in Egypt, Iraq, Jordan, Morocco, and elsewhere. Yet by the 1970s, most elections in the region were either suspended (Jordan, Morocco) or had become restricted to ruling parties (Algeria, Egypt, Iraq, Syria).

10. Military coups were attempted in Morocco in July 1971 and August 1972.

11. Sadat signed Egypt's first postindependence political parties law (law no. 40/1977) in June 1977. It provided a significant break from the single-party regime instituted by Gamal Abdel Nasser by stating that "Egyptians have the right to create political parties and every Egyptian has the right to belong to any political party." See Human Rights Watch, "Monopolizing Power: Egypt's Political Parties Law," January 4, 2007, available at http://www.unhcr.org/refworld/docid/45a4e0a92.html (accessed April 17, 2012).

12. Volker Perthes, "Syria: Difficult Inheritance," in *Arab Elites: Negotiating the Politics of Change*, ed. Volker Perthes (Boulder, Colo.: Lynne Rienner, 2004), 87–115.

13. The National Assembly elected in 1973 was dissolved in 1975, and the elections were suspended. The next elections in Bahrain were not held again until 2002.

14. Unfortunately, to date, far too little work has been done on the local elections in the Arab world. It is an area of likely fruitful theoretical and empirical study.

15. Blaydes, *Elections and Distributive Politics in Mubarak's Egypt*; Ellen Lust-Okar, "Legislative Elections in Hegemonic Authoritarian Regimes," in Democratization by Elections: A New Mode of Transition, ed. Staffan I. Lindberg (Baltimore: Johns Hopkins University Press, 2009), 226–45; Lust-Okar, "Elections Under Authoritarianism"; and Samer Shehata, "Inside an Egyptian Parliamentary Campaign," in *Political Participation in the Middle East*, ed. Ellen Lust-Okar and Saloua Magrawi (Boulder, Colo.: Lynne Rienner, 2008), 95–120.

16. Magaloni, *Voting for Autocracy*; Kenneth Greene, *Why Dominant Parties Lose: Mexico's Democratization in Comparative Perspective* (New York: Cambridge University Press, 2007); Blaydes, *Elections and Distributive Politics*.

17. Lust, "Competitive Clientelism." The same was true in other regions as well. On Kenya and Tanzania, see Joel Barkan, "Legislators, Elections and Political Linkages," in Politics and Public Policy in Kenya and Tanzania, ed. Joel Barkan (New York: Praeger, 1984).

18. Not surprisingly, oppositions can attempt to undermine legitimacy and challenge the regime's control by boycotting elections and challenging turnout figures. See Gail Jeanne Buttorff, "Legitimacy and the Politics of Opposition in the Middle East and North Africa," PhD diss., University of Iowa, 2011.

19. Barbara Geddes has argued more generally that this is a signaling mechanism. My interpretation differs from hers only slightly: While she sees this as a mechanism that elections can play at all levels—local and national, legislative and executive, I see it as a unique role of executive elections.

20. Lisa Wedeen, *Ambiguities of Domination: Politics, Rhetoric, and Symbols in Contemporary Syria* (Chicago: University of Chicago Press, 1999).

21. Alexander Baturo, "Presidential Succession and Democratic Transitions," Working Paper 209, Institute for International Integration Studies, 2007.

22. Valerie Bunce and Sharon Wolchik, "Favorable Conditions and Electoral Revolutions," *Journal of Democracy* 17, no. 4 (2006): 5–18; Mark Beissinger, "Structure and Example in Modular Political Phenomena: The Diffusion of Bulldozer/Rose/Orange/Tulip Revolutions," *Perspectives on Politics* 5, no. 2 (2007): 259–76; Mark Thompson and Philip Kuntz, "Stolen Elections: The Case of the Serbian," *Journal of Democracy* 15, no. 4 (October 2004): 159–72; Judith Tucker, "Enough! Electoral Fraud, Collective Action Problems, and Post-Communist Colored Revolutions," *Perspectives on Politics* 5, no. 3 (2007): 535–51.

23. To date, the closest experience to a color revolution in the Middle East, although not the Arab world, is found in Iran, which witnessed uprisings after the 2009 elections.

24. See Magaloni, *Voting for Autocracy*; Greene, *Why Dominant Parties Lose*.

25. For a careful case study of this relationship in Jordan, see Mustafa Hamarneh, "Ma'an: An Open Ended Crisis," University of Jordan, Center for Strategic Studies, September 2003; and Charles Schmitz, "Yemen's Spring: Whose Agenda?" in *Agents of Change*, vol. 1 of *Revolution and Political Transformation in the Middle East* (Washington, D.C.: Middle East Institute, August 2011), 19–24.

26. In most cases, participation declined over the past decade and a half: 65.6 percent in 1997, 46 percent in 2002, and 35.6 percent in 2007 in Algeria; 53 percent in 2002, 73.6 percent in 2006, and 67 percent in 2010 in Bahrain; 28 percent in 2005 and 27.5 percent in 2010 in Egypt; 58.3 percent in January 2005, 79.6 percent in December 2005, and 64 percent in Iraq; 57.8 percent in 2003, 54 percent in 2007, and 53 percent in 2010 in Jordan; 66.3 percent in 2006, 59.4 percent in 2008, and 59 percent in 2009 in Kuwait; 45 percent in 2000, 46.5 percent in 2005, and 54 percent in 2009; 58.3 percent in 1997, 51.6 percent in 2002, and 37 percent in 2007 in Morocco; 82.2 percent in 1998, 63.5 percent in 2003, and 56 percent in 2007 in Syria; 91.5 percent in 1999, 86.4 percent in 2004, and 89.4 percent in 2009 in Tunisia; and 80.7 percent in 1993, 60.7 percent in 1997, and 75 percent in 2003 in Yemen. Note that differences in registration levels and procedural difficulties make comparisons across time somewhat difficult. See IFES Election Guide and Institute for Democracy and Electoral Assistance, available at http://www.idea.int/vt/; and Dieter Nohlen, Michael Krennerich, and Bernhard Thibaut, eds., *Elections in Africa: A Data Handbook* (Oxford: Oxford University Press, 1999).

27. Not all elections were tied to promises of democracy, of course; Syria and Tunisia had long held elections but never promised extensive reforms. In Algeria, Jordan,

Yemen, and elsewhere, however, the reintroduction of elections or expansion had been heralded as democratization. Yet, decades later—and despite watching much of Africa, Asia, Eastern Europe and Latin America democratize, not only were such promises stale, but there was marked political de-liberalization.

28. For example, in the 2006 Arab Barometer Survey, only slightly more than 45 percent of Algerian respondents had voted in elections; nearly half of respondents believed the last presidential elections were not free and fair; and similarly, nearly half of them had no or little trust in elections. Similarly, more than 50 percent of Kuwaitis believed the 2006 elections had major problems or were not free and fair, and more than 50 percent of the respondents had little or no trust in parliament. Faith in elections appears higher among Jordanians, Lebanese, and Palestinians, with 56 percent, nearly 62 percent, and 73 percent, respectively, reported voting in the last elections. See the country reports and data available at www. http://www .arabbarometer.org/.

29. See Emily Beaulieu, *Electoral Protest and Democracy in the Developing World* (New York: Cambridge University Press, forthcoming).

30. For more on the potential role of elections in building opposition skills and institutions that help push for expansion of civil and political liberties and democratic consolidation, see Staffan I. Lindberg, *Democracy and Elections in Africa* (Baltimore: Johns Hopkins University Press, 2006); Staffan I. Lindberg, "The Power of Elections in Africa Revisited," in *Democratization by Elections: A New Mode of Transition*, ed. Staffan Lindberg (Baltimore: Johns Hopkins University Press, 2009), 25–46; Todd Eisenstadt, *Courting Democracy in Mexico: Party Strategies and Electoral Institutions* (New York: Cambridge University Press, 2004); Michael Bratton and Nicolas van de Walle, *Democratic Experiments in Africa: Regime Transitions in Comparative Perspective* (New York: Cambridge University Press, 1997); Jason Brownlee, "Portents of Pluralism: How Hybrid Regimes Affect Democratic Transitions," *American Journal of Political Science* 53, no. 3 (2009): 515–32. On the importance of cross-ideological alliances, see Philip Roessler and Marc Howard, "Post-Cold-War Political Regimes: When Do Elections Matter?" in *Democratization by Elections: A New Mode of Transition*, ed. Staffan I. Lindberg (Baltimore: Johns Hopkins University Press, 2009), 101–127.

31. Lisa Blaydes and James Lo, "One Man, One Vote, One Time? A Model of Democratization in the Middle East," *Journal of Theoretical Politics*, November 2011, 1–37; Ellen Lust, "Missing the Third Wave: Islam, Institutions and Democracy in the Middle East," *Studies in Comparative International Development* 46, no. 2 (June 2011): 163–90.

32. Edward P. Djerejian, "United States Policy Toward Islam and the Arc of Crisis," Baker Institute Study no. 1, 1995, available at http://bakerinstitute.org/publications/ study_1_arc_of_crisis.pdf (accessed April 17, 2012).

33. As they had before, Muslim Brotherhood candidates ran as independents. In part as a response to international pressure and regional insecurity after the 2003 war in

Iraq, the regime allowed these candidates more room to maneuver and more success at the polls in 2005.

34. Lust, "Missing the Third Wave."
35. Jason Brownlee, *Authoritarianism in an Age of Democratization* (New York: Cambridge University Press, 2007).
36. In fact, in 2005 more NDP-related candidates ran as independents and won than did NDP candidates running on the ruling party's ticket, and in 2010, the still-weak NDP could eliminate defections only by nominating several candidates per seat.
37. Guillermo O'Donnell, Philippe Schmitter, and Lawrence Whitehead, *Transitions from Authoritarian Rule: Tentative Conclusions About Uncertain Democracies* (Baltimore: Johns Hopkins University Press, 1986); Philippe Schmitter, "Twenty-Five Years, Fifteen Findings," *Journal of Democracy* 21, no. 1 (January 2010): 17–28.
38. For example, in Tunisia, seventy-three-year-old Ben Ali was determined to hang onto power and control succession, so he changed the constitution (increasing the age of president from seventy to seventy-five years old) to allow himself to run in elections. In Egypt, too, Mubarak implemented competitive presidential elections in 2005. This was a landmark decision—since previous presidential polls were referenda—but one in which the rules were clearly set to favor his son Gamal.
39. On the role of boycotts in undermining autocracies, see Beaulieu, "Protesting the contest."
40. Tarek Masoud, "The Upheavals in Egypt and Tunisia: The Road to (and from) Liberation Square," *Journal of Democracy* 22, no. 3 (July 2011): 20–34; Stephen Zunes, "Fraudulent Egyptian Election," *Foreign Policy in Focus*, December 7, 2010, available at http://fpif.org/fraudulent_egyptian_election/; Jason Brownlee and Joshua Stacher, "Change of Leader, Continuity of System: Nascent Liberalization in Post-Mubarak Egypt," *Comparative Politics-Democratization Newsletter*, May 2011, 1–9
41. This paragraph draws directly from Ellen Lust, "Why Now? Micro-Transitions and the Arab Uprisings," *Comparative Politics-Democratization Newsletter*, October 2011, 1–8.
42. The JMP was an alliance of five opposition parties that formed across regional and ideological divides, including Islah, the Yemeni Socialist Party (YSP), Hizb Al-Haq (a semireligious party), the Unionist Party, and the Popular Forces Union party. They had literally been at war with one another in 1994 but had joined forces out of their frustration with President Saleh and the GPC's increased hold on power.
43. In December 2010, a Yemeni official noted that the opposition was weak and unable to incite protest, and the government therefore "would not be influenced by opposition demands." See Reuters, "Opposition Threatens Yemen Polls Boycott," December 13, 2010.
44. The debate over the relationship between regime types, elections, and breakdown is fully unresolved. Geddes ("Authoritarian Breakdown") argues that single-party regimes last longer than military or personalistic regimes, and Jason Brownlee

("Portents of Pluralism") finds similar results, while Scott Gates and his colleagues contend that hybrid regimes are the most unstable. Brownlee's findings are consistent with my argument here, as he finds that monarchies are less likely to break down than are single-party and hybrid regimes, even when controlling for per capita GDP and Middle East (but not oil). See Scott Gates, Havard Hegre, Mark Jones, and Havard Strand, "Institutional Inconsistency and Political Instability: Polity Duration, 1800–2000," *American Journal of Political Science* 50, no. 4 (2006), 893–908.

45. Libya appears to be an outlier, since competitive elections have not been held and the regime is not officially a one-party state. Yet, the logic of Qaddafi's exceptional regime—with no parties, a revolutionary movement, and cell structures—most closely approximated a revolutionary, one-party state.

46. For a detailed analysis of the Algerian parliamentary elections, see Robert Parks, "Arab Uprisings and the Algerian Elections: Ghosts from the Past?" *Jadaliyya*, April 10, 2012, available at http://www.jadaliyya.com/pages/index/4979/arab-uprisings-and-the-algerian-elections_ghosts-f (accessed April 22, 2012].

47. For more on these challenges, see Ellen Lust, "Electoral Programming and Trade-Offs in Transitions: Lessons from Egypt and Tunisia," CDRL–Brooking Institution, May 2012, working paper.

48. At this writing, Yemen remains a notable exception. There, the election of Abd al-Rab Mansur al-Hadi, the sole contender for the presidency, can hardly be called competitive.

49. Bratton and van de Walle, *Democratic Experiments*; Lindberg, *Democracy and Elections*; Lindberg, *Democratization by Elections*; Brownlee, "Portents of Pluralism"; and Hadenius and Teorell, "Pathways from Authoritarianism."

PART III

Public Opinion

13

Political System Preferences of Arab Publics

MARK TESSLER AND MICHAEL ROBBINS

The roots of the Arab uprisings are multifaceted, but one of the key drivers is the widespread call by Arab publics for better governance. Central to this call is an emphasis on *karāma*, meaning "dignity," which reflects a desire for political leaders who respect their country's citizens and care about their welfare. But while the demand for dignity tells us what Arab publics want from their leaders and how these men and women insist on being treated, it leaves unclear the views of ordinary citizens about the kind of political system by which they wish to be governed. Do they favor democracy, or is this the rallying cry of liberal elites who are out of touch with mass opinion? Do they believe that Islam should play a significant role in government and political affairs, or do many believe that religion is a private matter that should be separated from politics?

The public opinion surveys by the Arab Barometer shed light on these questions about the political system preferences of ordinary citizens. The Arab Barometer, which is directed by an international team of scholars from the Arab world and the United States, conducts face-to-face interviews based on nationally representative samples of adults eighteen years of age and older. Basic information about the methodology of the Arab Barometer surveys is presented in the appendix. Additional information, including a number of country-specific reports, may be found on the Arab Barometer's website.[1]

The first wave of Arab Barometer surveys, conducted in 2006/2007, was carried out in Algeria, Iraq,[2] Jordan, Kuwait, Lebanon, Morocco, Palestine, and Yemen. A total of 10,823 men and women were interviewed. The second wave, conducted in 2010/2011, included surveys in Algeria, Bahrain,[3]

Egypt, Iraq, Jordan, Lebanon, Palestine, Saudi Arabia, Sudan, Tunisia, and Yemen. A total of 13,518 men and women were interviewed in this wave. Although neither wave was carried out in all Arab countries, both encompassed much of the Arab world's diversity; each wave included monarchies and republics, wealthier and poorer countries, and countries from the Maghrib, the Mashreq, and the Gulf.

We present the data from these surveys in two ways in order to show the political system preferences of Arab publics. First we look at the views of respondents from countries that were surveyed during both the first wave and the second wave of the Arab Barometer and compare them in order to assess continuity and change in political orientations during the last five years. Second we examine the views of respondents in all of the countries included in the second wave in order to provide a more detailed picture of the political tendencies that characterized the Arab world at the end of 2010 and the first part of 2011.

Support for democracy was and continues to be high in all the countries surveyed. Differences emerge, however, with regard to the degree to which Islam should play a role in government and political affairs, hereafter described as "political Islam." In most countries, support for political Islam has remained constant or declined over the last five years. Moreover, in 2010–2011 only a minority of respondents supported political Islam in most countries. Thus, despite the success of Islamist parties in recent elections in Egypt, Tunisia, and elsewhere, the majority of Arabs citizens surveyed preferred a system of governance that is democratic but also separates religion and politics.

Continuity and Change

Support for Democracy

Stated support for democracy has generally been very strong in the Arab world.[4] As can be seen in table 13.1, and as is later shown in table 13.2 as well, evidence from the Arab Barometer is consistent with these prior findings. Table 13.1 presents the political system preferences of respondents in the seven countries that were surveyed in both the first wave and the second wave of the Arab Barometer, with the respondents divided into four categories: (1) those who favor secular democracy; (2) those who support democracy but also believe that Islam should play an important role in government and political affairs; (3) those who do not support democracy

TABLE 13.1

COMPARISON OF POLITICAL SYSTEM PREFERENCES
IN 2006–2009 AND 2011–2012

COUNTRY	POLITICAL SYSTEM PREFERENCE/	AB1 (%)	AB2 (%)	DIFFERENCE
Jordan	Democratic secular	40.9	44.4	3.5
	Democratic with Islam	44.4	36.0	−8.4
	Authoritarian secular	7.3	10.3	3.0
	Authoritarian with Islam	7.5	9.3	1.8
Palestine	Democratic secular	37.5	49.1	11.6
	Democratic with Islam	45.1	35.1	-10.0
	Authoritarian secular	6.9	9.6	2.7
	Authoritarian with Islam	10.4	6.1	4.3
Algeria	Democratic secular	35.1	64.7	29.6
	Democratic with Islam	48.0	19.7	-28.3
	Authoritarian secular	5.3	8.2	2.9
	Authoritarian with Islam	11.6	7.4	-4.2
Lebanon	Democratic secular	75.4	70.3	-4.9
	Democratic with Islam	16.4	15.6	-0.8
	Authoritarian secular	6.9	12.0	5.1
	Authoritarian with Islam	1.3	2.1	0.8
Yemen	Democratic secular	35.4	30.5	-4.9
	Democratic with Islam	44.2	51.8	7.6
	Authoritarian secular	7.7	7.4	-0.3
	Authoritarian with Islam	12.7	10.3	-2.4
Iraq	Democratic secular	44.4	43.1	-1.3
	Democratic with Islam	42.9	43.7	0.8
	Authoritarian secular	4.9	9.1	4.2
	Authoritarian with Islam	7.8	4.1	-3.7

and also do not believe that Islam should play an important political role; and (4) those who not support democracy but do believe that Islam should play an important role in politics. The survey item used to measure support for democracy asked respondents whether or not they agreed with the following statement: "Democracy, despite its limitations, is the best political system." This item is part of a battery of questions that ask about democracy, and subsequent analysis has shown it to be reliable as well as valid. The survey item used to measure support for a political role for Islam asked respondents whether or not they agreed with the following statement: "Men of religion should have influence on the decisions of government." This item, too, is part of a battery of associated questions and has been shown to be valid and reliable.[5] Both items were dichotomized, and the two dichotomized items were then cross tabulated to derive the four categories shown in table 13.1.[6]

The level of support for democracy is reflected in the percentage of respondents in the first two categories, support for secular democracy and support for democracy with Islam, taken together. As seen in table 13.1, and as also may be seen in table 13.2, to be discussed later, every one of the surveys in each of the waves finds broad support for democracy. In one instance, in the Saudi survey in the second wave, the percentage of respondents in the two categories is 72.6. In two other instances, in Egypt in the second wave and Yemen in the first wave, the percentages are 78.1 percent and 79.6 percent, respectively. The percentage is 82 percent or higher, frequently much higher, in every other survey. As stated, these findings are in line with other survey research that reports consistently strong support for democracy among Arab publics.

As the preceding suggests, the difference between overall support for democracy in the first wave of Arab Barometer surveys and overall support for democracy in the second wave of Arab Barometer surveys was small. The biggest change was in Lebanon, where the support for democracy declined by 5.9 percent but still remained higher than in most other countries. In no other case was there a difference greater than 5 percent, and in most cases it was only two or three percentage points, which is within the margin of error for each survey, suggesting that attitudes were generally stable between the two waves.

Given the extensive support for democracy over time, and indeed in surveys in the Arab world that predate the Arab Barometer,[7] there is little need to formulate and test hypotheses about the country-level determinants of attitudes toward democracy. Even at the individual level, the breadth of support for democracy is such that it is high among almost all subsets of the population.

There are, however, some implications that arise from these findings about widespread public support for democracy in the Arab world. One is that it seems safe to conclude that the absence of public support for democracy is not where to look for an explanation of the persistence of authoritarianism in Arab countries and also that the presence of such support has not significantly affected the nature of the political system. Support for democracy is no higher overall in partly free countries than it is in countries that are not free at all, and accordingly, it is thus no lower in the latter countries than in the former. Another implication, or perhaps a question, is whether in the wake of the Arab uprisings these public attitudes will exert greater influence than in the past, helping sustain movements toward democracy in countries where a political transition has taken place or lead to change in countries where this has not occurred.

The Place of Islam

In contrast to support for democracy, which was widespread in the first wave of Arab Barometer surveys and remained so in the second wave, table 13.1 reveals a different pattern with respect to views about Islam's political role. In the first wave of Arab Barometer surveys, with the exception of Lebanon, there was a clear division of opinion on this issue in every country included in the table. Taking together those who believe Islam should play a significant role and also favor democracy and those who believe Islam should play a significant role but do not also favor democracy, in every country other than Lebanon the support ranges between 50 and 60 percent. Thus, Arab publics in 2006/2007 were clearly and for the most part quite evenly divided on the question of Islam's proper place in government and politics.

Although not shown in the table, this division is equally pronounced when only those respondents who support democracy are considered. These individuals, who represent the vast majority in every country, also were very divided on the question of Islam's place in politics. Of those men and women who support democracy, again with the exception of Lebanon, where only 17.8 percent favored a political role for Islam, the percentage of those who believe that Islam should have a place in political life was never less than 48.6 percent, which was the figure in Iraq, or more than 57.7 percent, the figure in Algeria. Thus, whether considering all respondents or only the 80 to 85 percent who support democracy, the data from the first wave of the Arab Barometer reveal a clear division of opinion on the question of Islam's political role.

Although this is not true in every country, data from the second wave of Arab Barometer surveys indicate that there have been some changes in views about Islam's place in political affairs. In Palestine and Algeria, and to a lesser extent in Jordan, the proportion of respondents who favor a political role for Islam has declined. Considering all respondents, that is, those who both do and do not support democracy, the drop was 14.3 percentage points in Palestine and a surprising 32.4 percentage points in Algeria. In Jordan the decline was 6.6 percentage points. In the second wave, Algeria thus approaches Lebanon in its preference for a political system that does not assign an important role to Islam; and in Palestine and Jordan, although opinion remains divided in both countries, there has been a notable decrease in the proportion who believe Islam should play a significant political role.

The decline in Palestine, Algeria, and Jordan is equally pronounced when only those respondents who support democracy are included in the analysis. Among these men and women, the decline is, respectively, 13.6 percent Palestine, 34.4 percent in Algeria, and 7.5 percent in Jordan.

In one country, the support for assigning a political role to Islam was greater in the second than in the first wave of the Arab Barometer, although the increase was modest and could be due to normal sampling variation. That country is Yemen, where the view that Islam should play a role in government and political affairs rose by 5.2 percentage points among all respondents and by 7.5 percentage points among men and women who support democracy.

These findings naturally raise the question of why views about Islam's political role changed in some countries but not others. Before turning to this question, however, it is important to recognize that the issue of Islam's political role remains both highly salient and strongly contested. This was forcefully expressed in the case of Iraq by Tariq Harb, an Iraqi constitutional lawyer and media personality. Harb wrote in 2010 that a central element in the struggle to define Iraq's emergent democracy is the question of how "to balance religion and secularism."[8]

Similar sentiments were expressed in many other countries, including and perhaps particularly, those in which the Arab spring offered hope of a transition to democracy. For example, Ali Gomaa, the grand mufti of Egypt, wrote in April 2011, in connection with the democratic transition struggling at the time to take shape in his country, that Egypt's revolution "has swept away decades of authoritarian rule but it has also highlighted an issue that Egyptians will grapple with as they consolidate their democracy: the role of religion in political life."[9] Thus despite an apparent decline in the overall breadth of popular support for political Islam in some Arab countries, and also notwithstanding an important measure of cross-country variation, public attitudes toward Islam's political role and the division of opinion around this question remain prominent, highly significant, and central to political contestation in many Arab countries.

Cross-National Variation

The question of why views about Islam's political role have changed in some countries but not others cannot be answered without looking more deeply than is possible in this short research report into the circumstances and experiences of each relevant population. A few thoughts may nonetheless be offered in the hope of encouraging reflection and further inquiry.

Lebanon and Iraq are the two countries in which views about Islam's political role were most similar in the first wave and the second wave of surveys, and the two countries share at least one attribute that is absent, or at least much less pronounced, in the other countries included in both waves of the Arab Barometer. This is a strong confessional divide, and one that has been central to intercommunal conflict. Furthermore, although the alignment is imperfect, Islamist political tendencies tend to be associated to disproportionate degree with a particular confessional community, and the communities themselves are the most important locus of political contestation. It therefore is possible that this pattern of confessionalism to at least some degree fixes assessments about the proper relationship between Islam and politics and makes people less likely to modify their views in response to political developments.[10] This is a plausible hypothesis that deserves further investigation and offers, if supported, the possibility of new insights into the impact of sectarianism on the formation of public attitudes toward one of the most important issues on the Arab world's political agenda at the present time.

Views about Islam's political role in Yemen and Jordan changed somewhat between 2006/2007 and 2010/2011, although support for political Islam rose in the former and fell in the latter. The differences between the two time periods are modest, however, and it is possible that the normal margin of error associated with probability-based sampling accounts for much, or perhaps even most, of this variation.

To the extent that more than sampling variation is at play, the increase among Yemenis believing that Islam should play a role in political affairs may be partly the result of the recent growing U.S. involvement in the country in the context of America's "war on terror." Popular resentment of the U.S. alliance with then President Ali Abdullah Saleh, as well as anger at the drone attacks inside the country that this alliance permitted, may have fueled pro-Islam political sentiments during the years between the two surveys. In Jordan, the increasing radicalization of the Islamic Action Front, the country's main Islamist party, could partly explain the drop in support for political Islam. In recent years, members of the more hawkish wing of the party have won key leadership roles in the party. As a result, the party leadership has been more vociferous in its opposition to the regime and seen as more supportive of Hamas.[11] This radicalization of leadership may have resulted in fears among many ordinary citizens about the true intentions of the Islamist movement, resulting in a decline in support for political Islam.

These explanations are only informed speculation, of course, but they do suggest several broader insights worthy of further reflection and investigation. First, in both cases, greater radicalization has accompanied, and very probably contributed to, a shift in public attitudes. Second, however, the direction of the shift is not the same, pushing toward more support for political Islam in Yemen and less support in Jordan. Third, this variation in the direction of the shift may be at least partly explained by the source of the radicalization, which was the result of actions by an external actor in the Yemeni case and a domestic actor in the Jordanian case. The causal story that results from these possibilities offers again the possibility of a deeper understanding of the dynamics shaping the views about political Islam held by Arab publics.

Palestine and Algeria are the two countries in which differences are larger than what might be the result of sampling variation. In Palestine, the decline in support for a political formula that incorporates Islam may be due at least partly to the timing of the first survey. In 2006, the first wave of the Arab Barometer was carried out less than three months after Hamas's government came to power following its January electoral victory, which very possibly represented a high point for support for political Islam. Hamas's subsequent break with Fatah and the nature of its rule in Gaza subsequently weakened Palestinian support for the party, however, and this in turn may have reduced public support for a political system in which an important place is assigned to Islam.

The reasons for the more dramatic shift in Algerian attitudes are not entirely clear. One possibility is the timing of the second survey, which was taken a few months after the fall of Zine al-Abdine Ben Ali in Tunisia and Hosni Mubarak in Egypt. In the past, support for political Islam in Algeria has to a substantial degree been strategic, with Islamist parties championed as vehicles for political and economic protest as well as, or perhaps even more than, a way to make Algeria more Islamic.[12] But in 2011, when the second wave survey was conducted in Algeria, it was clear that the changes in Tunisia and Egypt had not occurred in response to pressures from Islamists but were the result of uprisings in which progressive forces had played an equally, and probably a more, important role. Events in Tunisia and Egypt may thus help explain why many fewer Algerians were persuaded in 2011 than had been the case in 2006 by the Islamist rallying cry, "Islam is the solution." Along similar lines, the regime in Algiers has sought to limit the effectiveness of opposition Islamist parties and movements and brought the country's largest legalized Islamist party, the Movement of the Society for Peace, into the governing coalition. For these reasons, too, political Islam may have had less appeal in 2011 as a clear and preferable alternative to the existing political system.

The proposition that results from these assessments, which once again suggests a potentially productive avenue for future investigation, is that public support for political Islam is to a significant degree, although obviously not entirely, a function of the extent to which Islamist parties and movements are perceived as a consequential and, above all, a needed and credible alternative to the political status quo. This is not an entirely original insight, but it is notable that the availability of survey data from Algeria at different points in time provides more rigorous and representative evidence than is usually offered in support of this contention about the factors shaping individual-level views about political Islam.

In the Midst of the Arab Uprisings

Political System Preferences

Table 13.2 shows the distribution of political system preferences in each of the countries surveyed during the second wave of the Arab Barometer. In addition to the six countries just discussed, the second wave included surveys in Egypt, Saudi Arabia, Bahrain,[13] Tunisia, and Sudan.[14]

TABLE 13.2

POLITICAL SYSTEM PREFERENCES IN 2010–2011

COUNTRY	N	TIME OF SURVEY	DEMOCRATIC SECULAR	DEMOCRATIC WITH ISLAM	AUTHORITARIAN SECULAR	AUTHORITARIAN WITH ISLAM
Jordan	1188	December 2010	44.4%	36.0%	10.3%	9.3%
Palestine	1200	December 2010	49.1%	35.1%	9.6%	6.1%
Algeria	1216	April–May 2011	64.7%	19.7%	8.2%	7.4%
Lebanon	1387	Nov.–Dec. 2010; April 2011	70.3%	15.6%	12.0%	2.1%
Yemen	1200	Feb. 2011	30.5%	51.8%	7.4%	10.3%
Iraq	1236	Feb.–March 2011	43.1%	43.7%	9.1%	4.1%
Egypt	1220	June–July 2011	51.0%	27.1%	11.9%	10.0%
Saudi Arabia	1405	Jan.–Feb. 2011; March–April 2011	50.5%	22.1%	11.8%	15.6%
Bahrain	500	December 2009	47.0%	40.3%	5.7%	7.0%
Tunisia	1196	Sept.–Oct. 2011	66.8%	22.55	7.9%	2.8%

Support for democracy is as widespread in these other countries as table 13.1 showed it to be in 2010/2011 in the countries surveyed in both waves of the Arab Barometer. Only in Egypt and Saudi Arabia, where it was favored by 78.1 percent and 72.6 percent of those surveyed, respectively, does a preference for democracy fall below 80 percent. The Egyptian finding is interesting and may suggest a measure of political uncertainty in the months following Mubarak's departure. The Saudi finding, while lower than any other country in the second wave, is not only high in absolute terms but also higher than might be expected given how little experience Saudi citizens have had with democracy and how high nonetheless has been the country's overall standard of living. In any event, consistent with findings from all previous surveys, it is clear that democracy is the preferred political system of large majorities of Arab men and women.

The data presented in table 13.1 indicate a measurable increase in a preference for secular democracy over democracy with Islam in three of the countries included in both waves of surveys. They also reveal a modest but nonetheless measurable drop in support for democracy with Islam in one of countries. Without data from an earlier period, it is impossible to determine whether there has been movement in either direction in the countries included only in the second wave. Regardless of whether or not this constitutes a change from the past, however, table 13.2 reveals a clear preference for secular democracy in most of the countries surveyed during the second wave, in 2010/2011. Overall, considering all the countries included in the table, it is the political system preference of at least a plurality in all but two countries. Indeed, it is the form of government favored by an absolute majority in five countries: Algeria, Lebanon, Egypt, Saudi Arabia, and Tunisia.[15]

The two countries in which support for secular democracy is not greater than support for democracy with Islam are Yemen and Iraq, both of which were discussed earlier. Although it has been possible only to speculate about the reasons for this, it was suggested that Yemen's deep involvement in the U.S.-led war on terror may have increased support for political Islam in that country and that confessionalism in Iraq may have helped fix the views of a public deeply divided over the role that Islam should play in government and political affairs.

The findings about political attitudes in Saudi Arabia, Egypt and Tunisia shown in table 13.2 are particularly striking. Indeed, although consistent with the broader pattern of limited support for political Islam, the findings are in fact somewhat surprising. In all three cases, well under 30 percent of the respondents favor democracy with Islam, and well under 40 percent favor any kind of political system that assigns an important role to Islam.

Saudi Arabia is ruled by a conservative monarchy that claims *sharia* as its constitution. Yet the proportion of Saudis favoring secular democracy is more than twice the proportion favoring democracy with Islam. Reflecting the widespread desires for a government that differs from the one they have, this appears to parallel the protest-oriented support for political Islam that emerged in some countries governed by secular regimes. Events at the time of the survey may have also played a role in shaping Saudi views. Interviewed in early 2011, at a time when the Arab spring was registering gains and the Saudi regime was allocating resources in an effort to prevent local protests, many Saudis may have been inspired and influenced by the secular forces leading revolutions in Tunisia and Egypt. Whether the Saudi political preferences shown in table 13.2 are deep and stable or are confined to a particular historical moment is an interesting and important subject to be investigated in future research.

Findings from Tunisia and Egypt, the two countries that initially led the Arab spring, are equally noteworthy. In both cases, support for secular democracy is much greater than support for democracy with Islam. Due to a lack of earlier data, it is unclear whether this represents a change in political system preferences, although it is worth noting that in Algeria— the only other country where the entire survey was conducted after the fall of Ben Ali and Mubarak—support for political Islam fell dramatically. It is possible that this was the result of factors specific to Algeria, as discussed earlier, but it also is possible that the events of the Arab spring account for much of the change. If the latter is the case, it might suggest that political attitudes in Tunisia and Egypt also have shifted as a result of these dramatic events.

In any case, most Tunisians and Egyptians appear to favor a secular political system. Yet in both countries, this finding from the Arab Barometer surveys appears to be at odds with the results of post–Arab spring elections. The Islamist al-Nahda Party won by far the largest share of the vote in Tunisia, more than 40 forty percent, and in Egypt the Muslim Brotherhood–affiliated Freedom and Justice Party in Egypt and the Salafist al-Nour Party together took more than two-thirds of the vote. If Tunisians and Egyptians actually desire secular democracy, what accounts for these electoral outcomes?

One possible explanation is that the distinction between secular democracy and democracy with Islam is somewhat blurred in the minds of ordinary citizens. The leadership of both the al-Nahda and the Freedom and Justice Parties stated during their campaigns that their movements do not seek to impose Islamic prescriptions on the country in such areas as the status of women, for example, and both also indicated a willingness to share power with non-Islamist parties. Al-Nahda has often been described as "mildly" Islamist, and Freedom and Justice's former vice president, Rafiq Habib, is a Coptic Christian. If ordinary citizens believed the "mildly" Islamist campaign promises of the two parties, then these parties may have been able to appeal to many voters who actually prefer secular democracy.

A second explanation, which almost certainly is part of the story, is that by their very nature, elections are rarely fully reflective of public opinion. For example, in most Western democracies, poorer citizens and those in more rural areas tend to vote at lower rates than wealthier individuals in urban areas. Election results depend heavily on voter turnout, which in turn is a function of political parties' mobilization efforts to get their supporters to the polls. Turnout also depends on voter education and the ability of parties to appeal to uncommitted voters. Being well-established movements with a long history of communal involvement and political activism, al-Nahda in Tunisia and Freedom and Justice in Egypt were both much better organized and more effective in carrying out these functions than were their secular rivals. With less than a year between the fall of the old regime and the elections, the latter were unable to build comparable party infrastructures and grassroots organizations. Thus, the voting public was more likely to be supportive of the two Islamist parties than was the public as a whole.

A third consideration is that ideological or policy preferences may have been less important to many voters than al-Nahda's long-standing opposition to Ben Ali and the Muslim Brotherhood's history of opposition to the Mubarak regime.[16] This opposition, together with a perception that Islamist parties are less corrupt and more sincerely committed to the welfare of ordinary citizens, apparently earned a measure of trust from many Tunisians and Egyptians who did not factor ideology into their decisions about how to vote.[17] A related factor mentioned by some observers of Tunisia, which may also apply in Egypt, is that the Ben Ali regime's oppression of al-Nahda activists gave the latter a knowledge of the old regime that would make them better able than other political movements to prevent members of the old guard from regaining political influence.

Finally, the results of the Arab Barometer surveys and the Tunisian and Egyptian elections are not as inconsistent as they might appear at first. In Tunisia, the turnout was a little more than 50 percent, and al-Nahda won approximately 40 percent of the overall vote, which means that about 20 percent of all Tunisians voted for the party. This is not very different from the proportion of Tunisians who expressed a preference for political Islam in the Arab Barometer survey. Furthermore, the survey, conducted two weeks before the election, asked respondents to name the party for which they were mostly likely to vote, and a little less than 20 percent named al-Nahda.

The situation is similar in Egypt. The Freedom and Justice Party won approximately 40 percent of the overall vote, and al-Nour won about 25 percent of the vote. This means, with a turnout rate of around 60 percent, that approximately 35 percent of all Egyptian citizens cast their vote for one of the two primary Islamist parties. This is broadly consistent with the findings of the Arab Barometer survey, in which 37.1 percent expressed support for political Islam: 27 percent for democracy with Islam and 10 percent for an Islamic system that is not democratic. Thus, if turnout rates varied between supporters and opponents of political Islam, as is likely, these election results would not be significantly at odds with the findings from the Arab Barometer.

Highlighting and seeking to account for the difference between the vote share obtained by Islamist parties in Egypt and Tunisia and the degree of public support for political Islam in the two countries contributes in several ways to a deeper understanding of political affairs as these states emerge from a period of sustained authoritarianism. On the one hand, this illustrates and sheds light on the diverse and complex factors that shape voting behavior. As in established democracies, voters in these countries behave strategically, choosing among and balancing a variety of factors. This requires them not only to give priority to some interests over others but also sometimes to vote against their interests, or at least in a manner inconsistent with their preferences or even their values in order to offer support for something they consider equally or even more important at the time they go to the polls. In this sense, perhaps not surprisingly, Tunisian and Egyptian voters resemble voters everywhere.

On the other hand, and more specifically, the preceding discussion shows how Arab Barometer survey findings make it possible to offer an informed and reasonable estimate of how many of the recent Islamist victories in Egypt and Tunisia are due to the presence of a core constituency—voters who endorse and presumably are motivated by an Islamist platform—and how much is due to something else that draws ordinary citizens to the Freedom and Justice Party and al-Nahda. In the cases here, even if the explanations offered are incomplete, the findings presented in table 13.2 make clear that support for an Islamist political agenda is limited in both Egypt and Tunisia. Thus in future elections, assuming they are free and fair, the success of recently victorious parties will most likely depend on their performance in the political and economic domain and not on the degree to which their policies are faithful to a particular interpretation of Islam.

Attitudes Toward Women

A question commonly asked after the events of the Arab spring is whether or not there will be new polices and laws that hurt the rights and status of women. Worries that this might be the case have been fueled partly by the increasing political influence of Islamist parties in a number of countries. This is a much more relevant concern in some countries than others, however. Also, while Islamist victories in countries like Egypt and Tunisia have emboldened Salafi elements, who are seeking to impose on their societies a very restrictive interpretation of Islamic law as it pertains to women, mainstream Islamist movements in these countries and others for the most part are not of one mind on the question of women's rights in a society in which Islam exerts political influence.

Equally important, and in the long term perhaps more so, is the question of whether and to what degree various Arab governments will become more responsive to their citizens in the aftermath of the Arab spring. It will be possible to answer this question only in the years ahead, but to lay a foundation for such inquiries now and to provide information in the meantime about the attitudes toward women held by ordinary citizens, additional data from the second wave of the Arab Barometer are presented in table 13.3. Examining the views of men and women who support democracy, who are the vast majority of the respondents in every country, the table presents the responses to two questions about women by those respondents who favor secular democracy and those who favor democracy but also believe that Islam should play an important political role. Overall, the data presented in the table show, first, that in most countries, people hold more conservative views about women in some areas and more liberal views about women in other areas; and, second, that citizens who favor democracy with Islam sometimes, but only sometimes and frequently by only a small margin, hold more conservative views about women's role in society than do citizens who support secular democracy.

TABLE 13.3

POLITICAL SYSTEM PREFERENCES AND ATTITUDES TOWARD WOMEN

COUNTRY	AGREE THAT WOMEN CAN BE PRESIDENT OR PRIME MINISTER OF A MUSLIM COUNTRY			AGREE THAT UNIVERSITY EDUCATION IS MORE† IMPORTANT FOR A BOY THAN A GIRL		
	SUPPORTS SECULAR DEMOCRACY	SUPPORTS DEMOCRACY WITH ISLAM	DIFFERENCE	SUPPORTS SECULAR DEMOCRACY	SUPPORTS DEMOCRACY WITH ISLAM	DIFFERENCE
Jordan	71.7	66.8	4.9	26.6	34.7	-8.1
Palestine	66.9	55.9	11.0	15.0	19.6	-4.6
Algeria	53.8	42.5	11.3	18.8	29.8	-11.0
Lebanon	79.0	79.3	-0.3	15.7	22.9	-7.2
Yemen	65.0	49.9	15.1	30.2	38.2	-8.0
Iraq	44.5	38.8	5.7	21.7	23.4	-1.7
Egypt	28.1	22.6	5.5	30.4	44.6	-14.2
KSA	62.2	34.3	27.9	16.2	34.9	-18.7
Bahrain	79.3	61.6	17.7	13.7	18.2	-4.5
Tunisia	54.9	50.0	4.9	18.3	30.4	-12.1

One question asked of respondents is whether or not they agree with the statement that a woman can be the president or prime minister of a Muslim country. In eight of the ten countries surveyed, half or more of the secular democrats—meaning those who favor democracy and do not want Islam to exert influence in political affairs—say that a woman could be president or prime minister of a Muslim country. Indeed, this view is held by nearly eight in ten people in Bahrain (79.3%) and Lebanon (79.0%) and by more than six in ten in Palestine (66.9%), Yemen (65.0%) and, perhaps surprisingly, Saudi Arabia (62.2%). Only in Iraq (44.5%) and Egypt (28.1%), again perhaps surprisingly, did fewer than half the respondents agree with this statement about the political position a woman could hold.

Turning to Islamist democrats—meaning those who support both democracy and political Islam—several findings stand out. First, these respondents did not uniformly or overwhelmingly express opposition to the proposition that a woman could serve as president or prime minister of a Muslim country. On the contrary, in six of the countries included in the second wave of the Arab Barometer, half or more of these men and women said that a woman could be a prime minister or president. In fact, more than two-thirds in both Lebanon (79.3%) and Jordan (66.8%) held this view, and more than 60 percent of those in Bahrain (61.6%) said this as well.

Second, reinforcing the suggestion that the views of Islamist democrats are not as uniformly or disproportionately conservative as some might expect, the table shows that in five of the countries, the views of these respondents are not very different than those of secular democrats. This is the case in Jordan, Iraq, Lebanon, Egypt, and Tunisia. In some of these countries, most notably Jordan and Lebanon, the gap is small because there is strong support for gender equality in this area among Islamist democrats. In others, most notably Egypt, this is because relatively few secular democrats agree that a woman could be president or prime minister of a Muslim country.

Third, the preceding observations notwithstanding, in some instances, Islamist democrats are much less likely than secular democrats to agree that a woman could be president or prime minister of a Muslim country. The analysis reveals that in five of the ten countries surveyed, there is a difference of more than ten percentage points in the beliefs of the two categories of democrats, with Islamist democrats in all cases expressing a more conservative and traditional opinion. The largest difference is found in Saudi Arabia, where the proportion supporting gender equality pertaining to high political office is 27.9 percentage points higher among secular democrats. Sizable gaps were also found in Bahrain (17.7), Yemen (15.1), Algeria (11.3), and Palestine (11.0).

The Arab Barometer also included other items covering views about gender relations, one of which asked whether or not a respondent agrees that a university education is more important for a boy than for a girl. In all ten countries surveyed, fewer than half of all respondents—regardless of their political orientations—indicated that they did not agree with this statement. Thus, it is clear that among both secular democrats and Islamist democrats, a substantial majority believe that women should have equal access to higher education. Indeed, in only one case, that of Islamist democrats in Egypt, did fewer than 60 percent of the respondents favor equal access to higher education for women and men.

Although most respondents believe a university education is just as important for a girl as it is for a boy, in four countries the proportion of secular democrats who held this view was at least ten percentage points higher than the proportion of Islamist democrats who agreed with the statement. Again, the most dramatic gap was in Saudi Arabia, where secular democrats were 18.7 points less likely to hold this view than Islamist democrats. Important differences of the same direction also were found in Egypt (-14.2%), Tunisia (-12.1%), and Algeria (-11.0%). It is interesting that in the Saudi case, this difference reflects particularly widespread support for gender equality in higher education among secular democrats, whereas in Egypt it reflects disproportionately limited support for gender equality in higher education among Islamist democrats. The differing reasons for these gaps in Saudi Arabia and Egypt are illustrated by the fact that about as many Islamist democrats in Saudi Arabia as secular democrats in Egypt attach equal importance to higher education for boys and girls.

Taken together, these findings offer evidence that although Islamist democrats are sometimes more conservative than secular democrats on gender issues, this difference is neither uniform nor systematic. Indeed, it is the exception as much as, and perhaps even more than, it is the rule. In only two countries, Algeria and Saudi Arabia, is there a consistent difference in the beliefs about women's rights and status held by democrats who support and democrats who oppose a political role for Islam. By contrast, in three countries—Iraq, Jordan, and Lebanon—there are no substantial differences in the views of members of the two categories of democrats. Among democrats in the remaining five countries, there is a substantial difference on one of the two items considered, but it is not the same item, further indicating the absence of a systematic pattern. In Egypt and Tunisia, democrats who support and oppose political Islam differ on the question of a girl's education but not on the question of a woman holding high political office. In Palestine, Yemen, and Bahrain, the difference is in attitudes toward high political office and not toward a university education.

In sum, although political changes brought by the events of the Arab spring may result in policies or laws that limit the rights or roles of women, data from the Arab Barometer suggest that in most countries, these will not be driven by the demands of the populace or even, most notably, by the demands of those who support democracy but also want a Islam to play an important political role. With the exceptions of Egypt, Saudi Arabia, and, to a lesser extent, Iraq, majorities of both Islamist and secular democrats do not oppose, but in fact support, equality between women and men. Thus, the link between support for political Islam and opposition to gender equality is, at best, weak and inconsistent.

Conclusion

Although the degree to which this is a change from the past is unclear, and despite the electoral victories of Islamist parties in Tunisia and Egypt, the Arab Barometer surveys conducted in 2010/2011 suggest that large segments of the public in most Arab countries favor not only democracy but also a democratic political system in which Islam does not play a major role. It is possible only to speculate about why political formulas that assign a major role to Islam do not have more appeal, but some thoughts about factors that are not country specific but have a broader regional impact may be offered in conclusion as a stimulus to further reflection and inquiry.

Three sets of developments may have helped foster the political preferences revealed by the Arab Barometer. Each flows from the circumstances and experience of a particular country, and each also would appear to have regionwide implications. One is the Hamas victory in the 2006 Palestinian elections and the party's subsequent rule over Gaza. Interest in Palestine is widespread in the Arab world; and having campaigned under the banner of political Islam, the government under Hamas thus offered Arabs a picture of what Islamist rule in the Arab world might look like. But Hamas's performance did little to inspire confidence. While the party had its supporters, some of whom had political rather than ideological motivations, Hamas divided the Palestinians, failed to liberate any Palestinian land, and brought neither democracy nor economic progress. The character of the Palestinian situation is such that Hamas alone cannot be blamed for these failures.

The Israeli occupation in general and the blockade of Gaza in particular are the most important reasons for the Palestinians' problems. Nevertheless, Hamas's rule has not improved the situation in Gaza, and in some respects it has made things worse. Thus, the party's performance, guided as it is by its interpretation of Islam, has not only cost the party support among Palestinians, but it also may have inclined Arabs elsewhere to wonder whether the solution to their own country's problems is to be found in an Islamic political formula.

A second factor that may have dampened support for political Islam is the sectarian conflict in Iraq, which, like the situation in Palestine, received extensive media coverage throughout the region. During the conflict, which bordered on full-scale civil war, Shii and Sunni militias engaged in an armed struggle for control over the new Iraq. A number of holy shrines were attacked, and violence often targeted those observing religious festivals or attending mosque. Although relatively few Arab countries have such significant confessional divisions, the impact of this war between differing interpretations of Islam may have led many to conclude, as one of the Arab Barometer survey questions specifically asked, "Religion is a private matter and should be separated from political affairs." To the extent that the Iraqi experience thus served as a warning about the consequences of fusing religion and politics, it may also have led some, or perhaps even many, in other Arab countries to conclude, again, that Islam is not the solution.

Finally, the rise of Iran as a regional power may help explain the relatively low support for political Islam in many Arab countries, perhaps including the surprisingly low support for political Islam in Saudi Arabia. Iran's rise, long regarded as a competitor to Arab countries, is viewed with concern by many in the Arab world. Its involvement in a number of Arab countries, including Syria, Lebanon, Palestine, and Bahrain, is of concern not only to political elites but also to many ordinary Sunni Arabs.[18] Furthermore, Iran hardly offers an appealing model of governance for Arabs who favor democracy and want leaders who care about their welfare. Thus, given that the Iranian regime presents itself as the embodiment of governance in accordance with Islam, Arab perceptions of the regime in Tehran may also have made political Islam less appealing.

Much remains uncertain about what will emerge in various Arab countries by way of a new regional order. It also is impossible to predict with any certainty the degree to which the public attitudes expressed in 2010 and 2011 are likely to persist or whether, alternatively, the distribution of political system preferences will look very different in a few years' time. Indeed, one of the main findings of this chapter is that the preferences of ordinary citizens vary to at least some degree in response to domestic and regional developments, although more so in some circumstances than others. Nevertheless, uncertainty about the future notwithstanding, the Arab spring demonstrated that the views of ordinary men and women matter, and it follows that public opinion research in the Arab world is more important than ever. The third wave of Arab Barometer surveys will be completed in 2013, enriching, along with the political attitude surveys carried out by others, the data resources available both to track continuity and change across countries and over time and to carry out more and better research aimed at identifying and understanding the factors that play a role in shaping the political sentiments of Arab publics.

Appendix

In both waves of Arab Barometer surveys, national probability samples of adults eighteen and older were constructed to select respondents, to whom the survey instrument was then administered in face-to-face interviews. Most surveys employed a complex sample design that took into account stratification and clustering. The content of the interview schedule for each wave was determined at meetings convened by the Arab Barometer's steering committee and attended by most of the in-country partners responsible for carrying out the surveys. The interview schedule for each wave was finalized after pretesting in several countries.

The Center for Strategic Studies (CSS) at the University of Jordan, with assistance from the steering committee members and others, coordinated the postsurvey review of the data and the preparation of the final country and merged the data files. Specialists at CSS also reviewed sampling plans before conducting the surveys, and in several instances CSS specialists traveled to the coutnry to provide on-the-ground guidance to in-country partners on other aspects of the research.

The in-country team leaders and/or institutional partners are as follows:

- Jordan 2006 ($n = 1143$) and 2010 ($n = 1188$), Center for Strategic Studies at Jordan University. A stratified random-sampling technique was used for adults eighteen and over. The population was stratified proportionately by governorate. It was further divided into clusters based on maps of housing units from which blocks were randomly selected. The sample was further stratified by urban and rural areas.

- Palestine 2006 (n = 1270) and 2010 (n = 1200), Palestine Center for Policy and Survey Research. A stratified random-sampling technique was used for adults eighteen and older. The population was stratified proportionately between the West Bank and Gaza and then further subdivided into city, village, and refugee camp. Blocks were then randomly selected in proportion to the population parameters.

- Algeria 2006 (n = 1300), Abdallah Bedaida, University of Algiers; 2011 (n = 1216), Nasr Djabi, University of Algiers. A stratified random-sampling technique was used for adults eighteen and older. The sample was stratified proportionately by *wilaya* (province), and the primary sampling unit was the district. The sample was further stratified by urban and rural areas.

- Morocco 2006 (n = 1277), Mhammed Abderebbi Hassan II University-Mohammadia. Area probability sample with quotas provided by the National Bureau of Statistics in Morocco. They selected one hundred zones (sixty urban and forty rural) and took quotas for type of living situation, gender, age, whether married or not, socioeconomic level, and educational level.

- Yemen 2007 (n = 717) and 2011 (n = 1200), Tareq Almthagi, Yemeni Statistics Authority and Khalid Yasin, Interactions in Development A stratified random-sampling technique was used for adults eighteen and over. The population was stratified proportionately by governorate. It was further divided into clusters of housing units from which blocks were randmonly selected. It was further stratified by urban and rural areas.

- Lebanon 2007 (n = 1195) and 2010 (n = 1387), Rabih Haber, Statistics Lebanon. A stratified random-sampling technique was used for adults eighteen and over. The population was stratified proportionately by district. It was further divided into clusters based on maps of housing units from which blocks were randomly selected. The sample was further stratified by urban and rural areas.

- Iraq 2011 (n = 1234), Munqith Daghir, IIACSS. A stratified random-sampling technique was used for adults eighteen and older. The population was stratified proportionately by governorates. It was further stratified by *nahia* (administrative division). In urban areas, blocks were then selected based on probability proportional to size (PPS). In rural areas, respondents were selected using simple random samplin.

- Bahrain, 2009 (n = 435). The survey was coordinated by Justin Gengler, who used a random sample of five hundred households obtained for this study by the Bahrain Center for Studies and Research from the Central Informatics Organization. Given the small size of the Bahraini population, this meant that one of every 1,055 Bahraini citizens was interviewed. The survey instrument was administered in face-to-face interviews by field-workers that Gengler recruited and trained. As a rule, Shii interviewers conducted interviews in Shia-dominated areas and Sunni interviewers were sent to Sunni areas.

- Tunisia, 2011 (n = 1196), Sigma Conseil. A stratified random-sampling technique was used for adults eighteen and older. The population was stratified proportionately by governorate and then was divided into delegations from which sectors were randomly selected. The sample was further stratified by urban and rural areas.
- Egypt, 2011 (n = 1219), Al-Ahram Center for Political and Strategic Studies. A stratified random sampling technique was used for adults eighteen and older. The population was stratified proportionately by governorate and then by district. Blocks of households were randomly selected using PPS. The sample was further stratified by urban and rural areas. Five districts with large Christian populations were purposely selected.
- Saudi Arabia, 2011 (n = 1404), Ali Abdel Lateef, Qias. A stratified random-sampling technique was used for adults eighteen and older. The population was stratified proportionately by the five main regions of the country and then was divided into clusters based on maps of housing units from which blocks were randomly selected. The sample was further stratified by urban and rural areas.

For additional details, please visit the Arab Barometer website at http://www.arabbarometer.org.

NOTES

1. See http://arabbarometer.org. The website also includes the interview schedules used in the first and second wave of surveys.
2. The survey in Iraq, conducted in 2006, was part of the World Value Survey but included many of the items used in the Arab Barometer.
3. The survey in Bahrain was conducted in 2009.
4. Amaney A. Jamal and Mark Tessler, "Attitudes in the Arab World," *Journal of Democracy* 19 (2008): 97–110; Ronald Inglehart, "How Solid Is Support for Democracy and How Can We Measure It?" *PS: Political Science and Politics* 36 (2003): 51–57; Mark Tessler and Eleanor Gao, "Gauging Arab Support for Democracy," *Journal of Democracy* 16 (2005): 83–97.
5. Each item asked respondents whether they strongly agreed, agreed, disagreed, or strongly disagreed with the statement. In dichotomizing the items, those who agreed strongly and agreed were put in one category, and those who disagreed and disagreed strongly were put in the other. The items measuring attitudes toward democracy and the item measuring attitudes toward Islam's political role each correlated strongly with other relevant items, thus offering evidence of reliability and

validity. A single item was used in each case, rather than a multi-item scale, in order to increase clarity and reduce missing data.

6. Use of the term "secular" democracy is intended only to reference a particular pattern of responses but not necessarily the fuller sense of what the term "secular" might imply. For an analysis of the ways that "democracy" is understood by respondents, see Jamal and Tessler, "Attitudes in the Arab World."

7. Mark Tessler, "Islam and Democracy in the Middle East: The Impact of Religious Orientations on Attitudes Toward Democracy in Four Arab Countries," *Comparative Politics* 34 (April 2002): 337–54.

8. Quoted in Tim Arango, "In Iraq: Bottoms Up for Democracy," *New York Times*, April 16, 2011.

9. Ali Gomaa, "In Egypt's Democracy, Room for Islam," *New York Times*, April 2, 2011.

10. Despite the consistency in levels of support between these two cases over time, the overall levels of support vary greatly between these two cases. Most likely, this is due to Lebanon's sizable Christian population, which makes a significant role for political Islam less feasible than in Iraq.

11. Juan Jose Escobar Stemmann, "The Crossroads of Muslim Brothers in Jordan," *Middle East Review of International Affairs* 14, no. 1 (2010): 38–49.

12. Mark Tessler, "The Origins of Popular Support for Islamist Movements: A Political Economy Analysis," in *Islam, Democracy, and the State in North Africa*, ed. John P. Entelis (Bloomington: Indiana University Press, 1997), 93–126.

13. The Bahrain survey was conducted in 2009 and employed the interview schedule used in the first wave of the Arab Barometer.

14. Sudan is not discussed in this chapter.

15. In Iraq, one of the two countries in which a plurality does not support secular democracy, the difference in levels of support between secular democracy and democracy with Islam is only 0.6 percent. This difference is indistinguishable statistically, meaning that only in Yemen is it clear that the plurality of respondents does not support secular democracy.

16. A number of important secular political figures also have a long history of opposition to the Ben Ali regime, and al-Nahda was not alone in its opposition to Ben Ali's regime among the parties competing in the 2011 Constituent Assembly election.

17. In both Egypt and Tunisia, nearly half the respondents reported that they trusted the Muslim Brotherhood and al-Nahda, respectively. See Michael Robbins and Mark Tessler, "What Egyptians Mean by Democracy," *ForeignPolicy.com*, September 20, 2012, available at http://mideast.foreignpolicy.com/posts/2011/09/20/what_egyptians_mean _by_democracy (accessed on February 28, 2012); and Michael Robbins and Mark Tessler, "Tunisians Voted for Jobs, Not Islam," *ForeignPolicy.com*, December 7, 2012, available at http://mideast.foreignpolicy.com/posts/2011/12/07/tunisians_voted_for_ jobs_not_ islam (accessed on February 28, 2012).

18. The vast majority of Arabs are Sunni.

14

Political Attitudes of Youth Cohorts

MICHAEL HOFFMAN AND AMANEY JAMAL

The Arab revolutions have been painted in the popular media as youth revolutions in which young citizens—perhaps aided by social media—took to the streets in opposition to oppressive regimes. The sources driving youth discontent in the region are multifaceted, ranging from frustration with economic conditions to opposition to the political status quo to a lack of a sense of efficacy in general. What is not clear, however, is to what extent the youth population is distinct from other cohorts across societies in the Middle East and North Africa (MENA). In other words, do the youth populations in the Arab region feel less at ease with the status quo than do their older counterparts? And if so, were they indeed more likely to protest and demonstrate as a result of these grievances? Answering these questions sheds light on the recent cycle of protests across the Arab world.

In this chapter, we assess a variety of competing claims about whether and why the Arab youth became the leaders of the Arab spring. Using data from the Arab Barometer surveys in seven Arab countries, we dissected the political attitudes of the younger generations in comparison to other groups, asking, Are the youth more aggrieved? Are they more supportive of secular politics? Are they more opposed to incumbent regimes? Do they possess unique resources that make mobilization less costly, even if it is not any more desirable to them than to other age groups? We believe that a behavioral account of both the attitudes and the activities of this generation of Arab citizens is crucial to any thorough account of the Arab spring.

The current coverage of the events in the region attributes the growing grievances of a youth bulge without adequate employment as a major source of their tension and disillusionment. Ragui Assaad, for example, argues that the growing youth movement is particularly disenchanted:

> The region is facing a demographic bulge in which youth aged fifteen to twenty-nine comprise the largest proportion of the population. These young people, frustrated with the lack of jobs, have been at the forefront of anti-government protests. . . . So, demographics, simply by having a larger number of people who are very frustrated at their inability to turn their education into productive jobs, has really exacerbated the problems.[1]

In essence, scholars argue that the youth population has been awakened. Once considered a passive agent in the political sphere, the events of the Arab spring have galvanized this newfound momentum. As Rami Khoury says about the youth population that was once passive: "Today, they have sparked and manned one of the most important historical transformations anywhere in the world in modern history."[2]

The Youth Population in the Arab World

The youth population in the Arab world is growing expeditiously. Sixty percent of the region's people are under thirty, twice the percentage of that age group in North America.[3] Thirty percent of the population is between the ages of fourteen and twenty-four,[4] and more than half the people in the Arab world today are under age twenty-five.[5] The number of young people in the Middle East is the second highest in the world, behind only that of sub-Saharan Africa.

In the Middle East and North Africa, the rate of unemployment is four times as high for young people as for other age groups, and "North Africa and the Middle East have the highest regional rates of joblessness in the world."[6] In the MENA, the number of unemployed has risen steadily since 1996. Estimates suggest that each year, about 500,000 additional people in the MENA become unemployed.[7] Further exacerbating the problem is that for those first seeking employment, the rate is much higher;[8] indeed, in some areas, the youth unemployment rates are as high as 80 percent.[9] Few can afford to travel, so emigration is just a frustrating dream.[10] It is no surprise that a recent study found that about 70 percent of youth in the Arab world wanted to leave the region.[11]

Along with these economic concerns, the youth population is also quite frustrated with the political circumstances prevailing in the region. The lack of freedoms and abundance of political oppression has left a potentially dynamic youth population feeling rather sullen.[12] Not only are the regimes in their countries repressive, but the people are unable to express their political and social opinions openly. Many observers believe that this frustration is why social media have been so important to this youth population. Social media allow these youths to bypass political repression. After growing up being told that they could trust no one, social media have allowed them to come together in meaningful ways,[13] with some estimates putting the number of new users of some form of social media at 100 million. In Tunisia, for example, it was reported that 20 percent of the youth population use Facebook. To circumvent the government's censorship, youth movements distribute finger-length memory sticks, which permit users to log on anonymously. As a result, these youth groups have been able to create secret cyber communities away from the eyes of the authorities.[14] Facebook certainly helped Egyptians monitor the arrest and death of Khaled Said, a young Egyptian, in June 2010. In Morocco, more than three million users have now joined the social networking site. Accordingly, the youth population appears to be highly engaged in political and social affairs.

Besides being portrayed as frustrated with economic and political conditions, young people were described during the events of the Arab spring as being more liberal, less religious, and more supportive of secular politics. In fact, the coverage of the riots and protests made a concerted effort to distinguish between the protestors and the usual suspects: "Rather than the Arab world's usual suspects—bearded Islamists or jaded leftists—it is the young people, angry at the lack of economic opportunity available to them, who are risking their lives going up against police forces."[15] According to David Gardner, the main point is that under the old order, despotism and Islamism fed on each other and that there is nothing to lament about the passing of this perverse symbiosis and a lot to celebrate that in the young, dynamic middle classes of an awakening Arab world there are, against all odds, democrats with whom to democratize.[16] In a CNN op-ed, John Esposito wrote that the current wave of demonstrations were led by youth who were disillusioned with the "failures of Islamist authoritarian regimes in Sudan, Iran, the Taliban's Afghanistan and Saudi Arabia" and that the youth population was not interested in theocracy but in democracy.[17]

Yet juxtaposed with these accounts are patterns that may indicate that the youth are not necessarily different from earlier cohorts. Although young people in the region have more access to the Internet than their older counterparts do, it is still quite low.[18] Furthermore, researchers have found that persons aged eighteen to twenty-four tend to identify closely with traditional, religious, and familial ties. For example, the youth in Jordan still identify strongly with the army and the police, while the Lebanese youth demonstrate tight sectarian attachments.[19]

New studies have shown that although the youth are indeed a source of change, their messages lack coherence and direction. Just before the Tunisian elections, for example, they showed a lack of organization and involvement. A recent survey conducted by the International Foundation of Electoral Services revealed that only 38 percent of Tunisian youth aged eighteen to twenty-four correctly identified the purpose of their next election: to choose an assembly to write the constitution.[20]

Thus, on the one hand, the youth population has been portrayed as highly engaged, involved politically, upset about economic conditions, and distancing itself from existing forms of opposition movements, namely, Islamists. How true are these classifications? Fortunately, through cross-national survey data, we can compare the younger generations in the Arab world with others. To do so, the Arab Barometer provides the best source of data on political attitudes in the Arab world, as it allows us to observe changes in both political outlook and behavior across age groups.

We recognize that preferences are not always translated into behavior and that the protesters' demands are not always met. Political opportunities[21] have historically been a key component of social movements' success or failure and were undoubtedly of great importance during the Arab spring. We wish, however, to offer a *behavioral* account of these protests, describing and analyzing the groups that organized them. The character of the Arab revolutionaries dictates what types of questions we ought to be asking: If these revolutions were truly driven by young people, we would expect that the results would match the attitudes of these young citizens themselves. If the current generation of Arab citizens closely resembles older generations, then we would not expect their political outcomes to differ greatly; but if differences emerge between birth cohorts, then it is conceivable that these revolutions—if responsive to the protesters—could lead to significant political change.

Data and Analysis

The following analysis divides the respondents into five cohorts. The youngest cohort is labeled cohort 1, and the respondents are between the ages of eighteen and twenty-four. Cohort 2 covers ages twenty-five to thirty-four; cohort 3 covers ages thirty-five to forty-four; cohort 4 covers ages forty-five to fifty-four; and cohort 5 covers ages fifty-five and older.

Supposition 1:
Youth Population Is Less Religious Than Other Cohorts

First, it is useful to consider potential modernization effects. One of the main hypotheses of mainstream modernization theory is that as countries modernize, individuals tend to become less religious. In the Arab world, this trend seems to hold. Figure 14.1 depicts the proportion of people in each birth cohort who identify as religious and who participate in communal prayer. This figure suggests considerable differences among the cohorts: in the youngest cohort, less than 60 percent of respondents identify themselves as "religious," compared with nearly 80 percent in the oldest cohort. A similar trend exists in communal religious practice: slightly more than 40 percent of the youngest generation participates in communal worship, but only about 60 percent of the oldest cohort does. Unfortunately, the current data do not allow us to discover whether these differences are simply due to life-cycle effects; that is, individuals may become more religious as

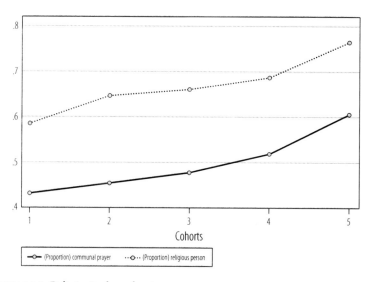

FIGURE 14.1 Religiosity, by cohort.

(Percentage of population under thirty in the Arab world)

they age, implying that the current older generations may have been just as secular when they were younger as the youth are today. We believe, however—admittedly without hard data capable of proving these claims beyond doubt—that there must be at least *some* secularization in order to produce the trends we see here.

Supposition 2:
Youth Population Is More Educated and Less Likely to Be Employed

Other evidence for a process of modernization can also be found in the data. Figure 14.2 plots the proportion of college-educated and unemployed individuals by cohort. As expected, there is a linear downward trend in the older cohorts of the likelihood of having had college education, except for the youngest cohort, many of whom are simply not old enough to have earned a college degree yet. Perhaps more interesting is the unemployment trend. A popular theory of youth mobilization in the Arab world attributes the recent protests to high unemployment among young people, as unemployment creates grievances that motivate antigovernment mobilization and also reduces the opportunity cost of protest.[22] While it is impossible to infer causality from these results, the data support the notion that younger Arabs are much more likely to be

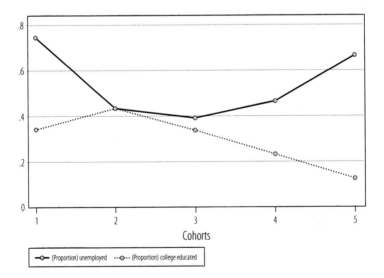

FIGURE 14.2 Education and unemployment, by cohort.

unemployed. Indeed, the youngest generation is nearly twice as likely to be unemployed as those in the middle age groups.

Supposition 3:
Youth Population Is Less Likely to Support Political Islam

We have yet to observe, however, how these social and economic changes translate into political attitudes. The lower levels of religiosity among younger Arabs could be associated with greater calls for secularization and a rejection of religious involvement in politics. Since younger individuals score lower, on average, in both belief and practice, we might expect that these same individuals would tend to call for separation of religion and state, tolerance of other religions, and moves toward secular law. Figure 14.3, however, presents patterns that do not match this expectation. Rather than promoting secularization and tolerance, younger generations are *more* likely to support Islamic law and *less* likely to say that they would be comfortable living near neighbors of other religions. It is evident that the decreases in personal piety associated with younger age groups have *not* translated into more secular or tolerant political attitudes.

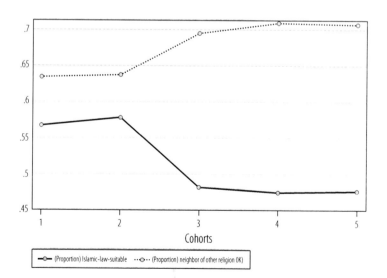

FIGURE 14.3 Support for religious law and religious tolerance, by cohort.

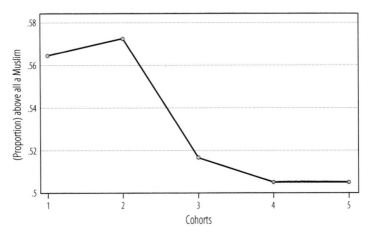

FIGURE 14.4 Muslim identity, by cohort.

Supposition 4:
Youth Population Is Less Likely to Identify as Muslim

Despite decreases in average individual religiosity, religion remains an important political identity. Figure 14.4 shows that younger individuals are, in fact, *more* likely to identify themselves primarily as Muslim rather than as citizens of country X or as Arabs. Taken together, these trends suggest that piety does not necessarily move in harmony with a religious political identity. Younger generations are at the same time more Muslim and less Muslim than their predecessors. While the political consequences of these attitudinal shifts are somewhat ambiguous, it is clear that analysts should not interpret decreases in religious belief or practice as indicating a decline in the importance of religion—specifically Islam—in public life.

Supposition 5:
Youth Population Is Less Likely to Participate Politically

How do these changes in both socioeconomic attributes and political attitudes relate to changes in political behavior? Younger generations appear to participate in politics in more informal ways. Figure 14.5 demonstrates that the youngest generation is around 50 percent more likely to

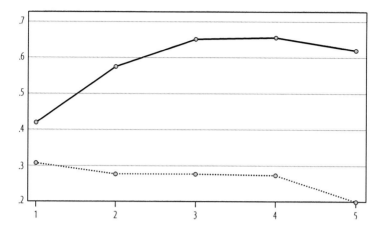

FIGURE 14.5 Political participation, by cohort.

participate in protests than is the oldest generation but that they are substantially less likely to vote. These findings lend some support—at least impressionistically—to the image of the Arab spring as a youth-based phenomenon. At the same time, it is important to consider that all these surveys were conducted several years before the Arab spring. Even before the recent spate of demonstrations, 30 percent of the youngest generation of Arabs had participated in an organized protest. In this sense, the Arab spring can be viewed as the culmination of a process that had *already begun*; even several years before the fall of Tunisia's president, Zine el-Abdine Ben Ali, younger Arabs were protesting in greater numbers than earlier generations did.

Supposition 6:
Youth Population Is Ambivalent Toward Government

Figure 14.6 shows that in general, attitudes toward the regime have remained fairly flat across cohorts (the *y*-axis on this graph is very small). The average citizen's satisfaction with the government (as measured on a ten-point scale) does not vary widely across cohorts. Interestingly, the youngest cohort is slightly *more* satisfied with the government on average than are the middle cohorts.

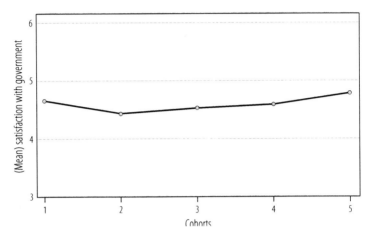

FIGURE 14.6 Attitudes toward government, by cohort.

Supposition 7:
Youth Population Is More Satisfied with Government

Figure 14.7 displays a surprising result: the youngest generation, on average, is *more* likely than other cohorts to believe both that leaders care about ordinary citizens and that the government creates conditions that allow for prospering. Contrary to the common image of youth populations in general—and Arab youths specifically—younger citizens in the Arab world are *more* sympathetic to their leaders, at least in their evaluations of those leaders' choices.

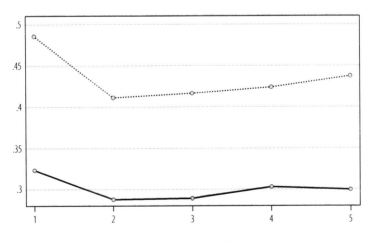

FIGURE 14.7 Satisfaction with government, by cohort.

Supposition 8:
Youth Population Is More Satisfied with Economic Conditions

Figure 14.8 shows a similar trend in the area of economic conditions. Despite their high level of unemployment, Arab youths are *more* satisfied with the current economic conditions of their countries and *more* optimistic that conditions will improve in the coming years. If deteriorating economic conditions led to a youth-led revolt in the Arab spring, as is commonly asserted, then attitudes toward these conditions must have changed sharply and rapidly in the few years before the Arab spring. When the first wave of the Arab Barometer was conducted, the youth population was substantially *happier* with their countries' economic conditions than were older generations. It is possible that the changing conditions (particularly the rise in global food prices that occurred after these data were collected) precipitated the youth mobilization against their regimes in the Arab world. Although these changes certainly might have inspired protest, we find little reason to believe that they would account for the relatively higher likelihood of protest among the youth. Since increasing food prices affect everyone, declining conditions should lead to lower levels of satisfaction among *all* respondents, simply shifting the graphs downward but not affecting the *relative* levels of satisfaction when comparing different age groups. Thus, poor economic conditions (at least those that do not disproportionately affect the youth) do not appear to explain mobilization of youths to protest.

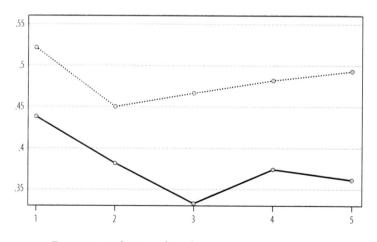

FIGURE 14.8 Economic evaluations, by cohort.

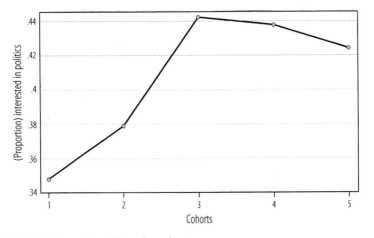

FIGURE 14.9 Interest in politics, by cohort.

Supposition 9:
Youth Population Is More Engaged in Politics

Figure 14.9 reveals a nearly monotonic decrease in interest in politics across age cohorts: the younger generations are, on average, much less interested in politics than are older citizens. This finding is consistent with the observation that younger citizens were substantially less likely to vote in elections. The Arab uprisings, then, pose a puzzle: What caused a fairly uninterested group of citizens to revolt, if indeed these revolts were primarily a youth-driven phenomenon? Clearly, if the Arab uprisings were brought about by the youth, something must have occurred that substantially raised their interest in politics.

Supposition 10:
Youth Population Understands Democracy to Be Something Different

Finally, figure 14.10 demonstrates that the youngest cohort understands democracy in largely the same way as do older cohorts. The youngest generation is slightly more likely than others to believe that elections are the primary characteristic of democracy, but this difference is minimal and not statistically significant. Likewise, the youth cohort is somewhat more likely to view democracy as a mechanism for income equality, but the effect is minimal. The only area in which the youth view democracy differently

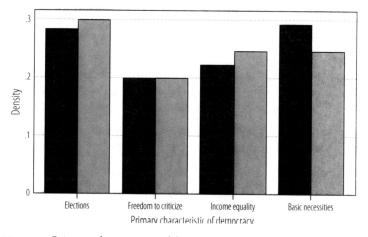

FIGURE 14.10 Primary characterisic of democracy, by cohort.

from others is in the question of providing basic necessities: the youngest cohort is less likely to view democracy as primarily a provider of basic necessities. This difference is perhaps attributable to the rise in living conditions in the region over time.

Basic Models

Next we examine more carefully two dependent variables: protest and support for political Islam. In particular we are interested in seeing, first, what factors were most likely to structure protest before the Arab spring and, second, what factors were most important to determining the levels of support for political Islam. In both models, we pay particular attention to the role of youth.

In analyzing the protest trends, some interesting patterns emerge. Table 14.1 presents the results of three logistic regressions where the dependent variable is scored as a 1 if the respondent had participated in at least one protest during the previous three years (2004–2007). All models include country-fixed effects (not reported) to account for any differences that might shift one country up or down, on average, on the dependent variable. In all three models, the coefficient estimate for the Youngest variable (which is a dummy variable indicating whether or not the respondent is in the youngest of the five cohorts) is highly significant and positive. This

TABLE 14.1
LOGISTIC REGRESSION RESULTS, PROTEST

	1	2	3	4
Youngest	0.465***	0.506***	0.514***	0.345**
	(0.0859)	(0.138)	(0.138)	(0.144)
Income	0.0677***	0.0680***	0.0680***	0.0484***
	(0.0123)	(0.0123)	(0.0123)	(0.0126)
Communal prayer	0.211***	0.212***	0.214***	0.208***
	(0.0777)	(0.0778)	(0.0778)	(0.0793)
Read Koran a lot	0.0498	0.0492	0.0505	0.0681
	(0.0693)	(0.0693)	(0.0694)	(0.0707)
Unemployed	-0.279***	-0.264***	-0.178*	-0.204**
	(0.0793)	(0.0883)	(0.0994)	(0.101)
College educated	0.241***	0.242***	0.343***	0.155
	(0.0771)	(0.0772)	(0.0939)	(0.0977)
Female	-0.524***	-0.525***	-0.533***	-0.469***
	(0.0770)	(0.0771)	(0.0773)	(0.0789)
Youngest* unemployed		-0.0688	-0.0572	-0.00144
		(0.179)	(0.179)	(0.184)
College-educated* unemployed			-0.292*	-0.203
			(0.155)	(0.158)
Internet usage				0.230***
				(0.0236)
Intercept	-2.353***	-2.360***	-2.407***	-1.268***
	(0.155)	(0.156)	(0.158)	(0.196)
N	5176	5176	5176	5051
R^2				

Standard errors in parentheses.

$*p < 0.10, **p < 0.05, ***p < 0.01.$

result holds up even when we include variables measuring unemployment status, college education, and their interaction. Contrary to what might be expected, unemployment does not seem to be driving protest (though this finding does not necessarily mean that unemployment was not a key factor in motivating protests during the Arab uprisings). In fact, the "unemployed" variable is *negatively* associated with protest in each model. College education, as expected, is positive and significant in each model, but the interaction between College educated and Unemployed yields a negative coefficient estimate in model 3. Based on these data, it does *not* appear that—in the few years before the Arab uprisings, at least—unemployed college graduates were the most likely to protest. However, protest does appear to be a youth-driven phenomenon, even when controlling for factors such as education, income, and unemployment status. Furthermore, model 4 accounts for the possibility that access to technology (as measured by Internet usage) might account for the youth cohort's greater likelihood of protest (see chapter 5). Indeed, the youngest group of respondents is about 50 percent more likely to use the Internet on at least a weekly basis, compared with all other respondents. The results from model 4 suggest that Internet users were substantially more likely to participate in protests than were non-Internet users, and the inclusion of this variable somewhat attenuates the effect of the Youngest variable. But even with the inclusion of this variable—which is highly correlated with the youth variable—the coefficient on the Youngest variable remains substantial and statistically significant. This result indicates that the youth's higher likelihood of protesting cannot be attributed only to Internet usage.

Table 14.2 shows the results of several regressions involving support for political Islam and Islamic law (for a more thorough treatment of political Islam, see chapter 11). The dependent variable in model 1 is a dummy variable indicating that the respondent believes that Islamic law is suitable for his or her country. In models 2 and 3, the dependent variable is a composite scale of support for political Islam, which is composed of three questions: the "Islamic law suitable" question in model 1 plus a religious tolerance question and a question about support for laws based only on *sharia* (for details, see the appendix).

The results in table 14.2 suggest that on average, the youngest cohort is substantially more supportive of political Islam than other cohorts are. This finding contrasts with modernization hypotheses, which claim that younger generations will become increasingly more tolerant, liberal, and secular than their older counterparts. Even though on average, the young generation

TABLE 14.2
REGRESSION RESULTS, SUPPORT FOR POLITICAL ISLAM

	1 ISLAMIC LAW SUITABLE (LOGIT)	2 POLITICAL ISLAM (OLS)	3 POLITICAL ISLAM (OLS) (OLS)
Youngest	0.242** (0.101)	0.109*** (0.0403)	0.149** (0.0684)
Income	-0.00861 (0.0136)	-0.00782 (0.00523)	-0.00748 (0.00525)
Internet usage	-0.0146 (0.0282)	-0.0217** (0.0107)	-0.0222** (0.0107)
Communal prayer	-0.0178 (0.0951)	-0.0830** (0.0352)	-0.0832** (0.0352)
Read Koran a lot	0.406*** (0.0758)	0.199*** (0.0301)	0.198*** (0.0301)
Unemployed	0.184** (0.0910)	0.0513 (0.0370)	0.0621 (0.0399)
College educated	-0.257*** (0.0870)	-0.0962*** (0.0329)	-0.0957*** (0.0329)
Female	-0.0732 (0.0952)	-0.0215 (0.0355)	-0.0234 (0.0356)
Youngest* Unemployed			-0.0612 (0.0843)
Intercept	0.745*** (0.203)	1.792*** (0.0769)	1.785*** (0.0776)
N	3701	2587	2587
R^2		0.484	0.484

Standard errors in parentheses.
*$p < 0.10$, **$p < 0.05$, ***$p < 0.01$.

is less religious than its predecessors, it is more supportive of both Islamic law and political Islam in general. Not surprisingly, Internet usage and especially college education mitigate this effect, as higher scores on each of these variables are associated with lower levels of support for political Islam. Unemployment is a significant predictor of support for *sharia* law and has a weaker, but still positive, effect on overall support for political Islam. The interaction between Youngest and Unemployed is nowhere near significance, suggesting that the effect of unemployment on support for political Islam is not conditional on age.

Table 14.3 presents the results of an important extension of our results using the second wave of the Arab Barometer. The second wave of the Arab Barometer survey was fielded in Egypt in July 2011 and in Tunisia in April 2011 shortly after the uprisings in these countries.[23] Using these second-wave data, we confirmed that the youngest cohort was substantially more likely than other citizens to participate in the *Arab spring* protests specifically, not simply to have participated in any type of protest, as we considered earlier in the first-wave analysis. For table 14.3, we used only respondents from Egypt and Tunisia, in order to ensure that our results were not simply artifacts of "Arab winter" countries, which dominated the earlier sample. Furthermore, we asked the respondents in this survey specifically if they had participated in the protests against Presidents Hosni Mubarak or Ben Ali, not simply if they had protested in the past several years. Some demographic variables found to be important in predicting protest during the first wave of the Arab Barometer remained relevant to the Arab spring: college-educated citizens were substantially more likely to protest than were citizens with lower levels of education, and women were far less likely to participate than were men. While unemployment does not appear to lessen the likelihood of protest in the second wave (as it did in the first wave), it does not have a statistically significant positive effect either. Likewise, the interaction between Youngest and College educated and between Unemployed and College educated do not suggest strong or significant interaction effects.

The results presented in this table provide very strong support for the claim that the Arab uprisings were heavily driven by youths. Regardless of the model's specification, the coefficient on our Youngest variable is large and statistically significant at the 0.01 level or better. Once again, the strength of this effect was mitigated somewhat by the inclusion of a measure of frequency of Internet usage. It is evident that Internet users were much more likely to participate in these protests, and since Internet usage

TABLE 14.3
REGRESSION RESULTS, PROTESTS (SECOND WAVE)

	1	2	3	4
Youngest	1.044***	1.008***	1.010***	0.566***
	(0.179)	(0.201)	(0.202)	(0.218)
Income	0.121**	0.121**	0.118*	0.0413
	(0.0607)	(0.0608)	(0.0607)	(0.0630)
Communal prayer	-0.548***	-0.548***	-0.546***	-0.430**
	(0.196)	(0.196)	(0.196)	(0.201)
Koran reading	0.471***	0.470***	0.472***	0.432***
	(0.0940)	(0.0941)	(0.0941)	(0.0972)
Unemployed	0.239	0.171	0.274	0.225
	(0.213)	(0.276)	(0.310)	(0.316)
College educated	1.058***	1.059***	1.109***	0.633***
	(0.168)	(0.168)	(0.182)	(0.201)
Female	-1.979***	-1.982***	-1.973***	-1.815***
	(0.204)	(0.205)	(0.205)	(0.208)
Youngest* unemployed		0.170	0.160	0.471
		(0.432)	(0.430)	(0.445)
College Educated* unemployed			-0.309	-0.420
			(0.445)	(0.453)
Internet Usage				0.293***
				(0.0514)
Egypt	-1.091***	-1.096***	-1.101***	-0.939***
	(0.180)	(0.180)	(0.180)	(0.186)
Intercept	-0.573*	-0.555	-0.587*	-1.226***
	(0.344)	(0.347)	(0.350)	(0.376)
N	1950	1950	1950	1934
R^2				

Standard errors in parentheses.

$^*p < 0.10$, $^{**}p < 0.05$, $^{***}p < 0.01$.

is highly collinear with youth, controlling for Internet use decreases the size of the coefficient on Youngest. Nonetheless, even when controlling for Internet usage, the coefficient on the Youngest variable remains both substantively large and statistically significant at the 1 percent level. When the Internet variable is included, respondents in the Youngest category are still more than five percentage points more likely than others to have protested, which represents a 45 percent increase in the likelihood of protest over those who are not in the youngest category (16.8% versus 11.2%). Thus, it is reasonable to conclude that the youth cohort was substantially more likely to participate in protests *during* the Arab spring, complementing our findings from surveys conducted before these uprisings.

Conclusion

After analyzing the characteristics of the Arab youth and comparing them with those of earlier generations, the image of the youth cohort in the Arab world remains complicated. Some common intuitions about the members of this cohort were confirmed: on average, they are less religious, more educated, more likely to be unemployed, more likely to protest, and less likely to vote. In other ways, however, our findings depart from the conventional wisdom about this generation. Young Arabs are generally more supportive of political Islam than are their older counterparts and tend to support *sharia* law more than do older citizens. They are more likely to identify themselves primarily as Muslims than are older generations. They are, in general, happier with their governments' efforts to create prosperity. Interestingly, despite their high unemployment rates, the Arab youth are both more satisfied with their countries' economic conditions and more optimistic about future economic prospects.

What do these findings imply about the role of the youth cohorts in the Arab spring? The data suggest that youth mobilization against the regime was not caused by *grievances* with the regime; in general, young people were more likely to be satisfied with the regime than others. On the contrary, it appears that *opportunities*—both real and perceived—may have motivated the youth to mobilize. The youth generation is more connected with the rest of the Arab world and the international community as a whole than any generation that preceded it, and it seems to be highly optimistic about what ordinary citizens can do. The opportunities presented by a mobilized citizenry seemed to play more of a role in motivating the Arab spring than did an elevated sense of antiregime sentiment among the youth.

Clearly, we can only go so far in characterizing the political attitudes and behaviors associated with the Arab spring using the available data, as the data used in this analysis predate the Arab spring by several years. We can, however, make considerable progress in describing the cohort that has been said to be the driving force behind the recent revolutions in the Arab World. It is unclear how the attitudes and behaviors of this cohort were affected by the events that led to the Arab spring or by the Arab spring itself. In the coming years, it will be useful and interesting to examine the *changes* in political attitudes before and after the Arab spring. For now, this study has attempted to draw a baseline for comparison and to describe how the Arab youth viewed politics *before* the Arab spring.

Future studies of the political outlooks of the Arab Youth should aim to make before-and-after comparisons that identify both the changes that led to the Arab spring and the impact of the Arab spring itself. In doing so, these studies can assess the relative importance of various factors that are said to have driven revolution: unemployment, corruption, repression, and others. By focusing on the microlevel attitudes of individual citizens, such analyses will be able to look into the minds of everyday Arab citizens. This type of analysis will prove invaluable for understanding both political changes in the Arab world and general theories of political behavior.

Appendix: Wording of Questions Used in the Analysis

101) How would you rate the current overall economic condition of [country name] today?
1.Very good 2. Good 3. Bad 4. Very bad

102) What do you think will be the state of [country name]'s economic condition a few years (3–5 years) from now?
1. Much better 2. A little better 3. About the same 4. A little worse
5. Much worse

207) Did you participate in the elections on [country name]?
1. Yes 2. No

215) Generally speaking, how interested would you say you are in politics?
1. Very interested 2. Interested 3. Little interested 4. Not interested

222) How often do you use the Internet?

1. Daily or almost daily 2. At least once a week 3. At least once a month
4. Several times a year 5. I do not use the Internet

230) Here is a list of actions that people sometimes take as citizens. For each of these please tell me whether you, personally, have ever done each of these things in the past three years:
2. Attend a demonstration or protest march
1. Once 2. More than once 3. Never

231) People often differ in their views on the characteristics that are essential to democracy. If you have to choose only one thing, what would you choose as the most important characteristic, and what would be the second most important?
1. Opportunity to change the government through elections
2. Freedom to criticize the government/ those in power
3. A small income gap between rich and poor
4. Basic necessities like food, clothing, shelter for everyone
5. Other (specify) ———

246) I'm going to describe various types of political systems that exist in the Middle East and ask what you think about each as a way of governing [country name]. For each one, would you say it is a very suitable, suitable, somewhat suitable, or not suitable at all way of governing [country name]?
4. A system governed by Islamic law in which there are no political parties or elections

301) Which of the following best describes you?
1. Above all I am a [nationality of country name]
2. Above all I am a Muslim
3. Above all I am an Arab
4. Above all I am a Christian
5. Other (please state)———

303) Which of the following groups you do wish to have as neighbors?
1. Followers of other religions
1. I don't wish 2. I don't mind

402) In your opinion, how important is each of the following principles as a guide for making the laws of our country?

2. The government should implement only the laws of the sharia
1. Strongly agree 2. Agree 3. Disagree 4. Strongly disagree

507) Do you agree/disagree with the following statements:
2. Our political leaders care about ordinary citizens
4. Our government creates conditions for people to be able to prosper through their own efforts
1. Strongly agree 2. Agree 3. Disagree 4. Strongly disagree

702) Gender:
1. Male 2. Female

703) Level of education:
1. Illiterate 2. Elementary 3. Primary 5. Secondary 6. College diploma, two years 7. BA 8. MA or higher

704) Employment status:
1. Yes 2. No

712) How often do you read the Koran?
1. Everyday or almost everyday 2. Several times a week 3. Sometimes 4. Rarely 5. I don't read

714) Do you pray at: 1. Mosque 2. Home 3. Both 4. Church

715) (Income includes all salaries, wages, and rent)
Monthly income for individual in [local currency]———

NOTES

1. Ragui Assaad, Demographics of Arab Protests, interview with Council on Foreign Relations, Washington, D.C., February 14, 2011.
2. UNICEF, *A Generation on the Move: Insights into the Conditions, Aspirations and Activism of Arab Youth* (Beirut: Issam Fares Institute for Public Policy & International Affairs, 2011).
3. Pew Forum on Religion and Public Life.
4. USAID Press Release, USAID Convenes Conference for Arab Youth Development, November 14, 2011.
5. Mounira Chaeib, "Young in the Arab World: Lebanon," *BBC World Service*, February 8, 2005.

6. Ellen Knickmeyer, "The Arab World's Youth Army," *Foreign Policy*, January 27, 2011, available at http://foreignpolicy.com/articles/2011/01/.

7. Nimrod Raphaeli, "Unemployment in the Middle East—Causes and Consequences," *Middle East Media Research Institute*, February 10, 2006, available at http://www.memri.org/report/en/print1606.htm.

8. Mehmet Huseyin Bilgin and Ismihan Kilicarslan, "An Analysis of the Unemployment in Selected MENA Countries and Turkey," *Journal of Third World Studies* 25, no. 2 (fall 2008): 189–205.

9. Jack Shenker, Angelique Chrisafis, Tom Finn, Giles Tremlett, and Martin Chulov, "Young Arabs Who Can't Wait to Throw Off Shackles of Tradition," *The Guardian*, February 14, 2011.

10. Ibid.

11. Gavriel Queenann, "Report: 70% of Arab Youth Want to Leave Region," *Arutz sheva*, November 16, 2011.

12. Shenker et al., "Young Arabs Who Can't Wait to Throw Off Shackles of Tradition."

13. Ibid.

14. Ibid.

15. Knickmeyer, "The Arab World's Youth Army."

16. David Gardner, "Arab Youth Steps in Where Islamism Failed," *Financial Times*, July 10, 2011.

17. John Esposito, "Arab Youth Want Democracy, Not Theocracy," CNN, February 28, 2011, available at http://www.cnn.com/2011/OPINION/02/28/pr.

18. The World Bank's figures on Internet usage suggest that in 2010, the Arab world was still lagging behind the global average of Internet users per capita by about 13 percent.

19. UNICEF, *A Generation on the Move.*

20. Sara Sorcher, "Arab Youth Still Want Change, but Won't Be Politicians," *National Journal*, August 4, 2011, available at http://www.nationaljournal.com/nationalsecurity/arab-youth-still-want-change-but-won-t-be-politicans-20110804.

21. See Doug McAdam, John D. McCarthy, and Mayer N. Zald, eds., "Introduction: Opportunities, Mobilizing Structures and Framing Processes—Toward a Synthetic, Comparative Perspective on Social Movements," in *Comparative Perspectives on Social Movements*, ed. Doug McAdam, John D. McCarthy, and Mayer N. Zald (New York: Cambridge: Cambridge University Press, 1996), 1–20.

22. International Labour Organization, "Youth Unemployment in the Arab World Is a Major Cause for Rebellion," April 5, 2011.

23. Other countries in the second wave are Algeria, Lebanon, Palestine, Jordan, Sudan, Saudi Arabia, Iraq, Lebanon, and Yemen.

15

Constitutional Revolutions and the Public Sphere

NATHAN J. BROWN

The profound gap between ruler and ruled in the Arab world before 2011 was hidden to nobody. But for many years the venality, aloofness, and unaccountability of rulers had been met not by revolutionary wrath but by resignation, despair, and alienation, sometimes tinged with sycophancy and opportunism. Why did the wave of uprisings take so many by surprise? Why did it take such surprising forms? Why did the initial Tunisian revolt inspire such disparate imitators and why did those would-be imitators follow such different paths? In this chapter, I try to explain the surprises for Egypt and to make some tentative claims about the uprisings more broadly.

For three reasons, the popular upheavals that shook the Arab world in 2011 shocked those who had closely observed those societies for years and even those who had worked to precipitate them. First, nobody expected that large numbers of people were willing to act with courage as well as significant (and growing) coordination to effect dramatic change.

A second surprise was that the agenda of the revolutionary crowds in Egypt was centered less on economic or social grievances (though these were voiced) than on constitutional reform. Dissident crowds wanted jobs and bread to be sure, but they also called for freedom and dignity. To secure these things, they demanded an end to the executive's domination of all sources of political authority. Their demands could be surprisingly specific and legal in nature, with apparently technical matters like the full judicial monitoring of elections emerging as a major issue. When the minimum wage figured loudly in the protests, the sense of economic injustice was deepened by legal outrage that the regime seemed to be ignoring the courts' decisions on the subject.

The third reason for surprise, or at least confusion, was that the Egyptian uprising came amid a series of rebellions, insurrections, and revolutions in the Arab world that quickly earned the name "Arab uprising" as if they were a single occurrence. Evidence for linkage, imitation, and similarities abounds. Although all these events centered on challenges to authoritarian regimes, they had varying levels of success and took different forms. More subtly, they also differed in their willingness and ability to render their goals in constitutional terms.

To answer the first question—why the uprisings surprised knowledgeable observers—many academics reached quickly for Timur Kuran's work on "preference falsification."[1] In authoritarian contexts, individuals are understandably reluctant to reveal what their true political preferences are; they feign loyalty or indifference so as not to draw attention and be singled out for repression. But when an authoritarian regime falters and the costs of revealing one's true feelings rapidly drop, these individuals can be bolder, and they might quickly find that their feelings are widely shared. As that happens, even larger numbers feel safer revealing their true preferences. As people suddenly discover one another's true feelings, they can achieve safety in numbers. Thus a sullen silence can be transformed into a revolutionary popular wave that surprises even those who participate in it.

In this chapter, I wish to draw on Kuran's framework and, in the process, suggest some of its limitations. Most significantly, his portrait of individual preferences fails to incorporate the social origins of those preferences, and his portrait of authoritarian regimes fails to incorporate the tremendous variations in how much free expression is allowed and where. Incorporating a more nuanced understanding of personal preferences and authoritarianism will not lead us to abandon Kuran's framework but, rather, to modify it. The Arab uprisings in general and the Egyptian uprising in particular exemplify a slightly different kind of cascade than the one Kuran describes. More important to this book, his framework—as modified—can help us understand the nature of the popular mobilization that occurred, differences in the agenda of mobilized populations, and the course of politics after the uprising.

Kuran originally described his framework right before the 1989 upheavals in the Soviet bloc,[2] so he immediately was able to draw on his ideas to explain why the downfall of communism came as such a surprise.[3] Kuran then developed his argument most fully in his book *Private Truth, Public Lies: The Social Consequences of Preference Falsification.*[4] As the upheaval began in the Arab world—and mere days before President

Hosni Mubarak's forced resignation—Kuran once again turned to the idea of "preference falsification" to explain the surprising nature of the Egyptian and Tunisian events:

> For decades, most Arabs, however unhappy, kept their political grievances private, for fear of persecution if they turned against their leaders publicly. Through private discussions with trusted friends, everyone sensed that discontent was common, yet no one knew, or could know, the extent of it.
>
> Even harder to gauge was what it would take for the disaffected to say "enough is enough" and begin challenging their regime openly, defiantly and in concert. If a sufficient number of Arabs reached that threshold at the right time, the long-docile Arab street would explode in anger, with each group of new protesters encouraging more to join in, giving people elsewhere in the Arab world the courage to initiate protests of their own.[5]

Kuran's "preference falsification" does help us understand some of the surprising events (and why they are essentially unpredictable), and it also suggests some of the reasons for the rapidity of the revolution's path. But it also has shortcomings.

First, "preference falsification" is designed for a full authoritarian context. (In his book, Kuran also applies it to a Tocquevillian democratic society in which the strong pressure of presumed public opinion silences dissent.) Some of the semiauthoritarian societies in the Arab world allowed for fuller airing of political preferences than Kuran suggests: although honesty could have a price, it was less uniformly punished than in those contexts for which Kuran developed his approach. The author of the book *I Hate Hosni Mubarak*—openly sold in the 2000s in Egypt—made his preferences alarmingly clear. Nobody who read an independent Egyptian newspaper in the 2000s would feel safe in claiming that political grievances were being kept private, and some of those newspapers became remarkable commercial successes.

Second, Kuran assumes—as perhaps befits his training as an economist—that preferences are fixed and individual (though in his book *Private Truths, Public Lies*, he does make some passing but still genuine allowances for social influences). He gives us few tools other than the coincidence of individual preferences for understanding how consensual agendas can quickly emerge and be enthusiastically embraced in situations in which individuals are just beginning to feel free to act on their private views.

In this chapter, I begin with these shortcomings to explore the three surprises of the uprising. Focusing primarily on Egypt, I argue that although political action was all but unthinkable before 2011, many political thoughts were very much thinkable, and indeed, they were not only thought but also explored and discussed in a variety of public forums. Seen in this way, it was not preferences but likely actions that were unknown. The relative clarity of preferences helped guide the revolutionary agenda as well. I define and address each of these puzzles in turn: why Egyptians acted, what they acted for, and why their would-be imitators acted differently. I close with some general observations about the implications of the Egyptian events for upheavals elsewhere.

Daring to Defy Gravity

I cannot remember the last time—or even if there was any time that I visited Egypt, beginning in 1983—that I heard an Egyptian express a positive sentiment about the Mubarak regime. Although I certainly met many Egyptians who had little interest in having a political discussion with a foreigner, I met many others who complained at length about corruption, the lack of personal freedoms, deep economic problems, the imperviousness of the country's leadership to the problems of its citizens, and the general failure of the political system to provide for the public welfare.

The quaking and pervasive private fear on which Kuran relies may bear some resemblance to Egypt in previous decades, but by the 1990s my impression was that the prevailing mood among the Egyptians I met (mainly in Cairo and mainly middle class or on the margins of the political elite) was closer to resigned disgust. By the 2000s, that disgust was easily and publicly expressed. I met Egyptians who seemed very much part of the prevailing political order who voiced disdain and sometimes more for the system they seemed to be helping to run. In a restaurant in the mid-2000s, a fairly senior figure told me (in a private conversation but in a public place), "Our problem in this country is corruption. Even the president is corrupt."

Such feelings were not merely the stuff of small-group conversations. They were the topics of seminars, workshops, and, most strikingly, discussions in the press. In some settings (generally those that were more public or written in a more permanent form), they often (but not always) avoided the person of the president, but they were far less likely to exempt the regime. My impression in the 1980s was that the legacy of authoritarianism still hung heavily over such discussions. Criticisms of the existing regime could be voiced in those years, but typically they came a bit elliptically or with some nervousness. In the 2000s, however, this reticence and caution were largely gone. I do not mean to imply that all Egyptians denounced the regime, just that the fear of doing so had greatly declined. Those who seemed to defend the regime came off as sycophantic (and often were). Of course, they could also come off as threatening; attempts to intimidate had not at all disappeared.

Indeed, pressure from the security services could still come in merely intimidating (an invitation to coffee) or far harsher (arrest and torture) form. This was particularly the case with the press, whose editors could confront both subtle and extremely heavy-handed pressure. Some topics were still especially likely to inspire indirect or impersonal wording at times (especially criticisms of the president). Yet despite such limitations, Egypt of the 2000s was a place where politics had returned, if by politics we mean very narrowly the public discussion of issues. Organized politics, by contrast, was still sharply constrained (and perhaps becoming more so as the Mubarak years ground on), even as political expression became far more open. Political life in Egypt owed less to Hannah Arendt's *Totalitarianism* and much more to the myth of Sisyphus: futility more than fear was the prevailing feeling. If Egyptians did little to improve their political situation, it was perhaps for the same reason that so few voted: there was simply no point. Working for change was like fighting gravity. Many Egyptians presumably would have been very happy to discover that they could fly—and none would have been surprised to find out that many of their fellow citizens would also fly if they could. But nobody expected to be able to defy gravity, so few tried.

This was the central reality of regime stability in Mubarak's Egypt. The regime continued not because it led people to conceal or falsify their preferences but because it led them to have no expectations that better possibilities could be realized. The regime had lost any ability to present itself as legitimate, just, or effective. But it had developed an impressive ability to represent itself as inevitable.

The result was something far milder than that described by Lisa Wedeen regarding Syria: in Egypt, the regime depressed more citizens than it oppressed.[6] Nobody was expected to mouth the regime's slogans (doing so might win contracts or specific positions, but silence or futile grumbling was rarely punished). It was not that the sycophantic pabulum of official media was to be echoed, only that it could communicate the system's

imperviousness to change. Similarly, electoral rules were carefully manipulated in order to guarantee that the opposition could not win (and those
rules were simply broken if it looked like the opposition might even do
well). The state-owned press built a Potemkin world in which Egyptians
were informed about the doings of high officials and in which wealthy individuals and companies could advertise their loyalty. Those who criticized
the system could be subject to scurrilous smear campaigns that seemed
designed more to throw dust in the eyes of readers than to persuade them.

The effect was likely to deepen the sense of political alienation. The sense
that Egypt was ruled by a small group who monopolized public institutions for private benefit was widespread. The words of Abbé Sieyès at the
outbreak of the French Revolution would have resonated with many Egyptians when they thought of their own nation and of the governing National
Democratic Party:

> What is a nation? A body of associates living under common laws and repre-
> sented by the same legislative assembly, etc.
>
> Is it not obvious that the nobility possesses privileges and exemptions,
> which it brazenly calls its rights and which stand distinct from the rights of
> the great body of citizens? Because of their special rights, the nobility does not
> belong to the common order, nor is it subjected to the common laws. Thus its
> private rights make it a people apart in the great nation. It is truly imperium
> in imperio.
>
> As for its political rights, it also exercises these separately from the nation.
> It has its own representatives who are charged with no mandate from the
> People. Its deputies sit separately, and even if they sat in the same chamber
> as the deputies of ordinary citizens they would still constitute a different and
> separate representation. They are foreign to the nation first because of their
> origin, since they do not owe their powers to the People; and secondly because
> of their aim, since this consists in defending not the general interest, but the
> private one.
>
> The Third Estate then contains everything that pertains to the nation while
> nobody outside the Third Estate can be considered as part of the nation. What
> is the Third Estate? Everything.[7]

In Egypt, the Third Estate was self-aware. What was missing, until
January 25, 2011, was the will to act. Egyptians required some help to
understand the leap from popular grumbling to mass uprising, and
Kuran could give them some of what they needed. That Egypt was a

society in which large numbers of people were discontent was wide-spread knowledge. But that Egypt was a society of people willing to act on that discontent was a surprise, even to the hardy group of people who spent much of the first decade of the 2000s trying to goad Egyptians to some form of action.

Everyone knew that the emperor was naked and even spoke about his lack of clothes, but few dared or cared to go beyond ridiculing to deposing him. What seems to have changed in January 2011 with astonishing rapidity was less people's understanding of one another's preferences than their understanding of one another's practical commitment to change. More than a half decade of protests had led Egyptians to regard public demonstrations and protest camps as occasional parts of the urban landscape. Then the events in Tunisia and the surprising turnout for the January 25 demonstrations allowed Egyptians to imagine that such protests on a larger scale might produce a different future.

A longtime friend told me that he left his workplace near Tahrir Square on January 25 stunned to find a large crowd of demonstrators. He told me later that he immediately called his wife to say, "Listen! There is a whole group of people cursing Hosni!" before holding up the phone so that she could hear. What surprised him was not the sentiment but the determination of the people who had gathered to express it in organized form. And he immediately joined them. Another demonstration leader told me that he was assigned to lead a group from a public square about half an hour away from Tahrir Square in a march to join the main demonstration. Only after he had been leading his group for a short distance did he turn around to see who was following him—and he was astounded to see a thousand people.

As soon as such determination was in evidence, demonstrations quickly snowballed. As more people publicly defied gravity, it seemed safer and more sensible to try to fly. The prior uprising in Tunisia, the series of miscalculations by the regime, and perhaps even the shutting down of cell phones and the Internet (communicating quite effectively to the entire population that the demonstrations were threatening the basis of the regime), and the "Battle of the Camel" (which made the regime look less inevitable and simply ridiculous; it was also a battle that the demonstrators were able to win). These were the events that seemed to make Egyptians rapidly shift their calculations of what was possible. Attending demonstrations was no longer eccentric behavior but, for many, became a way to participate fully in Egyptian society.

So in January 25, Egyptians suddenly realized a mutual ability to act. But act for what? Why did writing a new constitution become the order of the day?

Moving from the Fourth Estate to the Third: Revenge of the Nerds

When entering a restaurant, few of us think abstractly about the kind of meal we would most like at a particular moment; such an unstructured choice might bewilder us. Instead, the first question we generally ask ourselves is, "What is on the menu?" If we enter a restaurant with a group, the second question I often hear (or ask) before ordering is often, "What are you having?" We ask the first question even if it seems to narrow our choices, because it helps us think about the practical alternatives, and we ask the second question because the preferences of others—even in matters of personal taste in the very literal sense—can sometimes inform our own.

Kuran defines "preference falsification" as "the act of misrepresenting one's genuine wants under perceived social pressures."[8] But what if the line between the social and the personal origin of preferences is more difficult to draw, if our "genuine" wants are deeply informed by deliberations (and arguments) with our friends, families, and fellow citizens, if their preferences are in turn shaped in discussion with us, and if we sometimes even hesitate to answer a flight attendant's simple question "Chicken or beef?" until we know how our traveling companion has decided?

In the years before the Egyptian revolution, public deliberation on the country's deep political problems was not merely possible; it was, as I have said, the stuff of daily political discussion in the press. What it lacked in efficacy, it could compensate for in specificity.

In a totalitarian system, or even in a fully authoritarian one, the space for political speech and expression is sharply limited, as are the rules of political speech. But Egypt during the Mubarak years was not totalitarian; it was not even fully authoritarian. The president was inevitable, as was the regime, so there was no point in acting against them. Nonetheless, there was plenty of room for talk.

Beginning in the 1970s and 1980s, political speech became far more free and sophisticated. In the 1970s an opposition press emerged, and in the 1980s that press discovered its shrill voice. In the 1990s, pan-Arab newspapers, with their greater restraint in rhetoric, higher professional standards, and greater ability to cover news, entered the Egyptian market. Nongovernmental organizations, universities, and think tanks also stepped into the fray, holding discussions, workshops, forums, and conferences on a host of political matters. Satellite television carried the contents of similar discussions into coffeehouses and homes throughout the Arab world. Over the past decade, it seems that public discussion about politics may even have begun to edge out sports.

In the resulting public sphere in Mubarak's Egypt, red lines existed, to be sure, but they were constantly probed and tested. Criticism could be bitter and exacting as long as it was abstract; it also helped to be both elitist and slightly indirect. Organizing against the president was dangerous, but suggesting constitutional amendments to curb his power was fair game. Organizing an opposition political party was risky; documenting and decrying electoral abuses became routine. The rise of an independent press in the first decade of the twenty-first century—hamstrung in many ways, to be sure, but notable nonetheless especially compared with the modes and content of printed expression in the second half of the twentieth century—may have been the single most overlooked transformational force in Arab politics. The newspaper *al-Masri al-Yawm* spearheaded this trend in 2004, demonstrating that it was possible to have an independent voice and still sell papers. The speed with which it overtook most state-owned press in circulation is difficult to document (circulation figures are notoriously unreliable in Egypt) but is not denied by any observer. It was followed by other papers, some more obnoxious (*al-Dustur*)[9] and others relatively restrained (*al-Shuruq*).

The Arab world of the beginning of the twenty-first century saw the articulation of new political visions in a network of *nadwa*s (seminars) and newspapers—public discourse owed just as much to Jürgen Habermas as to George Orwell; it relied just as much on Johannes Guttenberg as on Mark Zuckerberg. These new political visions were expressed primarily in political terms, adopting concepts of human rights, democracy, and constitutionalism.

Indeed, what is remarkable is how widespread the new constitutionalist discourse could resonate in seemingly disparate settings. There were different strains, to be sure.[10] But when the General Guide of the Muslim Brotherhood summed up the organization's goal as "freedom," when Nasserists called for an independent judiciary (something their namesake did much to undermine), and when human rights organizations found their themes embraced by a wide variety of political forces, it was clear that constitutional reform was becoming the lingua franca of political debates. Across the spectrum, groups that felt able to accomplish little could still talk incessantly, and they used this opening to develop a set of overlapping diagnoses of Egypt's political predicament as lying in the basic framework according to which the country was governed.

This emergence of a public and very political sphere does not by itself explain the series of upheavals. But it does help us understand why people came to realize one another's revulsions so easily, why the opposition discovered its political voice, and why that voice expressed itself so easily (and with such detail) in constitutional terms. A decade of constitutionalist discourse lent a ready vocabulary and even detailed critiques and proposed remedies for the opposition leaders.

This emergence of a public sphere may also help explain why the upheaval of 2011 followed such a different and far more coherent path than previous outbursts of more inchoate urban unrest in 1977 and 1986 (or, as will be seen, some less cheery versions of the Arab spring in nearby countries). In 1977, economic grievances figured heavily; in 1986, institutions of state, National Democratic Party buildings, and tourist locations seem to have drawn special ire from the rioters. But in 2011, the more disciplined demonstrators focused a surprising amount of energy on shredding a piece of paper: the country's 1971 constitution. As the regime fragmented, a group of autodidact constitutional experts were poised to step into the breach.

When the Egyptian people spoke with a single voice in January 2011, their simple demand could be summed up as the fall of the regime and the departure of the president. But it was not always summed up so simply. Almost as frequent were calls for the judicial monitoring of elections, the transfer of authority from the presidency to the parliament, an end to the state of emergency, greater transparency and oversight over public finances, and more carefully structured instruments of horizontal accountability.

The demonstrators' constitutional sophistication was a surprise to everyone except those who had been reading Egyptian newspapers for the past decade. What had emerged in the press was a detailed set of constitutional arguments: how to restrain the power of the presidency, how to recover long-forgotten parts of Egypt's political history (such as the abortive 1954 draft constitution), and how to transform the 1971 constitution's bombastic and loquacious list of rights into real and effective guarantees for the rights of Egyptian citizens.

The number of producers in the most public aspects of this discussion was limited, as is often the case with the public sphere. But the number of consumers appears to have been considerable: opposition newspapers sold;

satellite television caught on; and these most widespread discussions gave birth to an uncountable number of private discussions and debates.

The discussions by the highbrow press had another effect as well: by diagnosing Egypt's political ills in constitutional terms, they made it much easier for many Egyptians to argue for a link between the problems in their own lives and fundamental issues of governance. If jobs were hard to find, public services in short supply, police a brutalizing rather than a protective force, and access to many institutions monopolized by those with wealth and social connections, the underlying disease could be diagnosed as a political order that rendered public authority beyond any mechanisms of accountability. A constitutional order that actually responded to popular voices and in which public institutions kept a watch over one another—in other words, one in which mechanisms of vertical and horizontal accountability worked—was a necessary condition for addressing the Egyptian citizens' problems. Thus, by 2011, when the Egyptian Third Estate spoke, it often did so in the language of a rather bookish constitutional law professor.

The Possibilities of Politics

I wrote this chapter to provide some clues to the success of the opposition movement in Egypt and the political and constitutional character of its program. But we need to restrain the underlying enthusiasm for the January 25 revolution and its constitutionalist agenda before we travel too far forward in time or too far away from Egypt.

In regard to moving forward in time, two years after the uprising we already have seen the mistakes of investing too much importance in Egypt's public sphere. When we move from the revolutionary politics of the public square to the electoral politics of the voting booth (as Egypt did in 2011 and 2012), much changes. And when we move from the public's speaking with one voice to fractious, angry, and even paranoid public debates (as Egypt also did in 2012 and 2013), it is difficult to establish new rules for political life.

Egypt's public sphere was able to bring down a regime and compel the military to sketch a plan for building a new democratic order, but it was unable to win an election. Under Mubarak, the problem was not that the preferences of people were falsified but that they were ignored. A public sphere arose that allowed them to speak with one voice. Elections, however, are not about people speaking with a single voice in public but about people expressing their individual voices (generally about a limited range

CONSTITUTIONAL REVOLUTIONS AND THE PUBLIC SPHERE 307

of options) in the privacy of the voting booth. The cacophony of elections is reduced to a single outcome by electoral rules; the result can be much different from what public discussion might suggest. Accordingly, in Egypt's referendum of March 2011, the Tahrir Square revolutionaries were as surprised as France's revolutionaries of 1848 to discover that when millions of citizens voiced their individual preferences, the results were different from the voices of the public sphere.

This process continued even to the point that the Egyptian public lost its single collective voice. The 2011 March referendum was followed by an extended and contentious process by which Egyptians argued and struggled, increasingly against one another, in a wide variety of fields. In public demonstrations, a variety of groups continued to claim the mantle of the January 25 revolution to press for their version of the political changes that united the crowds. Islamists turned their attention increasingly to the ballot box where they did well, winning control of both houses of parliament and the presidency. Unelected state actors—including the judiciary, the military, and even al-Azhar University—posed as the true defender of the nation; even though none could claim full revolutionary credentials, all could present themselves as acting consistently according to its values. By 2012, it seemed that Egypt's main political forces not only were not on the same team; they also were often playing different games. When it came time to realize the revolution's central demand—a new constitutional order—everyone agreed on the need for "consensus," but nobody could agree on what that consensus contained. In the end, Islamists came to have the most powerful voice in 2012, but they made only enough concessions to others to convince themselves of their own good intentions.

Thus, Egypt's 2012 constitution worked to give voice to some of the demands of January 2011. It paid more attention to defining fundamental freedoms and worked to specify the mechanisms of oversight of the executive. But its content and, even more, the process by which it was written proved deeply divisive. In the lead-up to its adoption, it would have been difficult to escape the conclusion that the public sphere of 2011 stood largely for the constitution's rejection, that most non-Islamist political forces were unified in rejecting the document. But the constitution was approved, with close to two-thirds of voters supporting it in a referendum in which fewer than one-third of eligible voters cast ballots. At least in the short run, the Third Estate was divided and perhaps defeated.

In 2013, Islamist electoral victories proved to be a useless weapon against a reenergized coalition of groups convinced (likely correctly) that they had come to represent the majority. After pulling off massive street demonstrations on June 30, 2013—and thus laying claim to the revolutionary mantle—the coalition was able to present itself as speaking once again with a single voice to tell the president to go and to take his constitution with him. When the military stepped in to arrest Mohamed Morsi, the Islamist president, and suspend the 2012 constitution, it also found it easy to mobilize almost all parts of the new public sphere to denounce the Brotherhood as terrorists and to demand a new (or at least significantly revised) constitutional order.

Across the Arab world, we find great variations in the vitality of the public sphere and the viability in constitutional institutions and procedures that help us understand some of the patterns that emerged in the 2011 upheavals. To be sure, the process in Egypt could be described in terms similar to those of one scholarly examination of contemporaneous political debates in Turkey among religious and secular elites: "The press plays a significant political role as a site where elite values change or are reproduced through discussion, deliberation, or silence."[11]

In the Arab world, those authoritarian regimes (which perhaps were the majority in the region by the early twenty-first century) that had converted to something like a semiauthoritarian system found that constitutional reform had become the language of politics, in ways that both helped and hurt them. Semiauthoritarian regimes are those that allow the opposition actors some room to organize and propagate their views and to contest elections but offer no possibility that the opposition can win them.[12] The rules of political life in such regimes is often unstable—and indeed often have a pattern of interspersing relative openness with bouts of repression—but they often show great ability to talk a democratic language, generally in constitutional form. They allow competitive elections, guarantee an accountable government and a range of political freedoms, and promise the possibility of political change at the ballot box but then rob these promises of much of their meaning by designing circular structures and procedures that place all authority in the hands of a president or monarch and use some combination of a ruling party, skewed elections, and a security apparatus beyond the instruments of accountability.

From the 1970s on, authoritarianism in many Arab countries often gave way to semiauthoritarianism. In 2011, such regimes found that the vague constitutional promises they had made gave them a vocabulary to deal with the opposition's demands. But these promises also gave the opposition a language with which to develop its own coherent vision, especially when allowed to operate in a more open public sphere (as in

Egypt). For some regimes, democratic talk was not cheap but proved to be extremely expensive.

The regimes in both Morocco and Jordan, for instance, seemed to have perfected the technique of offering piecemeal constitutional reform as a way of parrying the opposition's demands for change. Endless national dialogues, special commissions, and legal tinkering filled the political space with pledges for fundamental change whose promise was broken in the fine print or dilatory implementation; long shopping lists of liberalizing reforms were enacted only to the extent that underlying power relations were left untouched; and legal changes were carefully crafted to suggest improvements while leaving the leading figures outside all mechanisms of accountability.

The result was an opposition that grew both more cynical but also more expert, able to discern vague promises from real change. When the regimes were pressed in 2011, they could no longer respond with Potemkin promises. Instead, both offered constitutional concessions—ones that fell far short of full democratization (and thus failed to placate the opposition fully) but still opened politics and even the possibility of further change in the future. What Morocco and Jordan may have found, as Egypt had slightly earlier, was that regimes "ruling by law" while avoiding the "rule of law" can sometimes be bitten by law. The reforms in Morocco and Jordan reforms can be reversed, of course.

The course of reforms was quite different as well. Morocco offered deeper concessions that bought it respite from the revolutionary upsurge, but the extent to which those concessions brought real political change remains unclear. In Jordan, the regime failed to offer anything quite so significant. Already in 2011 the situation came to resemble Egypt in the late Mubarak years, with a regime that was resented and rejected but also inevitable. For Jordan, it was not so much the futility of action but the deep divisions regarding what action to take. Jordanians were deeply divided according to origin (East Banker / West Banker), ideology (Islamist/non-Islamist), class, and tribal status. Discussion in Jordan could be as free as in Egypt, and demonstrations could be held. Such discussions and demonstrations revealed, however, not only widespread disgust with the regime but also the lack of shared preferences among its citizens. Ultimately those divisions made a popular uprising far less likely.

Other regimes faced with a similar choice did not even feint in the direction of change. Bahrain's rulers, forced to choose between honoring their constitutional pretensions and abandoning them, hesitated briefly before choosing the latter with particular ferocity. Syria followed a similar path with even greater brutality.

The constitutionalist thrust of Egypt's revolution may therefore be difficult to replicate. Some places (such as in Lebanon and Kuwait) have a highly developed public sphere that may be freer than in Mubarak's Egypt but far less unified. Of the various countries experiencing upheavals in 2011, Egypt's public sphere was probably the most highly developed: it was more densely populated; its instruments were more diverse; and its adversaries in the regime were less imposing, not because they were gentle but just the opposite: their thuggishness rendered them a bit less concerned with highbrow discourse.

We should therefore expect the constitutionalism of the Egyptian uprising to be far more marked than in those countries (such as Libya and Syria) that were far more brutal in stamping out the dissident forces as well as politics more generally. Indeed, the Libyan and Syrian oppositions—the first one successful, the second not (as of this writing)—found themselves struggling to express their demands and programs in a constitutional language, often failing to find verbal formulas or consensus themes that could focus their energies. The Libyan opposition did manage to issue a particularly puzzling document, but its main symbolic rallying point turned out to be an old flag rather than a constitutional tradition.

Lest we rush to an overly bleak conclusion, however, the Tunisian example suggests that constitutional histories can be revived fairly quickly in favorable circumstances. In 2011, as the old regime collapsed, Tunisians would have been justified in abandoning any hope of a constitutionalist path. The overthrown (and soon banned) party had grabbed the name "Constitutional," and its governing document had descended from one written after independence in a mockery of a democratic process (a constituent assembly had drafted a constitution over several years, steadily guided by the dictatorial impulses of the Neo-Constitutional Party and its leader). But rather than abandon this example, those managing Tunisia's transition decided to try it over again, devising a nearly exact replica of the postindependence process, removing only the leading role of the self-styled constitutionalist party.

If analysts should exercise care before traveling with the lessons of Egypt's revolution, activists might want to be far less careful. One of the lessons of Egypt's upheaval is that revolution requires a change in what is deemed possible. Indeed, Egypt's revolutionaries spent much of the first decade of the 2000s targeting their fellow citizens' imaginations. They were aided in that task by the earlier Tunisian events. On a trip to Jordan and Palestine in February 2011, I was struck by how much events in Egypt and Tunisia had inspired people there with a sense of new possibilities. If our modification of Kuran's arguments holds true for those societies as well—that what matters in some semiauthoritarian settings is what actions people expect one another to take—then that inspiration may still be politically empowering.

NOTES

1. See, for instance, Stephen M. Walt, "Why the Tunisian Revolution Won't Spread," *Foreign Policy*, January 16, 2011, available at http://walt.foreignpolicy.com/posts/2011/01/15/why_the_tunisian_revolution_wont_spread. Walt's utterly inaccurate conclusion about revolutionary contagion only seemed to deepen Kuran's vindication; as Walt observed, Kuran had shown that "the actual revolutionary potential of any society is very difficult to read in advance."

2. Timur Kuran, "Sparks and Prairie Fires: A Theory of Unanticipated Political Revolution," *Public Choice* 61, no. 1 (April 1989): 41–74.

3. Timur Kuran, "Now Out of Never: The Element of Surprise in the East European Revolution of 1989," *World Politics* 44, no. 1 (October 1991): 7–48.

4. Timur Kuran, *Private Truth, Public Lies: The Social Consequences of Preference Falsification* (Cambridge, Mass.: Harvard University Press, 1995).

5. Timur Kuran, "The Politics of Revolutionary Surprise," *Daily News Egypt*, February 9, 2011, available at http://www.thedailynewsegypt.com/global-views/the-politics-of-revolutionary-surprise-dp2.html.

6. Lisa Wedeen, *Ambiguities of Domination: Politics, Rhetoric, and Symbols in Contemporary Syria* (Chicago: University of Chicago Press, 1999).

7. Abbe Emmanuel Joseph Sieyes, "What Is the Third Estate," available at http://faculty.smu.edu/rkemper/cf_3333/Sieyes_What_is_the_Third_Estate.pdf.

8. Kuran, *Private Truth, Public Lies*, 3.

9. *Al-Dustur* actually predates *al-Masri al-Yawm* but was shut down in the 1990s after a few years of operation. It was revived in 2005, but its editor paid for his stridency and served time in prison.

10. For an analysis of the various constitutionalist visions in Egypt, see Bruce Rutherford, *Egypt After Mubarak: Liberalism, Islam, and Democracy in the Arab World* (Princeton, N.J.: Princeton University Press, 2008).

11. Murat Somer, "Media Values and Democratization: What Unites and What Divides Religious-Conservative and Pro-Secular Elites?" *Turkish Studies* 11 (December 4, 2010): 555–77.

12. There now is a burgeoning literature on semiauthoritarian, hybrid, and electoral authoritarian regimes, which I analyzed and situated in an Arab context in the chapter "Dictatorship and Democracy Through the Prism of Arab Elections," in my *The Dynamics of Democratization* (Baltimore: Johns Hopkins University Press, 2011).

16

Conclusion

MARC LYNCH

The chapters in this volume present complex and dynamic accounts of the Arab uprisings that capture both the extraordinary surge of popular mobilization and the political struggles that followed. The introduction examined three topics: the unprecedented level of regional popular mobilization, the regimes' divergent responses, and the uncertain political outcomes. But we have not presented a single answer to any of these puzzles. Rather, we drew on a diverse array of literature, emphasized different dimensions of the uprisings, and ultimately did not always agree on key methodological and analytical issues. But collectively we offer a rich analysis bridging several levels of analysis and placing the uprisings into a theoretical framework.

I cannot summarize the volume's findings in this brief conclusion, so instead, I look at how this book's chapters might affect several of the theoretical and analytical debates that have dominated academic and popular discussions of the Arab uprisings.

The chapters offer little support to the common argument that the political science of the Middle East somehow missed the gathering force of the Arab uprisings. In fact, the literature, while diverse, generally did draw attention to the many sources of discontent across the Arab world and the rising incidence of public protest across multiple sectors in countries such as Egypt. Survey research, such as the Arab Barometer findings discussed in several chapters, revealed the depths of this discontent as well as the general desire for more democratic, just, and open political systems. Studies of the new media environment, including the rise of al-Jazeera and the political impact of the Internet, anticipated the unified nature of the regionwide mobilization and the effects of successful protests.

The literature's focus on authoritarian resilience likely did lead to overestimating the Arab regimes' ability to meet the rising popular challenges, however. Despite all their flaws, these regimes had managed to successfully repress, co-opt, or divert wave after wave of political protest, and there were few signs in the decade's waning years that their survival strategies had lost their efficacy. Those strategies continued to preserve regimes in a majority of the Arab states, with regimes falling in only four countries (Tunisia, Egypt, Yemen, and Libya) and with two others (Bahrain and Syria) surviving only through the brute application of extreme violence. As Robert Springborg pointed out in chapter 8, the military's decisions proved decisive, which in future research will accordingly demand far more analytical attention to its interests, organization, and behavioral patterns. The military coup on July 3, 2013, that brought down Egypt's elected president painfully vindicated the continued attention to the institutions and political forces of those old authoritarian regimes.

Although protesters across the region adopted a common language and followed a similar script, the political dynamics that ensued did not. Daniel Brumberg's argument in chapter 2 against applying a "democratic transitions" model to these cases is well taken. The "Arab uprising" model of rapid, unstoppable, and generally nonviolent mobilization forcing the president to step down actually happened only twice (in Tunisia and Egypt). In Bahrain, Libya, Syria, and Yemen, protracted violence or state failure overtook the wave of peaceful protests. Many of the wealthier Gulf states deflected the protest movements through a combination of repression and co-optation while learning from the mistakes of other regimes and taking steps to support one another's survival strategies. No Arab uprising has yet led to a real democratic transition, even as many countries in the region face persistent mobilization and political instability.

This authoritarian retrenchment, along with Syria's turn to extreme violence and the existential struggles of the Egyptian and Tunisian transitions, offers a sobering corrective to the early enthusiasm for sweeping revolutionary change. At some level, this retrenchment vindicates the last decade's close analysis of the practices and structures sustaining these authoritarian regimes, and it demonstrates the difficulty of moving past such deeply ingrained political and societal structures. But just as it is important not to rush too rapidly toward embracing the prospects for change, it also is important not to overcorrect back to assuming renewed authoritarian resilience. As Nathan Brown eloquently explained in chapter 15, the texture of politics has fundamentally and irrevocably changed.

Those structural, environmental changes have proven difficult for almost all actors to easily navigate. Islamist movements, for instance, have struggled to adapt ideologically or strategically to their new political opportunities. Although their electoral success in Egypt and Tunisia brought them unprecedented power, it was at the cost of a furious public backlash and uncomfortable questions about their ultimate objectives that had long been deferred. The Muslim Brotherhood's rise to power in Egypt ended with the 2013 military coup, which included sweeping arrests of Brotherhood members and the violent dispersal of its protests, all to broad public acclaim. Competing political trends have similarly struggled with the transition from protest movements to political parties, with many of the sources of their strength during the uprisings becoming weaknesses in the electoral and institutional political battles that followed.

This book demonstrates how an array of local factors, from urban geography to civil-military relations to political economy, account for the unfolding of the political struggles. It also shows that these outcomes were not structurally ordained. Morocco's relatively successful constitutional reform gambit and the disastrous Syrian and Libyan regimes' resort to outrageous violence demonstrate that the choices made by both regimes and opponents can change the course of the political process. But these changes also must be understood in their regional and international context, not simply as a series of comparative cases. As David Patel, Valerie Bunce, and Sharon Wolchik pointed out in chapter 3, regional demonstration effects had a powerful effect on the expectations and behavior of protest movements. Tunisia and Egypt galvanized the protests by publics who suddenly believed that they could succeed, whereas a year later Syria's horrors likely deterred others from pushing for a change that could have demonstrably led to something worse.

The regional effects were not only such indirect demonstration effects, of course. In chapter 6, Curtis Ryan clearly shows how the Arab uprisings have shaped the renewed Arab cold war defined by competitive proxy interventions and new patterns of regional alignment and conflict. Qatar's efforts to support the Muslim Brotherhood's movements across the region, interventions against the Libyan and Syrian regimes, and the use of al-Jazeera to shape regional public opinion were only one of the most obvious of such bids. The purpose of Saudi Arabia's moves to support friendly monarchical regimes financially, politically, and even militarily (in the case of Bahrain) was to defend and consolidate its conservative alliance structure. This recurrent logic of proxy wars and competitive mobilization within states that (perhaps temporarily) lack effective internal control has shaped the outcomes of several major waves of popular mobilization in the region's history.

The enthusiasm in the early months of 2011 has long since given way to a longer, grittier political struggle. It is far too soon to offer any definitive conclusions about the ultimate outcomes of the Arab uprisings. But this book's detailed, rigorous dissection of the dynamics of popular mobilization and regime responses during their first two years will have enduring value. Authoritarianism is rarely as stable as it appears during the days of normal politics, but equally rarely as ephemeral as it might seem during revolutionary moments. The dynamics of the early days of mass mobilization seldom fully predict the outcomes of the tough institutional and political battles to follow. Accordingly, political scientists need to be prepared to explain both those political struggles and those moments when popular mobilization surges to upend the system.

Contributors

Nathan J. Brown is a professor of political science at George Washington University.

Daniel Brumberg is a professor of government at Georgetown University and a senior program officer at the U.S. Institute of Peace.

Valerie Bunce is a professor of government at Cornell University.

Clement M. Henry is a professor and chair of the political science department at the American University of Cairo.

Steven Heydemann is the vice president for research at the U.S. Institute of Peace.

Michael Hoffmann is a doctoral candidate at Princeton University.

Amaney Jamal is an associate professor of politics at Princeton University.

Ryan King is a student at the University of Massachusetts, Amherst.

Vickie Langohr is an associate professor of political science at the College of the Holy Cross.

Reinoud Leenders is a reader in international relations and Middle East studies in the War Studies Department at King's College, London.

Ellen Lust is an associate professor of political science at Yale University.

Marc Lynch is a professor of political science at George Washington University.

Quinn Mecham is an assistant professor of political science at Brigham Young University.

David Patel is an assistant professor of government at Cornell University.

Michael Robbins is a doctoral candidate at the University of Michigan.

Curtis R. Ryan is an associate professor of political science at Appalachian State University.

Jillian Schwedler is a professor of political science at Hunter College.

Robert Springborg is a professor in the Department of National Security Affairs, School of International Graduate Studies, at the Naval Postgraduate School.

Mark Tessler is a professor of political science at the University of Michigan.

Sharon Wolchik is a professor of political science at George Washington University.

Index

protests (*continued*)
203–204; in Iran, 67; in Iraq,
70, 71; in Jordan, 9, 70, 179n53;
in Kazakhstan, 70; in Lebanon,
70; in Libya, 63, 67, 70; March
25, 174–75; in Morocco, 10; in
Oman, 69, 70; in Qatar, 69; role
of youth in shaping, 9–10; in
Russia, 70; in Saudi Arabia, 9,
68, 69, 88; spaces and, 164–68; in
Syria, 67–68, 70, 71; in Tunisia,
63, 70, 315; in Turkmenistan, 70;
in United Arab Emirates (UAE),
69; violence in, 9–10; in Yemen,
70; youth and, 285–87, 286*t*, 289,
290*t*, 291
proxy wars, 315–16
Przeworski, Adam: *Democracy
and The Market,* 77; on elected
institutions, 239n3; on levels
of society, 86; on military rule,
34
public spending increases, 77
public sphere: constitutional
revolutions and, 296–311;
diffusion and demonstration,
104–105; in Egypt, 306–307;
emergence of, 305–306
Putin, Vladimir, 61–62

Qaboos bin Said al-Said, 71
Qaddafi, Muammar, 22, 67, 70–71,
148, 206–207
Qaddafi, Muammar al-, 1, 82, 84,
86, 111, 147, 189, 227
Qaddafi, Saif-al-Islam, 232
Al-Qaida in the Arabian Peninsula
(AQAP), 208
Qasim, Abd al-Karim al-, 114

Qatar: calm in, 9; commercial
banking structures in, 129*t*;
competitive politics of, 118;
elections in, 221*t*, 231*t*, 234*t*;
electoral politics and outcomes
in, 237*t*; mobilization in, 228*t*;
protests in, 69; regimes in, 129*t*,
221*t*; regional leadership in, 117;
special forces troops, 158n26;
support of Muslim Brotherhood,
315

Rabbat, Nasser, 166
Rastan, 80–81
reactionary regimes, 115
reforms: about, 13; in Bahrain,
131; in Jordan, 309; in Morocco,
309; in Saudi Arabia, 13; Syrian
regime on, 82–83; in Yemen, 13
regime change, 10, 205
regime learning, process of, 78
regime manipulation, of identity
conflicts, 40
regimes: in Algeria, 13, 129*t*, 221*t*;
in Bahrain, 41, 129*t*, 221*t*; in
Egypt, 12, 13, 129*t*, 221*t*; hybrid,
244–45n44, 312n12; in Iraq,
129*t*, 221*t*; in Jordan, 129*t*, 221*t*,
309; in Kuwait, 10, 129*t*, 221*t*; in
Lebanon, 129*t*, 221*t*; in Libya,
13, 41, 129*t*, 221*t*; in Morocco,
129*t*, 221*t*, 309; in Oman, 129*t*,
221*t*; in Palestine, 221*t*; in Qatar,
129*t*, 221*t*; responses to, 3–4,
12–14; in Saudi Arabia, 129*t*,
221*t*; semiauthoritarian, 308,
312n12; single-party, 244n44;
in Syria, 13, 41, 129*t*, 221*t*; in
Tunisia, 12, 13, 129*t*, 221*t*; in

CPSIA information can be obtained
at www.ICGtesting.com
Printed in the USA
LVOW07s2224030417
529459LV00012B/50/P